The
HIDDEN PLACES

SOME OF THE
HIDDEN PLACES
WAITING TO BE
DISCOVERED
ON YOUR JOURNEY
THROUGH SCOTLAND

Chapter 1
Floors Castle, near Kelso

Chapter 2
Threave Castle, Castle Douglas

Chapter 3
Culzean Castle, Culzean

Chapter 4
Cloch Lighthouse, near Gourock

Chapter 5
Water of Leith , Dean Village

Chapter 6
Pitenweem Harbour

KING ROBERT THE BRUCE
JUNE 24 1314

Chapter 7
Robert the Bruce Monument, Stirling

Chapter 8
Oban Harbour & Mc Caig's Folly

Chapter 9
Glamis Castle

Chapter 11
Glen Coe

Chapter 11
Urquart Castle, Loch Ness

Chapter 11
Caledonian Canal

Chapter 12
Callanish Stone Circle, Lewis

Chapter 12
Dingwall Church & Graveyard, Shetland

The
HIDDEN PLACES

SCOTLAND

Front Cover:
Plockton Village by Loch Carron
by PAUL BENNETT

Acknowledgements

The Publishers would like to thank the following for their assistance in the production of this book: ;
Deborah , and Jean for Administration. Joanna, Gerald , Shane, and Sarah f or Writing. Craig for research, Simon at Graphix for the maps. Typesetting by Joanna Billing.

ALL MAPS COPYRIGHT MAPS IN MINUTES
RH Publications 1996

OTHER TITLES IN THE HIDDEN PLACES SERIES

© Featurepress Ltd. 118 Ashley Rd .Cheshire. U.K. WA14 2UN

Foreword

The Hidden Places Series

This is an established collection of travel guides which covers the U.K and Ireland in 16 titles.

The aim of the books is to introduce readers to some of the less well known attractions of each area whilst not ignoring the more established ones.

We have included in this book a number of hotels, inns, restaurants, various types of accommodation, historic houses, museums, and general attractions which are to be found in this part of the country, together with historical background information.

There is a map at the beginning of each chapter with line drawings of the places featured, along with a description of the services offered.

We hope that the book prompts you to discover some of the fascinating "Hidden Places" which we found on our journey, and we are sure the places featured would be pleased if you mentioned that our book prompted your visit.

We wish you an enjoyable and safe journey.

THE HIDDEN PLACES OF
SCOTLAND

CONTENTS

CHAPTER ONE

THE BORDERS

Hermitage Castle

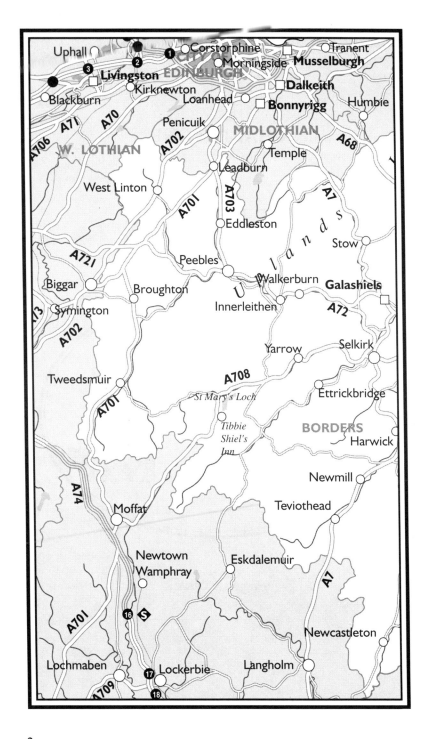

Dryburgh Abbey, near St Boswells

CHAPTER ONE

THE BORDERS

KELSO. Once described by the writer, Sir Walter Scott, as "the most beautiful town in the land", Kelso, set majestically at the junction of the Rivers Tweed and Teviot, must certainly be a contender for this coveted title. The town's name comes from the nearby chalk ridge, known once as Calchow or Kelkow and today as Kelsae. A busy market town with a relatively small population, Kelso has a lovely elegant square which is surrounded by fine buildings. The roofs, pinnacles and small streets of the town look strangely continental, with shop windows peering through arches, and grey and brown houses fronting the market square.

There is a bullring in the centre of the square, the point where bulls were once tethered during markets. Today markets and shows are no longer held here but in Springwood Park across the River Tweed. The arched bridge was built in 1800 and was, in fact, the model for the old Waterloo Bridge across the Thames in London. The two lamp posts were retrieved from London Bridge when it was demolished in 1930.

During World War II, Polish troops were stationed in Kelso and there is a plaque in the town which was presented by the visitors in gratitude for the hospitality they received during their stay.

The magnificent **Kelso Abbey** was built on the instructions of King David I and was started around 1128. Vatican records show that it was one of the largest of the Border abbeys. In 1545 it was used as a stronghold against the English invasion and the defendants, including the monks, were ruthlessly slaughtered and the Abbey all but destroyed.

If ever there was a jewel in the crown then **Floors Castle** must be a prime example. This superb mansion, overlooking Kelso and the River Tweed, is the home of the 10th Duke of Roxburghe and was used as the setting for the Tarzan film *Greystoke*. Built in 1721 by the builder and architect William Adam, Floors Castle became the Scottish seat of the 1st Duke of Roxburghe, an eminent gentleman who was bestowed with many titles by Queen Anne and became the first Secretary of State for Scotland following the Union of 1707.

The Castle occupies the site of the previous home of the Earls of

Roxburghe, Auld Floors, which had been their home since 1650 when they abandoned, the now ruined, Cessford Castle, which had been the principal seat of the Kers for four centuries. It is interesting to note that Auld Floors was sometimes known as Floris which in Scots tongue means flowers.

Floors Castle is rich in history, for Auld Floors was known to be a refuge for the Royalists in the days of 'Habbie' Ker, the 1st Earl. Another story tells of the present castle being used as a temporary lodging for Bonnie Prince Charlie's men during the 1745 Rebellion. At this time however, the castle was still under construction.

Romance is not far away either; romance connected with a drama that interrupted the family line. The 3rd Duke of Roxburghe, a man known for his great intellect, became deeply attached to Christina, the elder daughter of the Duke of Mecklenberg-Strelitze. Unfortunately for him, her younger sister, Charlotte, became George IV's Queen and court etiquette decreed that an elder sister could not become a subject of a younger sister. Their love was thwarted and in their despair both undertook a life of celibacy.

The Duke sublimated his affections by becoming the most discerning book collector of his time. Amongst his collection are such books as Caxton's *Recuyell of the History of Troy* and a first edition of *Decameron*.

A hiccough in the family line in the early 1800s, caused partly through Duke John's lack of issue, was the subject of a lengthy lawsuit which continued for seven years. As the 5th Duke took his rightful place, the lawsuit had to be funded from the sale of the Roxburghe library. However, this was not a total disaster, for the main components of the library were saved by a handful of peers who founded the Roxburghe Club. They each held originals and undertook to produce a number of facsimiles until they each had a complete collection.

Part of Scotland's heritage lies in the grounds of the Castle. There are the mounds of the old city of Roxburgh and of Roxburgh Castle; in its day one of Scotland's principal fortresses and home to many monarchs. Alas, all that remains now are the ruins of a postern gate. Much later, in 1460, King James II was killed when one of his own cannons exploded; a holly tree marks the spot in the parkland before the Castle.

The Castle is open to the public and during the summer the grounds host a number of events, from waupenschaus to hunter trails. Visitors can also enjoy the delights of the Castle's restaurant which offers food from the estate and river cooked on the premises. There is also a regular minibus from the estate to the Garden Centre which is enclosed within the walled garden.

Finally, the life of Sir Walter Scott is entwined with the town of Kelso. Rosebank was the home of his uncle, Robert Scott and his sister Jenny, where Scott spent his early years whilst attending the Old Grammar School in the shadow of Kelso Abbey. It was at the school that Scott first met the Ballantyne brothers, James and John, who figured prominently later as printers and publishers of his works.

AROUND KELSO

COLDSTREAM. This small border town is famous for the 2nd Regiment of Foot Guards of the British Army, founded here in 1639 by General Monk, and it gives the regiment their nickname: The Coldstream Guards. A plaque on the Guards' House, rebuilt in 1865, at the east end of the market place, indicates their original headquarters. Coldstream was also the family home of Alec Douglas-Home, Lord Home of the Hirsel. Widely held as one of Britain's finest Prime Ministers, he gave up his Earldom in order to become a Member of Parliament only to be deposed by his party shortly after being narrowly defeated in the General Election of 1964.

The Hirsel, to the northeast of the town, has been the home of the Douglas-Home family, descendants of the March Wardens of long ago, since the early 17th century. The house's name signifies the amount of land which could be tended by a single shepherd and the grounds have been open to the public for many years.

Like Gretna Green, Coldstream, being on the border, has had its fair share of runaway marriages. Although not as well known as Gretna, eloping couples used to cross at Smeaton's Bridge and make for the old marriage house that can still be seen.

A few miles from Coldstream lies the site of the **Battle of Flodden** where, in 1513, 10,000 Scotsmen, including their King James IV, perished at the hands of the English, despite outnumbering the enemy. It was one of the most fearful days in Scottish history where the flower of nobility was slain. The disastrous defeat was a result of some bad tactical decisions by the King who, at one stage, dismounted from his horse and fought hand-to-hand surrounded by his soldiers in a valiant attempt to turn the tide. This great loss is still remembered each year in Coldstream.

NORHAM. **Norham Castle**, which was apparently the inspiration for several landscapes by Turner, was built in 1157 and throughout its history has been repeatedly attacked. In his poem *Marmion*, Sir Walter Scott called it the most dangerous place in Britain.

Norham village itself is thoroughly charming, standing high above the River Tweed and with cottages lining each side of a lovely green. **St Cuthbert's Church** dates from AD 830 and, surprisingly, it has more than once been occupied as a base from which to besiege the castle. Its 17th century pulpit came from Durham Cathedral.

PAXTON. This small border village is home to **Paxton House**, a fine neo-Palladian mansion built in 1758 to the designs of the architect brothers John and James Adams. It was Patrick Home who had the House built as a home for the daughter of Frederick the Great whom he expected to marry. Unfortunately, the marriage plans fell through. The picture gallery, originally commissioned to house the collections Patrick Home made during his tour of Italy, has been restored and is now an outstation of the National Galleries of Scotland.

EYEMOUTH. This a picturesque and active herring fishing town which retains not only its cobbled streets but also a distinct old world charm. The harbour's breakwater dates from 1770 and is protected by the 'Hurkars' rocks. Overlooking the harbour, which was granted a free port charter in 1597, is **Gunsgreen House**, an 18th century mansion by Robert Adam and an old haunt of smugglers. The coast here is rich in smuggling legend, with numerous cliffs hiding caves and passages. Eyemouth harbour is still a busy place and a fascinating time can be had watching the fish being landed and auctioned here. The fishing is mainly for white fish, prawns, lobster and crab and it is possible to charter a boat for sea fishing.

During a great storm in 1881, Eyemouth endured a terrible tragedy when half of the fishing fleet was sunk and over 100 men lost. A marvellous tapestry depicting the disaster was sewn by local women in 1981 to mark the centenary. It is 15 feet long, containing one million stitches, and all of the women involved in the work were descendants of the men who were drowned. The tapestry can be seen in the **Eyemouth Museum**, together with the story of the storm and other exhibits, which show how both fishing and Eyemouth have changed over the years.

COLDINGHAM. This 18th century town, with a popular, fine sandy beach, has a priory that dates back to 1098 and now serves as a chapel. There are a wide range of activities available in Coldingham and, apart from numerous walks, there is a small art studio in the village where classes are held each summer. For the more energetic the waters here are ideal for diving and there are facilities for this very popular sport. Both sailing and sea angling are also available.

ST ABBS. This picturesque fishing village nestles around a tiny harbour that is still used by a small fleet of crab and lobster boats. **St Abbs Light**, built in 1860, is one of the few lighthouses remaining in use from the many that once acted as a vital guide into the Firth of Forth. The view of the 300 feet high red sandstone cliffs at **St Abb's Head** is truly spectacular. There are superb opportunities for painters and sketchers, with the landscapes and seabirds of the National Nature Reserve site on the Head. It is an important area for seabirds; many species can be seen here, especially between April and July, and these include guillemots, razorbills, kittiwakes, fulmars and even puffins. Birds on land include wheatears, meadow pipits and stonechats. The Nature Reserve is also an ideal stopping off place for the birds travelling south from the Arctic winter.

Three miles to the west of St Abb's Head is one of Scotland's most extraordinary ruined castles. **Fast Castle** is perched precariously on a stack of rock, barely accessible by the steep cliff footpath and it is best viewed from above by those unsure of their feet. Fast Castle was used by Sir Walter Scott as the model for Wolf's Crag in *The Bride of Lammermuir*. The 14 year old princess, Margaret Tudor, used the Castle as a resting place on her way to marry James IV, Flodden's tragic monarch.

CHIRNSIDE. The village was the home of famous racing driver Jim Clark (who lies buried in the churchyard) and also the philosopher David Hume.

DUNS. This small market town is situated right in the heart of Berwickshire. Its name is a strange one and derives from an old word for hill fort; the original settlement being situated on the slopes of Duns Law. The **Jim Clark Memorial Room**, in Newton Street, is a rather unusual museum. It commemorates the life and career of the Berwickshire farmer and racing driver who lived close by and was world champion in 1963 and again in 1965, before his tragic death at Hockenheim, Germany in 1968. The museum is open from Easter to October and contains many of the trophies and memorabilia of a driver held to be the finest of all time by his peers.

Built around a pele tower dating from 1320, **Duns Castle** was enlarged and embellished in the early 19th century by the architect James Gillespie Graham. Though the Castle is not normally open to the public, **Duns Castle Nature Reserve**, established in 1970 and the first such site to be organised by the Scottish Wildlife Trust, is well worth a visit, in particular to observe the artificial heron pond - Hen Poo.

In the public park at the lodges leading to Duns Castle can be found two bronze monuments erected in 1966 to commemorate the 700th anniversary of the birth of John Dunse Scotus, a famous scholar, theologian and philosopher.

A mile or so to the east of Duns is **Manderston House**. This is one of the finest examples of Edwardian country houses in Britain. There is much to see here, the 'downstairs' domestic quarters, which have been preserved, give visitors a real flavour of life in such a house 80 or 90 years ago. The house itself is a wonderful example of extravagance, and has a staircase which is a replica of the Petite Trianon at Versailles, the rails being plated in silver!

GREENLAW. Enjoying views of the Lammermuir Hills and Dirrington Great Law to the north, the ancient town of Greenlaw originated in 1147. Set against wooded country and on the Blackadder Water, the present town dates from the 17th century, replacing the older village that stood on a nearby hill. The church here was built in 1675 and has an interesting tower adjoining it that was originally used as a prison. A fire in 1545 destroyed much of the village, although it was subsequently rebuilt and, by 1698, had become the chief burgh of the shire. Greenlaw was of importance for two main reasons. Firstly, it was the market town of Berwickshire for over 150 years until Duns took over this role. Secondly, Greenlaw became a convenient stopping place for weary stage coach travellers on the route from Edinburgh to Newcastle in the days of horse-drawn transport.

Blackadder was not the invention of Rowan Atkinson and the Blackadder Water is well known for its trout and fishing permits are available from the post office or from hotels in Greenlaw.

The Horse Monument, Hawick

THE TURBULENT BORDER REGION

The shape of the border between Scotland and England is well worth a second look: rather than being a straightforward line from west to east, the divide between the two kingdoms runs broadly from southwest to northeast. Every yard of the border was fought over, right from Roman times, and, today, the crossing places are clearly marked and the traveller is well aware of the differences not only in speech but in many other aspects as he passes between the two countries.

What made the area so interesting to English invaders was not only the unsurpassed farmlands developed by the monks of the great abbeys at Jedburgh, Kelso, Melrose and Dryburgh, but also the ease with which they could make their way to Edinburgh. From the Scottish point of view, across the border, in England, there were only meagre settlements within easy marching distance and places further afield such as Durham, were greatly defended. An early move to bring peace to the area came when the English and Scottish Royal houses agreed to each provide three wardens of the Marches.

The violence and terror of the area during the turbulent years has given rise to many legends and ghosts. Many of the tales have been immortalised in the haunting ballads of the Border Region. Tradition, also, plays an important part in the lives of the Borderers. This is Scottish horse country, with roots going back to the time of the marauding freebooters or reivers of medieval times. The annual Common Ridings, an ancient custom, still take place in many of the border towns; most famously at Hawick. Originally, the riding round the boundaries of the common lands by the townsfolk acted as a reminder to the adjacent landowners.

In more peaceful times, the area is synonymous with tweed and the textile industry in general. The combination of lush sheep pasture, soft river water and the knowledge of clothworking that the monks brought with them from Flanders to the great abbeys of the region provided the Borderers with a cottage industry centred on weaving, tweed and knitwear that was only industrialised in the 19th century.

The Old Counties of Selkirkshire, Peebles and Roxburghshire

SELKIRK. Like so many Border towns Selkirk has a history linked to those fateful conflicts with the English. The town itself was actually destroyed by the English after the Battle of Flodden in 1513. Selkirk sent 80 men to fight in the battle for James IV but only one of them survived to come back to this saddened and decimated community. The story goes that he returned, however, bearing a captured English flag and, unable to speak of his sorrow and of the loss of his countrymen, he simply waved the flag down towards the ground. This act is symbolically re-enacted each year in the Common Riding, in remembrance of all those who have fallen in battle.

Selkirk is a fine and effective example of the blending of old and new crafts, which is never an easy task. This Borders' area excels in producing one of Scotland's most famous products: tweed. 'Tweed' is actually a misnomer: the weave's name does not originate from the River Tweed at all but is, in fact, the result of a misspelling of the word 'tweel' by, of course, an English clerk.

The town also has a long association with shoemaking, Selkirk natives were once known as 'souters', and on one famous occasion supplied Bonnie Prince Charlie and his army with 2000 pairs of shoes for their ill-fated march to Derby in 1745.

The story of poor Rabbie Heckspeckle, a soutar in the town is a peculiar tale. Rabbie was very hard working and used to be at his bench before dawn each day. Early one morning a stranger, dressed in a long black cloak and wearing a big hat pulled down low over his face, came into the shop. He tried on one of the shoes from Rabbie's workbench and found it fitted perfectly. He paid Rabbie in gold and said he would be back the next day, before day break, for the other shoe.

Rabbie, however, was suspicious of the strange gentleman. His clothes smelt mouldy and Rabbie had the impression that, although there was gold in his purse, it had also contained worms and beetles! Next day, true to his word, the stranger returned and paid for the second shoe. This time, Rabbie followed his from the shop. The cloaked figure walked across the churchyard and disappeared into a grave. Later that same day, Rabbie returned to the grave with some friends and they dug up the corpse and found it wearing new shoes - which Rabbie reclaimed. Early next morning, as usual, Rabbie was heard hard at work and singing away by his wife. Suddenly there was a loud screech and Rabbie's wife hurried down the stairs to find her husband gone. When the grave was reopened it was found to contain the corpse wearing, once more, the new shoes and clutching Rabbie's nightcap and Rabbie himself was never seen again.

Next to the post office is Robert Douglas' Bakery, where the baker made the original Selkirk 'bannock', a fruit loaf which is said to have been much favoured by Queen Victoria. Another extremely interesting place to visit is **Selkirk Glass**. As well as getting a birds-eye view of the glass-making process, all visitors are welcome to watch the craft in progress, producing the lovely glass products such as paperweights and perfume bottles that are exported all over the world.

Just four miles outside Selkirk lies **Bowhill**, a magnificent mansion and the home of the Scotts of Buccleuch. Erected by the 3rd Duke of Buccleuch in 1795, the house is open to the public during the summer months. The house contains many fine works of art, including paintings by Van Dyck, Reynolds, Raeburn and Claude Lorraine, and has the privilege of having the *Madonna and the Yarnwinder* which is the only painting by Leonardo da Vinci still in private hands in this country.

There are also many fine examples of 17th and 18th century furniture and clocks. One clock especially appeals, as it is able to play eight different Scottish airs, or tunes, though the mechanism was so set that the clock actually observes the Sabbath by not striking from midnight on Saturday until midnight on Sunday. In the grounds there are some fine gardens with nature trails and lovely woodland walks as well as an adventure playground for the children.

Sir Walter Scott was Sheriff of the county in the early 19th century and his statue stands in the Market Place, near to the **Courthouse** where he dispensed his justice. The Courthouse has recently been converted into a Museum/Visitors Centre and Scott's relationship with the area is explored in text panels and an AV presentation. Another visit to make in Selkirk is to the **Halliwells House Museum and Gallery**. Located on the west side of the main square, it consists of a row of late 18th century dwelling houses renovated to make a museum of Selkirk's colourful history. The buildings have links with the ironmongery trade and these have been renovated, providing a fascinating insight into the world of Edwardian shopping with a wonderful collection of domestic hardware from the period. In the adjoining Robson Gallery there is a range of touring exhibitions.

Scottish Borders Council, Municipal Buildings, High Street, Selkirk
Tel: 01750 20096

An ideal base for visiting the Border country, **The Glen Hotel** provides traditional Scottish hospitality for travellers from near and far. The building itself is substantial and attractive and stands only a few yards from the Ettrick Water, one of the best known and most attractive rivers of southern Scotland, and is ideally located for both holiday and business visitors. Now very much a family run hotel, The Glen provides both holidaymakers and business travellers with a range of comfortable and completely refurbished bedrooms, a spacious dining room, and a comfortable bar opening out on the hotel's own gardens. The Glen offers a full range of à la carte meals, both at lunch time and in the evenings. Smoked fish, beef and lamb, fresh vegetables and an appetising selection of other locally produced food. With the hearty Border breakfast giving the day a good start. The Glen has eight bedrooms, each one individually styled with its own private facilities and tea and coffee makers. The hotel also provides shoe cleaning, ironing facilities and hair dryers on request, and the resident proprietors are constantly available to ensure that a stay at The Glen is one to be recalled with pleasure.

The Glen Hotel, Yarrow Terrace, Selkirk Tel: 01750 20259

AROUND SELKIRK

ST BOSWELLS. The village, which boasts Scotland's largest village green, is situated on a common, with the main part of the village built in the local red sandstone. In the 18th and early 19th centuries, this common was the setting of the largest annual fair in the south of Scotland, with lambs, cattle, horses and wool all being sold.

Nearby is **Dryburgh Abbey**. Attacked by the English in 1322, 1358 and 1544, the ruins are still an impressive sight; the cloister buildings being some of the most intact of any monastery in Scotland. Sir Walter Scott and his biographer JG Lockhart are buried in the grounds as well as Field Marshal Earl Haig, Commander-in-Chief of the British Army during most of The Great War. A vault in the ruined Abbey also became the home of a woman who had lost her lover in the '45 Rebellion. The story goes that she vowed she would never look at the sun again until her lover returned. And, on hearing that he was dead, she only came out at night.

Merton House, just two miles east of St Boswells, is also well worth a visit. Designed by Sir William Bruce in 1703, it became the home of the 6th Duke of Sutherland and boasts 20 acres of beautiful grounds, with lovely walks and views of the River Tweed.

MELROSE. The beautiful ruins of **Melrose Abbey**, though impressive by day, are best viewed, according to Sir Walter Scott, by moonlight. Although badly damaged, some of the surviving parts are considered to be amongst the most splendid and detailed work of the time and include the famous jolly figure of a pig playing the bagpipes on the roof. The heart of Robert the Bruce is reputedly buried near the high altar. The **Abbey Museum** is housed in what was the commendator's house, built in 1590 on the site of the Abbot's Palace.

Melrose itself is a beautiful and intriguing Border town, steeped in history and with lots to offer the traveller. Of special note is the railway station; once described as the "handsomest provincial station in Scotland", **Melrose Station** lay derelict from 1969 when the Waverley Route from Edinburgh to Carlisle was axed. Now the only town station still standing in the Borders region, Melrose Station was saved from the same fate as its sister stations by the foresight of architect Dennis Rodwell, who purchased the building in 1985. The station houses a craft centre which is the focal point for skilled craftsmen and women throughout the Borders to display their skills and products. As well as the craft centre itself, the fine Jacobean-style building also has workshops where visitors can see hand-crafted articles during manufacture and the art gallery provides a changing programme of art and craft exhibitions, mainly featuring the work of Borders artists and craftspeople.

For railway enthusiasts, **The Waverley Route Heritage Centre and Model Railway** provides a fascinating reminder of the old Waverley Route and Borders branch lines. The Heritage Centre displays a wide variety of photos, posters, signs, lamps, documents and tickets. There is also a large working model railway and visitors can purchase general and specialist books, posters, cards and railway souvenirs.

Additionally there is an exhibition mounted by The Trimontium Trust which offers those interested in archaeology colourful and informative displays related to the Roman fort at Newstead.

Overlooking Old Melrose is **Scott's View**, a beauty spot so loved by Scott that his funeral cortege paused here on its way to Dryburgh Abbey.

Situated on the main street of Melrose you will find **Butterfly**, a delightful gift shop that sells an incredible selection of unusual presents. It is an Aladdin's cave of gifts ranging from the unusual to the sublime and all at very competitive prices. You can choose from pewter wear, jewellery, watches, pottery and ceramics and a grand selection of leather handbags and purses. There is always a choice of three Queen's China sets, with their extensive range of christening gifts also available. This wonderful shop has a large selection of children's toys in wood as well as silk and waxed flowers, candles, napkins and silk scarves.

Owned and run by Joanna Brownlie, Butterfly is simply filled to the brim with quaint gifts and a changing range of glassware, pictures, and record books for family tree, wedding anniversaries and engagements. So if you are visiting the area and need a keepsake of your stay, then look no further than Butterfly for probably one of the largest selection of presents in Scotland.

Butterfly, High Street, Melrose Tel: 01896 822045

One of Melrose's best loved inns is **The Kings Arms** in the High Street. A former coaching Inn which dates back almost 300 years, it was used as the original meeting place of the Melrose Rugby Football Club, the founders of Sevens Rugby and the current Scottish champions.

The Kings Arms

Owned and run by Mike and Helen Dalgetty, The Kings Arms is an establishment that is welcoming, fun and an excellent place to stay due to its very central location. There are six en-suite bedrooms which are comfortably furnished with a traditional feel and offer all the usual facilities for the weary traveller. For lovers of traditional Scottish dishes using only the finest quality beef and game, The Kings Arms Hotel offers an extensive menu with nearly 30 main course dishes available at one time, that's quite a choice! There are home-made dishes of all types including some very good Mexican Tacos, and with the cosy restaurant catering for up to 30 people and strictly non-smoking, you can guarantee that there will be something for everyone. This 17th century coaching inn provides guests with a warm welcome to this lovely area and comfortable surroundings in which to spend a delightful holiday.

The Kings Arms Hotel, High Street, Melrose Tel: 01896 822143

Standing only 50 yards from the magnificent Melrose Abbey, **Dunfermline House** is a friendly bed and breakfast owned and run by the proprietors, Susan and Ian Graham. There are five light and roomy bedrooms, all with en-suite facilities, central heating, colour television, hair dryers and tea and coffee making facilities. Each is individually decorated and furnished with a quiet and relaxed style and a bright and airy atmosphere. There is a comfortable dining room where a varied selection of cooked breakfasts can be enjoyed. If you wish to taste the real Scotland, traditionally-made porridge makes a delicious alternative to the usual. Susan and Ian also take pride in the home-made jams and marmalades that are made on the premises, these are definitely a must on that piece of breakfast toast. Although the Grahams don't serve dinner at the house, they do have a large selection of menus for many of the local eating establishments, so finding yourself a tasty dinner shouldn't be a problem. Dunfermline House is ideally situated for a touring holiday being convenient for many beauty spots and places of interest. Melrose itself is a small, attractive Border town nestling between the River Tweed and the Eildon Hills in the heart of the Scott Country. Melrose Abbey was founded in 1136 by David I and Priorwood Gardens, which are next to the Abbey, contain a special dry flower garden. Birthplace in 1883 of seven-a-side rugby, Melrose is a popular centre and excellent touring base.

Dunfermline House, Buccleuch Street, Melrose
Tel: 01896 822148 Fax: 01896 822148

ABBOTSFORD. Close to Melrose is Abbotsford, the home of Sir Walter Scott, whose fame has ensured that Melrose is now a busy tourist centre. There are many tributes to this man throughout the whole of this area; he was a well-loved figure who, through his writings, is credited with the preserving of the stories and ballads of the Borders.

Although Sir Walter Scott was actually born in Edinburgh, the area which has always been most associated with the poet and story-teller is the Scottish Borderlands where he made his home.

His family history is not without its own characters and tales. One of Scott's ancestors was captured by a rival hostile clan and offered a choice between marriage or hanging. He apparently took one look at the bride, who was the daughter of the clan's chief and not the most fortunate looking girl, and chose hanging! He was, though, persuaded to change his mind at a later date.

As Walter grew up and went to school, he became well-known as a teller of tales and a voracious reader of books, all the time developing a love of the beautiful countryside that surrounded him. He went to university in Edinburgh and on to practise law. He made good progress in his position and was appointed Sheriff of Selkirk in 1799.

With a good income and a stable position, he was able to work on his collection of ballads and poetry. Scott became well respected and among his admirers were the Wordsworths, who visited him at his home in the Borders. In 1812 Scott bought the farm that was later to develop into the extravagance of Abbotsford. The farm, as it was then, was unimpressive and was, in fact, known as 'Clartyhole', meaning 'dirty hole'. The place was renamed Abbotsford by Scott.

By 1825, Abbotsford was vastly expanded, taking in many surrounding farms and estates and it became Scott's pride and joy. However, the renovation severely drained Scott's finances and he was forced to work harder to pay the bills. His pace of work is said to have contributed to his death and, on 21 September 1832, he died at the age of 61.

Today the house is much as it was in Scott's day, with its remarkable collection of armour and historical relics, such as Rob Roy's sporran, Napoleon's cloak clasp, a lock of Bonnie Prince Charlie's hair and even a silver urn from Lord Byron. The library and study where Scott worked are fascinating to look at.

GALASHIELS. The name is an interesting one and it does have its roots in an associated trade, as it actually comes from the words 'gala' and 'sheiling' which mean 'huts of the shepherds'. The town is now famous for its woollens and textiles and the Scottish College of Textiles was founded here in 1909. To find out more about the industry, head for the **Woollen Museum**, at Waverley Mills, where, at Peter Andersons, there are guided tours showing the process of tartan weaving.

Galashiels is able to offer the visitor a superb choice of golf courses, both at Torwoodlee and at Ladhope. Fishing is also available on the Tweed and Gala waters, whilst horses can be hired for pony-trekking, if

SIR WALTER SCOTT

Sir Walter Scott's association with the Border region began early in his life when, at the age of three and a sickly child, he was sent to his grandparents' house at Sandyknowe, near Smailholm, and just a few miles from Kelso. It was here that, whilst dealing with his disability, the young Scott absorbed the ancient lore of the Borderland and listened to the old tales of wizardry, heroes and villains that were later to play such an important part in his writings. It was whilst at school, in the shadows of Kelso Abbey, that Scott met the Ballantyne brothers, James and John, whose friendship later developed into a business partnership. John Ballantyne became a printer and publisher in Kelso and this later formed the foundation of the Ballantyne Press. Scott, after leaving Kelso Grammar School, became a solicitor in Edinburgh.

Scott's first literary successes were written during his time in Edinburgh where he wrote a series of poems strongly influenced by the tales told to him as a child. His first work, *An Apology for Tales of Terror*, was published by his old school friend John Ballantyne and it was later followed by the volumes of *Minstrelsy of the Scottish Border*. Success and literary acclaim followed. Scott moved out of Edinburgh and built Abbotsford as well as injected large amounts of money into the Ballantyne Press. However, financial collapse of the publishing company in 1826, along with the excessive grandeur of his lifestyle at Abbotsford, lead Scott into a state of near bankruptcy. In order to pay his creditors, Scott turned to writing, this time with more purpose, and rather than staying with the epic poems that had originally brought him his fame, he turned to novels. Again, incorporating legendary figures from the past, Scott romanticised the lives of many Scottish heroes and heroines including, particularly, that of Robert Macgregor in his tale *Rob Roy*.

Intensely patriotic, it was Scott who instigated the search for the Scottish Crown Jewels in 1818, which had been missing since 1707. The occasion of the State Visit, in 1822, of George IV was also managed by Scott and it was at this event that marked the birth of the Highland culture that many tourist associate with Scotland today. Highland dress was worn, bagpipes played and the King even wore the Royal Stuart tartan.

desired. Every year in July, the town hosts the Braw Lads' gathering which, amongst other things, celebrates the marriage, in 1503, between James IV and Margaret Tudor, sister of Henry VIII. This union is commemorated by a symbolic mingling of a bouquet of red and white roses.

During the spring and summer months visitors can delight in the wonderful amount of flowers that seem to abound in the town centre, the fragrance and splendour of **Bank Street Gardens** in full bloom are wonderful. It's an ideal place for the traveller to stop and catch their breath, there is always the temptation to press on and see as much as possible, in the end missing so much.

LAUDER. **Thirlstane Castle** is possibly Scotland's finest grand symmetrical designed castle and it certainly has one of the most imposing frontages. What the visitor sees today was started, in 1670, by the first - and last - Duke of Lauderdale around the original castle. The Duke supported Charles II's attempts to foist his religious values on the Scots and he became the virtual 'uncrowned king' of the country. The castle features some very impressive Baroque plaster ceilings, as well as a huge historic toy collection and a Border life exhibition.

WALKERBURN. The village is home to the **Scottish Museum of Woollen Textiles** where, amongst its features, is an exhibition showing the growth of the country's textile trade.

The **George Hotel** is an attractive small hotel and eating place which lies on the A72 at the eastern end of the village of Walkerburn, midway between Peebles and Galashiels. Scottish Tourist Board 3 Crown Commended, this friendly family run establishment enjoys panoramic views of the Tweed Valley and is a paradise for walkers, anglers and golfers. Its eight centrally heated guest bedrooms are all comfortably appointed, with five having en-suite bathrooms and three showers and washbasins. Open all day, the lounge bar and restaurant serve delicious home-cooked dishes prepared from fresh local ingredients, with salmon a house speciality.

George Hotel, Galashiels Road, Walkerburn Tel & Fax: 01896 870336

Thirlstane Castle, Lauder

INNERLEITHEN. The Rivers Tweed and Leithen meet in this charming mill town which has a famous watering place known as **St Ronan's Well**. This was found in 1777 by local inhabitants who were drawn to it by the large number of pigeons sampling its waters. The fame of the spa spread and visitors are still able to sample the waters that are supposedly health giving. Another interesting visit to make in the town is to **Robert Smail's Printing Works**, in the High Street. This is a vintage printing press and printworks, formerly driven by water-wheels, now owned and displayed by the National Trust for Scotland and open as a museum.

Formerly known as Traquair Castle, **Traquair House**, just outside the town, has played host to 27 kings. Virtually unchanged since the 17th century, the house is home to a fascinating story concerning the 'Steekit Yetts' or Bear Gates, which were formerly the main entrance to the house. The gates were last closed after the departure of Bonnie Prince Charlie in 1745 and they have remained unopened since then; according to legend, they must remain so until a Stuart sits once again on the throne.

The current laird is a very industrious person, as he brews and sells his own brand of bottled ale, and, be warned, it is rather strong. A visit will always prove worthwhile, there is much to see in the house and, in the outbuildings, are housed a number of craftworkers, including potters, weavers and woodworkers. There are many woodland and riverside walks to choose from and a the garden dating from 1745. Before leaving this fascinating place, why not take a look around the maze?

Traquair Gates

PEEBLES epitomises everything enjoyable in the Border country; it is picturesque, full of history and yet has a thriving sense of its own character. A town built on the woollen industry, Peebles was granted a charter by David II, in 1367, nominating it a royal burgh.

The Tweed, one of the most famous salmon rivers, runs through its centre and helps give Peebles the impression that it was built for leisurely strolling, with fine buildings and open parklands going down to its banks. The wide shop-filled High Street has, as well as the usual chain

22

stores, many small craft shops and cafés.

Scrabble players and crossword fanatics may be interested to know that the Chamber brothers were born in Peebles. They were, of course, famous for their publications of encyclopaedias and dictionaries. William Chambers donated the Chambers Institute to Peebles and it is now a museum and civic centre. Thriller novel fans will be intrigued to know that John Buchan, who was the author of *The Thirty Nine Steps* (made into a celebrated film by Alfred Hitchcock) was associated with the town.

Until reorganization in 1974, Peebles was a county town and an agricultural show is held here each year in August and, in September, there are not only the Highland Games to look forward to but also the Peebles Arts Festival. It has been running for some seven years and is proving to be a wonderful myriad of drama, music, dance and exhibitions.

On the banks of the River Tweed, upstream from the town, is **Neidpath Castle**. This fortress of a palace reputedly has walls that are as thick as ten feet. Cromwell was at considerable pains to destroy it on account of this though it is now, fortunately, restored. The Queensbury family, who once owned the castle, incurred the wrath of the poet Wordsworth after they cut down every tree on the estate to pay off their gambling debts in 1795.

Situated just five minutes from Peebles town centre, the **Kingsmuir Hotel** is a delightful place to stay. This impressive family run establishment offers first-class accommodation in ten en-suite guest rooms, all recently refurbished and appointed to a very high standard.

Kingsmuir Hotel

The emphasis here is on hospitality and discreet but friendly service, and guests with children are particularly welcome. An award winner in the Best Eating Place competitions of 1992 and 1995, dining at the Kingsmuir is a treat. The restaurant is open to non-residents and offers a superb range of home-cooked dishes, including fresh local fish and game in season, plus a wide selection of vegetarian dishes.

Kingsmuir Hotel, Springhill Road, Peebles
Tel: 01721 720151 Fax: 01721 721795

Tucked away down an alley off Peebles High Street, the **Oven D'Or** serves the finest Scottish and Continental cuisine in an atmosphere which is relaxed and intimate. This delightful restaurant is housed in a handsome mid-19th century former bakery, outside which locals once queued in the early hours to buy rolls hot from the oven. Today, it is owned and run by Jo and Keith Hitchcock. Jo is an accomplished pasty chef and her menu features a number of mouthwatering pastry dishes, such as fresh salmon parcel served with a seafood sauce; all are freshly prepared and cooked to order. A veritable pot of gold, this outstanding eating place is open all day for morning coffees, lunches and evening meals.

The Oven D'Or, 24 High Street, Peebles Tel: 01721 723456

Hilary Forbes is an artist renowned for her beautiful **Hand-Painted Silks** which she produces in a studio located in a cobbled brae leading down from Peebles High Street to the River Tweed. Her output includes items of clothing such as ties, waistcoats and scarves, jewellery such as brooches and earrings, wall and window hangings, lamp shades, fans and cards.

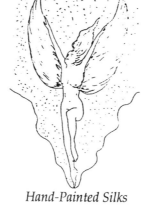

Hand-Painted Silks

All are hand-painted on to silk and are individually crafted so that no two items are the same. She also paints silk lids for wood and porcelain jewellery boxes and takes on illustration work and special commissions. Visitors are welcome to call and browse through her unique display of finished items.

Hilary Forbes Hand-Painted Silk, Unit 2 Craft Centre, School Brae, Peebles
Tel: 01721 720032

BROUGHTON. This pretty village, standing on Biggar Water, was the childhood home of the author John Buchan and also where his grandfather was minister. The **John Buchan Centre** is housed in the United Free Church and a popular locally brewed ale is called Greenmantle after one of his novels.

Set in one of the most breathtaking locations in southern Scotland, the **Broughton Gallery** occupies the ground floor of a large country mansion which stands on an isolated hillside in upper Tweeddale. Though looking much like a 17th century Scottish 'tower house', the turreted Broughton Place was, in fact, designed in the 1930s by Sir Basil Spence, the renowned Edinburgh architect who went on to design Coventry Cathedral. In 1976, Jane and Graham Buchanan-Dunlop founded a gallery in this magnificent setting to exhibit original paintings, prints, glassware, ceramics and jewellery by Scottish artists and craftspeople. Since then it has gone from strength to strength, thanks to their ongoing pledge to show top quality work which is well designed, well made and realistically priced. To complement their permanent display, Jane and Graham organise a series of special exhibitions based around a specific theme or the work of an individual artist. In summer, visitors can also walk in the beautiful walled garden with its spectacular views and superb collection of rare plants. Situated to the north of Broughton village on the A701 Moffat to Edinburgh road within an hour's drive of Carlisle, Edinburgh and Glasgow, the gallery is open daily except Wednesdays, 10.30 am to 6 pm from late March to mid-October, and from mid-November till Christmas.

Broughton Gallery, Broughton Place, Broughton Tel: 01899 830234

ST MARY'S LOCH. At the edge of the Ettrick Forest and set amongst rolling green hills, this is a truly beautiful spot. The loch is three miles long and these days it is commonly used for sailing, with a popular sailing club on the western end. The atmosphere is wonderfully peaceful here and it's great to just linger by the shores, skimming stones and generally letting time just pass by.

TIBBIE SHIEL'S INN. 'Tibbie Shiel' is a legendary name in these parts and on the neck of land that separates St Mary's Loch from the smaller Loch of the Lowes, is an inn with a tale to tell. Originally a cottage owned by Lord Napier, the Inn was rented by Tibbie and Robert Richardson, a mole catcher. It was St Mary's Cottage then, but, on the death of her husband, Tibbie reverted to her maiden name of Shiel and started to take in lodgers to support herself and her six children. Until her death in 1878, in her 96th year, Tibbie played host to such famous names as Sir Walter Scott, Professor Wilson, alias Christopher North, the publisher Robert Chambers and local poet James Hogg, the Ettrick Shepherd.

Tibbie Shiel's conjures up images of days gone by and of James Hogg penning his verse in the candlelit inn with only the log fires for company. There are certainly many references to Tibbie Shiel's in his poetry and literature: he obviously felt that Tibbie Shiel's Inn was worth writing home about.

NEWCASTLETON. Built in 1793, Newcastleton is one of the few planned village in the Borders and consists of a single long 'high' street astride the main road and a regular pattern street plan.

To the north of the village stands one of the Borders' most famous castles, **The Hermitage**. Aptly named, the Castle stands quite alone, grim and oppressive in the wild remote Liddesdale hills. Built in the 13th century it has an often bloody history. In October 1566 the 4th Earl of Bothwell, badly wounded in a skirmish with border rievers, was paid a surprise visit by Mary, Queen of Scots. She had been presiding over a Royal Court at Jedburgh but, on hearing of her lover's plight, she rode 20 furious miles to the Castle and two hours later back again; a feat that cost her a fever and nearly her life. Even on the sunniest day the castle's brooding presence makes the Queen's adventure all to easy to imagine and admire.

HAWICK. The largest of the Border burghs, Hawick has a thriving reputation for the manufacture of quality knitwear, clothing and carpets. The town is the home of such names as Pringle of Scotland, Lyle and Scott, Peter Scott and many other smaller firms producing knitwear in cashmere, lambswool and Shetland yarns.

The centre of a vibrant farming community, Hawick has an interest in animals both alive and dead, as it is the centre for the longest established auction mart in the whole of Britain. It also boasts a number of butchers producing that Scottish delicacy the Haggis, each to their own closely guarded recipe.

The Scottish Borders was, for centuries, an area of turmoil and intrigue. To the English, it was the area of first and last encounter with a traditional enemy and the target for quick and often bloody retribution. All of the Border towns were destroyed many times by raiders from England. Hawick was burned down no fewer than six times by the mid-1600s. On one occasion the natives of Hawick burned the town themselves to prevent the English from having the pleasure of extracting their vengeance. Traffic in marauding was by no means confined to the Scottish side - many English towns suffered a similar fate when the 'Rievers' of the Borders, on their small ponies, appeared from nowhere to burn, kill and rob.

Perhaps it is because Hawick was not stable enough that few ancient buildings exist - no abbey, castle or magnificent building has survived. **The Black Tower of Drumlanrig**, perhaps the oldest building, has suffered partial destruction on numerous occasions (the latest being dry-rot and vermin). Needle Street, in the town's west end, is the oldest remaining street. However, a dearth of ancient buildings does not mean a lack of ancient tradition and ceremony. Each year the town holds its colourful Common Riding Celebrations on the first and second weekends of June, a legacy of the aftermath of the Battle of Flodden in 1513. The **Horse Monument** in the High Street also commemorates the battle, a disaster for the town when nearly all the menfolk were killed. Riders visiting Hawick might like to try the 'Hawick Circular', which is a 27 mile ride running along minor roads, tracks and cross country sections.

First set up in 1984 to provide a place of rest, quiet and refreshment, **Whitchester Christian Guest House** is two miles south of Hawick town centre and run by Doreen and David Maybury, who have spent many years in ordained ministry. This comfortable country house stands in three and a half acres of magnificent gardens and offers its guests an opportunity to talk and pray through experiences and needs with trained counsellors. The house is elegantly furnished and preserves the atmosphere and comfort of a private home whilst offering the guest a time to worship in the modern and delightful chapel. A conservatory adjoins the lounge which has an open log fire, TV, video and audio equipment along with various records and tapes of Christian music and a wide selection of board games. All of the attractive guests rooms have hand basins, hair driers and drink making facilities, with four of the rooms being en-suite and the ground floor bedroom, equipped for the disabled, has its own shower. There is a library which has a wide selection of books and also a small shop that sells stamps, sweets and many other items for your convenience.

Much of the food used in the wonderful meals comes from Whitchester's own walled vegetable garden at the back of the house plus other local produce and game. The cuisine is recommended by A Taste of Scotland and a wide selection of Scottish cheeses are offered at the evening meal with special diets being catered for by prior arrangement. Enjoy a game of croquet on the main lawn at the front of the house or

27

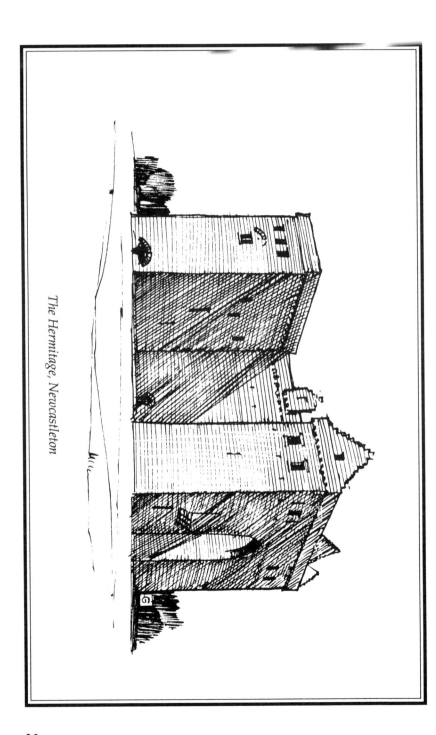

The Hermitage, Newcastleton

some energetic badminton, but whatever you choose to do with your time, we know that you will leave Whitchester Christian Guest House feeling rehabilitated and at peace.

Whitchester Christian Guest House, Borthaugh, Hawick
Tel & Fax: 01450 377477/371080

JEDBURGH. The town, which presents a pleasant and striking blend of old and new, is perhaps best known for its Abbey. Once rich and powerful, **Jedburgh Abbey** suffered the wrath of Henry VIII and his Reformation, along with many other abbeys in the region. Its majestic ruins, stand just outside the town, and are all that remain today.

In the middle of the High Street, looking rather modern, lies what is reputedly the oldest hotel in Scotland, and the fourth oldest in the British Isles; **The Spread Eagle**. In October 1566, Mary, Queen of Scots, travelled to Jedburgh to hold a Justice Ayres, or Circuit Court, in the Tolbooth that stood in Canongate, and as the Spread Eagle Hotel had already been established, she naturally sought lodging there. She remained until driven out by a fire next door, when she moved to Mary, Queen of Scots' House, which has been excellently preserved since its complete renovation in 1928.

Another distinguished guest at the hotel was Sir Walter Scott, who lodged there when engaged in the local circuit court, where he made his first appearance as an advocate. Robert Burns also lived in the town, for a short time, and it can be safely assume that he also had a knowledge of the 'Spread', as it is known locally, and of the fiery fluid purveyed therein.

Jedburgh Abbey

CHAPTER TWO

DUMFRIES & GALLOWAY

Caerlaverlock Castle

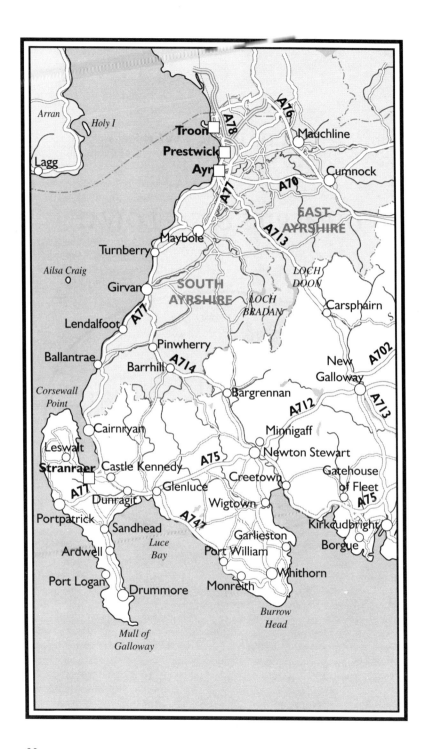

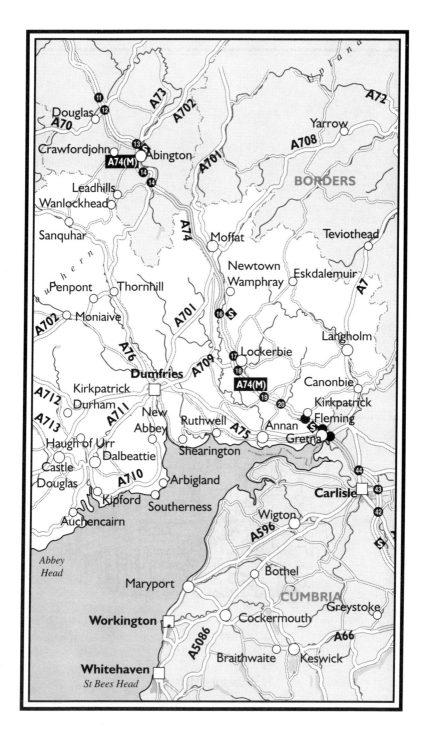

Dumfries Midsteeple

CHAPTER TWO

DUMFRIES & GALLOWAY

The Western Route to Scotland

DUMFRIES. If the Borders are associated with the tales and legends of Walter Scott, then Dumfries and Galloway are forever associated with the poet Robert Burns. He lived in Dumfries and worked as an exciseman here until his death in 1796. There is a statue in the High Street commemorating this town's most famous citizen. Many people come to Dumfries each year to visit the monuments and places associated with the poet and this period in his life is widely considered to be one of his most productive.

Whilst the French Revolution and the Napoleonic Wars were going on, and the country was alive with rumours and alarms, there were food shortages and riots in Dumfries. It was during this time that Burns produced some of his best work, despite being heavily in debt and suffering from a serious illness. He first came to Dumfries in 1787 but did not eventually settle here until some four years later, after finding his farm, Ellisand, to be uneconomical. He first lived in Bank Street, and the building can still be seen. In 1793 Burns moved to a larger house in what is now called Burns Street. Here he worked until his death three years later. The two storey house where he spent his last years is now **The Burns Museum**, with many items associated with the poet on display including some manuscripts. Burns is buried in the graveyard of nearby St Michael's Church.

During his time in Dumfries Burns was no stranger to its taverns, and one with special Burns links is the **Globe Inn**, just off the High Street. In the small panelled rooms it is fascinating to think of the poet sharing a glass of port or a tankard of ale with his friends. His favourite armchair is still there but before trying it out for size be warned, as anyone who sits in the chair can be called upon to buy a round of drinks for everyone present. In 1790 Burns had an affair with a young barmaid and she bore him a child, which his wife later took in and cared for as one of her own. For a full explanation of the poet's links with this town, why not take a look at the **Robbie Burns Centre** situated on the banks of the River Nith. This old mill building houses a permanent exhibition and an audio-visual presentation on the poet's life and works.

The most familiar landmark in Dumfries is the Midsteeple, a former tollbooth in the town centre which has been witness to some famous characters from the past. Bonnie Prince Charlie would have passed it on his way through Dumfries with the bedraggled remains of his army.

Apparently the soldiers needed some more shoes on their return journey, the ones from Selkirk being worn out, only this time the folk of Dumfries were not as forthcoming. A request for 1000 pairs of shoes only resulted in 225 being offered, whereupon, according to legend, the soldiers began to stop people in the street and take their shoes from them.

If the Midsteeple looks somewhat peculiar it is because it now leans over, although not so far as to risk of toppling. Walking around the town's old streets provides an opportunity to look at many interesting buildings, from the elegant Trades Hall to the quaint Queensberry Square with its old fashioned closes.

It comes as a surprise to learn that Dumfries was the inspiration for the story of Peter Pan. The young James M Barrie was a pupil at the predecessor of Dumfries Academy. In 1860 Barrie came to Dumfries and was, at one time, in the school's amateur dramatic club. He even wrote one of its earliest productions. When he returned to Dumfries, some years later as Sir James Barrie, he revealed that it was while playing in the gardens on the banks of the River Nith that he conceived the original basis for Peter Pan. The house in which he stayed whilst at the Academy is in Victoria Place and is marked with a plaque.

With a statue of Burns in front of it, **Greyfriars Church**, is a prominent red brick building of 1867 on the corner of Academy and Castle Streets. The Church occupies the site of the town's ancient castle and should not be confused with the 13th century **Greyfriars Friary**. The Franciscan Friary stood close by and it was here (at a spot now commemorated by a plaque) that Robert the Bruce and Kirkpatrick murdered Comyn in a dispute over the crown.

The River Nith, which runs through the centre of Dumfries, is crossed by several bridges and the six-arched **Old Footbridge**, dating in parts from the 15th century, is the last in a succession of bridges at this point. At the west end of this bridge stands the **Old Bridge House**, dating from 1660, and now home to a museum of local life, complete with period rooms.

Crichton Royal Hospital, to the southeast of the town, offers an unusual and interesting museum as it is dedicated principally to mental health care in southwest Scotland over the last 200 years. The Museum also contains a 19th century art gallery.

AROUND DUMFRIES

SHEARINGTON. Unique in Scotland with its triangular layout and moat **Caerlaverock Castle** proved a formidable fortress for the Maxwell family. It was taken by King Edward for 11 years, in 1301, and, in 1638, it fell to the Covenanters after a siege of some 13 weeks.

Nearby is the **Caerlaverock Nature Reserve**, covering some 13,594 acres of saltmarsh and sand along the coastline of the Solway Firth. The marshes and mudflats stretch for six miles along the coastline and, in winter, the reserve is home to great flocks of Barnacle Geese and other wildfowl. It also provides a breeding ground for the rare Natterjack toad. The wildfowl reserve is open from mid-summer until the end of April.

Caerlaverock Castle

RUTHWELL. This village is the unlikely home of the first savings bank in Britain. Founded in 1810 by the local minister, Henry Duncan, the building is now the **Duncan Savings Bank Museum**. Also worth a visit is **Ruthwell Church**, with its famous and impressive **Ruthwell Cross**. This 17 foot high cross is a testament to the faith of the early Christians and has survived many attempts to destroy it. Dating from the early 8th century, it features intricate and beautiful carvings, illustrating episodes from the Gospels.

A short drive from the village is **Comlongon Castle**. Exceptionally well preserved, it contains many original features including the great hall, kitchens, dungeons and bed chambers, with their 'privies'. A real opportunity to see how life was in a 15th century castle. A hotel is now attached to the keep.

ANNAN. This small red stone town sits overlooking the Solway Firth and the mountains of the Lake District. An ancient burgh, it was in fact founded by the family of King Robert the Bruce and the Bruce coat of arms is used by the town.

Standing close to the border as it does, Annan has been subjected to the unwelcome attentions of the English on many occasions and was destroyed repeatedly between 1298 and 1660. It was, however, the waters of the River Annan which brought about the first of many tragedies for this burgh. A curse was put on the town by the renowned mystic St Malachy, who was angered by the decision of one of the Lords of Annan to execute a robber on whose behalf he had interceded.

The town today, however, bears little sign of those turbulent years and is a pleasant and peaceful place in this lovely riverside setting. Once an important shipbuilding and trading centre, Annan now offers the visitor strolls around the attractive riverside park, many walks around nearby **Hoddom Castle** and there is a golf course with lovely views over the Solway.

GRETNA GREEN. Situated just across the Scottish border, Gretna Green is renowned for its runaway couples and hasty marriages. It's strange to think that marriages by declaration could in fact take place at any house or shop, provided there were two witnesses available.

In 1856, after much indignation from the Church and even local people, who were not too happy with what they saw as 'immoral practices', the law was changed. The new legislation demanded a residential qualification of a minimum of three weeks prior to the ceremony. Even when the couples had been married their problems were not always over and there have been several cases of bridegrooms being arrested on their return to England.

In one particular case, where a music master married his 12 year old pupil, the bridegroom was sentenced to nine months in jail for abduction. In 1940 marriage by declaration became illegal, although the age of consent was still lower than that in England, and the attraction of Gretna Green continued to lure young couples. This attraction only really declined when, in 1970, the age of marriage without parental consent was lowered in England from 21 to 18 years.

It is worth spending some time looking around this most famous place. The blacksmith's shop today has a range of curiosities and souvenirs from the marriage trade and there is also the opportunity to get involved in a mock ceremony.

KIRKPATRICK-FLEMING. A perfect example of a charming country inn can be found in this quiet village. The Station Inn is over 200 years old and inside the theme is, not surprisingly, railway based and there is plenty of fascinating memorabilia.

Some of this relates to **Quintinshill Signal Box**, scene of Britain's worst rail disaster. One busy morning in May 1915 a train carrying a regiment of the 7th Royal Scots struck a standing local train and the wreckage was run into by a north bound express. The following conflagration took an estimated 226 lives, the final number never being known as the regiment's records were destroyed in the train. Another 200 were badly injured. As the disaster involved troops during wartime it did not receive the publicity which usually attends such catastrophes, few people have heard of Quintinshill.

Kirkpatrick-Fleming is better known, however, as the site of **Bruce's Cave**. It was here, so the story goes, that Bruce hid and was inspired to carry on his struggle against the English by watching a spider persevere in making its web.

ECCLEFECHAN. The village is noted as the birthplace, in 1795, of the historian and essayist Thomas Carlyle. The **Arched House**, built by Carlyle's father and uncle, who were both master masons, is now a museum and features his letters and relics. The house is owned by the National Trust for Scotland.

CANONBIE. The parish church, in this picturesque village on the left bank of the River Esk, dates from 1822 and is situated on the opposite side of the River. Interestingly, it was designed by William Atkinson, the architect of Sir Walter Scott's Abbotsford.

LANGHOLM. A typical Border town in appearance, situated on the River Esk, like Edinburgh, Langholm is divided into a new and old town. It is hard to believe that three rivers join here and, not surprisingly, there are three bridges.

Being a true Border town, Langholm has an annual Common Riding which takes place on the last Friday in June. A feature of this day is that the colours worn by the Cornet for his ride are the same as the colours of that year's Epsom Derby winner. An unusual custom that is over 100 years old and must have a reason, now seemingly lost. This special event is a day full of the most exciting spectacles, including horse racing, foot racing, wrestling and Highland dancing; followed, in the evening, by open air dancing. Be warned though, the day's celebrations start at five o'clock in the morning.

Langholm is an excellent centre for exploring the quiet valleys and hill country on foot and there are marvellous opportunities for cycling and driving. There is also excellent fishing nearby.

ESKDALEMUIR. In the heart of some of the most magical forests and scenery lies the village of Eskdalemuir. In 1905 an observatory was built on the moors and there is also a weather station here. Some of the lowest temperatures in the winter are recorded at this station.

In this remote setting is the **Kagyu Samye Ling Tibetan Centre**, a Buddhist centre. This is a thriving international community and holds pottery, woodcarving and carpet-weaving workshops. There is an art studio and a printing press and meditation, healing and Buddhism are also taught. The centre is a highly unusual place, and promises an enjoyable visit.

MOFFAT. A picturesque town with wide main streets, attractive shops and hotels and fabulous gardens and parks which have helped earn Moffat the title of the 'Best Kept Village in Scotland' award twice in recent years.

In the centre of the town is a handsome square with the **Colvin Fountain**, surmounted by a ram. This statue proclaims the importance of sheep in this area and the role played by Moffat as a sheep and wool trading centre.

The **Moffat Museum** is housed in a traditional bakehouse in the old part of the town. The Scotch oven, an old furnace used for baking bread, is a particularly interesting feature on the ground floor. The museum also has an exhibition tracing local history which follows Moffat's rise as a health resort in the mid-18th century due to the discovery here of mineral springs. As a result of this, Moffat became famous as one of the few spa towns in Scotland. The **Old Well** and **Hartfell Spa** have both been restored and make fascinating visits.

Apart from fishing, Moffat can offer a wide variety of activities for the visitor. There are many beautiful walks around the surrounding countryside and horse riding, pony-trekking, cycle hire, sailing and swimming are all available locally. The annual South of Scotland Tennis Tournament held here actually pre-dates Wimbledon.

On the High Street in Moffat, you'll find the charming **Mulberry's Restaurant and Gift Shop**. Run by its new owners Phil and Agnes Smart, this attractively presented, family run, licensed Restaurant reflects the chef's international culinary skills. The widest range of tastes are catered for, whether your requirement is an appetising lunch or a romantic evening meal. Open for morning coffee, lighter snacks, afternoon teas and dinner, Mulberry's is a place to meet at any time of the day.

Mulberry's Restaurant & Gift Shop

In the Gift Shop, all manner of interesting goods are displayed; knitwear, ceramics, jewellery, china ornaments, Scottish clan ties and scarves are some of the very popular purchases to be made. Mulberry's is the only stockist of Acorn sweatshirts, hats and baseball caps in the town. Children are not forgotten and making a selection from the choice of soft toys, small toys and the many items to keep them happy is a pleasant task. Lots of gift ideas for young and old alike.

Mulberry's Restaurant & Gift Shop, High Street, Moffat Tel: 01683 220900

One of Moffat's hidden treasures and most unusual businesses is **Moffat Pottery**, your visit here may hold more surprises than the many interesting gifts on sale. The owner, Gerry Lyons, is known as 'The Singing Potter' and his smooth lirico spinto tenor voice regularly serenades his customers - quite a Continental experience and very enjoyable. Gerry has a range of hand-thrown pots, lamps, plates, teapots, mugs and other gift items which are all made on the premises, hand-painted and finished. He has been established for 28 years and you will delight in the many and varied gifts which carry his special hallmark and designs.

Moffat Pottery, 20 High Street, Moffat Tel: 01683 220793

NEWTON WAMPHRAY. Follow the old Carlisle road from Moffat signposted Newton Wamphray and turn right at the crossroads in the village, this will lead you to the **Red House Hotel**, the home of Val and Derrick Wilson for the past two years.

Red House Hotel

Here is a perfect place from which to enjoy touring the locality, walking, bird watching and some excellent fishing. Permits are available for the River Annan for the trout season from the 15th April to 15th September with a good run of sea trout in June and July. Salmon fishing takes place from 25th February to 15th November, the best time being September to November. The Red House is a comfortable, family run licensed hotel with bar meals always available and a wholesome dinner is served by arrangement. A peaceful country setting.

Red House Hotel, Newton Wamphray Tel: 01576 470470

LOCHMABEN. **Lochmaben Castle**, which dates from the early 14th century, is thought to have belonged to the family of Robert the Bruce and it later became a favourite residence of James IV. Today, unhappily, only the creeper-clad ruins remain.

LOCKERBIE. This small town has been important since the 17th century for its lamb fairs but, more recently, it is tragically associated with the terrorist destruction of an American civil airliner in December 1988. Now bypassed by the main road to Carlisle, much of the town's 17th and 18th century character has remained.

THORNHILL. The wide streets are lined with lime trees planted by the Duke of Buccleuch in 1861 and the monument at the end of the main street was erected by the Duke of Queensbury in 1714, Pegasus being his winged emblem. Thornhill is dominated by the magnificent Queensbury mountain which stands at 2,285 feet.

Just to the north is romantic **Drumlanrig Castle**, a beautiful stately mansion that is open to the public. The mansion was built by the 1st Duke of Queensbury between 1679 and 1690 and it was a departure from the style of most Scottish castles; more a fairy tale castle with its superb, pink sandstone walls and enchanting roof. Inside, there is the finest collection of furniture, paintings, silver and china in Scotland. Bonnie Prince Charlie slept here on his retreat northwards from Dumfries in 1745. His bedroom can still be seen as can a few of his mementoes and personal relics.

The castle has a magnificent setting and there are lovely views of the surrounding countryside. There are 40 acres of garden, craft shops and an adventure playground for the children.

PENPONT. A handsome and uncompromising example of the L-shaped fortified tower, **Barjarg Tower** forms the northeast corner of a mansion house lying on the west side of the River Nith some four miles south of Penpont. 'Barjarg' by the way means 'the red hill top'.

The original tower dates from the late 16th century when it was built by one of the Earls of Morton and gifted by him to Thomas Grierson. A later owner, a Mr Erskine, planted the magnificent Wellingtonia trees that have stood guard behind the house since the beginning of the 18th century.

In 1740, the property passed to a Reverend Hunter, a Doctor of Divinity from Edinburgh, who was related to the Hunters of Hunterston in Ayrshire; the remains of whose castle is now a near neighbour of a nuclear power station. Dr Hunter was the founder of the Hunter Arundell family who have owned the property and its surrounding estate for some 250 years.

Early in the 18th century the main part of the house was built with a symmetrical frontage and a matching tower at the west end. However the old tower is well preserved and visitors can see the original iron gate and many other features.

Robert Burns Monument, Dumfries.

ROBERT BURNS

Scotland's greatest poet, Robert Burns spent much of his life in the southwest of Scotland and, in particular, he and his works are most associated with the areas around Ayr and Dumfries. He was born, in 1759, at Alloway and the scene of his famous poem, *Tam o' Shanter*, is laid between Ayr and Alloway Brig o'Doon. In 1777 his family moved to Lochlea Farm near Tarbolton.

Along with his brother and father, Burns worked the farm but, after seven years, the farm was failing and Burns booked a passage to Jamaica. However, the first volume of his poetry was published in 1786 and proved to be so successful that Burns cancelled the passage and stayed in the area. During his time in Tarbolton, Burns founded, in 1780, a literary and debating society which became known as the Bachelors' Club.

Burns' early works such as *Highland Lassie* and *Highland Mary* were inspired by Mary Campbell of Dunoon, with whom Burns was in love. Fate though intervened and the couple were dealt a cruel blow when Mary died young.

In 1788, in nearby Mauchline, Burns married Jean Armour, the daughter of a local mason and the cottage in which they lived is now the Burns House Museum. After the wedding, Burns moved to Ellisland Farm, near Thornhill, where he, unsuccessfully, experimented with new farming methods. However, as a poet he flourished and it was during his time here that Burns wrote *Tam o' Shanter*, *Auld Lang Syne* and *Mary in Heaven*.

Once again moving on after the farm failed, Burns took up the post of excise officer in Dumfries in 1791. Here he remained until his death in 1796, in the meantime writing over 100 poems.

For many Robert Burns is most famous for his poem to the haggis, the 'great chieftain o' the pudden race'. Traditionally, on Burns' Night (24 January) the haggis is majestically piped into the dining room and Burns recited before the traditional feast of haggis, tatties and neeps are served, washed down with whisky.

MONIAIVE. Set between Craigdarroch and Dalwhat Waters, the village streets' are small and narrow with brightly painted houses. Moniaive is renowned for its peaceful atmosphere and beautiful surroundings.

There are many references to the Covenanters in these parts. They were Presbyterians who were persecuted for refusing to renounce their faith during the reigns of Charles II and James II. The Convenanters were often cruelly put to death without trial and due to this the 1680s later became known as the 'Killing Time'.

SANQUHAR. This name, which conjures up any number of exotic images, apparently means simply, 'old fort'. The post office here is the oldest in Britain and still retains some of its old world charm.

It is saddening to discover that at one time workers in the mines here were subject to laws of bondage, which meant that miners and their whole families could be bought and sold as slaves. They could only avoid this iniquitous system by escaping and staying free for a whole year and a day. Capture, however, would result in brutal punishment. It was not until the end of the 18th century that the final traces of this custom were removed by an Act of Parliament. There is an interesting local museum in the **Old Tolbooth** (1735), which is now a visitor and information centre.

The Solway Firth

NEWTON STEWART. Recently voted 'The Friendliest Town in the UK', Newton Stewart lies in the shadow of the Galloway Hills. A relatively modern town, it was built in the towards the end of the 17th century by William Stewart, son of the Earl of Galloway, after a charter had been granted by Charles II in 1677. The **Newton Stewart Museum**, housed in an old church, tells the story of the area as well as featuring period costumes, lace and a fine collection of photographs.

In the town centre of the bustling, ever popular Newton Stewart is Alexandra Wilson's **Chatterbox Coffee Shop**. An altogether ideal place to while away a little time relaxing and enjoying some of her very tasty and tempting home-baking. The mouthwatering meals and snacks set this coffee shop apart from the usual.

Alexandra has many delicious cakes and gateaux which, taken with one of the many speciality teas and coffees from around the world, will lift your spirits and tickle your taste buds. After a little shopping, call back and enjoy lunch or afternoon tea and savour more tempting savouries and sweets. Care is taken with children and disabled customers. A very popular and delightful respite.

The Chatterbox, 73 Victoria Street, Newton Stewart Tel: 01671 403967

AROUND NEWTON STEWART

MINNIGAFF is an ancient suburb of Newton Stewart, lying on the opposite bank of the River Cree.

'Good Golf and a Warm Welcome' is the promise of **Newton Stewart Golf Club**! With immaculate turf and true fairways this parkland course is set amidst the Galloway Hills with a pine forest backdrop affording stunning views from most tees. The recent addition of nine holes to this course has greatly added to its character with challenging shots and dramatic views. The new 9th hole, for example, provides a difficult test with options for the teeshot and the second shot for those golfers not willing or able to take on the carry over whins and a burn. This is followed by a dramatic short hole from an elevated tee over a burn and in a ravine. Distant views of Cairnsmore and Wigtown Bay add to the pleasure of a day's golf in this lovely setting. 18 Holes - Par 69. In whatever state you emerge from the golf course, a warm welcome awaits you in the Clubhouse. The bar and catering staff will attend to your needs whether it be refreshments, bar snacks and meals, or merely a shoulder to cry on! Accessible from the A75 Euroroute, in Minnigraff Village.

Newton Stewart Golf Club, Kirroughtree Avenue, Minnigaff
Tel: 01671 402172

NEW GALLOWAY. The road around Loch Ken is notable for its lovely scenic views of the waters and of the Galloway Forest. New Galloway is itself a very attractive little town which is actually the smallest Royal Burgh in Scotland and, standing on the River Ken, it is a popular base for anglers. To the south of the town, on the banks of the Loch, stand the ruins of **Kenmure Castle**, a Gordon stronghold.

To the west of New Galloway, along the A712, lies **Clatteringshaws Loch** in the Galloway Forest. The loch is surely one of the most scenic spots in Galloway with transfixing views over the waters to the hills beyond. This road runs through the Galloway Forest Park and the route was officially opened as 'The Queens Way' in commemoration of the Silver Jubilee of Queen Elizabeth II in 1977.

46

The park takes in a huge area and the road gives splendid views of mountains, lochs and waterfalls. To get thoroughly clued up on the park and its wildlife visit the **Galloway Deer Museum** at Clatteringshaws. Here there is a display on the history of the area and the wildlife in the park.

Opposite Clatteringshaws Loch is the famous 'Raiders Road' which is a trail following an old cattle rustler's route alongside the Blackwater at Dee.

KIRKPATRICK DURHAM. An unexpected surprise awaits those making a small detour into the hills between the A75 and B729 to the northwest of Dumfries. A minor road leads up to Glenkiln reservoir, and there on the hillsides surrounding the loch is a wonderful collection of sculptures by Henry Moore and other well-known artists. To observe these motionless figures in this remote setting is a strange and magical experience, although visitors are not allowed to approach them as they are on private land. From the Glenkiln sculptures, a road leads down to the southwest towards the A712 Crocketford to New Galloway road.

Close to this junction lies **Craigadam**, an impressive country residence which offers superb holiday accommodation throughout the year. Established in 1980 by Richard and Celia Pickup, this handsome white-painted house is attached to an 18th century hill farm which stands in a beautiful rural setting with lawns, orchards and woodland all around. As well as being open to all those wanting a break away from it all, Craigadam specialises in holidays for enthusiasts of the time-honoured country pursuits of hunting, shooting and fishing.

Craigadam

Among the many activities on offer are deer stalking, rough shooting, pheasant shooting, and trout and salmon fishing. Expert tuition is also available in fly casting, and rifle and shotgun shooting, as well as in the more up-to-date rural pursuit of 4 x 4 off-roading. Up to six guests can be accommodated in the house in three beautifully appointed en-suite bedrooms, and there is also a similarly well appointed self-catering cottage sleeping a further six (meals can be taken in the house, if required). The house itself has wonderfully comfortable atmosphere, with open log fires and a magnificent oak-panelled dining room.

The food at Craigadam is out of this world. Celia is renowned for her outstanding Scottish cuisine and makes the most of the many superb ingredients that are available to her, including locally caught trout and salmon, game in season, venison, and fresh vegetables and fruit from the farm and orchard. Whether a lover of the countryside or a keen outdoor sportsperson, Craigadam offers a superb holiday base for all those wanting a luxurious and highly enjoyable holiday in the heart of beautiful rural Scotland.

Craigadam, Kirkpatrick Durham Tel & Fax: 01556 650233

HAUGH OF URR. This village is ideally placed for many country pursuits such as fishing and shooting and, of course, walking. There is an abundance of forest, coastal and cliff walks to enjoy, with many fascinating Heritage Trails amidst the Galloway Hills and the Colvend Coast. The bridge here, built in 1760, straddles the small salmon river, the Urr, which also has a good run of sea trout in high summer.

Motte of Urr, to the south, is an impressive site and is the most extensive motte-and-bailey castle in Scotland. Its siting here is something of a mystery as there does not seem much to commend the position. It is possible however, that the river once surrounded it, making it an island. The circular mound here is 80 feet high.

NEW ABBEY. This picturesque village is a thoroughly charming and unspoilt haven with the impressive ruin of **Sweetheart Abbey** nearby. Right at the bottom of Criffel Hill, the Abbey was built in the 13th and 14th centuries by Lady Devorgilla in memory of her husband, John de Balliol: their son was the King of Scotland for a short while, chosen by Edward I.

There is a popular story that after her husband's death Lady Devorgilla carried his embalmed heart in an ivory casket wherever she went. When she eventually died, some 21 years later, the casket was buried with her in front of the high altar. The name of the Abbey comes from the Cistercians who, as a tribute to this lady, called it 'Dulce Cor' or Sweetheart.

After looking around the Abbey it is well worth paying a visit to the delightful **Shambellie House Museum of Costume**, which is just a quarter of a mile to the north of the village. The building itself is notable for having been designed by the architect David Bryce in 1854 and the house reflects the rich characteristics of Bryce's style, referred to as Scottish Baronial. Particularly fascinating are the crow-stepped gables, towers and turrets. The Scottish heritage is uniquely reflected in the appearance of the building with its suggestion of battlements, a reminder of the many castles seen in this part of the country.

Inside, the building houses the most fascinating exhibition of clothes, mainly from the 18th and 19th centuries, which were collected by Charles Stuart of Shambellie, an illustrator who developed this collection over a period of years starting before the Second World War.

Nearby, **Criffel Hill** is 1868 feet high and is not really a climb for the faint-hearted. The granite can be quite steep and rough in parts, making the wearing of a good pair of stout walking shoes advisable. Take it on good authority that the views at the summit are spectacular.

Taking the A710 Solway Coast route travelling south of Dumfries for seven miles, you arrive at the picturesque village of New Abbey with its 13th century Sweetheart Abbey, restored corn mill, and the very comfortable **Criffel Inn**. This unspoilt corner of the Scottish Borders offers easy access to many golf courses, sandy beaches and sea angling, loch and river fishing, and other holiday activities.

Criffel Inn

The owner-managed Inn has five en-suite bedrooms complete with colour televisions and tea making facilities. Home-baking and cooking are specialities of the Criffel Inn; traditional Scottish dishes are prepared from fresh local produce. Lunches, high teas and suppers are served daily in the dining room, bar and garden patio. With central heating throughout the inn and a selection of over 100 malt whiskies available at the bar, one can settle down to a most enjoyable and cosy evening! Egon Ronay Recommended for food and accommodation.

Criffel Inn, New Abbey Tel: 01387 850305

No visit to New Abbey would be complete without calling in at **Abbey Cottage Coffees and Crafts** which stands right beside the Abbey ruins. A non-smoking establishment, this is the perfect place to relax with a drink and a snack before purchasing a memento or gift. The combined efforts of Morag McKie and Jacqui Wilson ensure that all food is freshly prepared and of the highest quality, which has earned them an entry into various prestigious guides.

In addition to tea, coffee and soft drinks, you can enjoy a glass of wine or beer with your meal. After sampling the excellent food, the

Sweetheart Abbey, New Abbey

adjoining craft shop leaves you faced with the dilemma of what to choose from a wide range of locally produced, high quality arts and crafts.

Abbey Coffees and Crafts, New Abbey Tel: 01387 850377

ARBIGLAND. The gardens of **Arbigland House** are open to the public in the summer and John Paul Jones was born in one of the estate cottages in 1747. He was to become one of the area's most famous sons and became known as the 'father of the American Navy'. The story of John Paul Jones is very interesting and definitely worth a mention as he was not solely regarded as a hero. Indeed some people, including the British, branded him a pirate.

When he was only 13 he boarded a boat at nearby Carsethorn and began an apprenticeship in the Merchant Navy that was to last for seven years. His travels took him around the world visiting such beautiful places as Barbados and Virginia, and eventually he assumed command of his own ship. In Tobago, however, he killed a man in self defence whom he claimed had been a mutineer and, as a result, was forced to leave the navy, spending a year in America. When he discovered that officers were needed for the Congress' new navy he signed on as a first lieutenant. His most notable involvement in the colonial conflicts came when he staged raids against the port of Whitehaven and across the Solway at Kirkcudbright Bay.

Legend has it that he planned to seize the Earl of Selkirk as a hostage but, upon finding that the Laird was away from home, he gave his men permission to loot the family plate. After the conflicts were over Jones apparently purchased the plate and returned it to the family. John Paul Jones continued his exploits throughout America and Europe where his feats brought him recognition as a war hero. He was awarded a gold medal in recognition of his services by the US Congress and, in France, a dance was named in his honour. He was even invited to Russia where he helped the navy of the Empress Catherine defeat the Turks.

In 1953, the US Naval Historical Foundation and the Daughters of the American Revolution presented a plaque to be erected at his birth-place. At Carsethorn, where the Steam Packet Inn still stands, there are the remains of the old wooden jetty where John Paul Jones left to start his adventures.

Interestingly, once upon a time, a regular steam ship service left from here to go to Whitehaven and Liverpool. In addition although these old ports on the Solway seem to be relatively sheltered, they suffer from unusually high tides and strong currents, making them extremely difficult to navigate.

SOUTHERNESS. It is worth paying a visit to the lighthouse at Southerness which was built in 1748 and has the distinction of being the second oldest purpose built lighthouse in the country. Now no longer in use, many people come to Southerness today as it is a delightful holiday village with many attractions, including a famous golf course with 19 holes! With its many creeks and tidal rivers, it is not surprising to learn that the Solway was at one time notorious for smugglers.

This was especially true since, until 1876, the Isle of Man lay outside British Customs regulations, encouraging regular dealings in contraband goods. Sir Walter Scott wrote a vivid account of smuggling in this area in his book *Guy Mannering*.

KIPPFORD. Situated at the estuary of the River Urr, Kippford, or as it used to be known 'Scaur', is a fascinating place and at one time ships would set sail from here for the industrial areas of Northern England and Central Scotland with cargoes of barley, meal and potatoes. Kippford has a delightful setting and, with its old inn and jetty, is today one of the foremost yachting and sailing centres in the southwest. Across the estuary lies **Orchardston Tower** which is a unique circular towerhouse constructed in the 15th century.

DALBEATTIE. The town, close to Urr Water, is distinctive as it has been built mostly in the same colour granite. This is the grey granite that was quarried in the area and was a very useful source of income for the town, making it famous throughout the world. This striking material was shipped to many places and was used to construct London's Embankment.

The Maxwell Arms Hotel in the centre of Dalbeattie, having been purchased by Carolyn Maxwell, has recently undergone a major refurbishment and upgrading by the new owner. Patrons will find a comfortable lounge bar and dining room, a friendly public bar and a games room. The newly furnished bedrooms now have colour television and tea and coffee making facilities. All meals are prepared and cooked on the premises from fresh local produce and guests with special needs and diets are well cared for. This is a good area for hillwalking and sightseeing and the hotel will provide packed lunches upon request. Golf and fishing is nearby and The Maxwell Arms makes a good base for touring locally.

The Maxwell Arms, Maxwell Street, Dalbeattie Tel: 01556 610431

At the junction of the A710 at Sandyhills, approximately 18 miles from Dumfries, is **Cottage Crafts** offering a haven of interest for those seeking different and unusual gifts. The proprietor is Josephine Cockerill who has ensured that original arts and crafts are represented and indeed all the items on sale are produced in the region. Browse through the selection of paintings, prints and embroideries and look for the pottery, and turned and carved wood items. The painted silk scarves, jewellery items, sweaters, appliqué sweatshirts and hand-woven tweeds will certainly interest the ladies. You will also find a selection of narrowboat art, slatecraft, salt dough, books, maps, cards, shortbread, candles, a selection of aromatherapy oils and lots more to catch your eye. Well worth a diversion if you are not passing by. Open Easter to the end of October except Wednesdays.

Cottage Crafts, Sandyhills by Dalbeattie Tel: 01387 780220

CASTLE DOUGLAS. This market town is only ten miles from the Solway Coast and its sandy beaches. The surrounding area excels in natural beauty and fishing, sailing and riding are all available either locally or within easy motoring distance.

The streets of Castle Douglas have a certain planned elegance about them as a result of the town being developed by an enterprising landowner named William Douglas, who had made his fortune in America. He encouraged the development of the town as a cattle market and today it is still a focal point for the local farming community.

Not far away is the lovely **Carlingwark Loch**, where small boats can be hired out for visitors to look at the swans and take in the wonderful view of nearby Screel Mill. There was once an ancient causeway that led to a dwelling on an artificial island at the centre of this loch. A stones throw away from the Loch are the delightful **Threave Gardens**. These gardens and the visitor centre stand majestically in 60 acres surrounding a Victorian mansion. The house is used by the National Trust for Scotland for their School of Gardening. There is much to see here including rock gardens, heathers, herbaceous and rose beds and, in the spring time, nearly 200 varieties of daffodil provide a dazzling display.

On the River Dee there are many species of wild geese and duck.

The Posthorn is certainly one of the leading Glass and China Gift Shops in this most attractive region of southwest Scotland and is internationally famous for its stock of Border Fine Arts. In 'Border' they stock the entire James Herriot Range and also have their own exclusive editions. There is a collector's cabinet showing some of the oldies and 'Secondary Market' figurines are often available. In the Crystal department there is a well stocked range of Edinburgh, Waterford, Stuart, Royal Brierly, Dartington and Caithness. The Posthorn also stocks an exclusive range of Galloway Glass engraved by Frances McCallum. The China section has a huge selection representing the very best of British dinner and teasets from many famous makers including Wedgwood, Royal Doulton, Aynsley, Crown Derby, Spode, Worcester, Lladro and many more. Collectors of Moorcroft will want to spend time looking at the widest range to be seen in the region. The various departments regularly have a number of limited editions on sale. A look at the gift section reveals hundreds of ideas from shooting sticks to barometers; jewel cases to tablemats. All in all, a superb presentation of Britain's best craftsmen. Castle Douglas is a must for a day out and The Posthorn should be top of your list.

The Posthorn, 26/30 St Andrew Street, Castle Douglas
Tel: 01556 502531 Fax: 01556 503330

AUCHENCAIRN. This hillside village overlooks the bay from which it takes its name. **Hestan Island**, out in the Solway Firth, is associated with the McDowal and Balliol families and, in the 14th century, was a refuge to King Robert I's brother, Edward Bruce. Many tales of smuggling and of secret caverns are told of the island.

Vegetarians take note, here is a wonderful place to stay - **The Rossan**, an early Victorian ex-Manse owned by Mr and Mrs Bardsley. Special diets are Mrs Bardsley's forte; she caters for vegetarians, vegans (with a little advance notice) and special medical diets, as well as providing wholefoods, organically grown fruit and vegetables, free-range eggs and home-baked bread! Meat-eaters are well catered for too with local steak, salmon, trout or venison when in season. The Rossan was awarded 3 Star classification in the International Vegetarian Handbook. The house stands well back from the A711 in over an acre of grounds between the Screel Hills and the sea. The bedrooms are furnished as bed-sitting rooms with facilities for making hot drinks. The Rossan is a very relaxing house, with dinner an unhurried affair giving guests time to chat and enjoy themselves. This is a very convenient centre for touring Galloway, doing a spot of bird watching or painting or just enjoying the two sandy beaches close by. Within reach are 26 Golf Courses - a challenge to the keenest golfers!

The Rossan, Auchencairn Tel: 01566 640269

KIRKCUDBRIGHT. This beautiful county town and harbour has much to recommend it. There are many examples of fine 17th and 18th century buildings and particularly striking is the fabulous colour used throughout the town with reds, blues and blacks producing an effect that is almost Continental.

Kirkcudbright is an ancient place with quite a history. As far back as the 8th century the Vikings established the church of St Cuthbert near the town. The town seal today still reflects the rather bloody times of old with a picture of St Cuthbert with the head of the martyred St Oswald, King of Northumbria, in his lap. Facing England across the Solway Firth meant that the conflicts between the two countries were reflected in the fortifications and defences around the town. These included a water-filled ditch and wall enclosing the town.

The ruins of **Maclellans Castle** date from a period when building reflected a combination of the need for safety and a certain amount of comfort. It was built in the 16th century by Sir Thomas Maclellan who benefitted from the dissolution of the monasteries by acquiring the lands and buildings of the Greyfriar's convent on this site. He even built his castle with the stone from the dismantled buildings. It is worth taking a close look at the fireplace amongst the ruins. Some ten feet wide, it would have had a fire burning continuously throughout the winter months. A closer inspection reveals a rather puzzling small hole in the back of the fireplace. Apparently, this was a spy hole located in a small room reached from the stair. Here, Maclellan could watch and listen to what was being said, without fear of discovery

Besides Maclellan's Castle, the **Tolbooth** is another interesting building dating from the same period. Overlooking the market square, the Tolbooth was the point where taxes were paid and prisoners incarcerated. Pronouncements would have been made from its steps and it is fascinating to see the original manacles that were used to hold the prisoners during their punishment. The area was caught up in the persecution of both witches and, later, Covenanters. The case against witches usually began with a series of events or disasters occurring within the community until, eventually, someone came to be suspected of causing them. The case of Elspeth McEwen is a typical local example. She was accused of making her neighbour's hens stop laying and of having a moveable wooden pin at her command that was capable of drawing milk from their cows. The unfortunate woman was imprisoned and tortured in Kirkcudbright Tolbooth until she confessed and was subsequently found guilty "of a compact and correspondence with the devil and of charms and accession to malefices". She was executed in 1698.

Later in the 17th and 18th centuries the town developed along more civilized lines with smart new dwellings arising for the merchants and lawyers. A walk along Castle Street or Old High Street gives a clear indication of the elegance of Georgian Kirkcubright. It was an important town for shipping, trade went as far as the West Indies and the North American Colonies. As a result it became a centre for Customs and Excise Officers engaged in the capture of the smugglers who were operating from France, Ireland and the Isle of Man, running contraband along the shores of the Solway Firth.

In the late 19th century there was an artists' colony established here and the town has become associated with many fine painters and craftsmen. One famous resident was EA Hornel (1864-1930) and his house in the High Street contains a display of his paintings and furniture. Close by, is the house of the artist Jessie M King (1875-1949) and examples of her work can be seen at the **Stewartry Museum** in St Mary Street. There is also a host of articles and information on this pleasant town. Visitors during the mid July to August period will be in luck as there is an annual Summer Festival, which provides an extensive programme of entertainment.

BORGUE. This small village is home to the **Cow Palace**, a model dairy farm built at the turn of the century. Designed and built at great expense in a Gothic style, its grandest feature is the central water tower, which ironically failed as a means of water supply. Still a private farm it is visible from the road and a must for the folly spotter or those with a taste for the unusual.

TONGLAND. When crossing the River Dee at Tongland Bridge it is worth taking time to look closely at this structure. Although it is shrouded by trees and not immediately obvious to the traveller, this handsome bridge is a fine piece of engineering.

It was designed by Thomas Telford in collaboration with the famous Edinburgh architect and painter, Alexander Nasmyth. It is interesting to note that the single span bridge had to be built to cope with the tide which would rise six metres or more. The difficulty of this was brought home to the builders when the original foundations were washed away on the first attempt. The three small arches to either side are designed to help cope with the flow of water at high tides.

GATEHOUSE OF FLEET. This is a fascinating place with its brightly coloured buildings and scenic setting. It does not immediately spring to mind that this town was once at the forefront of Scotland's Industrial Revolution. However, a closer look reveals that many of these bright buildings were, at one time, working mills in a town that was built to rival the centres of industry in the north of England. The town was planned and built in the late 18th century as a centre for cotton manufacturing and other industries. It once boasted six cotton mills employing a workforce of more than 500 people. The industries did eventually decline in response to better transport related businesses elsewhere. There is a visitors' centre in one of the former mills.

The town also features one of the counties few follies, if indeed the **Jubilee Clock Tower** can be so described; surmounted by improbable castellations it is an impressive time-teller nevertheless. Finally, those interested in the haunts of the poet Burns will be pleased to find that the Murray Arms Hotel is reputedly the place where he wrote *Scots Wha Hae*.

Just a mile to the southwest of the town is **Cardoness Castle**, once the home of the McCullochs of Galloway; an unruly family who feuded with and plundered those around them. The family line ended in 1690 when Sir Gordon McCulloch was executed in Edinburgh for murder. Tall and gaunt with its four stories standing on a rocky mound, it must have seen much of the bloody troubles that beset the area for centuries.

The Cree Gallery and Bed and Breakfast

A wonderful discovery is **The Cree Gallery and Bed and Breakfast** establishment in Gatehouse of Fleet. This is an artist-run gallery and antique shop run by Rosemary Gascoyne and Linda Hepburn with artists' studio on the premises. Monthly exhibitions are featured throughout the year with changing artists. Rosemary studied and established her reputation in the south of England but has had a long association and love for Scotland. Their early Victorian house also serves as a charming setting for bed and breakfast accommodation with pleasant bedrooms where television and hot drink facilities are provided. Breakfast is served in the gallery or set amongst antiques elsewhere in the house. The lovely natural country garden is where most guests make for, to sit and enjoy the many flowers, trees and shrubs in this peaceful setting. An Information Centre for the Arts and Members of the Tourist Board.

The Cree Gallery, 56 High Street, Gatehouse of Fleet
Tel & Fax: 01557 814458

CREETOWN. This thoroughly charming, friendly village features as 'Port-an-Ferry' in Scott's *Guy Mannering* and has a history steeped in smuggling legend.

The village is built in the distinct and attractive local 'silver' granite. A great deal can be discovered about this and other rocks, minerals and gems at the **Gem Rock Museum**. This beautiful collection comes from all over the world and took over 50 years to amass. Recognised as one of the most comprehensive of its kind in the world, as well as precious stones, it contains many startling examples of the mineral forms created by nature.

Although only a small place, this lovely village has many facilities on offer to the visitor. There are many walks from along the Minnipool Burn, with its pleasant surroundings, to the slightly more ambitious **Cairnsmore of Fleet** which, at 2329 feet, is one of the highest hills in Galloway. The views are stunning and take in the Isle of Man, England and the Mountains of Mourne in Ireland.

It was said by Queen Victoria that the road from Creetown to Gatehouse of Fleet was 'the finest in the kingdom', the next finest being the road from Gatehouse of Fleet to Creetown.

WIGTOWN. This little town overlooks Wigtown Bay and the mouth of the River Cree. The feeling of calmness in the town today belies its previously fierce competitive spirit as the former county town of Wigtownshire, fighting for the royal burgh's trading 'freedoms' (which mean monopolies) over Whithorn and Stranraer.

The site of the ancient town reputedly lay more than a mile to the east which would have placed it firmly within the grasp of the sea! There is a small church on the east side of the town that was erected next to a ruined church dedicated to St Machitis.

There are some solemn reminders of the fate of the Covenanters here. A headstone, located in the burial ground, was erected in memory of the sad fate of 18 year old Margaret Wilson who, along with Margaret Lachlan (aged 63), was drowned for her religious beliefs by being tied to a stake in the sea. A stone post, now on dry land, marks the site of the drowning.

To the northwest of the town lies the **Torhouse Stone Circle** which is a captivating sight of 19 boulders on the edge of a low mound dating from the Bronze Age.

GARLIESTON. This small port, in Wigtown Bay, was founded in the 18th century by Lord Garlies. His father, the 6th Earl, built nearby Galloway House. The house is not open to the public, although a quiet afternoon can be spent in the gardens which cover nearly 30 acres and have superb displays of daffodils, rhododendrons and azaleas. There are lovely old trees here and the position of the garden, which leads down to a sandy beach by the sea, is delightful.

WHITHORN. The fact that this ancient town is on the very tail end of Scotland has not diminish its importance, for it existed as far back as the 2nd century. It was here, in AD 397, that St Ninian established the first Christian centre in Scotland. The site of the chapel, which he founded, is thought to have been a few miles further south, close to the Isle of Whithorn and the area has long since been the focus of pilgrimages. The present ruined priory dates from the 12th century and the local **Museum** contains displays of early Christian crosses, including the famous Monreith Cross.

Robert the Bruce came here in the last months of his life, severely weakened by years of hard campaigning and suffering from leprosy. He had, apparently, to be carried in a horse-litter as he was too weak to support himself. Another noted visitor had no such problem. He was James IV who came here many times, reputedly walking on foot from Edinburgh. Mary, Queen of Scots also made this journey in 1563. Indeed, such was the influence of this place that, after the Reformation, an Act of Parliament was passed to make illegal the practice of making a pilgrimage to the site.

ISLE OF WHITHORN. As the name implies, the Isle of Whithorn was originally an island, although this charming seaside village is now joined to the mainland and has become a popular spot for yachting. There are also a number of notable sites for the budding archaeologist, with a team digging here throughout the summer. There is a 'Dig' shop which provides a wide range of souvenirs and local crafts. There is also a visitor centre and museum providing much detailed information, with a guided tour of the site available.

MONREITH. Having travelled the A747 road towards Port William, we had heard of a small specialist restaurant in Monreith which is a tiny village set up on the cliffs overlooking Luce Bay and the Mull of Galloway. We found **The Glen Roy Restaurant** at one end of a row of delightful tiny white-washed cottages on the main road looking out to sea. The food is described by the owners, Patrick and Jenny, as 'best modern British'. All produce is freshly sourced with the emphasis on seafood whilst not forgetting good Galloway beef. A typical selection from the à la carte menu might be: Soufflé of Haggis and Black Pudding with apple and whisky sauce, followed by Symphony of Hot Seafood with two sauces, and finishing with Chocolate Marquise with Grand Marnier and chocolate sauce. With such a fine selection, it might be advisable to book ahead. Three guest bedrooms are planned to open for the 1997 season. Open all year except two weeks at the end of November. Closed Mondays and, from November to Easter, closed Mondays and Tuesdays. Facilities available for disabled visitors.

Glen Roy Restaurant, Monreith Tel: 01988 700466

PORT WILLIAM. This is a small and attractive fishing port on the eastern side of Luce Bay. At nearby Monreith Bay is a small statue of an otter overlooking the water. It is a tribute to the author Gavin Maxwell, who wrote lovingly about the area in his book *The House at Elrig*.

Close to this sleepy and attractive harbour village is **Monreith House**. Built in 1799, it has charming gardens and a park. The White Loch is here also and apparently even in the coldest of winters it never entirely freezes over

The area boasts an abundance of prehistoric sites and, in particular, the **Drumtrodden Standing Stones**, which were three upright stones (though one has now fallen) and, also nearby, the fascinating 'cup and ring' markings, which were probably carved during the Bronze Age. Theories abound as to the meaning of the cup and ring markings which can be found in many places in Scotland. One source lists a remarkable 104 theories that have been put forward to explain their meaning and usage. The most likely explanations are either that they had some connection with metal prospecting and smelting activities or that they had some religious meaning perhaps related to sun worship or astronomical observation.

GLENLUCE. This village sits on the edge of the Water of Luce and close to Luce Bay. It is fascinating to think that there has been a settlement in this area from as early as 6000 BC.

A mile to the north is **Glenluce Abbey** which was founded in 1190 and was visited by King Robert I, King James IV and Mary, Queen of Scots on their pilgrimages to Whithorn. The Abbey is said to have associations with a 13th century wizard named Michael Scott. Legend has it that he managed to persuade some witches, who were paying him too much close attention, to spend their time spinning ropes from the sands of Luce Bay. The results of their task can supposedly be seen at very low tides. Another interesting story was that of poor Gilbert Campbell, who was apparently haunted by the devil of Glenluce for four years from 1654 to 1658. Fortunately the local Presbytery was able to eventually rid him of his unfortunate possession.

Glenluce Motor Museum houses a splendid display of vintage cars, motorbikes and memorabilia. A great place for the fan of wheeled transport to while away an afternoon.

DUNRAGIT. **Glenwhan Gardens** has recently been described as "the latest gem in Scotland's crown of beautiful gardens", commanding spectacular views over Luce Bay and the Mull of Galloway. Started in 1979, this picturesque creation was hewn from a hillside covered in bracken and gorse by Mrs Tessa Knott. Two lochans were made by damming up the bogs to provide a rich habitat for rare species. The rocky outcrops are home to a wide variety of alpines, scree plants, heathers and conifers. One cannot adequately describe, in the space available here, the beauty of this lovely garden created in a 12 acre site; winding paths lead through rose arbours to enchanting woodland walks, the eyes stunned by the variety and colours of constant change. Not created by a team of landscape gardeners but principally by the incredible efforts of one lady. A richness of nature you should not miss! Open daily from 15th March until October, 10 am - 5 pm. Open out of season and for evening visits by appointment. Ample parking, refreshments, Visitors Centre and extensive Nursery and Plant Centre. Glenwhan is located seven miles east of Stranraer, one mile off the A75 at Dunragit.

Glenwhan Gardens, Dunragit Tel: 01581 400222

ASPECTS OF GALLOWAY

The name Galloway is still much used for the ancient territory which once covered virtually the whole of the southern part of the southwest of Scotland. This was the cradle of Christianity in Scotland as well as the starting point for the struggles of Robert Bruce. The Convenanters were staunchly supported in the region and, finally, this ancient territory was the home of Scotland's national poet, Robert Burns.

Christianity came to Scotland in around AD 400 when St Ninian built his church at Whithorn; though no longer visible, evidence of early Christian settlements litters the area. In particular, the Kirkmadrine Stones, dating from 5th-12th century, on the Rinns of Galloway and the cross at Ruthwell, near Dumfries. The remains of humble chapels and great medieval abbeys from the 12th century onwards can be found in abundance, but one of the earliest church buildings surviving is Chapel Finian, dating from the 10th or 11th century.

Robert Bruce began his struggle for Scottish independence in the region. Today, little physical evidence of the battles remain but the visitor is constantly reminded of his activity here. It was at Dumfries, in 1306, that Bruce killed Comyn, the act that rekindled the War of Independence. He is said to have hidden near Gretna, at Bruce's Cave, and, in Galloway Forest Park, two memorials mark the scene of his triumphs. It was to this area that Robert Bruce returned at the end of his life, when sick with leprosy, he founded a hospital there for lepers besides Bruce's Well, where he had been refreshed.

Though the crowns of England and Scotland were united in 1567 when James VI of Scotland and I of England was crowned, bitter quarrels, particularly about the Church, continued. The Convenanters believed in the Reformation and in the abolition of bishops created by James VI, and they refused to submit to the will of the Crown. By far the worst period for the Convenanters was the time between 1684 and 1688, known as the Killing Times. It is to the victims of those brutal times that many of the memorials in Galloway were erected. In particular, the stone tomb in Galloway Forest Park on which is engraved the names of six Convenanter martyrs and also with the names of their two killers.

CASTLE KENNEDY. This village, which lies close to White Loch, is home to some of the loveliest gardens in Scotland. Laid out by the Earl of Stair around the ruined 17th century Lochinch Castle (which was later restored) **Castle Kennedy Gardens** are well worth a visit. One of the main attractions is the broad avenue of monkey puzzle trees that are now over 100 years old and over 70 feet high.

CAIRNRYAN. This small coastal village was a base in the Second World War for handling transatlantic traffic. It was here, too, that the parts for the Mulberry Harbour, which was vital to the success of the Normandy landings in 1944, were made. It is fascinating to think that those massive Sunderland flying-boats also used Wig Bay as a base, the remains of which can still be seen.

The Rinns of Galloway

STRANRAER. Situated at the head of Loch Ryan, Stranraer is a busy seaport which attracts many visitors each year. It is, of course, the port which operates a regular ferry service to Ireland having taken over from Portpatrick. While the destroyed harbour in Portpatrick is a fitting testament to the power of the sea, there is a more solemn tribute in Stranraer's **Agnew Park**, which commemorates the loss of 133 lives in the sinking of the ferry in 1953.

Before the ferry came to Stranraer, the local people, in the 18th century, made a living from the seasonal shoals of herring in Loch Ryan, until the fish began to die out in the early 19th century.

There is a castle here and parts of it remained in use as prison cells until 1907. It was also used by John Graham of Calverhouse during his persecution of the Covenanters in the 17th century. The earliest surviving municipal building is the former Town Hall of 1776. There was a guide book published in 1877 which referred to the Town Hall as "like some ladies - not Stranraer ladies, however - very much indebted to paint for its good looks". The **Old Town Hall** is now an interesting museum with plenty of information on local history as well as changing exhibitions.

Arriving in the town of Stranraer and looking for interesting business places to feature, we were directed to **The Waterloo Gallery and Picture Framing Workshop** owned by Ann Mathewson. Although this is a relatively new business for Ann, she is already well into the stride of things. Exhibitions are a feature of the gallery displaying mainly original work by local artists which are changed on a six weekly cycle, most are offered for sale. It is an opportunity to discover interesting and accomplished work in all mediums, with exhibits in oils, watercolours, gouache and pastels. The picture frame workshop caters for all types of moulding requirements, the more exotic can be specially ordered to suit customers' exact requirements. As with the framing a full mounting service is executed on the premises and Ann is happy to guide customers in their choice.

The Waterloo Gallery & Framing Workshop, Wellington House, Princes Street, Stranraer Tel: 01776 702888

AROUND STRANRAER

SANDHEAD. The town's Main Street overlooks nine square miles of sandy beach, voted the cleanest, safest and warmest in the area.

ARDWELL. The Rinns of Galloway is certainly the place to come to for those interested in horticulture and viewing beautiful, exotic plants. **Ardwell House** offers wonderful daffodils and rhododendrons whilst, at the **Logan Botanical Gardens**, plants from much warmer, temperate regions of the world thrive.

Clachanmore Gallery and Tearoom

Follow the A716 (Stoneykirk Road) from Stranraer which is signposted Drummore and follow on to Sandhead. Take the next turning right after the school and continue for two miles to reach **Clachanmore**

Gallery and Tearoom. It is here that Meg McCall features a range of exhibitions throughout the year from Easter to October, each lasting approximately six weeks. Works include paintings in both oil and watercolour mediums by local and national artists.

Photography is also featured, along with ceramics, enamels and sculptures. The welcome Tearoom is open during Gallery hours for home-made snacks, home-baked confectionery and drinks. There is easy access for disabled visitors to the Tearoom, Gallery and toilets. Awarded - Achievement for Art - from the Regional Council. Well worth finding.

Clachanmore Gallery and Tearoom, Clachanmore School, Ardwell
Tel: 01776 860200

DRUMMORE. The people of Drummore are said to have visited the well of the 'Co' which is near St Medan's Cove on the Mull of Galloway. Supposedly on the first Sunday in May, they would come down to bathe in the waters which were widely accredited with having healing properties. Coins have been found in the well which date as far back as the reign of Charles I.

The most southerly village in Scotland, from the 19th century lighthouse, on a clear day, it is possible to see the Isle of Man and Ireland, some 26 miles away.

Rumour has it that the Picts brewed a drink from heather that was sweeter than honey and stronger than wine and when the Scots invaded from Ireland, they were most keen to learn the secret of this renowned brew. It was here, at The Double Dykes, that the secret is said to have died with the final defence of the Picts against the invaders. The story goes that a treacherous Druid betrayed the chief and his two sons, to whom only the secret of the drink was known. One son promised to reveal the secret, if his father and brother were first thrown off the cliffs, to prevent them witnessing his treachery. This request was duly obliged and then the remaining son flung himself off, shouting that the secret would die with him.

PORT LOGAN. On the western side of the peninsula, this small fishing village has a tidal pool in the bay. It was built, in 1800, by a McDougall laird as an artificial sea-water larder to keep himself supplied with cod. The pool is 30 feet deep and 53 feet in circumference. Today, however, the cod have no worse fate than being fed by hand and are so tame that they rise to the surface whenever a bell is rung.

PORTPATRICK. The largest village on the west coast this popular holiday resort is dominated by the impressive Victorian hotel on the cliff top. The village has the feeling of an amphitheatre about it and is in fact quite exposed to the winds and sea. There was an artificial harbour built here due to its proximity to Donaghadee, which is a mere 21 miles over the Irish Sea. Unfortunately, the harbour was constantly damaged by the elements, so trade was eventually moved to the safer haven of Stranraer. Children, young and old, will love **Little Whools**, a huge model railway, toy and transport exhibition in the village. The railway tracks extend for over 100 metres and would be train drivers can have ago.

This picturesque village has something to offer everyone, with golf, bowling and tennis among the many sports available or, for the more leisurely visitor, walks along the unspoilt harbour with its beautiful views across the Irish Channel.

CORSEWALL POINT. Some of Scotland's most spectacular coastline is found within and nearby the 20 acre grounds of **Corsewall Lighthouse Hotel**, one of the newest and most unique luxury hotels that Scotland has to offer. Your comfort is assured by the owner who personally runs and supervises the Hotel. The Lighthouse is a listed "A" building of major national importance and its light still beams a warning for ships approaching the mouth of Loch Ryan - as it has done for 180 years. Extensive restoration provides guests with bedrooms serviced with en-suite facilities, one of which is equipped for disabled guests, television central heating and all modern facilities. The restaurant caters for a wide variety of tastes including local beef, lamb, seafood and vegetarian dishes. Throughout this comfortable luxury hotel the standard of furnishing is very tasteful and thoughtfully designed. More recently the listed Stable Block has been converted into two luxury self-catering cottages both with tremendous views of the sea and with many outstanding facilities. Outdoor activities are available by prior arrangement as is collection from various points in the hotel Range Rover.

Corsewall Lighthouse Hotel, Corsewall Point
Tel: 01776 853220 Fax: 01776 854231

LESWALT. **Lochnaw Castle** dates back to 1426 and is one of the few 15th century castles still in existence. This charming and historic country residence was for centuries the ancestral home of the Agnew family, hereditary Sheriffs of Galloway. Built along simple Norman lines, the castle stands at the very edge of the loch, unspoilt and undisturbed.

CHAPTER THREE

AYRSHIRE, ARRAN & RENFREWSHIRE

Lochranza Castle, Arran

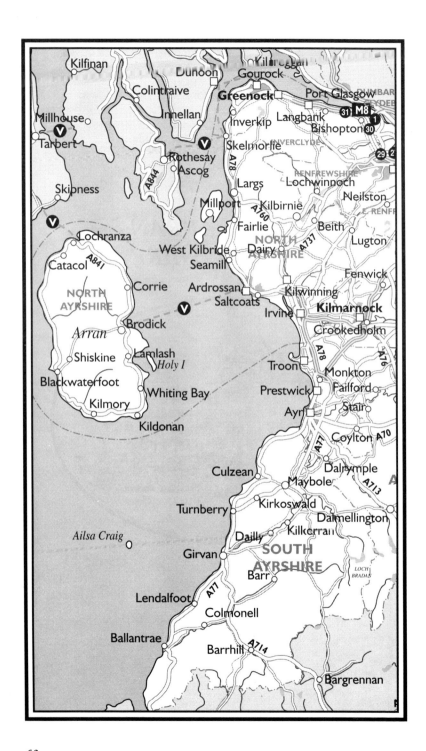

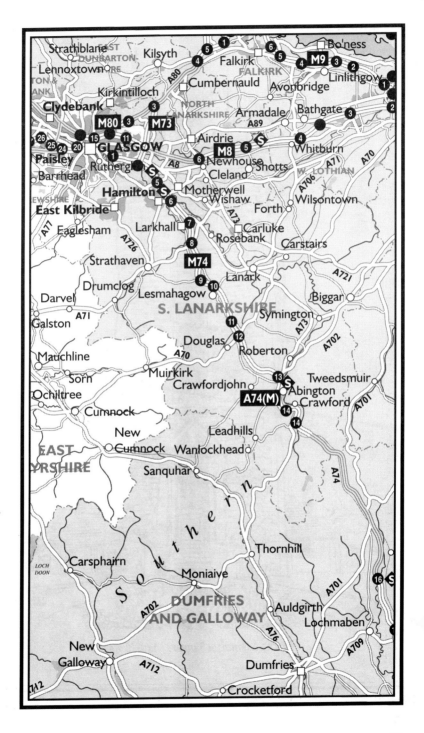

Burns Memorial Tower, Mauchline

CHAPTER THREE

AYRSHIRE, ARRAN & RENFREWSHIRE

South Ayrshire

AYR. This busy resort is one of the most popular and beautiful on the west coast of Scotland. The town developed from settlements in Roman times and has always retained an attraction due to its extensive sandy beaches, golf courses and many recreational activities. Visitors can choose to enjoy some of the traditional seaside entertainments or perhaps walk around the many colourful parks in the town. Here, of course, is the famous racecourse which hosts meetings throughout the year.

Ayr has a history of trading and markets and there is a busy fish market at the South Harbour which makes an interesting visit. Today, the Ayrshire Agricultural Show takes place every year in April. Around 1900 the cattle market in Ayr was relocated to its present site in the town's Castlehill Road. Here can be found the aptly named Market Inn, a well known watering hole for Ayrshire landowners and farmers seeking refreshment after a hard morning's bargaining.

There are two bridges that cross the river. The **Auld Brig** and **New Bridge** were written about by Burns in *The Brigs of Ayr* where he correctly forecasted that the old bridge would outlast the new. In the poem, the Old Bridge says to the New, "I'll be a brig when ye're a shapeless cairn". Indeed, the New Bridge fell down in a storm in 1870. The connections between Ayr and Burns are very strong, especially as Alloway, where the poet was born, is now a suburb of the town, though it was once separated by two miles of countryside.

The **Wallace Tower**, built in 1828, stands on the site of an ancient tower where, legend has it, Wallace was imprisoned and from which he made a daring escape.

Confusingly, **Auld Kirk** is also known as the **New Church of St John** because both the New Church and its gateway were built in 1654-56 using money given by Cromwell as compensation for absorbing the Old Church into his great fort, since demolished. It was here that Burns was baptised.

The oldest house in Ayr is **Loudoun Hall** and it dates from the turn of the 15th-16th century. Beautifully restored, the house which was once the home of a wealthy merchant, is a fine example of domestic architecture of the period.

Visitors to Alloway (now a suburb of Ayr) are able to go to the Burns Interpretation Centre; a permanent exhibition which displays events, characters and memories from the life of the poet. Nearby is the cottage where the poet was born, on 25th January 1759, and spent the first five years of his life. Just a few minutes walk away is the **Auld Brig O'Doon**, where the chase in the epic poem *Tam o' Shanter* took place, and **The Burns Monument**.

The **Maclaurin Gallery**, at Rozelle House, offers a change from Burns, and the exhibitions include fine art, sculpture, crafts and local history.

AROUND AYR

MAYBOLE. **Maybole Castle**, in the town itself, was the stronghold of the Kennedy's and their descendants now occupy **Cassillis House** which is situated four miles northeast of Maybole, high above the River Doon.

The position of Maybole is somewhat lofty, set 200 to 300 feet above sea level and the town, the fifth largest in Ayrshire, commands a wonderful view of the area. Apart from visiting the castle, the town offers splendid opportunities for walks as well as a golf course and an indoor heated swimming pool.

KILKERRAN. Situated in the Girvan Valley, **Kilkerran House**, the seat of the Fergusson Chiefs, is still the site of occasional clan gatherings. Built around an old tower in the 17th century it was enlarged in 1815.

Set within the historic Kilkerran Estate, home of the Fergusson family, the **Walled Garden Caravan Park** is a quiet and secluded park that offers the visitor a relaxing and enjoyable site. Surrounded by many specimen trees, the park is well sheltered and is a real suntrap in the long summer months, proving an ideal setting to unwind and relax. The establishment has been run by James McCosh for over three years and his aim is to provide the very best in personal service and Scottish hospitality; we feel he has achieved just this.

There is an attractive stone toilet facility block that supplies free hot water and showers complete with additional hairdryers and shaving points and an adjoining laundry which is fully equipped with washing, drying and ironing facilities. There are 30 pitches with electric hook-up points, a separate play area for children and also a Recreation room complete with pool table, television and table tennis table. A small site shop offers the visitor a choice of newspapers, milk and morning rolls that are delivered fresh each morning and Calor Gas is always available.

You can sit back and enjoy the beautiful views or roam through the woodland walks exploring the diversity of wildlife that is abundant all around. Try the putting green or golf practice net, there is local fishing on the River Girvan which runs through the estate and cycling on the safe and quiet roads. Nearby you will find swimming pools at Maybole, Girvan and Wondersplash Waterworld, the beaches at Girvan and Croy Bay are well worth an explore, and regular trips from Girvan to Ailsa Craig, a bird sanctuary and former granite quarry for curling stones. Whatever your interest you will always find something to do at the Walled Garden Caravan Park at Kilkerran, just follow the B741 from Dalmellington and you can't miss it.

Walled Garden Caravan Park, Kilkerran Tel: 01655 740323

DAILLY. This village grew up with the mining industry though there seems to be little evidence of this in the surrounding landscape. A good place to get some idea of the history of a place is in the churchyard. In Dailly churchyard there is a headstone to the memory of John Brown, a 66 year old collier who became trapped underground by a roof fall in the pit in 1835. He was eventually brought out alive, 'having been 23 days in utter seclusion from the world and without a particle of food'. However, John Brown only managed to survive for three days after being set free. Unmissable is the large mausoleum of the Bargany family in the churchyard; it is as high as the church.

At nearby **Old Dailly** are two large stones inside the churchyard. These were known as the **Charter Stones** and were used in local contests of strength to see who could lift them.

BARR is a charming little conservation village nestling on the banks of the River Stinchar, seven miles south of the fishing port of Girvan. This parish is the largest in the Scottish lowlands and around 60 years ago was said to have been populated by the most sheep and fewest people! In the churchyard are two headstones in memory of Covenanters who were put to death and, also, a richly sculptured stone showing Reverend John Campbell, whose unfortunate demise occurred in his own pulpit.

COLMONELL. The hill on which the village of Colmonell sits is known as Knockdolian which derives from the Gaelic words for hill, 'cnoc', and 'dall', meaning to mislead. It seems that in times past the hill was mistaken by mariners, in bad weather, for Ailsa Craig which lies off the coast. This pretty village takes its name from St Colmonella who died in AD 611 and the village has many old castles of interest.

Nearby, there is the one time hiding place of Robert the Bruce, **Craignell**, and marvellous views of the surrounding countryside and the River Stinchar are laid out below.

BALLANTRAE. Those familiar with Robert Louis Stevenson might recall his novel *The Master of Ballantrae*. Although Ballantrae was not the setting that he used for the plot, it is a pretty seaside town popular with visitors and is also the place where the River Stinchar, well known for its trout and salmon fishing, runs into the sea. It has a delightful harbour filled with both fishing and pleasure boats, whilst, above the river and the old bridge, stands the ruins of **Ardstinchar Castle**.

The small churchyard at Ballantrae bears witness to a vicious local feud that once took place between members of the Kennedy family. The Bargany Aisle in the churchyard is a memorial to Gilbert Kennedy of Bargany who was killed in a fight with his near relative, the Earl of Cassillis, in 1601. Theirs was a family torn by conflict for over 40 years, beginning when the 4th Earl of Cassillis kidnapped and roasted Allen Stuart until the unfortunate man signed over his lands. On a later occasion, the wicked Earl was only just persuaded not to blow up the castle at Ardstinchar, which was the home of the Bargany branch of the family, on the grounds that it might displease the King. The feud was ended in the High Court in Edinburgh in 1611, leaving the Earl a little chastised although still the supreme ruler in the family.

Just to the north of Ballantrae lies **Bennane Head**, the home, so the tale goes, of Sawney Bean, by all accounts a nasty piece of work. Apparently he and his family were cannibals and preyed on travellers passing their cave. The cave can still be visited by more intrepid visitors without, it should be added, the fear of being eaten.

LENDALFOOT. Along the coast, between the shore and the rising hills, is Lendalfoot which was once the haunt of smugglers and is overlooked by the ruins of **Carleton Castle**. One of a series of Kennedy watchtowers along the coast, it achieved minor notoriety in a ballad, as the seat of a Baron who rid himself of no less than seven wives by pushing them over the cliffs. His eighth wife, May, returned the gesture.

GIRVAN. The town can boast one and a half miles of safe sandy beach, which stretches southwards from the harbour, which is a hive of activity and a bustling centre for the fishing fleet. Although the necessary town charter was granted by Charles I in 1668, Girvan is known to have been occupied since at least 5000 BC. As late as 1961, archaeologists have been discovering more and more about Girvan's past, including a site of Bronze Age urnfields located off Coalpots Lane, to the east of the town.

In the town of Girvan, **The Mansfield Hotel** has been serving the needs of local and visitors for many years. This family run licensed hotel is well situated for many activities. For example, opposite the hotel are the Bowling Greens and there's the new Branson Castle Golf Course only five miles away. Sea-angling excursions and deep sea diving parties can be arranged by the owners and hosts Linda and Henry McEvoy. Guests will appreciate the choice from a full à la carte menu though lighter meals and snacks are available in the bar. Linda is happy to provide packed lunches ideal for the walkers and golfers! For those staying in the area, the ten guest bedrooms will be found comfortable and homely - some with en-suite facilities. Children are welcome and pets can generally be accommodated.

The Mansfield Hotel, 22 The Avenue, Girvan Tel: 01465 714268

AILSA CRAIG. No one looking out to sea along this stretch of the Ayrshire coast will fail to notice the large rock that is some ten miles offshore. Ailsa Craig is, in fact, the plug of an extinct volcano and the isle is sometimes known as 'Paddy's Milestone' as it lies halfway between Glasgow and Belfast. In Gaelic it is known as 'Fairy Rock' and, in medieval times, renegade monks were sent here in exile from Crossraguel Abbey.

A number of boatmen operate trips out to the island and it makes for an interesting excursion. The island's fine grained granite was mined, long ago, to make some of the highest quality curling stones and there was even a castle perched high on the rock, which was once the subject of an invasion by Hew Barclay of Ladyland, who attempted to seize the island for Philip of Spain.

Today Ailsa Craig is home to one of the largest colonies of gannets in the British Isles.

TURNBERRY. There are a few remains of the castle that was once the main seat of the ancient earldom of Carrick. It was inherited by Robert the Bruce and, indeed, it is believed to have been the place of this great man's birth. It was also where Bruce landed to begin his return to Scotland in 1307.

Turnberry, now, is more familiar as the home of one of Great Britain's Open Championship golf courses.

Culzean Castle Gatehouse

CULZEAN. **Culzean Castle and Country Park** is the most visited National Trust property in Britain and, with the range of interests and activities it offers, it is easy to see why. The castle itself was built by Robert Adam, between 1772 and 1792, and is noted for its magnificent oval staircase and round drawing room, which are now considered to be among Adam's most outstanding achievements.

Of course, there are many other permanent visitor attractions at Culzean, including the exhibition, shops and Visitor Centre. A visit to the fully licensed restaurant is a must, especially after a tour round the deer park, swan pond, adventure playground and walled garden!

One of Scotland's more unusual attractions is just a few miles north of Culzean on the A719. Croy Brae, also known as **Electric Brae**, gives the optical illusion that cars are travelling up hill when in fact they are going down! Well worth a visit as seeing is believing.

KIRKOSWALD. Burns studied surveying in the village for a short period. Visits can still be made to **Souter Johnnie's Cottage** which was built in 1785 and was occupied by John Davidson the shoemaker. Robert Burns took the real man and turned him into an immortal character of fiction in his celebrated poem *Tam o'Shanter*. Douglas Graham, the actual model for Tam o'Shanter lies buried, as does John Davidson, in the old parish churchyard. The ancient font, discovered at Chapel Donan and now in the churchyard at Kirkoswald, is rumoured to have been used for the baptism of Robert the Bruce.

Almost 200 years ago Burns himself wrote about the Kirkoswald hostelry, Kirkton Jean's, in his poem *Tam o'Shanter*. Since then Kirkoswald has been put firmly on the Burns heritage trail and Kirkton Jean's today is a popular watering hole for those exploring and living in Burns country.

Out of Kirkoswald and towards the town of Maybole are the fine ruins of **Crossraguel Abbey** now well preserved and giving an interesting insight into life during the 13th century. The abbots who lived here apparently made the most of the plentiful seabirds who nested on Ailsa Craig, as they were often served here on the dinner table. It was the unfortunate owner of the lands of Crossraguel after the Reformation, Allen Stuart, who was himself basted and roasted by the Kennedys. An interesting note about the monks who lived here was that they actually minted their own pennies and farthings. Not surprisingly, these coins are much sought after by collectors.

TROON. As far back as the beginning of the 18th century the attractions of coastal towns like Troon were becoming clear to those who lived in the cities and industrial areas. Indeed, Troon was considered at the time to possess "an excellent situation for sea bathing". Happily on this count Troon is unchanged, and this small fishing town is still a popular holiday resort that can boast two miles of soft, sandy beaches stretching from either side of the harbour.

The harbour itself is a fascinating place with much going on; the yachts arriving and hurtling, anglers trying their luck and children exploring all the nooks and crannies of the many rock pools.

The town's biggest association must, of course, be with golf. **Royal Troon Golf Club** was formed in 1878 and its course has hosted the Open Championship on several occasions.

Situated in the very centre of Troon, **Hopkins Coffee House** has been owned and personally run by Lisa Milne for the past four years. The atmosphere is warm and friendly, with the delicious aroma of home-baking wafting out onto the street and luring you into this attractive establishment. The menu is an extensive and varied one with light meals, open sandwiches, baked potatoes, pasta and pitta bread plus plenty of scrumptious home-baked creations for your delectation. All of the light meals are served with salad garnish and bread or toast with several being a little unusual, choose from cheese, mixed fruit and sultanas topped with curried fruit chutney, peach halves stuffed with tuna mayonnaise, sweetcorn, celery and apple or fruity ham salad topped with yoghurt, mint and honey dressing - delicious. The home-baked selection is superb, with such culinary delights as Chocolate Fudge and Biscuit Slice, Apple, Sultana, Cinnamon and Oat Slice and a selection of freshly made scones served with jam and fresh cream. If you are bringing the family to Hopkins Coffee House, it should be good to know that there is a special section of the menu just for kids, so you won't have to worry about any waste and it is all very reasonably priced.

Hopkins Coffee House, 9c Church Street, Troon
Tel: 01292 318750

DUNDONALD. This village developed beside the site of the castle which dates from 1390. The street of houses near the ruins are quite picturesque and there is a beautiful 19th century church. **Dundonald Castle**, the cradle of the Stuart line, stand on a hill, a rough and striking ruin.

FAILFORD. In this hamlet is a monument commemorating the last meeting between Burns and his lover, Highland Mary, who died the following autumn.

MONKTON. In the village, which lies just north of Prestwick airport, is a monument to James Macrae, a poor local boy who went to India and, after becoming the Governor of Madras, returned to his home to a wealthy man.

A friendly and welcoming place to stop and enjoy a drink or meal can be found in the pretty village of Monkton, by following the signs from Prestwick Airport you will come across **The Wheatsheaf**. This traditional Scottish pub was originally built in the 18th century as a coaching inn for weary travellers and still proves as popular today as it was back then. Owned and personally run by Michael and Douglas, The Wheatsheaf has lost none of its olde worlde charm and the greeting you receive will be a genuinely warm one. Douglas is the chef of this establishment and prepares some delicious and wholesome cuisine using only the freshest local ingredients, with vegetarian dishes being a speciality. The menu is changed daily and the local brew served at the wooden bar is the perfect accompaniment to your lunchtime or evening meal.

The Wheatsheaf Inn, 17-19 Main Street, Monkton Tel: 01292 470345

East Ayrshire

KILMARNOCK. The first edition of Burns' poetry was printed here and became known as the 'Kilmarnock' edition. In Burns' day the town was full of handloom weavers who lived and worked in their cottages. The industrial heritage has continued throughout the years and, at its peak during the 19th century, Kilmarnock was a bustling place with locomotive building, engineering and carpet manufacturing among the industries. Since the 1970s the town has suffered from decline although Johnnie Walker remains one of the world's largest whisky blending and bottling plants.

Just off the Kilmarnock bypass, north of the town centre, is **Dean Castle Country Park**. This is the sort of place where the whole family can spend a super day out. Apart from an adventure playground woodland walks, children's corner and riding school, there is **Dean Castle** itself with its dungeons and museum. The stronghold dates back to around 1360 when the main keep was built to defend the lands of the Boyd family, Lords of Kilmarnock. The castle then expanded along with the fortunes of the Boyds, until fire destroyed all but the shell of this once powerful family seat.

Now run by Kilmarnock and Loudon District Council, Dean Castle was superbly restored to its original grandeur by the 8th Howard de Walden and houses his collection of European arms, armour and tapestries. There is also the Van Raalte collection of early musical instruments.

There are, furthermore, exhibits and displays of medieval life, plus, of course, various artefacts from the life and works of none other than, Robert Burns.

The **Dick Institute** contains Kilmarnock's main library along with a museum and art collection that has many fine paintings, including works by Constable, Corot, Turner and members of the Glasgow School, as well as housing a variety of exhibitions throughout the year.

Situated in one of the oldest streets in Kilmarnock, opposite the Laigh Kirk, **The Coffee Club** offers something for everyone. There are three restaurants, all with separate menus, all housed under one roof and, although not licensed, you can bring your own wine and they will supply the glasses. Open from 9.30 am until 10 pm, Monday until Saturday and on Sunday from 12 noon until 5.30 pm with special menus for children, age 5 and under and then age 12 and under. The menus have lots of choice including grills and vegetarian dishes and a range of quick snack meals and even a party plan, so you don't have to do any work! For example you could start your meal with Spicy Chicken Wings, move on to a main course of Steak Mexico, with peppers and spicy tomato sauce and follow up with a delicious Ice-cream Marshmallow Munch - yummy! All the food is produced on the spot using fresh produce wherever possible and the home-baking is a speciality, including Chocolate Fudge Cake and fresh Spiced Apple Tart. Service is fast, friendly and efficient with a warm, welcoming and lively atmosphere from the moment that you step through the door.

The Coffee Club, 30 Bank Street, Kilmarnock Tel: 01563 22048

AROUND KILMARNOCK

CROOKEDHOLM. The main shopping centre of Kilmarnock is only ten minutes walk from the front door of **Westerlea House**, which offers the visitor superb bed and breakfast accommodation at a very reasonable price. Situated in a quiet location with rambling countryside and fields with sheep and cattle to the rear of the property, Westerlea is a family owned and run house that was built in 1992. Your hosts Margaret and Richard McAvoy offer their guests double, twin and single light and airy rooms, all with en-suite bathrooms and decorated to the highest standard. There is a very large dining room which is very well appointed and a luxurious lounge in which you may relax in total comfort in front of the roaring open fire that is always lit in those long, winter months.

The house has a very traditional Scottish style and theme, with Margaret and Richard offering a warm and very friendly welcome, making your stay as comfortable and enjoyable as possible. On waking from your pleasant night's slumber you will be greeted by a traditional full Scottish breakfast, with all the works and the menus vary on a weekly basis. The bus route is directly across the road to Kilmarnock town centre and Railway Station so getting about and exploring this beautiful part of Scotland shouldn't be a problem. In Ayrshire itself there are no less than 30 golf courses and also driven pheasant shooting, deer stalking, salmon fishing, bowling, tennis, football and many other leisure pursuits for you to enjoy.

Westerlea House, 34a Main Road, Crookedholm, Hurlford
Tel: 01563 574525

MAUCHLINE. Immortalised by the Burns, the town has a tall and rather grand **Burns Memorial Tower** celebrating the fact. It was here that the poet's family moved after his father's death and to which Burns returned to live with his new wife, Jean Armour, who came from the town. The house, on Castle Street, is now the **Burns House Museum** and it houses a wonderful collection of memorabilia. There is also the sad sight of the graves of four of Burns' daughters in Mauchline churchyard. Across the road from the museum is **Poosie Nansie's Ale House** (which inspired *The Jolly Beggars*) still in use today.

At one time Mauchline was a centre for the manufacture of curling stones. More information about this unusual sport and other local industries can be found in the museum.

South of the town lies **Ballochmyle Gorge** from which there are views of sweeping woodlands and the River Ayr far below. The railway viaduct here is, itself, of interest as a great feat of engineering, being the highest railway bridge in Britain, at 51 metres, and the main span being the widest masonry arch railway bridge in Britain, at 55 metres in length.

STAIR. Here, in this pretty little village standing on the banks of the River Ayr, is **The Stair Inn**. A listed building of considerable character and dating back to around 1670, this is a traditional country hostelry situated in a beautiful conservation area. Pictures of Robert Burns adorn the walls reminding visitors that this inn was frequented by the poet in his lifetime. Neighbouring the inn are the farmlands and woodlands of the Earl of Stair, and just across the river is the only hone stone mine works remaining in Britain. This still produces the celebrated Tam o'Shanter and Water of Ayr hone stones.

In the past the inn was used for church services when the local church roof leaked. After the service, every member of the congregation received a jar of ale and it has been said that these were the best attended services ever!

DALRYMPLE. A local legend has it that the heroine of the ballad *The Gypsy Laddie* was the wife of a 17th century Earl of Cassillis. The story goes that Johnnie Faa, a gypsy leader, and six accomplices stood outside the castle gates and sang so sweetly that Lady Cassillis came out to listen to them. When they had finished she then followed them into the forest. Her distraught husband searched high and low and eventually found her, with the gypsies, by a stream. He begged her to return home but she declared that she had finished with the fine life and wished to remain with Johnnie Faa and his companions. The Earl's answer was to arrest the gypsies and hang them all.

The Kirkton Inn

With its central position and ideal location for local shops and places of interest, **The Kirkton Inn** has long been a favourite of traveller's visiting the picturesque town of Dalrymple in Ayrshire. Your host is Ms June Cameron, who has owned and personally run the Kirkton Inn for many years, and it is down to her excellent Scottish hospitality that this pub is so welcoming. The splendid River Doon runs through the back of the premises and June holds fishing permits so that any guest can try their hand at Salmon fishing in these well stocked waters. Kirkton is very well known locally for its superb food and wines, the choice is extensive and varied with all meals being produced using only the finest local ingredients. For starters you could try Succulent Prawns smothered in a brandy-laced sauce, follow this with Roast Gigot of Lamb with redcurrant and rosemary sauce, and for dessert Alcoholic Meringue Glace, a wicked combination.

The Kirkton Inn, 1 Main Street Dalrymple Tel: 01292 560241

DALMELLINGTON makes an excellent base for exploring the River Doon, immortalised in verse by Burns. Its source is at **Loch Doon** and an enjoyable day is to be had with a picnic on its shores. The road actually follows the shoreline of the loch and provides ample opportunity to take a variety of invigorating walks.

Dalmellington Castle dates from the early 14th century, though it has actually been removed from its original site on an island in the middle of the loch. This ambitious scheme was undertaken as the waters of the loch were raised in the 1930s, and the castle was removed to the west bank to prevent it being lost forever. This must have been quite a task, since the walls are seven to nine feet thick. The island can still be seen from time to time as the water level tends to fluctuate. The loch has been the base for a number of schemes, one of which was the siting of a gunnery school during the First World War. The remains of the concrete blocks which carried the monorail target for the school can still be seen.

Back in the town, the **Cathcartson Interpretation Centre** contains an interesting display of weaving, mining and other aspects of the area's industry, and the town is full of fascinating buildings from the 18th and 19th centuries.

CUMNOCK. This village was once famous for the manufacture of snuff boxes. James Kier Hardy, regarded as the founder of the Labour Party, lived here and built himself a house nearby.

North Ayrshire

IRVINE. Many of the activities available in Irvine are based around the attractions of the sea and one of the most popular is the **Magnum Leisure Complex**. This dominates the harbour area and its features are too many for a complete list but include swimming pools, an ice rink, bowls hall, theatre, cinema, sauna and solarium, plus many other activities inside and outside in the 250 acre beach park.

A covered shopping mall spans the river connecting the town to the harbour area. In the latter is the Scottish Maritime Museum, which includes a shipyard worker's flat, which has been restored to its original 1910 decor. There are many fine historic ships moored in the harbour, which visitors are encouraged to board. Nearby is the enchanting **Sea World** which creates an underwater environment for observing marine life, housed in special tanks, ranging from sea anemones and starfish to lobsters and even giant conger eels.

Back in the town there are fascinating walks along the narrow cobbled streets of old Irvine, taking in the fine examples of 18th and 19th century buildings. Nearby, **Glasgow Vennel** was once the main route to Glasgow though it is now traffic free and was recently the winner of an award for its restoration.

This is Burns country and the Poet came here in 1781, not to pen his verse but to learn the flax dressing trade. The buildings where he worked, and stayed for two years, are now, some 200 years later, home to the Ayrshire Writers and Artists Society. His attic bedroom which is open to visitors and located at number four.

On the opposite side of the house is the **Buchanite Meeting House** which was once occupied by an infamous religious sect, led by Elizabeth Buchan. The agricultural revolution in the late 18th century brought many country folk into the towns in a desperate search for work. This led to an increase in the general instability and a result of this was the flourishing of religious cults. The most unusual of these were the Buchanites who set up their sect in Irvine. Elizabeth Buchan talked of the second coming of the Messiah when she and her followers would be taken up to heaven. The townspeople of Irvine were rather taken aback by all this and promptly ran the lady and her followers out of town.

AROUND IRVINE

SALTCOATS. As its name suggests, Saltcoats developed a salt panning industry established here by James V in the 16th century. The harbour was built in the 17th century and coal would come here via a canal for export to Ireland. Since the development of the harbour at Ardrossan however, the use of Saltcoats as a working port declined and only small boats are seen here today, although the place is very popular with holiday makers. At low tide, the fossilized remains of tree trunks are revealed in the harbour.

The tower above the school is a **Martello Tower**. There are examples these buildings all around the coast of Britain and they were gun positions built to protect the country from French warships during the Napoleonic Wars.

ARDROSSAN. Divided from Saltcoats by the Stanley Burn, Ardrossan is a 19th century town. There has, in fact, been a castle here since the 12th century though, despite its seemingly strong position, it was captured by Cromwell, who used its stones to build his castle in Ayr.

There was a very ambitious plan to connect the port and harbour at Ardrossan with Glasgow by linking the two with a canal. Both Telford and Rennie were engaged on the construction. Unfortunately their funding ran out in 1815 and the plan was abandoned. Had it gone ahead the town of Ardrossan might have been a very different place. Ardrossan has instead became important for its ferry crossings to the Isle of Arran and to Belfast, and developed into a popular resort boasting sandy beaches to rival the best of the west coast. **Horse Island**, just off the coast, is, not surprisingly, a bird sanctuary.

LARGS faces directly onto the sea and it was here, in 1263, that the Scots defeated an invasion force of Norsemen; in 1912, the **Pencil**, a distinctive monument on the coast of the southern end of Largs, was erected to commemorate the victory. In September each year, a Viking festival is held where, strange though it may seem, many Scandinavian entertainers return to celebrate the Vikings only defeat on mainland Scotland.

Kelburn Castle makes an impressive background here and there is much to do for all the family in its lovely grounds.

GREAT CUMBRAE ISLAND. Reached by boat from Largs,
Great Cumbrae Island lies between the Isle of Bute and the mainland. Small though the island is (just ten miles in circumference) a vehicle ferry service is available. It takes just ten minutes cross to this fascinating place, which offers some superb views of Scotland from its highest point, the Glaidstane.

MILLPORT, on the south side of Great Cumbrae Island, is a friendly town with the smallest cathedral in Europe. The Garrison House is now the **Museum of the Cumbraes**, which is packed with photos, memorabilia and articles telling the story of the island and its much smaller sister, not surprisingly called Little Cumbrae. **Garrison House**, was built by Captain Crauford in 1745, of the famous cutter 'The Royal George', as a barracks for his crew.

Millport is also the home of the **National Watersports Centre** which offers a wide choice of tuition courses in a variety of watersports for beginners and enthusiasts alike.

SKELMORLIE. **Skelmorlie Castle** was built in 1502 and very nearly destroyed in 1959 by a huge fire. Now restored, with the Victorian additions of 1852 removed, it is a private family home.

The family run **Mains Caravan and Camping Park** is situated just south of Skelmorlie on the hill overlooking the Firth of Clyde, behind Skelmorlie Castle, half a mile above the main A78 within a working Farm. Four miles from Largs and two miles from the Station and Pier at Wemyss Bay. The Park affords a panoramic vista of the islands of Bute, Arran, The Cumbraes and the Argyll Hills. Country walks, the scenery and natural beauty are readily available as well as the usual tourist attractions. Skelmorlie is centrally placed for ferries to the islands and as a base for discovering the west coast of Scotland. Sailing, water sports, golf, swimming, ice skating and entertainment are all available locally as well as historic places to visit. The Park facilities include shop and reception, showers, telephone, TV and games room, electric hook-up and gas. There's a holiday chalet available which sleeps six and is luxuriously fitted out including full central heating. A superb location for all the family. Tourist Board √√ Commended Site.

Mains Caravan and Camping Park, Skelmorlie Mains Farm, Skelmorlie
Tel & Fax: 01475 520794

DALRY. Situated on the River Garnock Dalry was developed principally as a weaving town in the 18th century. The grounds of the nearby Blair estate, to the southeast of the town, are well worth exploring and the house here is quite interesting. Standing on the bank of the River Bambo, it is based around an ancient tower and later developed into a T-shaped plan with three and four storeys. The Blair family can trace their antecedence back to 1165 and the house, started in the 1500s, is still in their hands. The estate is surrounded by a wall and there are attractive lodges and an interesting smithy worth looking at.

The Dusk Water flows through the estate and a trip to Cleaves Cove, on the south bank of the water, is well worthwhile. Excavations here in 1883 show that the caves were inhabited in prehistoric times! These are a series of limestone caves and contain some well known stalactites.

KILWINNING. Here there is the strange ancient custom of 'shooting the papingo'. A papingo, or wooden bird on a pole, is set up as a target from the clock tower of the Abbey Church for the Ancient Society of Kilwinning Archers to test their skills. This annual shoot is re-enacted each year and the table gravestones beside the church have been chipped by the arrows that presumably have missed the papingo! There is the magnificent Silver Arrow Trophy, dating back to 1724, displayed in the town's library.

The Isle of Arran

BRODICK. The Isle of Arran is a fascinating 10 by 20 mile island that is, perhaps, with some justification referred to as Scotland in miniature. The Island unfolds dramatically, from mountains in the north capped by Goat Fell to the farmlands and rolling moors of the south. Its history is turbulent, being held not only by the Dalriada Scots from Northern Ireland but also by the Vikings, whose links with the Isle are still celebrated, and finally by the Scottish Crown. Robert the Bruce stayed here in 1307 before leaving for the mainland to continue his struggle for Scottish Independence, which he finally achieved at Bannockburn after some seven years.

A regular services link the Isle with the Mainland and the ferry unloads the visitor at Brodick, after a journey time of about an hour. The name Brodick has Viking associations, as do many of the names of the Island, it is Norse for 'Broad Bay'. Brodick is the largest village on Arran, and lies to one side of Brodick Bay.

A mile and a half from the Brodick Pier is **Brodick Castle**, a fine National Trust for Scotland property. The Castle is the former seat of the Dukes of Hamilton and dates, in part, from the 13th century. Over the many following decades, additions to the Castle have included a gun battery erected in 1652 by Oliver Cromwell's troops, who occupied the Castle at that time.

A busy year for the masons was 1844 when they carried out work on the Castle in traditional Scottish Baronial style. Inside, there are many fine paintings, a large number of which depict sporting scenes and reflect the sporting nature of the Hamiltons. An indicator of the hunting skills of the family are the stag heads which line the walls of the grand staircase. There is also a fine collection of silver and porcelain to enjoy, as well as the valuable art collection.

The last owner of Brodick Castle was the Duchess of Montrose, daughter of the 12th Duke of Hamilton. It was she who created the magnificent rhododendron collection, now regarded as one of the finest in Europe. The Castle gardens these days form part of **Brodick Country Park** and, as well as the Woodland Garden which houses the rhododendrons, there is a Walled Garden which dates back to 1810.

Also in the Park is the mountain of **Goat Fell** (2618 feet high) and part of Glen Rosa and Cir Mhor. A thoughtful touch is the Nature Trail designed especially for wheelchair users, and for everyone, a Ranger Service is provided to answer the many questions posed by curious trekkers. Young visitors will love the Adventure Playground, and a visit to the Castle shop and tearoom rounds the day off perfectly.

Visitors to the castle will notice a strong Bruce connection as this stronghold has a room known as 'Bruce's Room'. The story goes that in 1307 Bruce, and his small band of colleagues, waited in hiding for a signal that it was safe to cross to the mainland. However, the King and his followers saw an unrelated light and set forth, across the waters. Luckily the misunderstanding did not hamper Bruce's arrival.

There is another version of the story which claims that the room, from which Bruce watched for the light, was in the now ruined Kildonan Castle, some nine miles to the south. Brodick at the time was the headquarters of King Edward's governor and, possibly, the last place that Bruce would find refuge, while Kildonan Castle was owned by a branch of the Clan Donald of the Isle, who were friends and supporters of Bruce. Whomever is right, it's a fascinating piece of history.

To get a real feel for life on the island before 1020 it's recommended that visitors make a trip to the **Isle of Arran Heritage Museum**, which is located between the Castle and the village. Here there are accurate representations of life on Arran, including a Smiddy and an Arran cottage. The museum also features a plaque in memory of the 112th Scottish Commando. The Isle was the training ground for the officers and men during the last war. It was this Commando Unit which was responsible for a daring raid on General Rommel's headquarters in the North African desert in November 1941.

Going back even further in time, the importance of Arran as an archaeological centre cannot be forgotten. There have been recently excavated sites, which have been dated back to 2500 BC, and are considered to be some of the most important remaining examples of Bronze and Iron Age finds in Europe. There are many ancient monument sites to see and the Isle can boast a rich choice of tombs from the Neolithic period and circles of standing stones from the Bronze Age.

The same must be said for Arran's importance as a geological centre. The local rock is Permian desert sandstone which is 250 million years old. James Hutton, who is regarded as the father of modern geology, made discoveries at Lochranza, which was the first certain proof of the great age of the Earth. The Douglas Hotel in the town often plays host to trainee submarine captains who come to Arran, twice a year, for simulated deep sea dives and attack manoeuvres around the island.

The beautiful Isle of Arran has much to offer the holiday maker, with splendid mountain scenery to the north and gently rolling farmland to the south, interspersed with little towns and villages providing a wealth of places to eat and shop.

Standing only 500 yards from Brodick Pier and with stunning views of the bay, **Tomderosa** offers the very best in self-catering accommodation. Owned and personally run by Thomas and Roseland Cooke, Tomderosa offers its guests a five bedroomed house with all the modern conveniences you will have come to expect. Two of the bedrooms are en-suite, whilst the kitchen is equipped with everything that you will need to make your stay in Brodick a relaxed one. In the large lounge area there is a warming open fire that is perfect for toasting marshmallows on those long winter nights and the general decor and furnishings have a definite Eastern feel that is quite captivating. The main bedroom has its very own private lounge with television just in case Mum and Dad fancy a quiet night in on their own and, in the beautiful garden, there are some superb facilities for the kids to keep them occupied over the holiday. Also in the garden is a Gas Barbecue, just ready for you to fire up and cook those sausages and steaks on those balmy, summer evenings. The views from the accommodation really are superb, the lounge looks out onto the magnificent Goat Fell and from the side there is the bay, colourful and bustling what ever the time of day.

Tomderosa, 2 Manse Crescent, Brodick Tel: 01770 302480

The **Good Food Shop** stands on the banks of the Cloy Burn 3/4 mile from the ferry port of Brodick where Geoff Collins and family will welcome you to their interesting business.

The Good Food Shop

They have been here for eight years supplying fresh fruit and vegetables and fresh fish, daily, all year round to locals and local business people. Take a look at the rear of the shop and you'll find the refreshment area and patio overlooking the Cloy Burn where you can sit back and enjoy snacks, meals to suit all tastes including vegetarians (menu changed daily), tea, cakes or bakery products all freshly make on the premises. The shop also sells specialist foods, herbal and health food and Homeopathy medicine. There's even a launderette facility available here.

Children are welcome and assistance will be given to the less-abled customers. Situated just across the road from the Brodick Golf Club.

Good Food Shop, Auchrannie Road, Brodick Tel: 01770 302427

Situated just 1 mile from the charming village of Brodick, you will find **The Sheilin**, which offers the visitor some splendid self catering accommodation. Owned and run for the past 29 years by Janie and John Maclure, this beautiful hideaway establishment consists of 2 flats and a cottage. The cottage has a light and airy dining room, bedroom, bathroom, lounge and fully equipped kitchen with some stunning views of Arran's highest peak. There is also a pretty garden at the rear of the property, perfect for those summer barbecues. Both flats are fully self contained with double bedrooms, living room, kitchen and shower and toilet room. The views from the upstairs flat are breathtaking, with the downstairs flat having their own sun terrace and garden area from which to sit and enjoy those balmy summer evenings. The furnishings are very comfortable, with the atmosphere being both warm and relaxed you are guaranteed a friendly welcome when you visit this super example of self catering holidays at their best.

The Sheilin, Corriegills, Brodick Tel: 01770 302456

Overlooking the ever changing Brodick Bay and Goat Fell, stands the **Glenflorol Guest House**. You will be warmly welcomed by Andy and Mary, the proprietors to this homely bed and breakfast, who will make your stay in this pleasant establishment a memorable one. There are five light and airy bedrooms, each decorated with a definite feel for comfort and relaxation. One of the rooms is en-suite with the other four sharing a guest only bathroom. On waking you will be treated to one of Mary's full Scottish breakfasts that are guaranteed to keep you going until lunchtime, with a full vegetarian alternative also available on request.

Out of season you can visit Glenflorol Guest House on an accommodation only tariff that is at a reduced rate, perfect for exploring the magnificent scenery that surrounds the town without the hustle and bustle of the many tourists that visit Brodick every year. The ferry and pier are only a few minutes walk away from this family Guest House which is great for convenience and an uncooked breakfast can be supplied on request for those early boat departures.

Glenflorol Guest House, Shore Road, Brodick Tel: 01770 302707

Delightful bed and breakfast accommodation in Brodick can be found in **Glenard House**, a small guesthouse which lies within easy reach of the Ardrossan ferry. The house stands within a beautiful secluded garden and has magnificent views over the sea in one direction and the dramatic mountain landscape of Goat Fell and the Three Bens in the other.

Glanard House

Built in 1928 by a long-standing resident of Arran, today it is the home of Sandra and Iain MacMillan, two charming hosts who offer their guests the warmest of welcomes and superb hospitality. Their three spacious guest bedrooms are comfortable, well appointed and fitted with an appealing mixture of antique and other quality furniture. Three rooms are situated in the main house with their own private facilities, whilst the cottage adjoining the house is both self-catering and fully self-contained with two bedrooms that sleep up to four. The MacMillans are renowned for serving one of the most delicious full Scottish breakfasts on Arran. More a feast than a meal, it is guaranteed to satisfy the heartiest appetite for most of the day. Both born and bred on Arran, Sandra and Iain have accumulated a wealth of knowledge on the geography, history and natural science of the island, making this the ideal base for hill-walkers, bird-watchers and wildlife enthusiasts.

Glenard House, Brodick Tel: 01770 302318

Quietly situated in the main village of Brodick and commanding spectacular views over Brodick Bay and the mountains beyond, **The Glenartney** is a comfortable, family hotel run by resident Scottish proprietors, Wren and Marion Gentleman. It is the ideal location to take advantage of the many splendid activities the island has to offer or to simply relax amid the finest scenery in Scotland.

The Glanartney Hotel

The Glenartney offers comfortable accommodation in 14 bed-rooms, all with central heating, electric blankets, wash hand basins and tea and coffee makers. Most rooms have TV with private shower and WC facilities. There is a cozy lounge with a real log fire and colour TV and a residents only bar featuring a fine selection of imported wines and malt whiskies. Whilst staying at Glenartney it is a must to explore the magnificent local countryside. In the north of the Island, Golden Eagles roam the skies and large herds of Red Deer are regularly sighted. Along the shore you will see many species of native and migrating birds. Seals and Basking Shark are regular visitors to the island whilst the semi-tropical plants that grow in abundance can be quite breathtaking.

There are also seven golf courses, three pony trekking centres, bowling, tennis, rambling, hill walking, climbing, fishing - you name it and it's near at hand! For a warm, friendly welcome, the best in home cooking and value for money, phone not to arrange your holiday.

Glenartney Hotel, Brodick Tel: 01770 302220

Boasting some spectacular views over Goat Fell and the surrounding bay, the **Kingsley Hotel** is one of Arran's most premier establishments. Having been owned and family run by the Duncan's for the last 50 years, you can guarantee only the very best in service and hospitality which makes many of its guests want to return year after year to sample this unique style of conviviality. The Kingsley also houses one of the largest bars on the Island, **Duncan's Bar**, a relaxing spot where you can enjoy freshly prepared bar lunches and suppers whilst enjoying a cup of real Italian coffee or sampling one of over 40 malt whiskies. If you wish for a more formal meal then the attractive Kingsley dining room will prove ideal. Overlooking the picturesque bay, you can sit and enjoy some of the best Scottish fayre which has been created using only the freshest local ingredients. There are 27 individually decorated and comfortably furnished guest bedrooms, each having full en-suite facilities with the added benefit of a colour TV, tea and coffee maker, direct dial telephone and full central heating. Kingsley Hotel has a glorious sun lounge, the ideal location to sit and soak up the rays, or if you are looking for something a little more energetic then the heated indoor swimming pool will prove very popular. And in the summer on those long and sunny days you can relax in the green and lush gardens with a meal and a pint of excellent cask conditioned ale that is served throughout the day at Duncan's Bar.

Kingsley Hotel, Brodick Tel: 01770 302226

AROUND BRODICK

LAMLASH. It was here, in 1263, that a naval battle was fought between the Norwegians and the Scots. Prior to the battle, the Viking King Haakon's fleet was anchored off the shore, and every year the village of Corrie, which in fact is to the north of Brodick, holds the 'Corrie Capers' to remember this time by burning the replica of a Viking long ship. The Vikings lost the battle to Alexander III of Scotland, who effectively ended centuries of Norse control of the Western Isles.

The small island off the shore of Lamlash is called **Holy Isle** and is a paradise for bird lovers. Visits to the Island, which is only a short boat trip away, can be made and as well as seeing many breeds of bird there is also a herd of wild goats which roam around its rocky crags. Holy Isle also contains **St Molio's Cave** (to the west of the island) along with **St Molio's Well** and the **Judgement Stone** which is a 7 foot sandstone table. The Island takes its name from the 7th century St Molaise who is said to have lived to be 120; perhaps this is a testament to the healthy life here in the Isles. Graffiti on the walls in runic, the old Norse alphabet, was carved by Norwegian sailors who were here before the battle in 1263.

In 1829 the brig, 'Caledonian', stopped at Lamlash Bay. It's purpose was to pick up 86 emigres who had lost their places on the land as a result of the clearances, when they were forced to leave their homes to make way for more profitable sheep which the landowners were bringing in. There is a monument here to these unfortunate people.

Visitors to Lamlash will also find a lively marina and boats can be hired for those who like a spot of sea fishing. Alternatively, those with a taste for the underwater world may like to hire some diving equipment and excellent advice can be found on the best places to drive locally.

The cottages along Hamilton Terrace were originally built for estate workers, who would move to the backs of their houses each summer in order to let the main front house to visitors. Another interesting shop in Lamlash is the **Arran Provisions** factory which produces a world famous range of jams, jellies, chutneys and mustards.

Set amidst mature, sloping gardens, **Blairbeg House** occupies an elevated situation and offers breathtaking views across Lamlash Bay to Holy Island where the sun rises in the summer. In this most beautiful of settings, you can choose accommodation in either the upper level villa apartment built around 1840 or the newly built lodge.

Blairbeg House

Both are designed and equipped to standards of excellence with three bedroomed accommodation. The kitchens are fitted with every luxury appliance you could wish for from carefully chosen china, glass and cutlery to microwave oven and dishwasher; even the thermos flasks are included. The interiors are spacious, light and airy with soft colours, furnished with rich fabrics and supremely comfortable furniture, cosy beds and fine linen. Blairbeg House is quality all the way. The Lodge is awarded 5 Crowns De Luxe by the STB while the upper level Villa Apartment has 5 Crowns Highly Commended. Need we say more?

Blairbeg House, Lamlash Tel: 01770 600383

WHITING BAY. This is a truly lovely spot and it is close to the Glenashdale Falls, a picturesque place of sparkling waters which makes a pleasant excursion on foot from the other side of Whiting Bay.

There is a rich abundance of sea-life around the Island and it is quite common, in the earlier part of the summer, for sightings to be made of basking sharks in the waters. These huge plankton-eating fish can grow up to 40 feet in length and swim around for six to eight weeks before taking their leave. It is amazing to think that little is known about the habits of these creatures, which are harmless. Another visitor to the Isle is the whale, and both killer and bottlenosed have been sighted around the shores. There can be few more stirring sights.

Located in the very beautiful Whiting Bay, you will stumble across the wonderful **Grange House Hotel**. This Grade B Listed Building is owned and managed by Janet and Clive Hughes, who bring to the Grange a range of expertise which should ensure that the hospitality you receive will be second to none. Each of the nine bedrooms has its own unique character with furnishings of the Victorian period but not the inadequacies and chill! Seven of the rooms have en-suite facilities and some can be grouped to give family privacy, with eight having spectacular sea views of Holy Isle and the Ayrshire coast. Each room has a colour television and tea and coffee makers, with the downstairs bedroom also having full facilities for the disabled.

Grange House Hotel

Food and drink are both important contributions to an enjoyable stay and you will find the menus incorporate all that is best. The food is so fresh that it has been picked or caught that very afternoon to grace your table in the evening. To make your trips out even more enjoyable, packed lunches are available and are suitable for fishing or mountain climbing. The atmosphere of the attractive dining room is informal and relaxed, with coffee and drinks being served in the lounge, where on cooler evenings a warming fire awaits you. In the garden you will find an eight hole putting lawn and there are suntraps where you can read or watch the activities of the many birds from gannets to Eider ducks. Your stay at The Grange House Hotel will recharge your batteries and the service is an amiable blend of individual attention and unobtrusive caring. The Hotel is totally non-smoking.

Grange House Hotel, Whiting Bay
Tel & Fax: 01770 700263

Whilst taking a stroll along Whiting Bay's Sea Promenade you are bound to come across the perfectly located **Argentine House Hotel**. This family run hotel has the typical cosy ambiance of a turn of the century dwelling and was built, in 1904, by a seafaring Captain who made his fortune with trade to Argentina. The imposing staircase, which you will notice on entering this splendid property, is made of Argentine oak that was imported from the tropics by the Captain on one of his many voyages. All of the six bedrooms are tastefully decorated and furnished, many with breathtaking views of the sea and promenade. All rooms have either a private shower or bath, as well as colour TV, hair-dryers and tea and coffee making facilities, with refreshments available at any time.

The food is lovingly produced by the Swiss chef and owner who blends the best of her native cuisine with that of Switzerland's neighbours, France, Italy and Austria, including traditional Scottish fayre for a fresh, new and balanced menu, also to note is the fact that the Hotel is a member of the Taste of Scotland scheme.

Argentine House Hotel

The scenic surroundings make a stay at Argentine House Hotel very worthwhile, with waterfalls and quiet valleys to walk and explore.

There are also seven challenging golf courses in Arran with tennis, mini-golf, lawn bowling and boating also available for those energetic ones among you. The Argentine House Hotel really is the perfect location for those wanting to travel and explore this beautiful part of Arran.

Argentine House Hotel, Whiting Bay Tel: 01770 700662

The Burlington Hotel now has a new look having been totally refurbished by its new owners John and Doreen Lamont. This Edwardian seafront hotel is ideally placed opposite a sandy beach with magnificent views of the bay and Holy Isle and has one of the most attractive positions in Whiting Bay.

Burlington Hotel

The new look Burlington has individually styled bedrooms all with private facilities, electric blankets, Continental quilts, TV and hospitality trays. The Burlington licensed restaurant is also open to non-residents and chef Robin Gray is well known to visitors to the island. Drawing on his extensive repertoire he produces dishes to tempt all palates with specialities such as free range ducklings, seafood and organic vegetables. Carefully selected wines compliment his culinary delights. Guests are offered a choice of evening meal from a varied table d'hôte menu to individually priced à la carte; special diets are given personal attention. The Burlington Bistro will take care of your lighter meal requirements offering flavoursome food, a glass of wine, patisseries and coffee. Children are welcome and dogs by arrangement. Guests can be collected from the ferry at Brodick.

Burlington Hotel, Shore Road, Whiting Bay
Tel: 01770 700255 Fax: 0374 595327

KILDONAN and its castle are situated at the southern tip of the Island and the harbour is another centre for diving as well as having opportunities for boat hire.

KILMORY. Around Bennan Head at Kilmory is the creamery that manufactures the prize winning Arran cheddar cheese, all 300 tons of it each year!

Situated in Kilmory on the beautiful Isle of Arran is **The Lagg Hotel**, a splendid country house hotel that offers its guests the very best in service and amenities. Owned and very capably run by Ronald and Sheila Moore, the Lagg Hotel has 14 light and airy guest rooms with private bathroom and full facilities for making tea and coffee. All prices charged are inclusive of a traditional Scottish breakfast that is guaranteed to keep any guest going until lunchtime when they can return to the hotel and indulge in some of the delicious food that is served in the thriving Wishing Well Restaurant. Situated adjacent to the Hotel, the Wishing Well serves morning coffee, snack lunches, afternoon teas, high teas and a full à la carte restaurant menu throughout the day at very competitive prices. Reservations may prove essential if a preference is made to dine there as opposed to the main Hotel dining room. As well as a superb dining room, the Lagg Hotel also offers its guests a very warm welcome at its large public bar, which stays open from 11.00 am until 1.00 am seven days a week and proves very popular with locals and guests alike.

The Lagg Hotel, Kilmory Tel: 01770 870255

BLACKWATERFOOT. With much of the Island open country, exploring from the back of a horse is an excellent way to see the delights of Arran and, in Blackwaterfoot, there is a choice of pony trekking and riding centres

A short sea crossing is all it takes to enjoy the enchantment of one of Scotland's loveliest Islands and located in the glorious scenery of Blackwaterfoot is the **Kinloch Hotel**. The Hotel has been family owned and run for over 42 years by the Crawfords, who pride themselves on offering their guests the very best in Scottish hospitality. The fact that so many guests return to Kinloch Hotel year after year is testimony to the very special pleasure it provides, a warm and friendly welcome coupled with excellent food in a relaxed and quiet comfort on the beautiful west coast of Arran. Kinloch is the largest Hotel on the Island and offers superb accommodation on three floors, with 44 en-suite guest rooms that each have colour TV, direct-dial telephone, tea and coffee making facilities, hair dryer and room service is always available.

Enjoying an imposing location facing out to the picturesque panorama of Kilbrannan Sound and the Mull of Kintyre, the Hotel has a unique location providing the valuable seclusion and privacy for conducting your conference in a relaxed and efficient manner. To help your conference to be as successful as possible they also provide the following support facilities, O/H projector, slide projector, TV/video, audio equipment, photocopying/fax, flip charts / display boards and controlled lighting which includes spotlights. A must for corporate entertainment is the unrivalled wealth of leisure pursuits that Kinloch offers delegates, from quad biking, paragliding and paintball games to pony trekking and visits to Lochranza Distillery, where sampling is positively encouraged. For more leisurely pursuits you can enjoy the birdwatching opportunities or explore the rich wealth of ancient historic sites in which the Island abounds. You could treat yourself to a leisurely trip on The Waverly, the world's last ocean-going paddle steamer, or simply laze the time away on Blackwaterfoot's beautiful sandy beach.

Kinloch Hotel

The Crawford family have also added seven beautiful self-contained suites that are situated on the second floor of the Hotel. There are five two bedroom suites with lounge and small kitchen area, with the two single bed settees in the lounge giving the suite a total occupancy of six. Also on this floor are two one bedroom suites with four poster double bed, lounge, complete with two single bed settees and a small kitchen area, this suite has a total occupancy of four. A rare blend of pleasure awaits you in a landscape of unrivalled natural beauty, from the rugged drama of its northern mountains offering splendid hill walking or challenging rock climbs to the gentle moorland and fields of the south, Arran's unspoiled beauty will cast its spell on you.

Kinloch Hotel, Blackwaterfoot Tel: 01770 860444

SHISKINE. The village claims to be the last resting place of St Molaise. Despite deliberately catching some 130 diseases in expiation of his sins, the Saint is nevertheless believed to have died at the age of 120!

Just off the main road in the charming parish of old Kilpatrick and within easy walking distance of Blackwaterfoot stands **Bellevue**. This self-catering accommodation has been tastefully converted from an old barn, adjoining the main farmhouse in the grounds of a working farm. The two modern, but characteristic apartments which are fully self-contained, offer the holidaymaker two bedrooms, one room with double bed and one with a single and bunk beds; a cot is also available on request.

Bellevue

Both apartments also have a fully equipped kitchen with electric cooker, microwave and automatic washing machine, there is also a tumble dryer that can be made available if you so wish. The lounge has a colour television and patio doors that open out onto the superb garden which is shared by both apartments and offers the kids a great play area and for the adults, a superb view across the sea to Campbeltown. Central heating is installed throughout, with electricity being charged by coin meter, also available at a modest weekly charge are bed linen and towels. The village itself boasts a magnificent 12 hole golf course surrounded by beautiful views of Carradale, tennis courts, a bowling green and riding stables so there is plenty to do without even leaving your own doorstep.

Bellevue, Shiskine Tel: 01770 860251

MACHRIE BAY. The approach to Machrie Bay features some fine examples of standing stones; some 15 feet tall they are a reminder that the Island has been settled since the Bronze Age. The Bay itself has lovely sands and is an ideal place for a walk or picnic.

The sighting of wild red deer is not unusual as the Isle can boast over 2,000 of the species in the wild hill country. They wander around at will and are a most impressive sight. The Island is also famous for its Golden Eagles, as well as a wealth of other birds of prey including hawks, buzzards, peregrines and kestrels. Bird watchers will enjoy a rewarding time here.

Located on the unspoiled west coast of Arran, with spectacular views of Kilbrannan Sound and the Mull of Kintyre, stands **Machrie House**. Previously used as a hotel, Machrie House has been fully converted and offers its guests four quality self-contained apartments, one on the ground floor which sleeps two in a double bedroom, and three on the first floor. The apartments on this floor all sleep four people in two bedrooms, with every apartment offering private bath or shower room, open plan kitchen, lounge/dining room and are equipped to a very high standard. The kitchen includes a cooker, fridge and microwave whilst the lounge has a colour TV that is linked to the satellite movie channel. There is also a separate utility room with a washing machine and tumble dryer for the convenience of all apartments. From October through to April there is storage heating available free of charge, all other electricity is provided by coin meter.

Machrie House

The decor is comfortable and welcoming, with light and airy rooms allowing you some magnificent views of the surrounding countryside and on a clear day you can even see Ireland. All bed linen, duvet covers and towels are available at a weekly hire charge and there is a large garden with picnic tables so that you can sit outside and soak up the sun on those hot summer days. Machrie House is also adjacent to Machrie Golf Course, a very popular nine hole course where visitors are always welcome, there is also a modern all-weather tennis court and children's play area adjoining the golf clubhouse.

Machrie House, Machrie Tel: 01770 840223 Fax: 01770 840600

Standing in the quiet village of Machrie is **Ashlar Farm** which is owned and run by Angus and Aase Smith. This Victorian farmhouse provides self-catering accommodation in the traditional environment of a working farm. The facilities include a full equipped modern kitchen with washing machine, dining and sitting rooms, both with open fires, four large bedrooms for sleeping up to 11 guests and a large, private garden. The property is fully centrally heated and all fuels are provided free. Ashlar Farm is very close to local attractions including Kings Caves and The Machrie Moor Standing Stones. You are also very close to the local beaches and the village of Blackwaterfoot with its shops and hotels. Your hosts for your stay also speak Norwegian and a little French.

Ashlar Farm, Machrie Tel: 01770 840246

CATACOL. Here there is a rather intriguing row of identical terraced cottages know locally as The Twelve Apostles.

Situated on the seashore, overlooking the Kilbrannan Sound and Kintyre, the **Catacol Bay Hotel** is a small, friendly, fully licensed hotel nestling in the hills at the picturesque north end of Arran. Dave Ashcroft has been the owner for 17 years and is your convivial host making everyone welcome and comfortable. The hotel is open all year and is centrally heated throughout so even if the weather turns, you will be cosy and warm. All bedrooms have wash hand basins, shaver points, Continental quilts and tea and coffee making facilities. The residents lounge has colour television and the public bar makes a good meeting point. Children and dogs are very welcome. **The Green** is 200 yards from the

Catacol Bay Hotel

hotel and is a newly built, split level bungalow offering family accommodation with everything provided for up to six guests. Charges are very reasonable and special rates apply to children in the hotel. Food is served all day from 12 noon until 10 pm with a special buffet served on Sundays.

Catacol Bay Hotel, Catacol Tel: 01770 830231 Fax: 01770 830350

LOCHRANZA. A delightful community situated around the shores of Loch Ranza. Here stand the ruins of **Lochranza Castle**, which was once the hunting seat of Scottish kings, and was built in the 16th century. Situated on a sand spit in the middle of the Loch, the Castle was used by James VI as a base during his struggles with the Lords of the Isles in the early 1600s and, later garrisoned by Cromwell the Castle fell into disuse by the end of the 18th century. Today there are many fine craft industries based here, visitors to Arran Pottery are able to watch the craftsmen at work and the gold and silver jewellery produced at the Castle Workshop is both intricate and beautiful.

The A841 road weaves its way through Glen Chalmadale and gently starts to descend towards the sea and the picturesque village of Lochranza unfolds before you. The hills and shore which cradle Lochranza abound with wildlife. Large herds of red deer can be seen all year round; birds of prey, including the golden eagle, can be seen soaring above the hills; red squirrels, seals, oyster catchers, swans and numerous varieties of duck are just a few of the wonders on offer in this magnificent part of Scotland. **Lochranza Hotel** stands amidst this timeless village and has a spectacular panoramic view across the bay.

Lochranza Hotel

One of Arran's original hotels, George and Fiona Stewart, the proprietors of this beautiful property, have refurbished all the rooms to incorporate en-suite facilities, colour television and tea and coffee makers. Residents are offered a table d'hôte menu, to be taken in the pleasantly appointed dining room. Alternatively they also offer a large selection of bar meals with specials available every day for more variety and suiting all tastes and pockets. To relax at the end of a busy day, Lochranza Hotel has a very friendly, atmospheric bar, where you can make a choice from the enviable collection of malt whiskies and superb selection of real ales. Whether your holiday choice is fishing, golf, hillwalking, birdwatching or just a get away from it all holiday, Lochranza Hotel is an ideal base offering comfort and hospitality.

Lochranza Hotel, Lochranza Tel: 01770 830223

CORRIE, previously mentioned for holding the 'Corrie Capers', is a small village of closely packed white cottages. It makes an excellent base for hill walking and climbing and is ideal, for instance, for attempting the majestic challenge of Goat Fell or Glen Sannox which can be seen from the village.

Lovers of self-catering will be spoilt for choice when they call Gillian Langley, for she manages a dozen properties on the island. One of these is **Burnside Cottage** in the picturesque village of Corrie, five miles from Brodick. The properties are all fully equipped and the accommodation provided is of a very high standard. Two houses, which have a Scottish Tourist Board 5 Crown, Highly Commended rating have disabled facilities.

Gillian Langley, Kirn Point, Lochranza Tel: 01770 830224

Inverclyde

GREENOCK. Until the 17th century, Greenock was a small fishing village which then benefited from the herring boom. By 1711, the Clyde's first dock was opened here and this lead to a period of phenomenal growth which made Greenock the foremost port in Scotland by 1840. Badly damaged during World War II, the docks have declined as has the town's ship building industry.

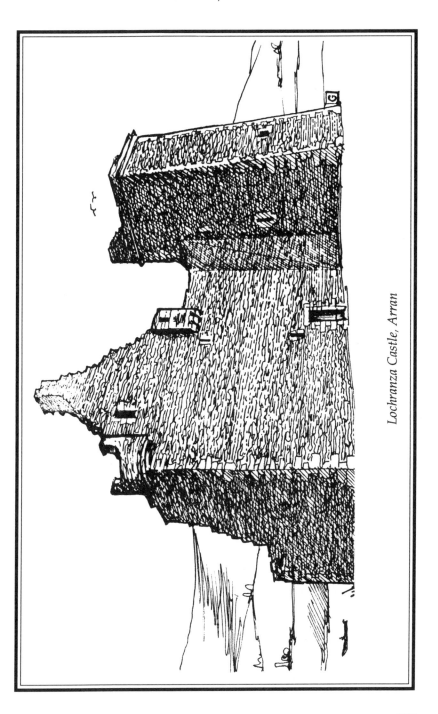

Lochranza Castle, Arran

Pride of place in the **Maclean Museum and Art Gallery** is taken by a collection of model ships. These were often built at the same time as the real thing and either kept on display at the shipyard offices or presented to the ships owners. There are also items relating to James Watt, born in Greenock, who pioneered the condensing steam engine and gave his name to the measurement of Power.

To discover more about the town's entrepreneurs of the past it is well worth visiting the **Smugglers Museum** housed, ironically, in the Custom House.

AROUND GREENOCK

INVERKIP. Just a short journey from Inverkip, into the hills, is **Cornalees Bridge Centre**. Part of the Clyde Muirisheil Regional Park, the centre offers a series of delightful walks and trails along the banks of Loch Thom as well as one that utilises the Greenock Cut, an historic aqueduct that once supplied the houses and factories of the town.

CLOCH POINT. North of Lunderston Bay lies **Cloch Lighthouse**, standing on Cloch Point. This white painted lighthouse was built in 1797, and whilst not open to the public it offers magnificent views of the Firth of Clyde and the hills of Argyll beyond.

Cloch Point marks the start of the famous Firth of Clyde, the life blood of the area; for over 200 years ships from up the river have sailed the world and now, with shipbuilding almost at an end, these waters offer excellent leisure sailing with many international yachting and watersports events held each year.

GOUROCK. The **Kempock Stone** at the Castle Mansions of Gourock is also know as Granny Kempock's Stone. It stands over six feet high and was undoubtedly of great significance in prehistoric times. More recently it was used in fair weather rites ceremonies by local fishermen, and couples intending to marry would encircle the stone to gain Granny's blessing. Gourock also offers the traveller ferry services to Dunoon and Argyllshire.

PORT GLASGOW. Despite being surrounded by shipyards and their attendant industries, **Newark Castle** remains an impressive example of the fortified baronial residence. Though not complete, this former home of the Maxwells is well worth a visit which stands proudly on a spit of land jutting out into the river.

Port Glasgow was originally called Newark until Sir Patrick Maxwell sold the land and village to the magistrates of Glasgow in 1668. They built a port to facilitate the transfer of goods from ocean going vessels to those which could navigate the then shallow Clyde.

Cloch Lighthouse, Cloch Point

Renfrewshire

PAISLEY. There is a wealth of architectural gems in this city, from an impressive selection of Victorian churches to the restored Sma'Shot cottages, where once local artisans plied their trade. These are in George Place and consist of a traditional 19th century millworkers' two-storey cottage, with back of the house iron staircase, and an 18th century weavers's cottage. They give a valuable insight into the lives and living conditions of Paisley's working community over a hundred years ago.

The town has benefited from its commercial past, not least in the outstanding architectural legacies of the Coats and Clark families, whose names are synonymous with the textile industry. The striking Renaissance style **Town Hall** is a lasting testament to the Clarks, while the stunning Gothic spire of **Thomas Coats Memorial Church** marks it out as one of the finest Baptist churches in Europe. Those interested in the world famous Paisley cloth can discover much more at **Paisley Museum and Art Gallery** in the High Street. It houses the world famous collection of Paisley shawls as well as displays that trace the history of the Paisley pattern, the development of weaving techniques and the social aspects of what was a tightly-knit weaving community. There are also fine collections of local history, natural history, ceramics and Scottish painting. Paisley also boasts a fine **Cluniac Abbey Church** founded in 1163 and the birthplace of the Stuart dynasty. In 1307 Edward I of England ordered its destruction. After victory at Bannockburn it was rebuilt and restored in the following century. The choir has a fine stone-vaulted roof and features some beautiful stained glass, as well as the tombs of Princess Marjory Bruce and King Robert III. Outside there is an impressive Norman doorway, cloisters and Place of Paisley. The Barochan Cross, a weathered Celtic cross, 11 feet high and attributed to 10th century is also in the Abbey.

Nearby is **Coats Observatory** on Oakshaw Street. Since it opened in 1882 there has been continuous astronomical observation and meteorological recording. The recent addition of the latest seismology equipment and a satellite weather picture receiver has made it one of the best equipped observatories in the country. Those tired by all this exploring may like to pay a visit to the **Lagoon Leisure Centre**, off Mill Street. This modern swimming pool complex has saunas, steam room and jacuzzi as well as bar and cafeteria.

The **Brabloch Hotel** is a pleasant family run hotel and restaurant which is situated just half a mile south of junction 27 on the M8; Paisley town centre and railway station lie only half a mile away to the south, and Glasgow Airport only two miles away to the northwest. An imposing building standing within four acres of attractive landscaped grounds, this former mansion house has been refurbished and extended over the years and now offers 30 well appointed guest bedrooms, all with en-suite facilities, satellite television and a number of impressive extras. Proprietors Patricia and Lewis Grant provide a warm welcome and excellent food and accommodation. The restaurant is renowned for its Continental cuisine and offers a top class table d'hôte menu; first rate snacks and meals are also available in the lounge bar.

Paisley's famous 12th century abbey, the birthplace of the Stewart dynasty, lies within a mile of the hotel, and there are many other historic buildings in the town, including the Coats Observatory and Coats Memorial Church, which were built when Paisley was an internationally renowned centre of the textile industry. Part of the Minotel consortium of privately owned hotels, the Brabloch Hotel is Scottish Tourist Board 4 Crown Commended, RAC 2 Star and Les Routiers recommended.

Brabloch Hotel, 62 Renfrew Road, Paisley
Tel: 0141 889 5577 Fax: 0141 561 7012

AROUND PAISLEY

LANGBANK. **Finlaystone**, the home of the Clan MacMillian, has beautiful formal gardens and woodland walks, picnic sites and children's play areas. The visitors centre also offers a ranger service as well as a Celtic art exhibition. The House, which has historical connections with 16th century preacher John Knox and poet Robert Burns, has a large doll collection and display of Victoriana. Enchanting and relaxing the estate offers the visitor a break from the hurley burley of the outside world.

BISHOPSTON. Another ideal place to escape the 20th century for just few hours is **Formakin Estate** along the riverside at Bishopston. This 150 acre estate was designed by Sir Robert Lorimer between 1903-1913. The Mansion house is incomplete internally and set in landscaped gardens and grounds which though overgrown are being restored. There is plenty to explore: the estate workers bothy and stable block with courtyard, craft workshops, towerhouse, gatelodges and a derelict mealmill. The estate also runs a rare breeds farm and if all the exploring makes you peckish there is restaurant.

LOCHWINNOCH. Lochwinnoch Nature Reserve, run by the RSPB, offers magnificent views from its observation tower and a wealth of information on the local wildlife in the Nature Centre. For twitchers there are hides within a short walk; two overlook the marshes and a third gives excellent views over Loch Barr. As with so many lochs Barr has its castle, albeit a somewhat dilapidated one.

In the village is the community museum which features a series of changing exhibitions reflecting the life and times of Lochwinnoch and the surrounding area. **Muirsheil Country Park**, to the north, covers several square miles and offers a huge choice of trails and walks. There is something for everyone, from the afternoon stroller to the committed hikers, and peace and tranquillity just a half hours drive from Glasgow.

EAGLESHAM. It was near this model village, laid out in 1769 by the Earl of Eglinton, that Rudolf Hess, the Nazi leader, made his sensational parachute landing in 1941.

Those looking for an outlet offering a wide selection unusual gift ideas should make a point of finding **Eaglesham Gifts** in Eaglesham, a large and scattered village which stands around the junction of the B764 and B767, three miles southwest of East Kilbride. The street plan of this historic community is laid out in the shape of an 'A', and Angela Forbes' fascinating business is situated near its centre in Montgomery Street. The gift shop occupies a handsome Georgian building almost two centuries old which has a white-painted façade and an interior full of character and charm. Someone with an eye for the unusual, Angela has assembled a delightful collection of top quality gifts, including fine china, crystal, basketware, scented candles, soaps, soft toys and linen. She also stocks an interesting selection of crafts, including brass, copper and leather goods, as well as a range of beautiful greetings cards for all occasions. With its charming Aladdin's Cave atmosphere, Eaglesham gifts is the perfect place to go to find that special present or souvenir.

Eaglesham Gifts, 14 Montgomery Street, Eaglesham
Tel: 01355 303003 Fax: 0141 429 5229

CHAPTER FOUR

GLASGOW & LANARKSHIRE

SS Waverley

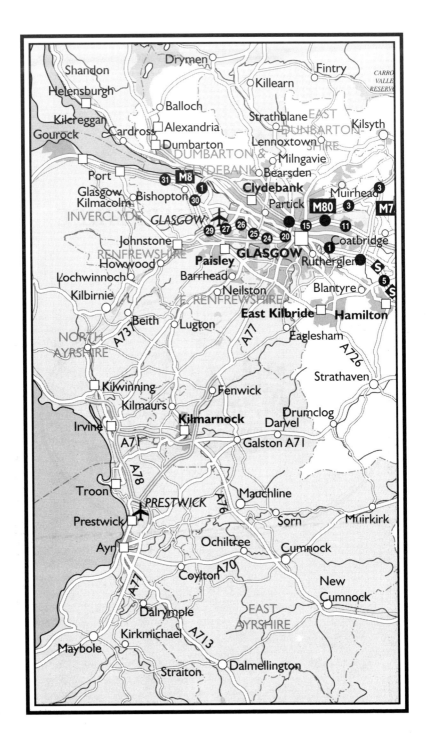

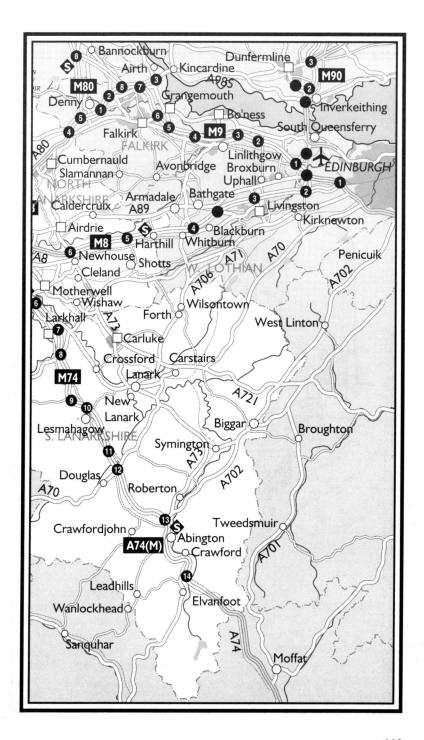

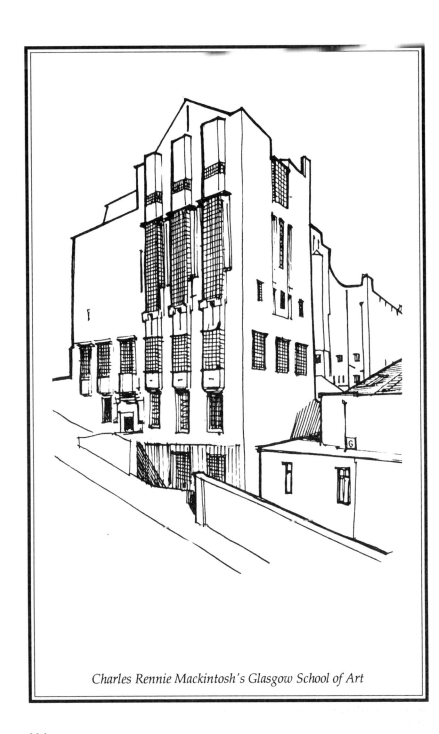

Charles Rennie Mackintosh's Glasgow School of Art

CHAPTER FOUR

GLASGOW & LANARKSHIRE

The City of Glasgow

GLASGOW has a character and flavour all of its own and is full of opulent 19th century architecture and wonderful museums and galleries. Once considered the jewel of western Scotland, the city's very name, from the Celtic 'glas glu', means 'dear green place'.

Charles Rennie Mackintosh designed the **Glasgow School of Art** in Renfrew Street and in the famous Sauchiehall Street, much beloved by that famous old variety artist Harry Lauder, is his **Willow Tea Room**. If Mackintosh's style appeals then take a look at his church at Queen's Cross which has recently been restored and the **Hunterian Art Gallery**, Hillhead Street, where there is the opportunity to see reconstructions of his Glasgow home's interiors. Another opportunity to see his work can be found in **Bellahouston Park** where his domestic house design for a competition in Darmstadt in 1900 has been recreated. In Glasgow particularly, but throughout Scotland, Mackintosh's influence can be seen and his designs are copied on everything from furniture to restaurant menus. Charles Rennie Mackintosh was the leading spirit of what became known as the 'Glasgow Style', which earned the city a place in the world of Art Nouveau comparable with Paris. Comparison with the French capital is only natural. It is easy to forget that since the days of Mary, Queen of Scots, it has been the French and not the English who have been the dominant influence in Scottish cultural life. Towards the end of the last century buying Impressionist paintings without crossing the Channel, brought people to Glasgow and not London or Edinburgh, in order to meet several distinguished and highly respected dealers. The greatest of whom was Alexander Reid, a personal friend of many of the Impressionists.

The most famous collection in Glasgow is the **Burrell Collection**. On his death in 1944 Sir William Burrell, a Clyde ship-owner, bequeathed his magnificent collection of 8000 items of the ancient world, paintings and oriental art to the city. He was quite specific in his will about how the collection should be housed and this resulted in a superb gallery being built in **Pollock Country Park**. There is no question that this is a must for anyone visiting Glasgow. Leave plenty of time as it is easy to spend a day here.

Henry Moore Sculpture, Burrell Collection

The **Glasgow Art Gallery and Museum** in Kelvingrove Park has one of the finest municipal collections in Britain, ranging from Rembrandt to Dali. There are also impressive collections of ceramics, glass, silver, clocks, snuff boxes, pewter, Egyptian antiquities and rare arms and armour. More unusual is **The Tenement House** on Buccleuch Street. A Victorian flat, it has remained unchanged since 1892, right down to the smallest detail. For those who like oddities, especially of the Gothic variety, Glasgow is full of them but perhaps the most memorable is the **Necropolis**, a hill crowned with obelisks, monuments, statues, columns and miniature temples; in Victorian Glasgow it was the burial place chosen by the fashionable and wealthy citizens.

Alongside the Necropolis is **St Mungo's Cathedral**, which has a long history. It was around the little church founded here in the 6th century by St Mungo which the city of Glasgow grew. It is worth taking a look at the Lower Church which has what is considered to be one of the very best vaulted crypts of Gothic Europe. It is of beautiful proportions and very graceful. In the centre is the simple tomb of St Mungo who was buried on the site beside an ancient well in 603. The Cathedral now has a museum that celebrates the world's religions, the only one of its kind in Britain. Tradition has it that, in about AD 550, after he had finished his training under St Serf, Mungo travelled to the house of a holy man named Fergus, at Kernach. Previously, Fergus had been told that he would not die until he had seen someone who would convert the whole district to Christianity. Soon after Mungo arrived, Fergus died. Placing his body in a cart pulled by two wild bulls, Mungo ordered them to take the body to the place ordained by God. The cart stopped at Cathures and this is where Mungo buried Fergus and founded the original church.

So many people just expect Glasgow to be an industrial city but it wasn't picked as a European City of culture on a whim. Its University, for example, was founded by Pope Nicholas V in 1451, which makes it the fourth oldest in Britain, after Oxford, Cambridge and St Andrews. It is also home to Scottish Opera, Scottish Ballet and the Royal Scottish Orchestra. Glasgow is a city of fun as well as culture, there are good theatres, concert halls, good eating houses and hotels, and there is even an underground system to travelling around.

Of course the city will be forever associated with the mighty River Clyde, yet the river was for centuries shallow and unnavigable. The city had to rely on the harbours at Greenock and Dumbarton both over 20 miles away; a short journey today but then heavy goods could take several days to cover it. After the union of England and Scotland in 1707 the city was able to trade freely with the Americas and it was clear to the city fathers that fortunes could be made. However, unless the ships could bring their cargos into the heart of Glasgow, those fortunes would come no nearer than the other ports.

So an ambitious project to deepen the Clyde was begun. After many false starts in 1781 an engineer, John Golborne, discovered that by narrowing the river the water could be made to flow faster, and 'scour' out its own channel. He achieved this by building a series of dykes into the river. His work was continued later by famous engineer Thomas Telford; who joined the ends of Golbourne's dykes to contain the Clyde within stone banks, rather like a canal. During the 19th century dredgers took over the task of deepening the river. By the 1930s some of the world's largest vessels were being launched from Clydebank and over 40 feet of water flowed where people had once walked across the river at low tide.

It was this feat of engineering that made Glasgow the greatest ship-building centre in the world. One of the most famous yards was that of John Brown & Co at Clydebank. Established in 1871, opposite the mouth of the River Cart, it had the extra room to launch larger ships. The Lusitania, whose sinking drew the United States into the First World War, was launched here in 1906 and, in 1934, they needed every inch for the launch of the Queen Mary, over 1000 feet long and with a draft of over 35 feet. Her sistership, the Queen Elizabeth, and her famous successor, Queen Elizabeth II, also came from the yard.

The world's first steam ferry started on the Clyde between the city and Greenock on 14th August 1812. The ship (the Comet) was wrecked in 1820, but a replica of her can be seen at Port Glasgow. Things have almost come full circle on the Clyde, where once it was said people could walk across the river on the dense mass of shipping it is now quiet and much cleaner.

SS Waverley, Clyde Paddle Steamer

Today it is well worth taking a trip down to the Firth of Clyde, and what better way than on the **Waverley**, the world's last sea-going paddle steamer. Built in 1946 to replace her 1899 predecessor lost at Dunkirk and retired in 1973, she now spends the summer months cruising the Clyde and the islands of the Firth. Just along the waterfront from Anderston Quay where the Waverley docks is the impressive **Finnieston Crane**, erected in 1932 and still in use, it is Glasgow's largest ever dockside crane and can lift 175 tons.

Glasgow's rich transport history reaches far beyond the river. The **Museum of Transport**, at Kelvin Hall, has a wonderful collection of vintage cars, old locomotives and trams; the city once having one of the finest tram networks in the world. And its factories built locomotives that not only pulled trains the length and breadth of the country but move passengers and goods on every continent. **Springburn Museum**, on Ayr Street, preserves the heritage of the locomotive builders of the Springburn plant by recording the memories of the local people at work and at home.

A short journey from the city centre lies the **Botanic Gardens** which feature over 40 acres of woodlands and open lawns, crossed by the River Kelvin. Here, also, is the magnificent **Kibble Palace**, a great cast iron glasshouse that could only be Victorian. Inside amongst the tropical ferns are white marble statues. A gem of a different kind is the Barras Street market which has stalls heaving with collectables and bric-a-brac, full of local colour, and not to be missed.

Dunbartonshire

DUMBARTON. Guarding the Clyde approaches Dumbarton, like Stirling, has its origins in its fortified rocks and was once the capital of the ancient kingdom of the North Britons, a Pictish tribe. The name Dumbarton is derived from 'Dun-Briton' which literally means the fort of the Britons. There was a castle on the rock in medieval days and William Wallace was reputedly imprisoned here for a short time and it was from here that Mary, Queen of Scots set sail for France to marry the Dauphin. **Dumbarton Castle** was last used as a barracks during the First World War and is now a museum which makes an interesting visit.

Being situated on the river, the town developed an important position, controlling the pass into the Highlands and was formerly a port for Glasgow until the deepening of the River Clyde in the 19th century. There were many shipyards along the banks and one great ship that was launched from here was the famous clipper Cutty Sark. The name incidentally was taken from an incident in Robert Burns' *Tam o'Shanter*, and means 'short shift' or 'skirt'. Another maritime gem in the town is the fascinating **Denny Ship Model Experiment Tank**. This was the first purpose built experimental tank to be used commercially and it was built for the renowned Denny Shipbuilding Company in 1882. For over 100 years it was used to test designs for hulls and propellers until it was taken over in 1984 by the **Scottish Maritime Museum**. The tank itself is over 300 feet long with a depth of 10 feet and there are many other interesting exhibits from this fascinating industry including workshops, model making processes and the drawing office.

AROUND DUMBARTON

ALEXANDRIA, just south of Loch Lomond, holds a piece of motoring history. The Argyll was Scotland's first home-produced car, the first being built in 1899 and proving a great success. The magnificent neo-Baroque factory built on the company's early success still stands: unfortunately, it proved rather too magnificent. The Italian marble interior, 500 washbasins for the workforce and a resident Italian works choirmaster proved the company's undoing and it collapsed in 1908.

BALLOCH. This resort, on the River Leven, lies at the southern end of Loch Lomond and was the base for the first steamer on the waters, launched in 1816.

Formed in 1988, the Loch Lomond Park Authority is responsible for managing the **Loch Lomond Regional Park**, 170 square miles of dramatic countryside which encompass beautiful Loch Lomond. Standing on the geological boundary of the Highlands and the Lowlands, the loch has long been recognised for its special atmosphere and beauty. Its narrow northern section is characterised by steep conical mountains plunging dramatically to the shore, and its wider southern part by tree covered islands rising from the clear shallow water of the Loch. Shaped by glacier and invaded by the sea, the Loch's diverse habitat is home to a huge variety of wildlife, from the rare wildcat, otter, osprey and golden eagle, to the less secretive species which inhabit the lakes and woodland of northern Britain. The lands around Loch Lomond also show evidence thousands of years of human occupation.

Loch Lomond Park Authority

Balloch Castle, at the southern end of the Loch, is the ancient seat of the Earls of Lennox, although the original 13th century castle has all but disappeared. In 1808, its place was taken by a neo-Gothic castellated country mansion built for John Buchanan of Ardoch, and it was this building and its surrounding estate that was purchased by Glasgow City Council in 1914 to provide a clean recreational amenity for its citizens. Now known as **Balloch Castle Country Park**, it contains a variety of attractive features, including a lochside walk, walled garden, fairy glen and rose garden. The ground floor of the mansion is now a popular visitor centre containing a small gift shop, audio-visual presentation and exhibitions which provide a good introduction to the area. (Open between Easter and the end of October.)

In 1994, the Park Authority opened a second visitor centre at **Luss** on the western shore of the loch which provides a fascinating insight into the landscape, wildlife and cultural history of the locality. This historic village is known for its Viking remains and stands at the foot of Glen Luss, one of the first places in Scotland to be subjected to the Highland clearances. Most of the houses in the village were built in the 18th and 19th centuries to house workers employed at the local slate quarries and cotton mill.

Further north, **Firkin Point** picnic site between Inverbeg and Tarbet gives direct access to a three mile stretch of the old A82, providing a safe level pathway which is ideal for wheelchair users, pushchairs and cyclists. The views from here across the loch to Ben Lomond are breathtaking. A new visitor centre at Balmaha on the eastern shore of the loch is due to open in April 1997.

Loch Lomond Park Authority, Balloch Castle, Balloch Tel: 01389 758216
Fax: 01389 755721

BEARSDEN. Lying to the northwest of Glasgow, Bearsden has the country's finest example of a visible Roman building in its bath house; built around AD 140 for the troops manning the Antonine Wall. It is all too often forgotten that the influence of Rome progressed a lot further north than Hadrian's Wall.

MILNGAVIE. The purpose built **Lillie Art Gallery** features an impressive collection of 20th century paintings, sculptures and ceramics, as well as hosting exhibitions of contemporary art.

CLACHAN OF CAMPSIE. It is possible to step back in time at the Clachan of Campsie Conservation Area, a small arts and crafts community that nestles at the foot of **Campsie Glen**.

Originally The Crown Inn, then the Red Tub Tea Rooms, **The Aldessan Gallery and Batik Studio** nestles at the foot of the Campsie Hills, in picturesque and historic Clachan of Campsie. This beautiful and unspoilt part of Scotland offers a living landscape that is studded with numerous picturesque villages cradled among the hills, yet whisky distilling is the closest you'll find to any form of manufacturing industry. The Gallery, run by husband and wife team Melanie and Martin Brickley, provides a relaxed and comfortable atmosphere for browsing.

Melanie runs her batik studio next door to the Gallery and organises the monthly exhibition including paintings, embroidery, batiks and mixed media. There is an exciting range of Scottish crafts, the majority of which have been hand-made by the country's finest crafts people. The Aldessan Gallery is for everybody, not just professional artists. Classes have been organised for anyone wanting to know more about painting, etc, and have proved very popular, with people travelling from as far afield as Ayrshire, Lanarkshire, Cumbernauld and Bearsden to take part.

The Aldessan Coffee Shop is the ideal place to meet for a cup of tea, snack or a meal, with the varied menu offering a tantalising selection of dishes, all freshly cooked and prepared using only the freshest local ingredients wherever possible. Care and attention is paid to detail and even the simplest sandwich is a work of art in itself, from soup to salads, coffee to cakes, the highest standards are met. In good weather you can enjoy sitting outside in the picturesque courtyard, or there is a comfortable and cosy seating area inside the Gallery. Meals are served all day from 11 am-5 pm, Monday to Friday all year; 11 am-8 pm on Saturdays and Sundays from April-September; and 11 am-5 pm in winter. Hundreds of art lovers and day visitors have already discovered the many delights of the Aldessan Gallery, why not pay them a visit the next time you are in the area, we guarantee that you won't be disappointed.

Aldessan Gallery and Batik Studio, The Clachan, Campsie Glen
Tel & Fax: 01360 313049

North Lanarkshire

COATBRIDGE. For the more energetic Coatbridge has plenty to offer the visitor. **The Time Capsule** is Scotland's largest leisure centre; being half ice and half water, it has a choice of ice skating, tropical wave pool, curling, a thrilling rubber ring ride and high speed glacier run. If all that sounds a little to cold or wet then nearby **Drumpellier Country Park** has golf, fishing and a superb tropical Butterfly House. It is also an outdoor pursuits centre with orienteering courses available.

Summerlee Heritage Park is designed around the archaeological remains of the Summerlee Ironworks, which emerged form under six metres of slag and industrial waste, and in 1986 won the British Council for Archaeology Scotland's coveted Robertson's Award. Put into blast in the 1830s the ironworks was served by a branch of the Monklands Canal, which has now been restored. The pioneering Monklands & Kirkintilloch

Traction Engine Rally, Summerlee Heritage Trust, Coatbridge

railway bounds part of the site, and the Howes Basin, built for transshipping coal from rail to canal, has also been uncovered. Part of the site had been used since the 1950s by a crane manufacturer, and the framework of their factory building has been stripped, repaired and reclad to form the museum's impressive Exhibition Hall. This massive hall houses Scotland's largest collection of historic machinery operating daily. Permanent displays include reconstructed working environments such as a Tinsmiths shop, a Brass Foundry, a Brassfinishers Shop and a Spade Forge. Also within the Exhibition Hall are Social History interiors including a Co-op Shop, an Edwardian Photographers Studio and a Bicycle and Radio Shop.

Summerlee Heritage Park

In April 1990 the Ironworks Gallery opened at Summerlee and it has established a reputation as an exciting exhibition venue. Fully environmentally controlled, this substantial exhibition space houses a programme of temporary exhibitions throughout the year with displays covering a range of disciplines from photography to sculpture, and from fine arts to local crafts. Summerlee operates Scotland's first preserved electric tramway, recently extended to run a distance of three quarters of a mile, the tramway is in use daily. Many of the collected trams are both driven and partly restored by the Summerlee Transport Group and include a newly restored double-decker open topped Lanarkshire tram. The tramway carries visitors to the site of Summerlee's newest and most ambitious development to date: a reconstructed 19th century shallow-level stoop and room coal mine where visitors go underground and see the workings, a reconstructed miners row of typical Lanarkshire style, a range of 20th century workers houses and the Engine House featuring the 1810 beam engine from the Farme Colliery. The Museum also offers a wide range of gifts including postcards, books, souvenirs, children's toys and games.

Summerlee's Tearoom is housed within a building which was once the Summerlee Ironworks offices originally constructed in Whifflet in 1830s and re-erected at Summerlee in 1990. It serves a selection of both savoury and sweet dishes throughout the day from 10 am until 4.30 pm.

The Conference Room can be hired for all forms of corporate and private events, including functions, meetings, training courses and dinners. A selection of audio-visual equipment is available for use if required and catering can be arranged to suit a variety of tastes.

Summerlee Heritage Park, West Canal Street, Coatbridge Tel: 01236 431261 Fax: 01236 440429

AROUND COATBRIDGE

AIRDRIE. The early day's of the region's industrial past can be glimpsed at in the **Weaver's Cottage Museum**. Here, two cottages of 1780 have been restored, one as a master weavers house and the other for displaying artefacts and exhibitions. Visitors get a fascinating insight into one of the area's oldest traditions, as well the daily lives of the weavers.

KILSYTH. Full of rural charm and set amongst the southern Campsie Fells this is one of many picturesque towns and villages which have a rich heritage that stretches back to Roman times. The **Antonine Wall** runs through the area. This turf and ditch rampart stretches between the Clyde at Old Kilpatrick and Bo'ness on the Forth. At Bar Hill near Twechar the remains of one of the wall's forts can still be viewed and the **Kirkintilloch's Barony Chambers Museum** has many absorbing exhibitions depicting the area's social and industrial history.

Set in 68 acres of attractive woodlands and lawns, which feature a walled garden and arboretum, curling pond and children's zoo, **Colzium House** is a delight. As well as so much outside, in the house is a museum of local history as well as function rooms.

CUMBERNAULD. One of Scotland's most renown venues, **Cumbernauld Theatre** hosts a wide variety of concerts and productions throughout the year. Southeast of the town is **Palacerigg Country Park**, once a hilltop farmland, the park offers nature trails, pony riding and a children's farm.

MOTHERWELL. At the turn of the century, Motherwell was the largest steel producer in Scotland but after 1914 it suffered a steady decline and, in particular, the Ravenscraig project in the 1950s.

Lying on both sides of the River Clyde, the **Strathclyde Country Park** features a man-made lake, complete with sandy beaches, and a nature reserve as well as plenty of open space. There once stood here one of the largest palaces ever to have been built in Scotland. Hamilton Palace was originally started in 1591 and was substantially added to over the years but it was not to everyone's taste. Dorothy Wordsworth has been known to call it a heavy lumpish mass. However, good or bad, the Palace was demolished in 1927 after underground mine workings had caused the foundations to sink.

South Lanarkshire

HAMILTON. Although seen as a fairly modern town, which grew up in the heart of the coalfields of central Scotland, there has been a settlement here since prehistoric times. Originally known as Cadzow, in 1445 James II awarded a charter to the 1st Lord Hamilton and the town's name was changed to that of the family.

In the northern part of the town, **Hamilton District Museum** is housed in an old coaching inn that was enlarged, in 1790, to provide an assembly hall. The museum recalls the industrial and social development of the town and includes a reconstruction of a Victorian kitchen, a transport section and an area devoted to Sir Harry Lauder, who is buried in the town's Bent Cemetery.

The **Hamilton Mausoleum**, which can be clearly seen from the M74, was built by the 10th Duke of Hamilton, who was considered to be an eccentric. The building dates back to the mid 19th century and took four years to complete, costing over one hundred and fifty thousand pounds. A large portion of this sum was spent on the floor alone, a wheel mosaic containing almost every known variety of marble, many of them rare. The building is famous for its 15 second echo, which made using it as a chapel, as intended, impossible.

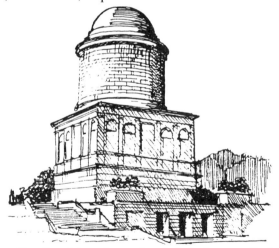

Hamilton Mausoleum, Strathclyde Country Park

Opened in June 1995, the **Hamilton Water Palace** is one of the most impressive and up-to-date leisure facilities in Scotland. Situated opposite Bell College in Almada Street, in the heart of Hamilton, this superb amenity combines all the fun of a leisure pool with a competition pool for more serious swimmers. The facilities include a six lane 25 metre competition standard pool, a children's play pool and a magnificent leisure pool incorporating such features as a flume, tyre ride, lazy river, bubble beds and outdoor lagoon. Thanks to its movable floor, the depth of the water in one-third of the 25 metre pool can be changed, allowing swimmers of all ages and abilities to participate in safety. The children's play pool is fitted with slides, a swing and a number of interactive water features which activate a sequence of showers and cascades. The Hamilton Water Palace also provides a fully equipped health suite, incorporating a sauna, steamroom, spa pool and tanning suite. There is also a function room which is ideal for business presentations and children's parties. With its excellent recreational and catering facilities, this is the ideal place for a fun day out, whatever the weather.

Hamilton Water Palace, 35 Almada Street, Hamilton
Tel: 01698 459950 Fax: 01698 307107

AROUND HAMILTON

BOTHWELL. The Battle of Bothwell Bridge (which spans the Clyde) in 1679 is commemorated by a monument here. Some 300 years earlier, in 1398, the **Church of St Bride** was founded here by Archibald, 3rd Earl of Douglas. From the outside the original choir with stone-slab roof and its generous buttresses can still be seen whilst, inside, is the grave-slab of Walter de Moravia, the builder of Bothwell Castle.

Bothwell Castle, now a sprawling red ruin situated amongst woodland high above the Clyde, is said by many to be the finest 13th century castle in Scotland. Built in the 1200s and rebuilt by the Douglases in the 15th century, the Castle was constructed on a massive scale and has walls 15 feet thick, the central donjon or keep is 65 feet in diameter and stands 90 feet tall. The name donjon interestingly comes from the Latin dominus (meaning lord); hence the dwelling of the lord.

BLANTYRE. The David Livingstone Centre offers a very different day out. Subject of perhaps the most famous quote ever, the story of this remarkable man's life is told in the very tenement in which he was born. An adventurer and missionary his legendary journeys amongst

Bothwell Castle

the people he loved, respected and helped are described here: his battles with slave traders, search for the source of the Nile and, naturally, that meeting with Stanley. There is a fascinating African Pavilion, which features a Zambian Bazaar, where many of the crafts are for sale.

STRATHAVEN. Pronounced 'Straiven', this former weaving centres has its own castle as well as **East Church**, built in 1777, which acts as one of the town's best landmarks. The **John Hastie Museum** contains displays of weaving and ceramics as well as relics of the Convenanters and the radical rising of 1820. **Calderglen Country Park** consists of 300 acres of wooded gorge and parkland and makes for a very enjoyable day out. There are many lovely marked routes around the park, as well as the woodlands and river with waterfalls, which are very picturesque. There is also a children's zoo for the young ones, an ornamental garden and an adventure playground.

The Toffee Shop

Since 1904 Gilmour's have made sweets and hand-dipped chocolates at Strathaven in Lanarkshire, you can purchase these delicious confections at **Straven Toffee Shop** in Strathaven's central shopping street. Strathaven, known locally as Stra'ven is an historic town of character set in the valley of the River Avon among the hills and moors southeast of Glasgow. The business was started over a century ago by the Gilmour family and is run today by the grandson of the founder, Ian Gilmour. The toffees and chocolates are world renowned and have been loved by Scottish families for generations. Stra'ven toffee is as individually characteristic as the town, with the sweets being hand-made using traditional methods. They are rich and tasty due to the use of pure ingredients and the slow cooking process not normally found in the modern mass production. The whole selection of Stra'ven toffee is a sweet delight for all ages.

SW Gilmour, The Toffee Shop, 33 Common Green, Strathaven
Tel: 01357 521158

One of the most impressive hotels in central Scotland can be found on the outskirts of Strathaven, a small market town lying six miles southwest of junction 8 on the M74. Well located for touring this attractive part of the country, the **Strathaven Hotel** is situated only half an hour from central Glasgow, 45 minutes from Edinburgh and an hour from Gretna Green. The main building is a handsome Georgian structure dating back to 1797 which was designed by Robert Adam for a wealthy Glasgow merchant. Now category 'B' listed, it is privately owned and managed by the Macintyre family, friendly and experienced hosts who provide a warm welcome, first class service, and superb food and accommodation. The guest lounges are comfortable and elegant, and the ten beautifully appointed guest bedrooms all have en-suite facilities, direct dial telephones, satellite television and several impressive extras. The award winning Avon Restaurant is renowned for its cuisine, and serves the finest Scottish and Continental dishes using fresh local produce wherever possible. Scottish Tourist Board 4 Crown Highly Commended, the Strathaven Hotel is also a popular venue for business meetings, private functions and wedding receptions.

Strathaven Hotel, Hamilton Road, Strathaven Tel: 01357 521778
Fax: 01357 520789

CROSSFORD. Craignethan Castle was a Hamilton stronghold of the 16th century. It was once a refuge of Mary, Queen of Scots and is said to be haunted by the Queen, minus her head, of course.

CARLUKE. Thanks to recent housing developments, this is the largest town in Clydesdale and it is famous for is jam, made from fruit grown in the area. The town also has what is claimed to be the most complete windmill in Scotland. **Highland House** was built in 1795 and became a steam powered mill in 1895. Now privately owned it has not worked since the 1930s. Once a small community Carluke has the distinction of having three of its citizens receive the Victoria Cross. And just outside the town, at Miltonhead, a plaque commemorates a man dear to all seekers of hidden places. General William Roy was born here in 1729 and went on the become the 'father' of the Ordnance Survey.

Craignethan Castle, Crossford

CARNWATH. **Carnwath House**, where Bonnie Prince Charlie supposedly slept at one time, is now a golf course clubhouse and nearby **Couthally Castle** was originally the stronghold of the Sommerville family. The Castle is known for providing James V with a mistress, Katherine Carmicheal, whom he first met at a wedding party there.

Lanarkshire provides some of Scotland's biggest contrasts; from the hurly burly of metropolitan Glasgow to the wild isolation of the Lowther hills and their quiet unspoilt hamlets.

BIGGAR. This town, with its broad main street, can trace its history back to Roman times. It is a colourful town with brightly painted shops and hotels and is well known for its markets and fairs. Every Hogmanay on the main street the townsfolk gather around a huge bonfire to 'burn out the old year' and welcome in the new. The town is also rightly proud for its many fascinating museums. The family of the British prime minister Gladstone came from Biggar and the **Gladstone Court Museum**, open from Easter to October, features an interesting 19th century town with shops, a library and a schoolroom.

Behind the museum is the **Albion Archive**. The Albion Motor company started on a local farm in 1899 and went on the become the largest truck manufacturer in the British Empire before being absorbed into Leyland Trucks. There are plans to build a motor museum but in the meantime, every August, the town plays host to a multitude of vintage and classic cars, motorcycles, commercial and military vehicles at a commemorative rally. Almost next door is **Biggar Kirk** built by Mary, Queen of Scots' uncle, Lord Fleming. Finished in 1546 it was the last pre-Reformation church in Scotland.

Across Kirkstyle is **Moat Park Heritage Centre**, which depicts life in the Clyde Valley over the past 6000 years. As well as figures from its turbulent past there are many splendid models and a magnificent Victorian patchwork, with some 80 colourful figures stitched into place by a rather eccentric local tailor during the Crimean War. The Moat Park is open everyday between Easter and the end of October.

Above Kirkstyle lies **Greenhill Covenanters House** where visitors can step back in time to the 17th century and the 'killing times' The signing of the National Covenant forced many to worship in open fields rather than attend state controlled churches. These Covenanters were hunted down and many put to death for their beliefs. The house, which was moved to its present site to save it from dereliction, contains many relics of this bloody period in Scotland's history. Visitors will find the house open between 2 pm and 5 pm everyday from Easter through to late October.

The last rural gasworks in Britain, **Biggar Gas Works** were built in 1839 and rebuilt in 1914, before finally closing in 1973 with the arrival of North Sea gas. Fortunately the works were saved from the fate of every other town gasworks and are now open to the public. Here visitors can watch the hot and filthy work of turning coal into the gas that kept Biggar's (and Britain's) kettles boiling for over a century. The works are open daily between Easter and October and on Sundays in July and August. For full details of the admission costs and opening times of Biggar's excellent museums call Biggar Museum Trust on 01899 21050.

Finally, the town also boasts a beautiful Victorian **Puppet Theatre**, a must for the children and a relaxing respite after all the museums. A last curiosity about this small town is the occasional and ancient contest for the Biggar Jug; which is open only to the Queen's bodyguard in Scotland, the Royal Company of Archers.

The **Elphinstone Hotel** in Biggar High Street is renowned throughout the area for its excellent food and accommodation. Situated in the heart of town, this handsome 15th century building has recently been taken over by Janette and Robert Allen, friendly and experienced hosts who provide a warm welcome, good service and superb food and drink. Frequented by visitors and locals alike, the restaurant offers an outstanding choice of freshly prepared Scottish and Continental dishes.

Elphinstone Hotel

On the evening we visited, starters included 'Cullen Skink' (traditional Scottish smoked haddock and potato soup with cream), chicken pakora, and deep-fried Brie with cranberry sauce. Main courses included such regional Scottish dishes such as herring in oatmeal, and steak and ale pie, along with more exotic specialities such as cajun chicken, Italian beef and turkey char sui. There was also a wide choice of steaks, fish and vegetarian dishes, a special children's menu, and a variety of light meals including baked potatoes, toasted sandwiches, wholemeal hoagies and ciabatta rolls. The Elphinstone also has a pleasant lounge bar and three well appointed guest bedrooms equipped with en suite bathrooms, colour television and tea and coffee making facilities.

Elphinstone Hotel, 145 High Street, Biggar Tel: 01899 220044/221165

CARMICHAEL. This village takes its name from a church which was situated on a hill or 'caer'. The present Church's stained glass windows are of particular interest as they depict the heroic achievements of the local lairds.

To the south of the village lie the Tinto Hills; 'tinto' is derived from the Gaelic 'tienteach' or 'place of fire' and there are ancient rhymes and stories which connect this place with fire raising powers. **Tinto Hill** itself is, at 2320 feet, the highest in Lanarkshire.

Carmichael Visitor Centre

A visitor centre which is both interesting and educational can be found beside the A73 Clyde Valley Tourist Route, midway between Lanark and Biggar. Situated on the beautiful Carmichael Estate on the northern edge of Tinto Hill, the **Discover Carmichael Visitor Centre** is a fascinating attraction which lies within 50 minutes of both Glasgow and Edinburgh. The centre is home to the relocated Edinburgh Wax Museum which chronicles the turbulent history of Scotland in a series of life-size wax models. Episodes depicted include the execution of Mary, Queen of Scots and the massacre at Culloden, and there are also replicas of the many Scottish men and women who have made important contributions to the world of science, literature, philosophy and economics throughout history. The visitor centre incorporates an adventure playground, baby animal farm, 'eco-friendly' house, gift shop and licensed restaurant, and is also the starting point for a number of dramatic walks and pony rides through the Carmichael estate.

The Laird of Carmichael is an enthusiastic advocate of an integrated approach to land management and amongst his recent innovations is a flourishing meat-rearing business specialising in farmed venison, one of the most lean, tender and versatile meats on the market. Advice is available at the visitor centre on the best ways to prepare and serve this increasingly popular ingredient. Over a dozen buildings across the estate have been restored and equipped as top quality holiday cottages. These luxuriously appointed traditional stone cottages are set in beautiful unspoilt surroundings which are a paradise for walkers and anglers. Open all year round, they are rated 3 to 5 Crowns by the Scottish Tourist Board and provide an ideal base for touring southern Scotland.

Carmichael Visitor Centre, Carmichael, By Biggar
Tel: 01899 308169 Fax: 01899 308481

LANARK. Here are the famous **Falls of Clyde**, which start where the river becomes swollen with the waters of the Douglas. There are three falls; the first being **Bonnington** which surges over a drop of 30 feet then the river presses on for another half mile before coming to Corra Linn, the middle fall. Although the waters of **Corra Linn** fall 90 feet they do not seem as impressive as those of Bonnington, as the drop is not quite so sheer, but is a series of very beautiful cascades. Two miles further down are the broadest of the falls at **Stonebryes**. Surrounding the Falls is a nature reserve run by the Scottish Wildlife Trust, where red squirrels, kingfishers, otters and badgers can be seen.

Lanark itself is one of the original four royal burghs of Scotland created by David I, who built a castle here in the 12th century. **Lanark Castle** saw the start of William Wallace's great fight to free Scotland when, in 1227, he laid a raid against the English garrison here in revenge for the death of his wife. In so doing, the governor, Haselrig, was fatally stabbed. Lanark's most famous son is commemorated by a statue at the front of St Nicholas' Church.

The town is well known for its traditional ceremonies, one in particular, called 'Whuppity Scoorie', takes place on the first day of March each year. This ceremony is believed to drive the harsh winter away. A crowd gathers at the parish church of St Nicholas and the children of the crowd are each given a tightly wadded paper ball on the end of a piece of string. At the sounding of the six o'clock bell, the children run around the church three times hitting each other with the paper balls on the way.

An attractive retail shop offering a surprisingly wide selection unusual gift ideas is **Thyme of Lanark**, which is situated in Hyndford Place, off the main A73 Lanark High Street. Customers are invited to 'rediscover the past' in a handsome Victorian building near the town centre. The interior retains its original character and charm, and has an enchanting period atmosphere which is a delight to browse around. A place for those with an eye for the interesting, there is a superb collection of top quality gifts, including silk flowers, scented candles, tableware, white linen and limited edition prints, all with a distinct period feel inspired by a bygone age. There is also a selection of beautiful period style occasional furniture which will lend comfort and style to any living space. Thyme is happy to provide information about the many unusual items in stock, or offer advice on the ideal gift for any occasion. With its congenial Aladdin's Cave atmosphere, Thyme of Lanark is the perfect place to browse and perhaps discover that special present or long sought after item for the home.

Thyme of Lanark, 1 Hyndford Place, Lanark Tel: 01555 664391

Daisies Coffee Shop

An exceptionally pleasant place to enjoy a delicious morning coffee, light lunch or afternoon tea can be found in Broomgate, close to the main church in the heart of Lanark. **Daisies Coffee Shop** is a delightful family run business which was established in 1983 by the present proprietors, Margaret and Jim Raeside. Since the 1980s, they have been awarded a series of food and hygiene awards. They have also created an atmosphere which is relaxed and welcoming. On entering, customers are greeted with a friendly smile and the enticing aroma of freshly brewed coffee. A surprising variety of hot and cold beverages is offered, including speciality teas and wines. The menu contains an extensive range of appetising snacks, including home-made soup, filled rolls, sandwiches, baked potatoes, burgers and quiche, and there is also a tempting selection of home-baked cakes and pastries, the speciality of the house for which Daisies is renowned. Margaret and Jim also offer an efficient service for customers wishing to take items away. Their coffee shop is open from 9 am to 4.45 pm on Mondays to Saturdays and from 12 noon to 4.30 pm on Sundays, and is totally non-smoking.

Daisies Coffee Shop, 18-22 Broomgate, Lanark Tel: 01555 665209

SCOTTISH HEROES - WILLIAM WALLACE & ROBERT BRUCE

Scotland's rich past has given rise to an wide collection of legendary heroes who have, in peacetime or during conflict, become household names the world over. Throughout this book, the places that acted as a backdrop to lives of such people as Mary, Queen of Scots, Bonnie Prince Charlie and others are highlighted. Often seen in a romantic light, particularly those who have been immortalised on film by Hollywood, the determination and courage shown throughout the ages is truly the stuff of heroes.

In the last few years of the 13th century, as Edward I of England was earning his reputation as 'Hammer of the Scots', **William Wallace** came to prominence. Born around 1270, Wallace came from Dunipace near Stirling and, after the death of his wife at the hands of Edward's men, he was outlawed for killing an Englishman. His life became dedicated to expelling the English forces from Scotland and, with an army of followers, he frequently attacked English positions including the famous burning of the barracks at Ayr. Following a confrontation at Irvine, where many of his supporters left him, Wallace turned northwards and recruited a new army in the Highlands.

His finest hour came at Stirling Bridge, in 1297, where he was victorious and also succeeded in expelling the English. The ecstatic Scots appointed him sole Guardian of Scotland but the their triumph was short-lived when, less than a year later, Wallace took on the seasoned English army in their overpowering numbers. Under the personal command of the King, the English army annihilated the Scots battalions at Falkirk and Wallace was never to lead an army in the field again.

For the next seven years Wallace became a fugitive and, for some of that time, he may have gone abroad to raise support for the Scottish cause. In 1305 he was betrayed in Glasgow, taken to London and tried for treason at Westminster Hall. One of the few people to be put to death by hanging, drawing and quartering, a barbaric method only introduced in 1284, his head was spiked on London Bridge and other fragments of his body were distributed among several Scottish cities.

During the Wars of Succession and Independence (from 1286 to 1371) **Robert Bruce** came to power. Born in 1274, at either Lochmaben or Turnberry, Robert, who was of Norman ancestry and had land in England, had grown up at the court of Edward I and, as the Earl of Carrick, had fought alongside Wallace before deserting him at Irvine. After murdering Comyn the Red, his only rival to the Scottish throne, in Greyfriars Church, Dumfries, Robert Bruce was crowned King of Scotland at Scone in 1306. Following crushing defeats at the hands of the English, being proclaimed an outlaw and being excommunicated Bruce's cause seemed hopeless. It was during his time as a fugitive that the story of the persistent spider came about, probably whilst Bruce was hiding on Rathlin Island.

The story goes that Bruce was hiding from his pursuers in a cave when he caught sight of a spider attempting to make a web. Six times the spider tried to find an anchor for its work of art and on the seventh try it succeeded. Bruce took this to be a good omen and resolved to continue the struggle for independence once again.

After Edward I was succeeded by his incompetent son in 1307, Bruce returned to Scotland and there followed seven years of fighting during which Bruce and his supporters defeated their rivals. This violent time culminated in the defeat of Edward II at Bannockburn in 1314.

Bruce succeeded where Wallace had failed and Scotland became, once again, an independent kingdom. His skill as a soldier certainly played an important part, not only in expelling the English from Scotland, but also in defeating further attempts to reconquer. However, it was not until 1323, six years before his death probably from leprosy, that Bruce was recognised as King of Scotland by the Pope.

When Bruce's tomb in Dunfermline Abbey was opened in 1819, the skeleton was found wrapped in sheets of lead and the breastbone had been cut down the centre. This goes some way to prove the legend that, before he died, Bruce instructed the Black Douglas to carry his heart to the Holy Land and bury it there. Though he had been excommunicated Bruce had always regretted he had never made a pilgrimage to Jerusalem.

Diners travel from miles around to enjoy the outstanding cuisine at the **Ristorante La Vigna**, a superb establishment which is considered to be one of the two best Italian restaurants in Scotland. Situated in Wellgate, off the High Street in the centre of Lanark, it is a recent winner of the *Scottish Field* Restaurant of the Year.

Ristorante La Vigna

Since founding the restaurant in 1982, proprietors June and Tiziano Barelli have established an enviable reputation for providing the finest food, wine and service in an atmosphere which is stylish and congenial. Fresh fish and seafood are the speciality of the house, and the menu features an impressive choice of seasonal specialities. On the evening we visited, dishes included fresh lobster from the tank, Dover sole, sea bass, red mullet, crayfish and halibut, all individually prepared in a mouthwatering variety of styles. There is also an extensive range of beef, veal, poultry and pasta dishes, many of which are prepared to regional Italian recipes which have been perfected by the Barellis over the years, plus a wide choice of carefully selected wines, spirits and liqueurs. June and Tiziano also have a well appointed holiday flat available to let; rated 4 Star Highly Commended by the Scottish Tourist Board, it provides an excellent base for exploring this lovely part of Scotland.

Ristorante La Vigna, 40 Wellgate, Lanark Tel: 01555 664320
Fax: 01555 661400

Conveniently situated off the High Street in the heart of Lanark, **Valerio's** is a lively restaurant and take-away which was originally established in 1932 by the present proprietor's forebears. Now owned and personally run by Dario Bianco and his family, it has a pleasant Continental feel, with large picture windows and a recently remodelled shop front in striking burgundy and white. The menu features an extensive range of dishes, including pizzas and traditional Scottish fish and chips for which Valerio's is renowned throughout the area. Another house speciality is fresh dairy ice cream, a continuing tradition for which the family is justifiably proud. Look out for the certificate of merit on the wall which was awarded back in 1937 and for the photograph of the present owner's great-grandfather who is shown selling ice cream from the back of a horse-drawn cart! Situated in Bannatyne Street near the busy bus and rail stations, Valerio's is the ideal place to sit back and enjoy excellent food while watching the hustle and bustle of Lanark go by. A friendly and efficient take-away service is also available from the shop which adjoins the seating area.

Valerio's Restaurant, Bannatyne Street, Lanark Tel: 01555 665818

NEW LANARK. This 'new' town has a fascinating origin. It was built in the 18th century as an experimental cotton spinning village by an entrepreneur called David Dale, working in partnership with Richard Arkwright. Although there is nothing particularly uncommon in this, when the partners fell out, allegedly over the hanging of a bell on the belfry of the church, Robert Owen took over the project and it became an experiment in community living with work, housing and education organized on socialist principles. It is well worth visiting today, as it has become a conservation project with craft industries and a famous heritage trail. As the site is so well preserved in the style of the Industrial Revolution it has been used many times as the background for films and television programmes.

DOUGLAS. Taking its name from one of Scotland's most prominent families, the town has been a centre of medieval power and, later, a hotbed of Convenanting activity.

Douglas Castle was destroyed in the 1940s because mining works were found to have damaged its foundations. The chapel however can still be seen, and it contains the tombs of the famous Douglas chiefs including Good Sir James, the Black Douglas, who took King Robert the Bruce's heart on the Crusade against the Moors in Spain. Sir James' story is an interesting one, as he was Bruce's friend and the greatest of his lieutenants, much feared by the English. Apparently, on his death bed Bruce charged him with the task of removing his heart from his dead body and taking it on the crusade. Sir James obeyed his King's command and got as far as Spain before being killed. His body and the King's heart were retrieved and the heart is reputedly buried in Melrose Abbey. Since that time the Douglas coat of arms has carried a red heart beneath the three stars on blue.

There is also a memorial in the town to the Earl of Angus, son of the Marquis of Douglas, who founded the Angus, or Covenanters, Regiment. Later renamed the Cameronians the regiment earned many battle honours before being disbanded in the town in 1968, the spot being marked by a monument. Coal mining dominated the local economy from before the First World War until 1967, when the last mine closed.

ELVANFOOT. This village stands at the source of two of Scotland's greatest rivers, the Forth and the Clyde, and lies in some of the wildest lowland country in Scotland. There is a lovely red sandstone church here, with a stained glass window commemorating the actor-manager Wilton Barrat, whose drama productions achieved fame before the advent of television.

LEADHILLS. This village has two claims to fame: it is one of the highest villages in Scotland and, also, it is also the birthplace of Allan Ramsay (1686-1758), an important poet in the 18th century revival. The **Allan Ramsey Library**, founded by miners in 1741, is the oldest subscription library in Britain and probably Europe. It also holds many rare books and detailed records of mining in the area.

The **Hopetoun Arms Hotel** at Leadhills is a handsome former shooting lodge which is well worth making a detour to find. It lies in the heart of the beautiful Southern Uplands, and is easily reached from the main A74/M74 Carlisle to Glasgow road via the B7040 from Elvanfoot, or the B797 from Abington.

Hopetoun Arms Hotel

An imposing gabled structure built of local stone, it stands in the Main Street of this famous old mining centre. Throughout its history, shooting parties have come here from all over the world for the abundant pheasant and grouse on the local moors. In the past, the Hopetoun Arms has played host to such famous patrons as Prince Charles and Zsa Zsa Gabor, and inside it still retains a relaxed genteel atmosphere which is reminiscent of a country house. Proprietors Helen and Jim McKenzie offer warm hospitality, excellent food and drink, and comfortable accommodation. The nine guest bedrooms are spacious and well appointed, and the lounge and bar are full of traditional character and charm. Helen and Jim serve a superb full Scottish breakfast and a wide selection of delicious bar meals at lunchtimes and in the evening which are prepared to order from fresh local produce.

Hopetoun Arms Hotel, 37 Main Street, Leadhills Tel: 01659 74234

WANLOCKHEAD is, in fact, the highest village in the Lowlands of Scotland, standing at 1500 feet above sea level, and it is almost completely isolated in its setting amongst the Lowther Hills. The mines were closed in the 1930s, after some 400 years of production. The **Museum of Scottish Lead Mining** depicts how lead was mined and smelted, as well as displaying local gold, silver and rare minerals. Every half hour a guide takes visitors to explore the Loch Nell Mine. Worked between the 1700s and 1860, this walk-in mine gives a true impression of the conditions underground. The picture of life in the village is completed at the Miner's Cottages, where visitors step back in time and contrast a miner's home in 1740 and 1890. The village also has a unique water powered beam engine, which was used to drain the Straitsteps Mine in the 19th century.

Wanlockhead Lead Mining Museum

Finnieston Crane, Glasgow Waterfront

CHAPTER FIVE

EDINBURGH & THE LOTHIANS

Forth Bridge

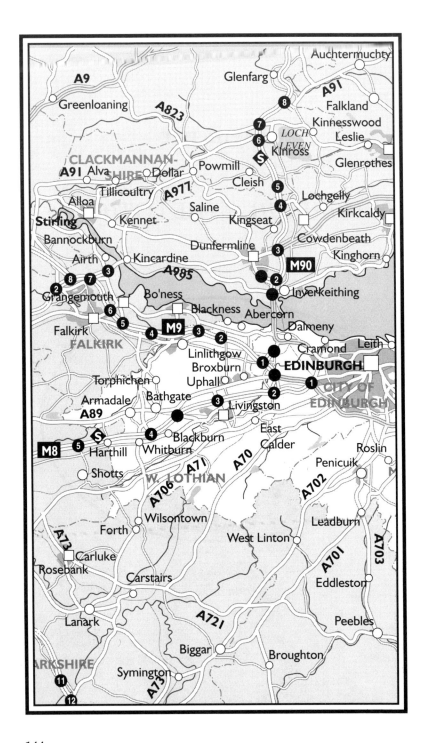

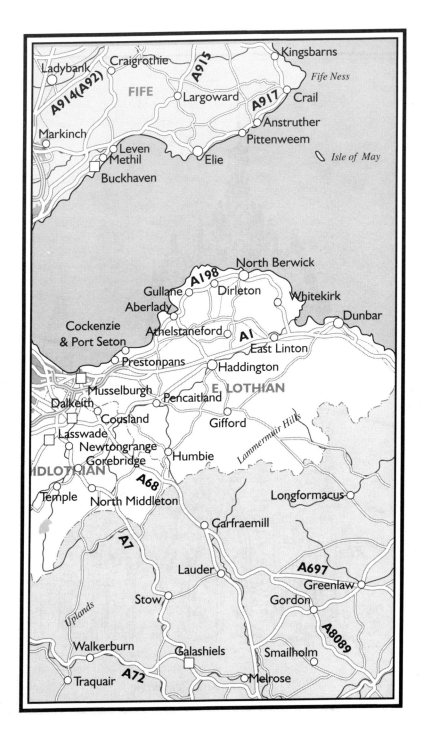

St Giles' Kirk, Edinburgh

CHAPTER FIVE

EDINBURGH AND THE LOTHIANS

The City of Edinburgh

EDINBURGH. The story of Edinburgh is almost the story of Scotland itself and on every corner there is a tale to be told. This is a truly lovely city, full of beauty and character, and there is so much pleasure to be gained from its vast range of attractions which draw visitors each year from all around the world.

It would be difficult to do Scotland's capital city justice in a few pages, instead the aim of this book it to guide the reader to some of the hidden places and to tell a few of the stories that lie behind this dramatic place.

Edinburgh, like Rome, is built on seven hills and at the centre of these is the Castle Rock. This, together with the other main promontory, Arthur's Seat, helps to give a unique and splendid skyscape which has acted as a backdrop for some of the most poignant events in history.

At the centre of the city lie the Royal Mile, running from the castle at one end to Holyrood Palace at the other, and Princes Street, which divides the city into the Old Town and the New. The most dominant feature in Edinburgh is, of course, the famous castle; perched high as it is, this great defender of the city features in every view. There has been a castle here for over a thousand years and its dominance and important position has never been lost.

The name 'Edinburgh' stems from an encampment created by a former King of Northumbria called Edwin, whose building on top of the rock became known as Edwin's Burgh. In the years that followed, the town developed, clinging at first to the **Castle Rock** and then stretching to the site of the palace and former abbey at Holyrood.

Edinburgh Castle is an ideal place to begin a tour of the city; it was here that Mary, Queen of Scots gave birth to her young son, James VI of Scotland, who was eventually to become James I of England. There were many who were not happy at the birth of a Catholic king and stories abound of his early life. One tells that the infant James did in fact die when he was on a tour of the Borders with his mother and that the Countess of Mar, who had charge of the young prince, substituted her own child in his place.

Some say that James bore little resemblance to the facial characteristics of the Stuarts but showed a startling likeness to the Earl of Mar.

This theory was revived in 1830 when rumour has it that a small oak coffin was found in the wall of Mary's apartments in the Castle. It contained the body of a small infant, wrapped in an embroidered silk covering bearing the initial 'J'.

Queen Mary's apartments can be seen in the castle, and her story is one that is linked vividly to the castles and abbeys of Edinburgh and the Borders. Indeed she seems to have been an unfortunate victim of circumstances and events who led a life doomed to be tragic. At 17, Mary Stuart was Queen of France but a year later, after her husband had died, she was taken home to Edinburgh as the 'Queen of Scots', taking up residence in Holyrood Palace.

She was reputedly a great beauty and, with all the power of Scotland in her hand, she was victim to the struggles and scheming of all those who meant to take advantage of her position. She met and fell in love with Lord Darnley and they married in 1565. This proved to be a disastrous mistake as Darnley was a callous and vain person. Mary was vulnerable and fell in love again, this time with the Earl of Bothwell. Again, tragedy struck when Darnley was killed in Kirk o'Field in 1567. Bothwell was blamed for the death of Darnley and, although he married Mary in secret in her own council chamber, he had many enemies who were powerful people. Mary was taken prisoner, forced to abdicate and held on a tiny island on the shores of Loch Leven. In 1568 she escaped only to eventually run into the hands of the English, where she was to face 19 years of captivity and finally death at the hands of the axeman.

In the Crown Room of the Castle the 'Honours of Scotland', the equivalent of the crown jewels, can be seen. They include the Crown worn by Robert the Bruce, the Sceptre and the Sword of State. Many attempts have been made to have these precious items removed to London. Even a request by Charles I was turned down and he was forced to come to Edinburgh to be crowned King of Scotland. Cromwell was determined to get his hands on these symbols of royalty, but they were smuggled away from him to Dunnotter Castle for safe-keeping. After being buried in a churchyard they were eventually returned to Edinburgh Castle and sealed up in a room until Sir Walter Scott made a search and rediscovered them in 1818.

Of the large iron cannons that sit in the Castle, the most famous is 'Mons Meg' and, though it now sits indoors, this cannon was renowned for its use at the siege of Norham and it could blast a five hundredweight stone at a target more than a mile away. Today on the high ramparts a slightly newer 25 pounder gun is fired at one o'clock everyday.

The broad esplanade fronting the Castle has always been used as a drilling ground. Today the Edinburgh Military Tattoo revives some of its former glories for three weeks in the autumn. This military spectacle is world famous, the massed pipes and drums conjuring up memories of the campaigns and heroism of centuries gone by. A wondrous spectacle of military precision not to be missed.

The streets and narrow alleys, or closes, off the **Royal Mile**, contain some of the most fascinating tales and the character of the old town. Across the street is **Cannonball House** with its two cannonballs lodged in the wall. These were supposedly fired from the castle at the time of the 1745 Rising, when Prince Charles Stuart was about to enter the city.

Castlehill has many tales to tell, some quite chilling. A bronze plaque fixed to the wall recalls that, between 1479 and 1722, more than 300 terrified women were branded as witches and cruelly put to death on this spot. One unique way to view the city from here is the **Camera Obscura**. Built in Victorian times this optical device projects an amazing live view of the city on to a table placed at the top of an outlook tower.

In the early days the supply of water to Edinburgh had serious problems. Most families owned a pair of 'stoups' for collecting water. These were two wooden vessels about two feet high which narrowed towards the top and they were popular wedding presents at the time. Queues would form around the various wells in the city at around six in the evening and the wait for water might last until as late as three in the morning, with the possibility of nothing to show for it if the wells ran dry.

Brodies Close was the home of a real life 'Jekyll and Hyde' character: Deacon William Brodie was a respected member of the town council by day and an extremely clever house burglar by night. However, unfortunately for him, he ventured out once too often and was recognised, arrested and hanged. If his ghost ever passes he may well be amused to see that an inn bearing his name stands by the site of the gallows where he was executed.

In nearby **Tanners Close** there once lived two rogues, much loved by the makers of horror films. The famous couple, Burke and Hare, being enterprising gentlemen, found that there was a trade in the supply of dead bodies for the purposes of medical research. Then, as now, the city had a reputation for medical research and bodies for dissection fetched a high price. The infamous duo took to grave robbing and then, ultimately, murder to meet the demand. They murdered and sold 18 victims before being caught and hanged in 1828. The churchyard at **Greyfriars** has many elaborate graves enclosed in heavy iron cages, known as mortsafes and intended to prevent bodysnatchers going about their work. The churchyard also provided the venue for the signing of the National Covenant in 1638, during the persecution that followed over 1400 covenanters were held in the yard.

Perhaps the best known grave in the yard is that of John Gray. When he died in 1848 his faithful Skye terrier, Bobby, watched over his master's grave for 14 years. Just outside the yard is a statue of **Greyfriar's Bobby**, a small monument to the little dog's loyalty, opposite the pub of the same name.

Passing through Lawnmarket into the High Street the visitor comes to the **High Kirk of St Giles**. In the early days of Edinburgh there was little room for shops, so traders would set up stalls wherever they could find room around St Giles. This is where both rich and poor would do their shopping for meat, bread, fish and other groceries. When the congestion reached the point of chaos the magistrates decided to act, allocating various places where the traders could do business. Today the old places of these traders can still be seen in the street names: Grassmarket, Lawnmarket, Flesher's Close, Candlemaker Row, etc.

The **Royal Mile** is rich with history, full of stories about kings, queens and dramatic turns of events and eventually leads to **Holyrood Palace** and the ruins of the abbey. Across the road at intervals the letter 'S' can be seen. This marks the sanctuary line of Holyrood Abbey, a line that many a debtor has been chased across by pursuing bailiffs.

Holyrood Abbey was destroyed by the English under orders from Henry VIII when his demand for the return of the infant Mary, Queen of Scots was refused. Also destroyed were the palaces and the abbeys of Melrose, Kelso and Jedburgh on the Borders. The palace was eventually restored and Mary's chambers can be seen. Queen Victoria visited here in 1842 and today the Queen stays here when she visits Edinburgh. The Palace and Abbey remains sit in the perfect setting of Holyrood Park, dominated by **Arthur's Seat**, rising up to some 822 feet at the summit and providing views across the city roofs.

The exposed rocks on the west side are known as Samson's Ribs and below this point is a road that runs to **Duddingston**, a pretty village on a loch in the shadow of Arthur's Seat and the home of **The Sheep Heid Inn**. The Inn is the oldest and most historic in Edinburgh and it dates back to 1360. Patronised by Bonnie Prince Charlie when he lodged in Duddingston village; Mary, Queen of Scots is also known to have stopped here for refreshments on her way to Craigmillar Castle. The Inn's present name comes from an ornate snuff box in the shape of a ram's head, which was presented to the pub by James VI in 1580. He considered the Sheep Heid to be one of his favourite hostelries and although the snuff box was proudly displayed in the bar for many years its whereabouts are now unknown.

This exploration of the city now leads into the New Town of Edinburgh. In 1752 steps were taken to oversee the development of Edinburgh in a style in keeping with the city's status. Designers and architects were employed to ensure the quality of the work and they began to construct the spacious and elegant streets that make Edinburgh famous throughout the world today. It is without doubt one of the finest Georgian urban landscapes in the country, an opulent mixture of classical, Gothic and baroque architecture in the grand style. Craiglieth stone, used extensively in the New Town, is particularly attractive, and much of it was sent south to provide building materials for Buckingham Palace and the British Museum. The area was planned and laid out by a young architect, the winner of a competition for the submission of the best design. Remarkably James Craig was only 23 at the time.

Princes Street is of course one of the most famous shopping streets anywhere in Britain and, with its buildings on just one side of the street, it must surely rank as one of the most picturesque. Another feature of Princes Street is the **Scott Monument** which was begun in 1840, eight

Greyfriar's Churchyard

years after the death of Edinburgh's most famous son. Surprisingly it was designed by an untrained joiner called George Kemp, who was unfortunately drowned before he had a chance to see the finished result. For those with a head for heights, and the energy, there is a 287 step climb to the top where the reward is a magnificent view over the city. The monument itself has much of interest to look at, including over 60 small statues of the figures in Scott's books. **Princes Street Gardens** offer pleasant walks and a respite from the teeming shops. Along with the fine floral displays is, reputedly, the oldest floral clock in the world, dating from 1903. There are more than 20,000 plants used in the display on the clock, which are changed several times a year.

There is, of course, so much more to see and do: there are a great many fine churches and historical houses to explore, art lovers will enjoy the profusion of galleries and theatres and there are fine parks to wander around. Those with a love of animals are sure to enjoy the Zoo, with its world famous penguin colony. No visit to Edinburgh would be complete, however, without reference to the spectacular **Edinburgh Arts Festival** that takes place every summer. The festival includes music, opera, ballet, theatre, dance, poetry and of course the fringe events that take place on every corner. All in all Edinburgh is a wonderful melting pot, rich in character and charm. The city is an experience not to be missed, but accommodation around Festival time, the last three weeks in August, can be difficult to find.

The place to go to enjoy some of the best coffee and tea in the city is **The Elephant House**, a superb establishment with a relaxed and stylish atmosphere which is situated in the heart of historic Edinburgh, just a few yards from the Royal Mile and Castle.

The Elephant House

This friendly café offers one of the finest ranges of gourmet filter and espresso coffees, and traditional, speciality and herbal teas in Scotland. A must to visit, this is a place where tea and coffee making is taken seriously, with all the ingredients being selected, stored and prepared to ensure the best results. Proprietor Ian Fraser has successfully created an environment which is tasteful, informal and popular with the young at heart. The walls are covered in an eclectic assortment of paintings, prints and memorabilia, and there is also a collection of over 600 elephants in all shapes and sizes, some of which are for sale. Along with the extensive choice of beverages, there is an impressive food menu offering a range of delicious light meals, including baked potatoes, home-made soups, filled rolls, salads, savoury platters, and an appetising all-day breakfast. A selection of arabica coffees can also be purchased, ground to the customer's own specification.

The Elephant House, 21 George IV Bridge, Edinburgh
Tel: 0131 220 5355 Fax: 0131 220 4272

The **Ben Doran Guest House** is a handsome Georgian listed residence which lies on the southern edge of the city centre, close to the Olympic-sized Royal Commonwealth swimming pool and the Meadows area of Edinburgh. This impressive family run bed and breakfast establishment has plenty of off-street parking, allowing guests to leave their cars and either walk or take the frequent local bus service into the centre.

Ben Doran Guest House

The ten centrally heated guest bedrooms are spacious, cheerfully decorated and appointed to a high standard; all are equipped with colour televisions and hospitality trays, and five have the added benefit of en-suite facilities. Proprietor Dr Joseph Labaki provides charming hospitality and a hearty full Scottish breakfast, with vegetarian options available if required. He is also full of useful information on Edinburgh's many superb visitor attractions and is always on hand to ensure guests get the most from their visit to this beautiful city. AA recommended and Scottish Tourist Board commended, the Ben Doran Guest House is ideal for those wanting a holiday or business base which lies within easy striking distance of the city centre.

Ben Doran Guest House, 11 Mayfield Gardens, Edinburgh
Tel: 0131 667 8488 Fax: 0131 667 0076

Barony House is run by Susie Berkengoff as a family home and Guest House. The decor and feeling in the house is very much a home-from-home atmosphere. There are eight guest bedrooms, two of which are single rooms and four with en-suite facilities. Served in a very large and spacious dining room, breakfast is a choice of buffet style, incorporating the full traditional Scottish breakfast or fresh fruit, juices, and other lower calorie foods. Breakfasts for vegetarians, vegans and people with special diets can also be provided. Freshly ground and decaffeinated coffee is a nice touch. A facsimile facility is on hand for business users. The house is Victorian and set in a very tranquil area of Edinburgh yet close to all the amenities. Ideal for sight-seeing and with very easy access to all the attractions of Edinburgh and surrounding areas. Awarded 2 Crowns Commended by the Scottish Tourist Board.

Barony House, 4 Queens Crescent, Edinburgh
Tel: 0131 667 5806 Fax: 0131 667 6835

From the town centre of Edinburgh, we headed in the general direction of Morningside where we had been recommended to seek out very comfortable bed and breakfast, at **Braid Hills Road**.

2 Braid Hills Road

Jean Roland has been providing a home-from-home for travellers and visitors to the area for 14 years now and has many returning guests year after year. Her well presented stone built house overlooks the Braidburn Valley and is within easy reach of three local golf courses. Equidistant between Edinburgh centre and open countryside, it is a perfect location for town and country. Jean has a warm and welcoming manner, as you might expect after so many years experience, and looks after each guest as though they were personal friends - which many have become over the years. The optional evening meal is freshly prepared and is served in pleasant homely surroundings. A very tasty traditional Scottish breakfast greets you in the morning and, if you have a good breakfast appetite, Jean's cooking will set you up for the day.

2 Braid Hills Road, Edinburgh Tel: 0131 447 8849

Offering some of the most attractive bed and breakfast accommodation in Edinburgh, **The Hollies** is ideally situated on the main bus route and only two miles from the city centre, so shopping and entertainment are only a stones throw away. This large and imposing Georgian property has two spacious en-suite guest rooms, each having been individually decorated to a very high standard and offering all the usual home comforts including your own sitting area. The facilities are also suitable for disabled guests as the rooms are on ground level.

The Hollies

One of the most unique features of The Hollies is the fact that you can have your breakfast in bed each morning, served to you by your very capable host Rita Coleman. Rita ensures that all tastes are catered for and offers a comprehensive range of breakfasts including full Scottish, Continental and for the vegetarians, fresh fruit and juices. The Hollies is a true home from home and the traditional Scottish hospitality guarantees that you will return again and again to this most splendid house. There is private parking.

The Hollies, 54 Craigmillar Park, Edinburgh
Tel & Fax: 0131 668 3408

AROUND EDINBURGH

LEITH. The port for Edinburgh, this village straddles the Water of Leith which flows into its sizeable harbour. The dock area has undergone some refurbishment and now features a couple of very good seafood bistros and a fine Indian restaurant, making it well worth the detour. The **Clan Tartan Centre** on Bangor Road makes a very interesting visit. As well as offering information about the clans themselves, the Centre will research, for any given surname, if there are any clan connections.

PORTOBELLO. This once stylish and famous resort has gained a new lease of life as a watersports centre with water and jet skiing available on the waterfront. For the more adventurous there is parascending. With its easy access to and from the A1, an excellent place to stay on the eastern side of Edinburgh city centre is the **Ardgarth Guest House** in Portobello. This charming family run establishment is situated in a quiet residential street just a short stroll from the seafront with its impressive beach and promenade. A spacious Victorian residence, the property has been tastefully converted to bring it up to the standard of a Scottish Tourist Board 2 Crowns Commended guest house.

Ardgarth Guest House

Resident proprietors Ursula and Richard Wright are friendly and experienced hosts who provide a warm welcome, comfortable accommodation and a delicious Continental or full Scottish breakfast, with vegetarian choices available on request. They create a real home from home atmosphere, and offer choice of single, double, twin and family rooms, either with washbasins or full en-suite facilities; all have TVs and tea and coffee making facilities. Children are most welcome. Cots and high chairs are available and a baby listening service can be arranged, if required. There is also good level access for disabled people, with the property being listed as Category 1.

Ardgarth Guest House, 1 St Mary's Place, Portobello, Edinburgh
Tel & Fax: 0131 669 3021

CRAMOND. This village, with its huddle of cottages and narrow winding steps, is a quiet and attractive place at the mouth of the River Almond. The foundation of a Roman fort, built around 142 to guard the harbour, can still be seen laid out by the mid 17th century church. **Cramond Old Bridge**, over the River Almond, was built in 1619 on the site of an older bridge.

Many years ago, a local miller, Jack Howieson, rescued James V after he had attacked the bridge and Jack brought him some water to quench his thirst. In gratitude James V granted land to the family on condition that they always have a basin and ewer ready whenever a sovereign should be passing. Such were offered, in 1952, to the present Queen.

DALMENY. **Dalmeny House** has been the home of the Primrose family and the Earls of Rosebery for over 300 years. The splendid Tudor Gothic house seen today was largely built in 1815 by William Wilkins. Along with hammerbeam roofed hall, vaulted corridors and classical main rooms, the interior also features a collection of 18th century portraits, tapestries, many pieces of 18th century French furniture, porcelain from the Rothschild Mentmore collection and the Napoleon collection. The grounds feature a four mile walk along the shoreline to Cramond. Still in the Primrose family the house is open to the public 2 pm to 5.30 pm Sunday to Thursday between May and September.

SOUTH QUEENSFERRY. The town is dominated by the two **Forth Bridges**. The rail bridge comes right over the town and is best viewed from the shore front - which incidentally has an original hexagonal Victorian post box. Built over 100 years ago it is still a breathtakingly audacious structure: a mile and more long this double cantilever bridge is 361 feet high, takes three years to paint from end to end and has 135 acres of exposed steel. Magnificent though it is, the modern road suspension bridge somewhat lives in the shadow of its neighbour; opened in 1964 by the Queen, it ended 800 years of ferrying people and goods across the Firth.

East Lothian

MUSSELBURGH. Almost adjoining Portobello is the small town of Musselburgh, which was once known as Eskmouth and is situated on the mouth of the River Esk. The modern name derives from a profitable mussel bank in the river's estuary. Musselburgh is a place of very independent character.

The tollbooth dates from 1590 and has an interesting story behind it, as it was built from the ruins of the Chapel of our Lady of Loretto which was destroyed by the English in 1544. Unfortunately, the act of building the tollbooth from the sacred ruins was considered to be sacrilege and brought the citizens under sentence of Papal excommunication for over 200 years.

There is a race course and golf course here, on which King James IV is said to have played in 1504. The actual golf club was founded in 1774 and used to offer a prize for the best fish-wife golfer. If it was unusual to find women on a golf course in the 18th century though it was not considered so in Musselburgh as the womenfolk had a tough reputation. One such woman was hanged at the Grassmarket in Edinburgh in 1728, only to be taken down to be buried in Musselburgh. The jolting of the wagon on her last journey however revived the spirit of this indomitable woman and she is said to have lived on to get married and produce many children.

AROUND MUSSELBURGH

PRESTONPANS. The **Scottish Mining Museum**, on a former colliery site, has a beam pumping engine that kept the mine from flooding as the miners dug out under the sea, as well as a colliery winding engine and steam engines. The 'Cutting the Coal' exhibition tells the story of mechanical coal extraction from the mid 1800s.

Prestonpans provided the setting for one of Bonnie Prince Charlie's victories during the '45 Jacobite Rising. The market place also features an impressive cross, one of few that survives as built and in its original position. Probably dating from around 1617, when the Hamiltons of Preston obtained the right to hold a fair.

PORT SETON. Along with a picture postcard harbour, complete with colourful fishing smacks and lobster pots, this village also has an interesting late 15th century church which features a fine vaulted chancel and apse.

LONGNIDDRY. Overlooking the Firth of Forth the impressive **Gosford House** features a central section by Robert Adam built in 1800 and north and south wings completed in 1890 by William Young. The south wing has a celebrated marble hall and the grounds ornamental waters have nesting wild geese. The house is open in June and July on Wednesday, Saturday and Sunday between 2 pm and 5 pm.

ABERLADY. Just east of the village is **Luffness Castle**, standing at the head of Aberlady Bay. With origins in the 13th century it was built to defend nearby Haddington. Bought by the Earl of Hopetoun in 1739 for £8350, it remains the Hope family home.

DIRLETON. Now by-passed by the main road, this is a village with a very pretty green and an impressive ruined castle. **Dirleton Castle** dates back to 1225 and was destroyed in 1650. The gardens enclose a 17th century yew-lined bowling green. Refreshment can be had and the view enjoyed admirably from the Castle Inn on the other side of the green.

NORTH BERWICK is a popular yachting resort and centre for tourism. Offshore is the fascinating **Bass Rock**, rising some 312 feet from the sea, which is now a famous bird sanctuary providing a home for one of the few nesting colonies of gannet, a bird with legendary diving abilities and, surprisingly, once a sought after dish. Many other birds nest on the rocky cliffs and slopes. Boat trips can be made by arrangement from North Berwick and the trip guarantees an amazing view of the sights and sounds of the birds on this spectacular rock, the third largest gannetry in the world.

Inland from the town, the country rises to **North Berwick Law** which is 613 feet above sea level and can be seen from as far away as Edinburgh and Fife. On the top of this ancient volcano are the jaw bones of a whale, a watch tower dating from Napoleonic times and stunning vistas on a clear day.

General Monk, who destroyed Dirleton Castle, also severely damaged **Tantallon Castle**. A few miles east of the town, the Castle, built by the Douglases, has a curtain wall that blocks off a promontory from cliff to cliff. Once considered impregnable it is now, along with The Hermitage and Bothwell, one of the most striking castle ruins in Scotland.

WHITEKIRK. The rather special parish church, St Mary's, dates back to the 6th century and has a Norman high square tower. This large red sandstone place of worship was, in medieval times, a place of pilgrimage famed for its healing well. The tithe barn to the rear of the church is one of the oldest still standing in Britain.

DUNBAR. Here is a town which boasts more sunshine hours than any other location in Scotland. It is also a popular holiday resort, with Belhaven Beach to the west and White Sands to the east. Dunbar has a history of brewing which goes back to the Middle Ages and today boasts a number of brewing firms renowned for their real ales, still brewed in the traditional manner.

Dunbar was, at one time, a prosperous fishing centre and, in 1879, could boast a fishing fleet of over 300 boats. The wide high street and big solid sandstone buildings are evidence of the prosperity that was brought to the town through the industry. Indeed, a walk around Dunbar will be a rewarding experience.

Dunbar Castle overlooks one of the town's two harbours. It was here that Mary, Queen of Scots was brought by the Earl of Bothwell in April 1567 and where they remained for ten days prior to their marriage.

To the western side of the town and located on a beautiful stretch of coastline is the **John Muir Country Park**. American patrons, will feel at home here for this park was named in honour of the man who himself emigrated to the States and founded America's first national park. Dunbar is his home town and today the Sierra Club of America regularly visit the town in memory of the man who provided them with perhaps one of the most important elements of their national heritage.

EAST LINTON. Here is **Preston Mill and Phantassie Doocot**. The watermill is probably the last of its kind still in working order in

Preston Mill, East Linton

The Pulpit, St Mary's Kirk, Haddington

Scotland and the Doocot or dovecote is, without doubt, one of the strangest looking buildings in Scotland.

The now ruined **Hailes Castle** dates from the 13th and 15th centuries. Mary, Queen of Scots was brought here by the Earl of Bothwell, her third husband, on her flight from Borthwick Castle in 1567.

ATHELSTANEFORD. The village is traditionally associated with the origin of Scotland's flag. The story goes that the Scots, fighting the Northumbrians under Athelstane in the 10th century, saw a white St Andrew's Cross against the blue sky. Thus encouraged to victory, the Scots made a banner which became the Scottish flag and a flag flies beside the village church.

HADDINGTON is one of those rare towns that has come into the 20th century with its elegance and character intact. This magnificent town has many lovingly restored houses and shops as well as the beautiful late medieval Parish Church of **St Mary**. Unfortunately, the town lay directly in the path of invading English armies and was repeatedly destroyed before reaching more prosperous days in the 18th century. Since then, its biggest threat came from the River Tyne that runs around it, flooding Haddington in 1775 when the River rose to a height of 17 feet above its normal level. As recently as 1948 the Tyne rose above all recorded levels, forming a torrent some 800 yards across.

To the south of Haddington on the B6369 is **Lennoxlove House**. Originally named Lethington, it was owned for centuries by the Maitland family, one of whom was secretary to Mary, Queen of Scots. In 1672 the Duchess of Lennox, La Belle Stewart who was model for Britannia on the coinage, bequeathed it to Lord Blantyre, stipulating it be renamed in memory of her love for her husband. Now owned by the Duke of Hamilton it is open on Easter weekend and on Wednesdays, Saturdays and Sundays from May to September.

HUMBIE. At the foot of the Lammermuir Hills, the village is famous for the Children's Village, a charitable institution founded in 1886 for the disabled children of Edinburgh.

It has taken the best part of four centuries to create the unique setting of **Johnstounburn House**. Built in 1625, but lovingly extended by successive proud owners, this historic family house - just 15 miles from the centre of Edinburgh - is now an extraordinary country house hotel. The earliest trace of Johnstounburn is found in 1260 when the lands of some thousand acres were given by John de Keith to the great hospital and church of the Holy Trinity at Soutra Hill. The present mansion house was part of an original inn, undoubtedly built around a Medieval structure, in 1625. It was known as the 'Highwayman's Haunt', being frequented by professionals who used it as a rendezvous prior to moving up to Soutra Hill where they would hold up the London to Edinburgh stage coaches.

At the beginning of the 20th century, Johnstounburn was purchased by a well known brewer, Andrew Usher who was the first man to blend whisky and thus make his fortune with which he built Edinburgh's famous Usher Hall.

A peaceful yet convenient retreat beside the Johnstoun Burn, this beautiful manor is surrounded by attractive gardens enclosed by traditional walls and formal yew hedges, while beyond lies lightly wooded parkland running up into the Lammermuir Hills overlooking the busy Firth of Forth. The hotel has a great charm and character which although refurbished with all modern day comforts, essentially retains its historic heritage and impressive features. The Drawing Room has a welcoming open log and peat fire and is just the place to curl up with a good book or relax over coffee and liqueurs. An elegant 18th century panelled dining room is the setting for some of the best cuisine in Scotland. Chef Bryan Thom selects only the very best from Scotland's sumptuous larder, and he is only too happy to prepare special dishes on request. The carefully selected wine list features wines from the old and new worlds. Each of the 20 well appointed bedrooms are either in the main house or in the original coach house, situated some 300 metres through the formal gardens. They are attractively furnished and provide a level of comfort befitting such a country mansion. All have a private bathroom, satellite television, radio and direct dial telephone. Many diversionary pursuits are close at hand; a dozen or so golf courses, access to some of the best shooting in the Lothians. Clay shooting, off road driving, a practice golf fairway, and a trout-filled pond for fishing - all on the estate. A hotel of grace and courtesy awaits!

Johnstounburn House Hotel, Humbie, near Edinburgh
Tel: 01875 833696 Fax: 01875 833626

Midlothian

DALKEITH once stood on a Roman road and today it stands, by the River Esk, on one of the main routes to Edinburgh. There are interesting houses here to look at, most notably **Dalkeith Palace** which, although not open to visitors, has had celebrated guests such as James IV, George IV and Queen Victoria. **Dalkeith Park**, surrounding the Palace, is open to visitors and has woodland walks along the banks of the Esk.

AROUND DALKEITH

COUSLAND. The White House is situated in the heart of the village of Cousland and is found from the A68, approximately two miles from Dalkeith. The house was custom built for Dorothy and Jimmy Stevenson in 1980 and the local views are over the Pentland Hills and towards Edinburgh Castle. Dorothy and Jimmy provide great value bed and breakfast accommodation in three guest rooms; two double en-suite rooms and one twin-bedded room with private bathroom. Each has a television and tea and coffee making facilities. Dorothy will cater for vegetarians upon request and cooks a really excellent breakfast to individual requirements. There are pleasant and peaceful walks locally. Commended by Scottish Tourist Board.

White House, 1 Hadfast Road, Cousland Tel: 0131 663 1294

NEWTONGRANGE. This whole town was built around the **Lady Victoria Colliery**. Everything was built and run by the mine company; the mines own powerhouse supplied the town's electricity and they provided homes, baths, a cinema and institute (pub) for their employees. The mine manager's word was law and a man fired would never work in the Scottish coalfields again. One manager inspected his employees' gardens every Sunday and any found wanting would be seen to, at the miners expense. Another forced the miners' sons underground by threatening their fathers with the sack. The colliery which closed in 1981 is now the **Scottish Mining Museum**.

The pithead is much as it was the day it closed, around ten years ago, covered in coaldust and a fitting tribute to the men who toiled deep underground to win coal. There is a magnificent pit winding engine in working order, though the shaft has been filled, and tours are conducted by former miners. The visitors centre, in the old mine offices, describes life in a Victorian pit village. Keep an eye out for Pick and Shovel, the museum's canaries. This type of bird was once the miner's best friend, being used to detect the presence of dangerous gases and some are still used today.

GOREBRIDGE. Arniston House is a gem of an historic house in an outstanding setting between the villages of Gorebridge and Temple. Temple was the headquarters of the Knights Templars who owned the lands, now part of Arniston estate, in the 1100s. The Dundas family bought the property in 1571 and the family still own and live in the house. The family rose to great heights in the 18th century and, in 1726, commissioned William Adam, father of the famous Robert, to commence the present mansion house. Robert Dundas who organised the Adam commission eventually became Lord President of the Court of Session as did his son, also named Robert. Arniston contains portraits of the generations of the family from the 16th century up to the present day, by artists including Ramsay and Raeburn. Also to be enjoyed at Arniston are fine examples of Adam architecture, stucco work, furniture and other fascinating contents.

Arniston House

The present owners have been involved in a long programme of restoration work, over a number of years, which is still continuing. The house has been beset by dry rot problems. Despite this as much public access as possible is made available. The house is open from July to mid September each Tuesday, Thursday and Sunday of these months between 2-5 pm. Parties of 10-50 outside these dates are accepted throughout the year by prior arrangement. Althea Dundas-Bekker likes, whenever possible, to take visitors round the house herself and visitors enjoy the ethos of a real home. Directions: Take the A7 route south of Edinburgh and turn into the B6372 signposted Penicuik and Temple. Arniston is the second turning on the right which is about one mile from the A7.

Arniston House, Gorebridge Tel: 01875 830238 Fax: 01875 830573

An excellent place to stay which offers easy access to central Edinburgh and the beautiful countryside of the Scottish Borders is **Ivory House** at Gorebridge, a pleasant community lying ten miles from the city centre off the main A7 Galashiels road. A handsome Victorian residence dating from 1880, it stands within an extensive lawned garden which enjoys fine views of the Pentland Hills. The beautifully decorated interior has a warm and welcoming atmosphere, enhanced by a number of attractive original features. The three centrally heated guest bedrooms (one family, one twin, one double) are spacious, well appointed and fully updated throughout; the last named has a charming romantic feel, complete with brass bedstead and antique furnishings. Resident proprietors Barbara and Jack Maton are very friendly hosts who provide first class hospitality and a superb Scottish breakfast. Vegetarians choices are available and many of the ingredients are picked fresh from the greenhouse and garden. Jack is a mine of information on the many attractions, both rural and urban, of the surrounding area, making this an ideal holiday base for walkers, golfers and those wishing to sample the unique character and culture of the Scottish capital.

Ivory House, 14 Vogrie Road, Gorebridge Tel: 01875 820755

NORTH MIDDLETON. Borthwick Castle is the highest tower house in Scotland and, in many respects, one of the best preserved and most impressive of the country's medieval buildings. Bothwell and Mary, Queen of Scots came here a month after their marriage before being forced to flee. In 1650 Cromwell sent the 10th Lord Borthwick, a Royalist, a letter threatening to 'bend his cannon' unless he capitulate. Cromwell did indeed need his cannons but Borthwick surrendered before any substantial damage was done. Today the castle, so full of Royal tragedy and treachery, is a hotel and surely one of the most exciting and romantic places to stay in the Lothians.

The local church, associated with the Borthwick family and clan, is mainly Victorian; though it does retain an aisle and vault from the 15th century, an apse from the 12th century and two 15th century effigies, amongst the best preserved in Scotland.

LASSWADE. Sir Walter Scott lived at Lasswade Cottage for the first six years of his married life and, during this time, Scott began to establish himself as a poet and was, in turn, visited by William and Dorothy Wordsworth. Lasswade is said to be the location of Gandercleugh in Scott's *Tales of my Landlord* and while Dorothy Wordsworth stayed here she recorded, in her diary, her impressions of this part of the Esk Valley, noting that she had "never passed through a more pleasant dell".

Now for something completely different - how about a visit to a tropical paradise? - yes in Edinburgh! Whatever the weather, stroll through the wonderful world of an exotic rainforest, a landscape of tropical plants surrounding splashing waterfalls and pools. At **Butterfly World** you can enjoy the unique pleasure of watching hundreds of the world's most spectacular and colourful butterflies flying all around you. See their entire life cycle at first-hand and marvel at nature's ingenuity. It's a fascinating place to visit for all ages and especially interesting for children is the strange worlds of the creepy crawlies! Yes, you can also enter another fascinating and strange world and observe at close quarters the habits of live scorpions, tarantulas, leaf-cutting ants, stick insects, beetles and other remarkable insects.

Butterfly World

Butterfly and Insect World is located at Dobbies Gardening World off the bypass at the Gilmerton exit. Open from March to January 10 am to 5.30 pm seven days a week. The gift shop has a lovely range of quality gifts, many with a butterfly theme. The garden tearoom serves a variety of snacks and delicious home-baking. Full facilities for disabled visitors. An exciting experience not to be missed.

Butterfly World at Dobbies Gardening World, Melville Nursery, Lasswade
Tel: 0131 663 4932 Fax: 0131 654 2548

In a converted 17th century stable block, designed by James Playfair for Lord Dundas of Melville, the dwelling, now called **Chestnut House**, derives its name from the 500 year old Spanish chestnut tree planted by Mary, Queen of Scots' lover, David Rizzio. The property stands by the River North Esk in 150 acres of mature woodland and meadows on the outskirts of Edinburgh (approximately 20 minutes drive). The private gardens extend to a terrace on the banks of the river and there is a luxurious 16 metre indoor heated swimming pool with spa, gym and conservatory. Trout fishing in the river is permitted.

Chestnut House

By careful restoration, the 17th century character of Chestnut House has been retained. The spacious rooms, all with log fires, wrought iron chandeliers and Jacobean furniture, offer a warm and welcoming atmosphere. The guest rooms have en-suite facilities. Take the A772 Gilmerton Road and travel past Butterfly Farm to the Melvillegate Roundabout, turn right into Melville Castle and Chestnut House drive. Chestnut House is past the castle on the left.

Chestnut House by Melville Castle, Lasswade
Tel: 0131 6541339

ROSLIN. **Rosslyn Castle** is believed to have been founded by Sir William St Clair, having reputedly won the lands in a wager he made, betting his head against the lands, that two of his hounds would bring down a deer by the time it reached a certain spot. Fortunately for Sir William the deer was killed and he was awarded the estate. The Lady Chapel was the beginning of a much larger project that Sir William had intended as a monument of himself. Unfortunately he died when the project was only partially completed. The remains are somewhat dilapidated, though what is left gives indications that, had it been finished, the church would have been one of the most remarkable medieval buildings in Europe.

Housed in a cottage built in and around 1660, The Old Roslin Inn had, in its day, many famous patrons including King Edward VII when he was Prince of Wales, Sir Walter Scott, Robert Burns and William and Dorothy Wordsworth. The inn is though to have closed its doors for the last time in 1866. Also in the glen is **Hawthornden Castle**, which dates from the 15th century. It was the birth place of William Drummond the poet (1585-1649) and remained in the Drummond family until the 1970s. It is now a retreat for poets and writers.

Rosslyn Chapel is unique and famed world wide for the beauty of its carvings and for the aura of mystery and magic that surrounds it. Built in 1446 by William St Clair, 3rd and last Prince of Orkney, the Chapel conforms neither to contemporary architecture nor to any fashion. Rich in ornament; the carvings include the famous Prentice Pillar and also carvings of plants from the New World which pre-date the discovery of that land by Columbus by 100 years.

Rosslyn Chapel

Rosslyn Chapel stands on the edge of the steeply wooded Esk Valley. The narrow rocky gorge below with its fast flowing water gives Rosslyn its name. The richly wooded Rosslyn Glen offers pleasant walks and magnificent views of Rosslyn Castle. The Chapel has been a place of pilgrimage over the centuries and has much to delight, intrigue and inspire today's visitors. The Chapel is used for weekly services, can be booked for Weddings and is a venue for Musical Evenings. Rosslyn Chapel, its Shop and Tea Room are open all year 10.00 am to 5.00 pm (Sundays 12.00 am to 4.45 pm). Located six miles south of Edinburgh's Princes Street and three miles from the city bypass. The A701 to Penicuik has Roslin signposted, once in Roslin Village the Chapel is signposted.

Rosslyn Chapel, Roslin Tel: 0131 440 2159 Fax: 0131 440 1979

PENICUIK. This small Midlothian town has its fair share of visitors, many of them attracted to the **Edinburgh Crystal Visitor Centre** on the edge of the town. As well as a visitor centre and shop, Edinburgh Crystal also organises interesting and informative factory tours. Penicuik is an excellent centre for the Pentland Hills, which are a long stretch of uplands that run south from the edge of Edinburgh.

West Lothian

LINLITHGOW. This ancient burgh was once one of Scotland's four main towns. An important industrial centre it had a reputation as the place that 'was smelt before it was seen'. The local industries included mining, textiles, milling and brewing. On Linlithgow lochside stands the solid and imposing **Linlithgow Palace** which has its origins back in the 1200s. Ruined in 1313 and rebuilt in 1350 by King David II, the Palace went on to become a favourite residence of the Scottish kings. Burnt out in 1424 it was again rebuilt much as we see it today. When Mary, Queen of Scots was born here in 1542, her father, James V, lay dying in Falkland Palace across the Forth. Mary's son, James VI, had much done to the Palace, having the north wing, where his mother was born, rescued from dereliction. Later Cromwell garrisoned it, Bonnie Prince Charlie captured and abandoned it and, finally, men defeated by the Prince sought sanctuary there and accidentally burnt it down. And so it remains today, there have been various projects mooted to re-roof it but in the meantime it stands massive and gaunt, brooding over the past. Next door to the palace is St Michael's, one of Scotland's finest examples of a medieval church.

Linlithgow stands on the Union Canal, built 1822, which joined Edinburgh to the Forth-Clyde Canal near Falkirk. Some of the 31 miles of the canal can be enjoyed aboard the Victoria, a replica Victorian Steam Packet that takes half hour trips along it. The boat can be found at the Manse Road basin along with the **Canal Museum**. Sited in the former Canal stables the/museum features records, photographs, audio-visual displays and relics of the history of the Union Canal.

Beecraigs Country Park is the largest of its kind in West Lothian and offers a whole range of activities and outdoor pursuits to appeal to the whole family. The beautiful surrounding countryside is home to a wide variety of birds and wildlife and provides a wealth of lovely walks. The nearby Deer Farm with its pedestrian walkway and viewing platform gives visitors the opportunity to observe the majestic red deer while they graze undisturbed and at the Trout Farm, the rearing ponds detail the life cycle of the trout. Beecraigs also has a lot to offer the sports enthusiast with a wide variety of activities and courses available, ranging from canoeing and climbing to archery and mountain biking.

Thornton is an impressive family home which offers exceptionally comfortable bed and breakfast accommodation to those visiting historic Linlithgow. This handsome Victorian residence lies in the heart of the town midway between the railway station and the Union canal, within easy walking distance of the royal palace. Built in 1870, it is set within a large attractive garden which incorporates a private parking area. The interior has a wonderful relaxed atmosphere, with many original features having been retained, most notably in the magnificent drawing room. The guest bedrooms (one double, one twin) are centrally heated and beautifully appointed, with en-suite facilities, colour televisions and a number of thoughtful extras. Resident proprietors Jill and Rob Inglis provide a superb full Scottish breakfast. The extensive menu includes freshly squeezed fruit juice, fresh fruit compote, porridge, eggs cooked in any way and, given prior notice, Arbroath smokies, kedgeree or scrambled eggs with smoked salmon. With its excellent connections to Edinburgh airport, Stirling and Glasgow, Thornton is the ideal holiday base from which to explore the many attractions of central Scotland. Scottish Tourist Board 2 Crown Highly Commended, the house is unsuitable for smokers.

Thornton, Edinburgh Road, Linlithgow Tel: 01506 844216

The Cedars is a delightful bed and breakfast establishment situated in the High Street, a short walk from the local railway station. An original Merchant's house built in 1829 by a local shoe manufacturer for the princely sum of £325. Owned and operated by the Mitchell family for 16 years, The Cedars offers a warm welcome, comfortable accommodation and hearty Scottish breakfasts. Within sight and three minutes walk from historic Linlithgow Palace, birthplace of Mary, Queen of Scots; this is an ideal base from which to explore central Scotland.

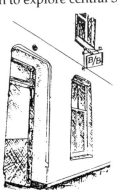

The Cedars, 135 High Street, Linlithgow Tel: 01506 845952

BLACKNESS. One of the great houses along the southern shores of the Firth of Forth **The House of Binns** is situated just off the A904 south of Blackness and not surprisingly it offers extensive views over the Firth. Built between 1612 and 1633, by the Dalyells, the house admirably reflects the transition of Scottish manor house architecture from fortification to mansion. One famous occupant of the House was Tam Dalyell, a Royalist general known as 'Bloody Tam' or the 'Muscovy Brute' (as he was supposed to have brought the thumbscrews into Scotland from Russia) Tam was feared, particularly by Convenanters, and he was thought to be in league with the Devil. According to legend, the terrible twosome played cards together and one night, after Tam had won, the Devil picked up a marble table and threw it at the General. Tam ducked and the table flew through the window and landed in Sergeant Pond at the foot of Binns Hill. Much later, in 1878, when the pond was being cleaned, the table was found amongst the mud and it was returned to the house.

The interior has fine plaster ceilings and an outstanding family collection of paintings, furniture and porcelain. Occupied for over 350 years the house is now in the capable hands of the National Trust for Scotland and open everyday except Friday from 1st May to 30th September between 2 pm and 5 pm.

ABERCORN. **Hopetoun House**, the family home of the Hopes, was built in the grand manner. Started in 1699 to a design by Sir William Bruce it was considerably enlarged between 1721 and 1754 by William Adam and his son, John. With paintings by Canaletto, Gainsborough, Rubens and Titian on display inside, a rooftop viewing platform with panoramic views and magnificent gardens and deer parks in the grounds, it is certainly one of the great houses of Scotland. Looked after by a preservation trust the house and grounds are open daily between Easter and September from 10 am to 5 pm.

LIVINGSTON. This new town, established in 1962 in a previously coal mining area, is now a successful centre for manufacturing and high technology industries.

EAST CALDER. **Almondell and Calderwood Country Park** resides here and offers the visitor extensive riverside and woodland walks as well as displays on nature, local history and a large freshwater aquaria in the visitors centre.

BATHGATE. This industrial town was the birthplace of James Simpson, a pioneer of anaesthesia, who first used chloroform in 1847. The local **Bennie Museum** features both Simpson and James 'Paraffin' Young.

ARMADALE. The Dale, as it is better known to most of its inhabitants, is situated in an area once famous for its wild pig hunting.

Before 1790, when Lord Armadale purchased a house in the area as a weekend retreat from his law practice in Edinburgh, there was nothing much here. Following completion of the Glasgow to Edinburgh highway, Armadale became perfectly situated and turned into one of the new towns of the Industrial Revolution. Armadale contains a wealth of stories and characters from the past, and its development over the last century is fascinating. Being halfway between the two cities, a regular stage coach route was established and passengers would break for a rest and perhaps have a meal while the horses were changed in the middle of this twelve hour journey. There was also a toll house here and it was once described as a "small one-roomed hut with a window lookout in each wall". Presumably this was to keep an eye open for those who might try to slip by without paying.

TORPHICHEN. **Torphichen Preceptory** was founded in 1153 by the Knights of St John of Jerusalem as their centre in Scotland. An interesting site to visit, the ruins dating from the 13th to the 15th century can be seen along with an 18th century parish church that was built over the original Norman nave. Full of atmosphere and with the air of a small and elegant castle, Torphichen Preceptory also has an exhibition which tells the history of the order.

Originally a Neolithic sanctuary **Cairnpapple Hill** was rebuilt in the early Bronze Age, around 1800 BC, as a monumental open-air temple with stone circle. Later, around 1500 BC, the site was despoiled and built over with a cairn, which in itself was enlarged several centuries later.

Cairnpapple's significance to early man may be explained by its position on the summit of the Bathgate Hills. On a clear day the view extends right across Scotland, from the Isle of May in the Firth to Goat Fell on distant Arran. The site has now been excavated and laid out but still retains the mystery of its ancient worshippers and their rites.

Forth Bridge

174

CHAPTER SIX

THE KINGDOM OF FIFE

Falkland Castle

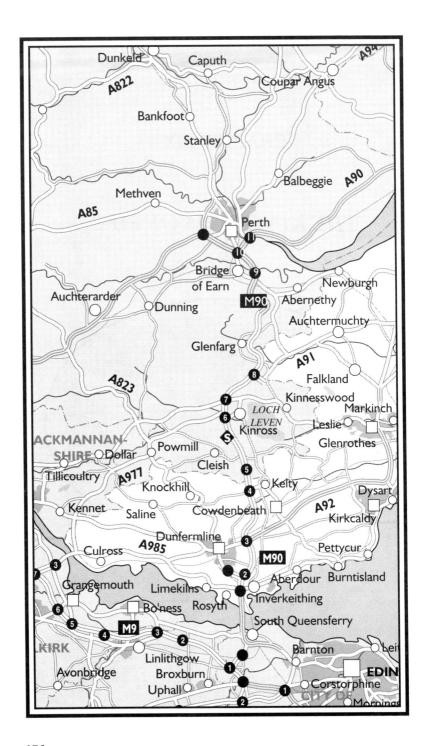

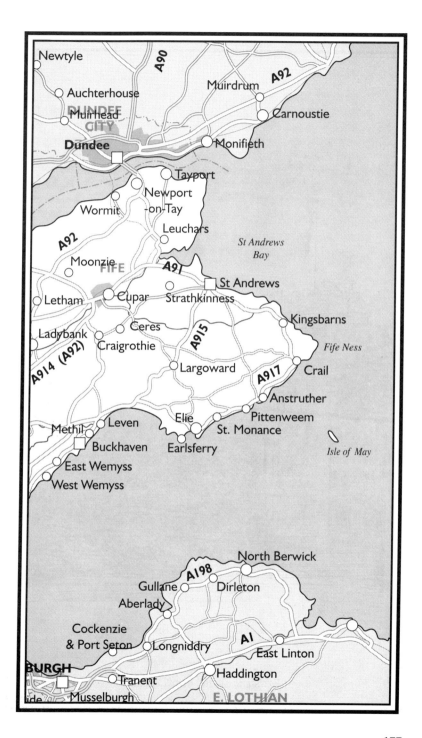

Earlshall Castle, near Leuchars

CHAPTER SIX

THE KINGDOM OF FIFE

The Firth of Forth

KIRKCALDY. This is a thriving town that developed through the linen trade into the manufacture of linoleum. The latter was apparently discovered when a local family had the idea of making a more durable cloth that would be suitable for the covering of floors. It was originally made from cork, imported from Spain, and whale oil. This combination, at one time, gave the town a rather unique smell.

There is a wealth of interesting buildings throughout the town, including Raith, probably built by MacDuff and Balwearie, which has strong connections with the renowned wizard, Michael Scott, whose practices and proficiency in alchemy and astrology earned him a fearful reputation. He even has a mention in the eighth Circle of Dante's *Inferno*.

Adam Smith, the economist, was born in the town and it was here that he retired to write his famous book *The Wealth of Nations* which appeared in 1776. Incidentally, the last two duels to be fought in Scotland, in 1822 and 1826, took place in Kirkcaldy.

Kirkcaldy is also known as "the long town" and, with a four mile long main street, it is easy to see how it got this name. There are libraries, an award winning museum and galleries throughout, which make interesting viewing. **Ravenscraig Castle** stands on a promontory between Kirkcaldy and Dysart. Though of no great historical significance it does have perhaps two claims to fame; it is probably the first castle in Britain designed and built to deliver and withstand artillery attack and, undoubtedly, the first to be overlooked by a high-rise blocks of flats. Built in the 15th century, the ruins are reached via a flight of steps leading up from the beach. The flight is said to be the inspiration behind John Buchan's *The Thirty-Nine Steps*.

AROUND KIRKCALDY

GLENROTHES. The Kingdom of Fife is rich in arable land and its coastal waters teem with life but the prize its hinterland holds is deep underground - coal. Though coal is still being mined there is little evidence of the area's industrial past. The second of Scotland's new towns, Glenrothes was established in 1949 though most of the buildings date from the 1960s. New industries are replacing the old though and the town has a fast developing electronics industry.

KELTY. **The Butterchurn Restaurant** is set in 25 acres, part of a working farm dating back to 1773. It is housed within old cowsheds and dairy buildings and, due to its popularity, has recently been extended to provide 40 extra covers - in effect, doubling the seating capacity of this very special place. The fully licensed Restaurant is run and supervised by the owners, Jennifer and Kenneth Thomson.

A warm welcome is assured and, with friendly waitress service, you can enjoy anything from morning coffee to afternoon tea. A full meal menu is available at anytime throughout the day; choose from the blackboard selection of freshly prepared and home-cooked meals to the highest standards.

The quality of the food is exceptional - beautifully arranged on display you will see home-baking, special recipe preserves and local fresh produce. To complete your meal, the adjacent display houses an equally mouthwatering selection of sweets, all home-made and very tempting. With panoramic views on all sides and a wonderful relaxed atmosphere, this really is a gastronomic haven. **The Butterchurn Pantry** stocks a wide range of quality Scottish craft and gift products. Delicious Scottish food such as Scottish cheeses and wines are available as well as baked fayre and dishes from The Butterchurn's own kitchen. Children are always welcome and enjoy seeing and feeding the farmyard pets. This is not a place to be missed. Closed during January. Leave the M90 at Junction 4 and take the B914 Dollar road.

The Butterchurn, Cocklaw Mains Farm, Kelty
Tel: 01383 830169 Fax: 01383 831614

KNOCK HILL. **Knock Hill Racing Circuit** is Scotland's national motorsport centre and, between Easter and October, scarcely a weekend goes by without the roar of engines and the screech of tyres. Every sort of car, motorcycle and even trucks can be seen being pushed to the limit and beyond! There is also a race and rally school where visitors can try their hand behind the wheel for a circuit or two. For details of the racing programme call 01383 723337, budding Nigel Mansells should call 01383 622090.

CULROSS. Pronounced 'Cooross' this fascinating village has been very carefully looked after by the National Trust for Scotland. It is a remarkable example of a 16th and 17th century small town, having changed little in 300 years. The small **Culross Palace** was built between 1597 and 1611 by Sir William Bruce, who developed the seagoing trade in salt and coal from Culross. Featuring crow stepped gables and pantiled roofs outside and painted ceilings inside, it is indeed an outstanding building. Others well worth finding include The Study, Town House, The Ark and The Nunnery. On the outskirts of the village there is also the remains of the 13th century Cistercian abbey, the choir of which is the present Parish Church.

DUNFERMLINE. This ancient town was the seat of many Scottish kings and queens and, in fact, was once itself the capital of Scotland (before the Union of the Crowns in 1603). The palace now lies in ruins beside **Dunfermline Abbey**, which contains many royal graves including, most notably, that of Robert the Bruce who died in 1327. During restoration work on the abbey in 1818, workmen who were excavating came across a vault containing a stone coffin, in which was a skeleton wrapped in thin lead. Some of the teeth were still in the head and there were shreds of gold cloth still clinging to the bones. Any doubt that this was the body of Robert the Bruce was removed when it was noticed that the breastbone was sawn away so that his heart could be removed by Sir James Douglas (Sir James was pledged to take the heart of the King for burial in the Holy Land). Before the new tomb was ready the King lay in state and many hundreds of people came to pay their respects.

Dunfermline boasts a list of interesting buildings and some lovely parks. One of the town's most famous sons was Andrew Carnegie who went to America and became a self-made millionaire in the iron and steel industry. The cottage where he was born in 1835 is now **The Andrew Carnegie Birthplace Museum** and the town contains many fine buildings housing galleries and museums donated by Carnegie.

Opposite the abbey church is **Pittencrieff Glen**, a large ornamental estate with magnificent gardens that was presented to the town by Carnegie in 1903.

LIMEKILNS. The natural seaport for Dunfermline, the village was originally called Gellald or Gellet. Of similar age as the Parish Church is the building known as the **King's Cellar**. More properly, it should be called the Monk's Cellar or Grange as it was a place where rents and tithes were collected.

The pretty village of Limekilns lies off the main road between the Forth Road Bridge and the Kincardine Bridge. It is well worth a stop here to eat at **Il Pescatore Restaurant**. Working as a team, the Restaurant is run by Celia and Reza Bazazi who have been at Il Pescatore for the past three and a half years. The cuisine is classical Italian with also steaks and fish dishes, all freshly cooked to order. The excellent wine list features a great house wine and Italian beers. Reza is renowned for his colourful personality and waistcoats to match! There's a sincere welcome for all their guests, many of whom return again and again to enjoy the good food and great hospitality. Celia and Reza are in the process of converting the building next door into an exclusive hotel which will have six en-suite bedrooms, with the friendly guy in the waistcoat on breakfast patrol! There are many things to do and places to visit in the area so you might want to book early in the new hotel - but don't miss the food.

Il Pescatore, Main Street, Limekilns Tel: 01383 872999

ROSYTH. From the high bridge over the Forth the first views of Fife are of the once great naval dockyards of Rosyth. Here in the glory days, when Britannia did rule the waves, the battleships of the fleet were built and maintained. It was from Rosyth that Admiral Beattie's ill-fated fleet of battlecruisers sailed; joining Jellicoe's Home Fleet to meet the German Grand Fleet at Jutland in 1916. Three ships were lost; Invincible, Indefatigable and Queen Mary, together with their 3000 crew. Only the selfless actions of a turret gunner, who flooded a burning magazine, saved Beattie's own flagship, Lion, from a similar fate. The day's losses led to Beattie's oft quoted understatement: "There appears to be something wrong with our bloody ships today". Times have changed since the days when the Navy could muster over 40 dreadnoughts and Rosyth is now a shadow of its former self.

ABERDOUR. This small town is famous for its silver sands and its attractive position between dramatic cliffs. It was here that an amorous young Frenchman propositioned the young Mary, Queen of Scots, and was beheaded for his unwelcome attentions. The village itself is steeped in history. The quaint harbour is still here and there is also a 12th century church, 14th century castle and an interesting circular doocot, or dovecote.

PETTYCUR. Curiously the name Pettycur appears on many old roadside milestones throughout the Kingdom of Fife, for it was once the

Robinson Crusoe Memorial, Lower Largo

North Carr Lightboat, Anstruther

northern end of a long gone ferry route across the Firth to Leith. It was from the nearby towering cliffs that the last Celtic King of Scotland, Alexander III, accidentally plunged to his death in the spring of 1286.

DYSART. The name Dysart itself actually means desert or hermitage, and it was in the 6th century that St Serf settled at Culross and established a retreat at Dysart. St Serf is credited with the conversion of Fife to Christianity and he reputedly kept a pet robin. His life abounds with rumour and legend; one source claims that he was the son of a Caanite king and an Arab princess, while another says that he was Pope for seven years. Dysart once did a brisk trade in salt with the Continent, though by the end of the 18th century, nailmaking had become its principal industry, with over twelve million nails produced each year.

EAST and **WEST WEMYSS**. These two villages take their name from the old word for sea caves, as does Pittenweem along the coast. The story of the caves is told by the environmental education centre in East village. During the summer months the centre holds occasional open days that include walks and displays on the history, wildlife and industry of the area. The ruins of **Macduff's Castle** stand nearby, probably once occupied by the historical original of the Thane of Fife in Shakespeare's *Macbeth*.

LEVEN. Here a Mr Bissett adorned his cottage garden with seashells, eventually covering it from top to bottom. Sadly the late Mr Bissett's efforts are no more but his shell covered bus remains triumphant, every square inch bar the windows adorned with crustaceans.

LOWER LARGO. This village was the birthplace of Alexander Selkirk whose experiences marooned on the island of Juan Fernandez, off the coast of Chile, inspired Daniel Defoe's *Robinson Crusoe*. A statue of Selkirk, in the dress of a castaway, looks out over the sea from the village. As well as its fine beaches, there are many delightful walks in the area and, for the energetic, the climb to the summit of Largo Law is particularly rewarding.

ELIE and **EARLSFERRY**. These two villages nestle between Chapel Ness and Sauchar Point. Together they are one of Fife's favourite resorts, offering a mile and more of safe sandy beach and a large harbour popular with yachtsmen and windsurfers. There is history here as well. Earlsferry took its name from the time when Macduff, in flight from the murderous King Macbeth, took a ferry from here. In slightly more recent times Elie gained its **Lady's Tower**, built as a bathing box for the noted 17th century beauty, Lady Janet Anstruther. Legend has it that she would send a servant through the streets, ringing a bell and warning villagers to avert their eyes whilst she bathed. How times have changed!

For a refreshing drink or a tasty home-cooked meal, visitors to the delightful coastal town of Elie would be well advised to call in at **The Ship Inn**. Situated in the heart of the town overlooking the beach, as well as being a popular watering hole, this is one of the most well patronised restaurants in the area. Originally built as a cottage in 1794, it has been an inn since 1838 and is beautifully decorated throughout, with lovely pew style seating and wooden tables enhancing its character and charm. The 'ship' theme is emphasised with new and old ships photographs adorning the walls and the cosy restaurant provides an intimate setting in which to enjoy the excellent menu whilst admiring the wonderful views over the Firth of Forth.

The Ship Inn, The Toft, Elie Tel: 01333 330246

ST MONANS. It is hard to image, gazing over the now tranquil sea-lapped harbour, that this was once one of the busiest harbours in Scotland with scarcely a quiet hour. Not that the sea has been forgotten here, for the 18th century boatyard still builds and repairs wooden fishing vessels. The ancient church of St Monan was founded here as long ago as AD 400 and it has been long regarded as a place of healing ever since David I was reputedly cured here of an arrow wound. Above the village, on a headland, are the remains of **Newark Castle** that once belonged to General Leslie, 1st Earl of Leven, a key Covenanter.

With its superb seafood menu and magnificent south-facing view across the Firth of Forth, the **Cabin Restaurant and Bar** is one of the most celebrated eating places on the Fife coast. The sheltered terrace is a real suntrap in fine weather, and from here customers can watch the crab and lobster-boats coming in to land at nearby St Monans harbour. Since taking over in 1993, Angela, Shuna, and now Tim and Sophie, have established a reputation for serving some of the finest seafood in the locality. Both the restaurant and bar menus feature a superb range of dishes, including fresh Pittenweem haddock, halibut, turbot, lemon sole and 'smokies' from the St Monans smokehouse. However, the crowning glory is the Cabin's spectacular seafood platter - a breathtaking feast which includes fresh lobster, crab, oysters, prawns, scallops and smoked salmon. There is also a good selection of steaks, meat and vegetarian dishes, as well as a choice of daily specials on the chalkboard. The bar provides a pleasant atmosphere to enjoy an aperitif or after dinner drink, and is usually filled with a lively assortment of visitors and locals who meet to exchange tales of the day's activities over a relaxing drink or bite to eat.

The Cabin Restaurant and Bar, 16 West End, St Monans Tel: 01333 730327

PITTENWEEM. Many of the little houses in the village have been restored by the National Trust for Scotland and, away from the harbour, the quiet streets and lanes invite exploration. Its name is derived from an ancient word for sea caves and, sure enough, amongst the houses is **St Fillan's Cave**. Once a retreat of the early Christian missionary it has for the most part been respected as a shrine for many centuries, though fishermen did once store nets in it. Re-dedicated in the 1930s, services are still held in this unusual holy place.

ANSTRUTHER. Pronounced 'Anster', the town has strong connections with the sea and it is fitting that it is home to the **Scottish Fisheries Museum**. Established in 1969 in buildings dating back as far as the 16th century, the Museum offers the visitor a vivid insight into the hard and dangerous world of the fisherman. Using tableaux, models and striking paintings their story is told. The Museum covers every aspect of the fishing industry, including whaling and industrial salmon farming, as well as the lives of those who worked ashore; in the industry's heyday there were four ashore for every one at sea. In the harbour are 'Reaper' and 'Zulu' a pair of lovingly restored fishing vessels. The Museum also has the poignant Memorial to Scottish Fishermen Lost at Sea.

Anstruther's other maritime museum spent 40 years helping protect seafarers. **North Carr Lightship** was stationed at the notorious Carr Rocks off the Fife coast and is now a tribute to the men who served on lightships all around the coastline. From 1933 to 1975 her 500,000 candlepower lamp swept the Firth of Forth and her foghorn boomed out a melancholy note. They were a rare breed the men who manned her through the worst the North Sea storms, keeping her vital generators running, standing four hour watches on her open deck and living with the non-stop clamour of her engines and the crashing of the waves.

Exploring the streets is a rewarding experience and one of Anstruther's curiosities is **Buckie House**. 'Buckie' is the local dialect for shell and the eccentric who owned the house covered it inside and out with shells. He even requested that he be buried in a shell-encrusted coffin.

Housed in the former Tollbooth gaol building on the shore at Anstruther, the **Bakehouse Tearoom** specialises in home-cooking and baking, fresh local seafood and a wide variety of snacks and meals. A homely family atmosphere makes this a popular spot with both locals and visitors alike - most patrons returning time after time. Call in and see why! Adjoining the Tearoom is **Family A Fayre** and the sister shop **Lady Fayre**, these two charming shops are run by local sisters Jenny Watson and Mary Hutchinson. They cater for all dress senses and tastes from baby, through childhood, to adults. As well as a wide variety of quality and individual ladies dresses, tops, coats, blouses and skirts; there's a wide choice of fashion accessories - scarves, earrings, pedants, chains and other costume jewellery. Hand-crafted jewellery boxes and trinket cases, perfume sprays and atomisers are a popular choice for the discerning lady's dressing table. Wedding outfits are a speciality. Fashion shows are regularly organised for charities so do ask Jenny for details of forthcoming shows.

Bakery Tearoom, Family A Fayre and Lady Fayre, Shore Street, Anstruther
Tel: 01333 310106

ISLE OF MAY. Lying out in the Firth, the island was, centuries ago, the home of Benedictine priors dedicated to St Adrian, murdered on the island in AD 870 and it is now a haven for razorbills, shags and guillemots. The island is also the site of Scotland's first lighthouse, built in 1636 and now preserved as an ancient monument. There is still a light on the island which dates from 1816 but is no longer manned. During World War II the waters around the island were used as practice ranges by torpedo bomber crews.

CRAIL itself is the last and most easterly of the East Neuk ports. It has one of the most photographed harbours in Scotland; picture postcard as it may be Crail is also home to Fife's crab and lobster fleet and remains a working port. The red tiled houses tumble down to the harbour and it is indeed a delightful sight. During the summer, on Sundays, the town's small museum runs guided walks which give a real flavour of life in the port over the centuries. Amongst the many fascinating buildings are the early 16th century Tollbooth, which now doubles as library and Town Hall, with it fishy weather vane and the striking Dutch Tower which has a bell cast in Holland and dated 1520.

Crail churchyard not only holds the graves of 21 brave airmen who used the practice ranges at the Isle of May but also a large boulder that, so the story goes, the Devil hurled from the Isle of May. Why he threw it no one knows but he missed the Church; a good thing too, as the church is one of the oldest and most interesting buildings in the village.

The **Hazelton Guest House** is situated in the heart of the lovely old fishing port of Crail, opposite the tourist information centre and famous 16th century Tollbooth. This delightful establishment is owned and personally run by Rita and Alan Brown, charming hosts who extend a warm welcome and some of the most impressive hospitality in the area. The seven centrally heated guest bedrooms are all comfortably furnished and equipped with colour televisions, tea and coffee making facilities and washbasins. A number also have a view of the old Mercat Cross in Marketgate, a scene of serenity which was once one of the busiest market places in Europe. Rita is an award winning chef who has recently earned the Hazelton a place in the coveted Taste of Scotland scheme. She is renowned for providing the very finest Scottish cuisine from the best local ingredients, including fresh fish, vegetables and locally raised beef and lamb. The menu changes daily and there is also a wine list offering a selection of quality wines at reasonable prices. Diners should call in advance to reserve their table. The Hazelton also offers excellent value inclusive breaks during the off-peak autumn, winter and spring season.

Hazelton Guest House, 29 Marketgate, Crail Tel: 01333 450250

FIFE NESS. With its nature rambles, seashore walks and adventure play area **Cambo Country Park** is a great place for all the family to relax. Cambo is also an important rare breeds centre helping to preserve many of the less common breeds of farm animal once familiar sights all over Scotland.

FALFIELD. Ideally located half a mile south of Peat Inn village and seven miles from St Andrews, **Millhouse** has proved itself to be a superb base for golf fanatics and those visiting the East Neuk fishing villages and other historic attractions.

Millhouse

The house was originally an old steading, but has been lovingly converted by its owners Andrew and Ann Small, into the splendid family home that you see before you today. Offering full bed and breakfast facilities, Ann and Andrew do all they can to ensure your every comfort has been catered for. Each of the three individually decorated bedrooms have full en-suite facilities and all guests have free use of the comfortable TV lounge and spacious, beamed dining area.

The professional refurbishment of this lavish property can be seen at its best in the lounge and dining room, each having a large, open stone fireplace and quality antique furnishings. The Millhouse also has a large adjoining building which is home to a superb collection of old farming tools and machinery, many dating back centuries. A traditional Scottish breakfast is a speciality of the house and consists of cereal or porridge followed by eggs, bacon, sausage, potato, scones and tomatoes, but we do recommend a bit of exercise after this delicious feast! Andrew and Ann also cater for the vegetarian guest and offer a fresh selection of stewed fruits followed by kippers or haddock when available, and evening meals are provided with prior arrangement.

Millhouse, Falfield, Peat Inn Tel: 01334 840609

The Firth of Tay

ST ANDREWS. The calm of this ancient burgh today gives no hint of the violent and bloody struggles that took place here during the Reformation. One particular churchman, Cardinal David Beaton, was particularly relentless in the punishment of considered heretics, watching more than one victim burning at the stake. He, in turn, was murdered by the Reformers, who were joined by John Knox and occupied the castle, until the French attacked in 1547 forcing a surrender. Knox was taken away and subjected to the life of a galley slave for 18 months. He swore to return to St Andrews for vengeance upon the places of worship and, indeed, came back to Scotland eventually in 1559 to incite his followers to destroy the cathedral.

Despite Knox's attentions the remains of **St Andrew's Cathedral** still give a vivid impression of the scale and splendour of what was once Scotland's biggest church. From St Rule's Tower, in the grounds, there are superb views of the town and surrounding countryside.

Today there is a far more peaceful air in the town and the place attracts holidaymakers and visitors to its stretches of safe, sandy beaches with delightful dunes and wonderfully clear waters. St Andrews is also home to Scotland's oldest university, founded by Papal decree in 1411. It has many fine old buildings right in the centre of the town; which are only accessible to the public during July and August when twice daily guided tours operate, the Tourist Information Office on South Street will have the details.

GOLF

Golf is Scotland's national game and courses can be found almost anywhere with there being little need for visitors to be introduced and the cost is less than most countries, including England. The British Open is held at many famous Scottish courses including Troon, Turnberry and St Andrews.

The exact origins of golf and when and by whom the first game of golf was played is open to dispute but there is no question that the game, in terms of the facilities, equipment and formulation of the rules, is entirely Scottish. By the 16th century, the game had become so popular that three Acts of Parliament were passed, to no great effect, insisting that more time be devoted to archery practice and less time to hitting a small ball into a hole with a long stick.

Courses in Scotland, as in many parts of the world, are divided into those on coastal links and those inland, usually in a parkland setting. Of the coastal courses, the ones at St Andrews and Dornoch are among the finest in the world. Just to get a flavour of how passionate Scotsmen and women are about golf, Ayr has three courses whilst Troon, just up the coast, has five. And there are, in Glasgow, more than a dozen courses within the city limits.

However, the most famous golfing location of all has to be St Andrews with its five courses and a new one just opening. The Old Course is a British Open venue and, though there are no fancy trimmings here like specially planted trees or flamboyant shrubbery, there are some curiously named bunkers, Hell, Coffin and Grave, which have been known to live up to their names.

The Royal and Ancient Golf Club at St Andrews was founded, as the Society of St Andrews Golfers, in 1754 by 22 gentlemen who admired the ancient and healthy exercise of golf. The annual playing in of the captain remains the key event of the Club's calendar. Now the world's premier club, it shares the framing of the rules of golf with the very much younger United States Golf Association.

During term time Sunday afternoons are colourful affairs as the students stroll up and down the stone piers of the harbour in their red robes, a tradition that goes back centuries. The pier, incidentally, contains stone from both the cathedral and the castle.

No Scottish town with so rich a history could be complete without a castle. St Andrews is no exception and the **Castle** has as a long and bloody history as any. There is a bottle dungeon hollowed out of solid rock, from which death was the only release, as well as a mine and counter-mine hacked out beneath it during one of several sieges. Cardinal Beaton was murdered here in 1546 and the first round of the Reformation was fought out in the siege that followed.

And, of course, there is golf, with St Andrews, home to possibly the most famous golf course in the world at the **Royal and Ancient Golf Course** founded in 1754. The history of the game is much older and has its origins in the 14th century. Its popularity in the 1400s led to its banning in 1457, the Scottish parliament feeling it took people away from archery practice. The ban was repeated by James IV as he found the game 'unprofitabill' for his subjects. The Stuart kings were ardent players and so to, it was rumoured, was Mary, Queen of Scots. St Andrews naturally is home to the **British Golf Museum**, which uses the latest in audio-visual displays and touch activation to tell the 500 year story of Golf, fascinating even for non-players.

Grange Inn

Set on a hillside overlooking St Andrews Bay and the hills beyond, **Grange Inn** has served local people and visitors alike since the mid-sixties. In that time it has been operated by a number of people but is now in the guiding hands of Peter Aretz whose wealth of experience in the hotel and catering world is recognised as being amongst the best. The buildings which originally formed the Inn date back to the 17th, 18th and 19th centuries. The views from the Inn are stunning, complemented by the well kept gardens and small kitchen garden to supplement the fresh produce always used in the kitchen. Fresh locally caught fish are generally available and on occasions the local fishermen come up with a whopping 100 kilogram halibut. Pork, beef, lamb, venison and poultry are on most occasions bought from Scottish suppliers to provide the freshest of produce.

Three restaurant areas present a welcoming ambiance and, particularly in winter, when the open fires are ablaze. Local people in particular like the Caddies' and Ploughman's bars. The former is a dining area for smokers whereas the Patio and Bay Rooms are exclusively for non-smokers. The comparatively small wine list of 44 wines is carefully selected each year by attending wine tastings and wines from France, Italy, Australia, New Zealand, South Africa, Germany and other countries world wide are featured on the list. Malt whiskies are well represented too, as are grain and blended whiskies, and the popular draught and bottled beers. The Grange has maintained and improved on its reputation for good food and drink, attractive surroundings and excellent service. Featured in Egon Ronay and Taste of Scotland guides.

The Grange Inn, Grange Road, St Andrews Tel: 01334 472670
Fax: 01334 472604

Described in the Los Angeles Times as being "as famous for its wine card as for its menu", **Aikman's Bar-Bistro** was conceived as a result of tempting aromas of freshly ground coffee emanating from this building, then a grocery firm named Aikman and Terras, which attracted the present graduate owners in their student days at St Andrews University. However, the fresh coffee aromas have been replaced by the equally tempting aromas of the freshly prepared meals and bar snacks - reflecting a truly cosmopolitan and international menu.

Aikman's Bar-Bistro

The evening menu features such favourite 'Starters' as Pate, Melon and Gaspacho and Cullen Skink soups and Brie wedges to more exotic ideas such as Chinese Dimsum and Jalapos from Mexico. The Main Course offers 'home grown' specialities such as Tay Salmon, Trout, Venison and other game dishes alongside dishes from Europe, Mexico, Scandinavia and many other places. Over the past ten years, Aikman's have represented over 300 different Real Ales in its Cellar Bar. Their quality and variety has played a large part in their continued presence in the CAMRA 'Good Beer Guide' since 1987. Malt whiskies are also well represented with a continually changing list of some 30 malts, and the owners will consider it a pleasure to guide you through the range at a leisurely pace! Aikman's opens from 11 am to 11 pm daily; Sunday 12.30 pm to 10 pm.

Aikman's Bar-Bistro, 32 Bell Street, St Andrews Tel: 01334 477425

One of the most delightful eating places in St Andrews can be found in the heart of the town at No 49 South Street. **The Merchant's House** is a handsome town house whose impressive stone-flagged barrel vault dates back to the late 16th century. Charles II is reputed to have visited the house in the mid 17th century, and it is from around this period that its distinctive painted ceiling is believed to date. This features a charming design of fruit and flowers and is thought to have been moved to its current position at a later date where it lay undisturbed behind panelling for many decades until the 1930s. Today, the Merchant's House is a stylish licensed restaurant and coffee shop which is owned and personally run by Jennifer and Angus Mitchell. The atmosphere is delightful with old pine furniture, a conservatory, and sepia-tinted photographs of university professors looking down from the walls. The food too is superb. The lunchtime menu features an impressive range of international dishes, including many suitable for vegetarians, all of which are freshly prepared each day on the premises. It also features widest choice of teas available in St Andrews, along with a good selection of alcoholic beverages. The Merchant's House is open from 10 am to 5.30 pm, seven days a week.

The Merchant's House, 49 South Street, St Andrews Tel: 01334 472595

Snicket Ceramics is a delightful small working pottery situated down a narrow alley (or snicket) just off South Street, St Andrews. Open all year round, and every day during the summer months, the pottery produces a superb range of hand-made items, many of which are for sale. Although this is first and foremost a workshop, there is also an attractive display area where visitors are welcome to browse. The work of potter Ian Wood is bright, cheerful and full of humour: among the many shapes and designs on view is a charming range of ceramic pigs, sheep and chickens, each of which has its own unique hand-painted expression. From the display area, visitors are usually able to see Ian at work, perhaps throwing on the wheel or decorating work prior to firing in the kiln. He is constantly developing new ideas and is happy to undertake special commissions for items produced to a client's own specifications. Snicket Ceramics is the ideal place, not only for those wishing to buy something special from Scotland, but also for those wishing to observe a genuine craftsman at work using traditional techniques in a unique fashion.

Snicket Ceramics, 57a South Street, St Andrews Tel: 01344 472985

AROUND ST ANDREWS

LEUCHARS. The village is perhaps best known for its RAF base from which jets fly overhead on their way to and from the training grounds in the north. The airbase annually hosts the Battle of Britain Airshow in September, an opportunity to marvel at the planes of old and the latest flying technology. History of an older but no less dramatic kind can be found at **Earlshall Castle**, a mile or so east of the village.

Earlshall, despite its five foot thick walls, battlements and musket loops, has a feeling of warmth and welcome about it. It is relatively new as Scottish castles go, being built in 1546 by Sir William Bruce. His ancestors, the Baron and Baroness Earlshall, retain the Castle as their private family home to this day.

Inside the Castle has a renown long gallery, it coved painted ceiling depicts the arms of the principle families of Scotland, together with many fabulous and fanciful mythical beasts. The walls are lined with over a hundred Scottish broadswords, reminders of a more bloody age. Here too can be seen the romantic 'Lynkit' hearts symbol, which incorporated the initials of Sir William Bruce, great grandson of the builder, and his wife Dame Agnes Lindsey. The motif is still used, over 350 years later, on the estates signs.

In 1561 Mary, Queen of Scots visited the Castle and her bedchamber, with its period furnishings, is on view. There are many other articles and artifacts from the Jacobite period displayed throughout the Castle. Sir Andrew, The Bloody Bruce, is said to haunt the Castle, his ghost's footfall is heard on the staircase from time to time. The pastimes of hunting, shooting and fishing are celebrated in the rod and gun room, with its antique firearms, old sporting guns and fishing tackle from past generations. The museum room contains many military trophies, including a set of bagpipes played at Waterloo in 1815.

The Castle grounds were relaid over 100 years ago by renown Scottish architect Sir Robert Lorimer. They feature magnificent yew topiary, herbaceous borders and a series of small gardens within gardens. There is also a fine herb garden and a 'secret garden'.

Northeast of Leuchars is the **Tentsmuir Point National Nature Reserve**. It is a large reserve of some 47 acres that runs from Tentsmuir forest down to the foreshore at Abertay Sands, and is a haven for a wide variety of birds and animals.

WORMIT. The village lies at the point where the railway from Edinburgh to Dundee crosses the Firth on the infamous Tay Bridge.

MOONZIE. The name is a probable derivation of the Gaelic for corn plain and, indeed, this area (known as the Howe of Fife) is a fertile land of rolling hills covered with the checkerboard fields of arable farming. The old kirk of Moonzie, standing on a hilltop, used to be known as the 'Visible Kirk' by sailors who caught sight of it on the skyline as they sailed the Tay. Ruined **Lordscairnie Castle** was the stronghold of a 15th century Earl of Crawford; a fearsomely hirsute character, called Earl Beardie behind his back. His involvement in a failed attempt to overthrow James II saw him forced to dress in beggars' rags and grovel for forgiveness before the King's court.

NEWBURGH. This is a town of many fine buildings and, in particular, keep an eye out for the marriage lintel at 60 High Street, where the names of the newlyweds has been carved alongside a sailing ship, showing the husband was a master mariner. The harbour looks across the Tay to wide expanses of reed bed on the north shore. These are still harvested every winter for roofing thatch.

AUCHTERMUCHTY. This delightful sounding name is actually Gaelic for 'Upland for Swine'! To the southwest of the town lie the Lomond Hills, which contain a number of weird rock formations, formed by the erosion of soft underlying rock leaving sandstone boulders doing a balancing act. Easiest to get to is the **Bannet Stane** or Bonnet Stone, so named for its shape. On the west side of the hills is Carlin Maggie; Maggie the Witch, who so irritated the Devil that he turned her into stone for all eternity. She stands here, a 40 foot column of shattered basalt, admiring the view.

FALKLAND. The splendid buildings, in Renaissance style, of **Falkland Palace** date from 1501-41 and it was the favourite seat of James V, who died here in 1542, and of his daughter, Mary, Queen of Scots. There is a rather grisly story that Robert II died here after being imprisoned and forced, by starvation, to eat his own flesh. A woman in an adjoining cell, who is said to have fed him for a while from her own breasts, was put to death for her trouble. When James VI was here he was forced to listen to the preachings of John Knox the reformist. Legend has it that the King kept interrupting the preacher until he was reminded in no uncertain terms that the King was merely "God's silly Vassal". Apart from being a fine palace with some exemplary architecture of the period, the gardens contain the original royal tennis court, the oldest in Britain, built in 1539.

The Malt Barn Inn has quite a history with roots back in the 17th century when, as a brewery, it was in the hands of the Bonthrone family until it was eventually sold to the Distillers Company in 1947 and became a malting. Local residents are regulars in the welcoming lounge bar and are more than happy to regale visitors with tales of yesteryear about Falkland and the surrounding area. The village of Newton of Falkland grew up around the Maltings which is today the Malt Barn Inn. It is very central to many of Fife's charming attractions including Falkland Palace, the Scottish Deer Park and St Andrews Golf Club. The Inn's recent new owners are Mark and Monica Henderson; Mark is Scottish and Monica, the chef, hails from Sweden. The food therefore shows a marked emphasis towards Swedish cuisine. A regular feature being plank steaks (the food is served on a Swedish oak plank) on which is served a range of succulent steaks or fish, surrounded by a selection of fresh vegetables and topped with an accompanying sauce. Lunchtime brings 'Smorgasbord' - open sandwiches with a choice of fillings such as prawns, seafood, mussels, salads and more. Unique to Scotland, this Scottish/ Swedish blend of cuisines creates a wide choice of mouthwatering dishes. The bar has a selection of real ales, malt and blended whiskies, bottled and draught beers, spirits and a comprehensive wine cellar.

Malt Barn Inn, Main Street, Newton of Falkland
Tel & Fax: 01337 857589

CUPAR. Here, in Duffus Park, is the **Sir Douglas Bader Garden for the Disabled**. This famous World War II fighter pilot worked tirelessly for the cause of the disabled until his death a few years ago and this garden is a tribute to his works. Designed to be worked on and enjoyed by the disabled, it features raised beds, water gardens, aviary and rock garden.

There are several interesting places to explore within striking distance of Cupar. On the A916 two miles south of the town is the unusually named **Hill of Tarvit**. An Edwardian country mansion designed by Sir Robert Lorimar (who rebuilt Earlshall Castle) for Fredrick Bonar Sharp. Bonar Sharp was a noted art collector and the furnishings, paintings, tapestries, Chinese porcelain and bronzes reflect his admirable tastes. The house also has well laid out gardens. Almost next door to the house is **Scotstarvit Tower**, a finely preserved five storey L-plan castle which lost one of its heraldic fireplaces to the Hill of Tarvit.

Near to Cupar, on the A91, is the **Scottish Deer Centre**, which offers a unique opportunity to see, and even feed and touch, these noble beasts.

A real find in Cupar is **Ostlers Close Restaurant**, a small and intimate establishment which lies hidden in a narrow lane off the main street. This enchanting eating place is housed in a 17th century building which is full of genuine character and atmosphere.

Ostlers Close Restaurant

Proprietors Jimmy and Amanda Graham specialise in the finest modern-style cuisine which they lovingly prepare using the best of Scotland's natural larder. Regular ingredients include fresh seafood and prawns from Pittenweem, salmon from the River Tay, free range ducks, local game birds in season, venison, and wild local mushrooms; special diets can be catered for on request. A winner of the 1996 Chef of the Year Award, Jimmy is renowned for his cooking throughout Scotland. The menu changes daily according to the availability of produce and features an imaginative selection of Scottish dishes with a Continental style influence. The restaurant is licensed and offers an impressive list of fine wines, making this the perfect place to enjoy an appetising lunch or romantic candlelit dinner. It has been awarded 3 Rosettes by the AA and is featured in all major restaurant guides. Open Tuesdays to Saturdays, 12.15 pm to 2 pm and 7 pm till late, with last orders taken at 9.30 pm. (Booking essential at lunchtimes.)

Ostlers Close Restaurant, 25 Bonnygate, Cupar Tel: 01334 655574

CERES. This pretty village, pronounced 'Series', is home to the **Fife Folk Museum**, which is housed in 18th and 19th century cottages and a 17th century weighhouse.

STRATHKINNESS. Just two miles west of St Andrews, we found the truly superb **Fossil House and Cottage** at Strathkinness. The home of Alistair and Kornelia, it was built in 1876 and together with Fossil Cottage, it forms a pleasant, mature courtyard development in this peaceful village. The property has been tastefully converted to offer quality bed and breakfast facilities in very pleasing surroundings. All the en-suite bedrooms are at ground level and have direct access to the courtyard, beautiful garden and car park. The rooms are tastefully decorated and delightfully colour co-ordinated in warm welcoming colours with facilities more akin to hotel standard, with remote colour television, radio clock alarm, hair dryer, trouser press, hot drinks facilities and, believe it or not, guest refrigerator. By prior arrangement, a three course evening meal is prepared from a choice of home-cooked dishes using as much home grown produce as possible and reviving some long forgotten recipes. You will be impressed by the quality and amazed by the reasonable price. In the evening, a warm comfortable guest lounge and conservatory awaits with well-stocked mini library of books and video tapes. Alistair and Kornelia have their own Inverarity Whisky, so - enjoy a nightcap! The big breakfast is a real challenge though you may choose exactly what you wish from the very detailed breakfast menu. All in all, one cannot fail to be impressed with the facilities, quality and warmth of this first class holiday home. Scottish Tourist Board awarded 3 Crowns Highly Commended, AA QQQQ selected and RAC acclaimed.

Fossil House, 12-14 Main Street, Strathkinness Tel: 01334 850639

Falkland Palace

CHAPTER SEVEN

STIRLING, FALKIRK &
CLACKMANNANSHIRE

Stirling Castle

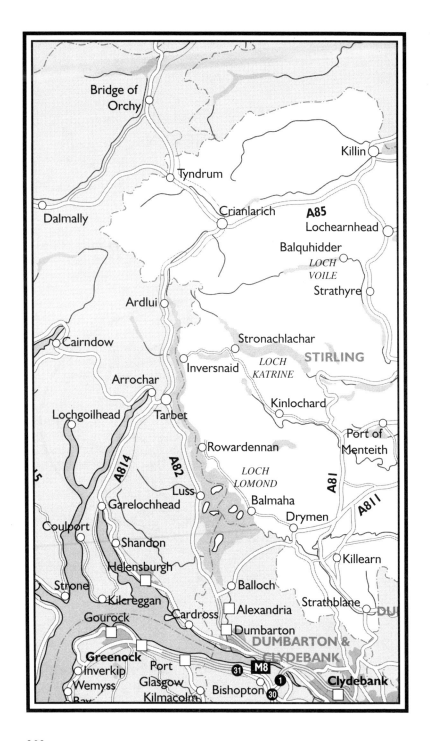

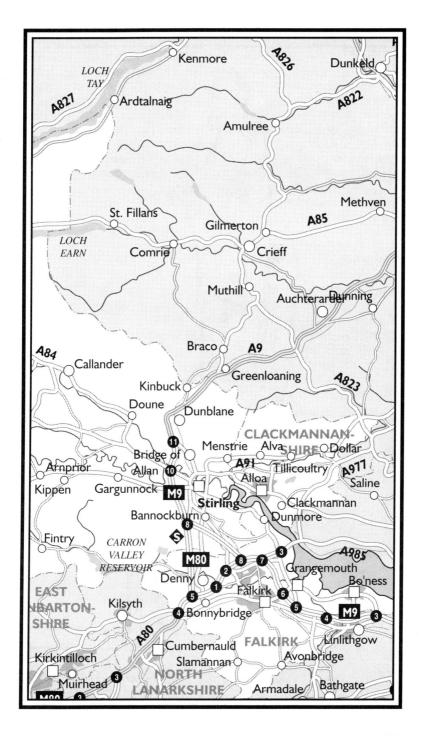

Robert the Bruce, Stirling Castle

CHAPTER SEVEN

STIRLING, FALKIRK &
CLACKMANNANSHIRE

Falkirk

FALKIRK. An industrial town today, Falkirk is historically known for two battles fought here in 1298 and 1746. In the first, Edward I defeated Wallace and, in the second, the retreating Young Pretender inflicted a severe repulse on pursuing Government forces. **Falkirk Museum** has displays covering the archaeology and history of the area.

Good sections of the Roman **Antonine Wall**, built between the Firth of Forth and Kilpatrick, lie close to Falkirk. Built around AD 140, it was planned by Emperor Antonius Pius who wished to abandon Hadrian's Wall, recently completed, and adopt a more forward policy towards Scotland. Unlike Hadrian's Wall, which was built of stone, the Antonine was a turf rampart on a stone base with a ditch to the north and a military road to the south. At **Callendar Park** a good length of the Antonine Wall ditch can be found and, at **Callendar House** next to the park, an exhibition tells the long history of the house. **Rough Castle**, four miles west of Falkirk near Bonnybridge, is by far the best preserved fortified site on the Wall.

This town boasts Britain's shortest street: **Tolbooth Street** which still manages to accommodate a tearoom, pub and shoe shop in its 20 paces end-to-end.

Ideally situated for visitors wishing a central base, (Edinburgh, Stirling, Glasgow, Perth, Fife, The Trossachs and Loch Lomond are all readily accessible) **Darroch House** is a well proportioned Victorian Manor set in nine acres of garden and woodland yet only a short walk from Falkirk's attractive town centre. Built in 1838, this family home was bought in the 1900s by the proprietors Great Grandfather and has been handed down through the generations ever since. Today it is owned and run by Rod and Heather Mitchell, who have the ability to make their guests feel at home the moment that they step through the front door. There are three large and well appointed guest rooms, each offering its visitor spacious en-suite facilities with Sky TV, radio/alarm, telephone, hairdryer and a complimentary tea and coffee tray, there is also a fax machine available if needed. A plentiful Scottish breakfast is served in the original dining room of the house, which is filled with traditional Victorian furniture and overlooks the tennis lawn and a pasture which is home to two donkeys. An evening meal is also available by prior arrangement and the overall atmosphere of this charming house is a friendly, relaxed and comfortable one.

Darroch House, Camelon Road, Falkirk
Tel: 01324 623041 Fax: 01324 626288

Situated in Falkirk, only five minutes walk from the town centre, **The Hotel Cladhan** is the perfect base for a visit to Scotland's Central Region. Built in 1971 by the family who still owns and runs it, the Cladhan is set in the grounds of the Callendar Estate, adjacent to the beautiful Callendar House. The 39 comfortable and spacious guest rooms all have en-suite facilities and offer an in-house video, colour TV, telephone, hairdryer, trouser press and complimentary tea and coffee tray.

The Cladhan Hotel

The Hotel has a first class restaurant that is Egon Ronay Recommended and offers a varied and delicious menu. For your starter you might choose Deep Fried Brie with a Cumberland sauce and, for main course, Fillet of Lamb Arlene, served in its own juices with a hint of mint and garlic. There are also a good selection of snacks and children's courses if you only want a light lunch or wish to save yourself for the evening meal! The attractive bars serve a wide variety of beverages, including a good selection of fine malt whiskies, which you can sit and enjoy at your leisure in the pleasant, Bistro-style surroundings. The Hotel is within walking distance of Falkirk's exciting new shopping centre, yet most of the bedrooms overlook the beautiful Callendar Estate and its gardens. Within minutes you can be on cool forest walks and nature trails or boating on the lake. Business or pleasure, the emphasis on comfort and service is evident, so if you are in the area why not visit Cladhan Hotel and see just what can be achieved with a little thought and a lot of experience.

Cladhan Hotel, Kemper Avenue, Falkirk Tel: 01324 627421

AROUND FALKIRK

GRANGEMOUTH. Lying on the Firth of Forth, it was here that the world's petroleum industry had its humble beginnings. In 1851 Dr James 'Paraffin' Young established Young's Paraffin and Mineral Oil Company. At its height the Scottish shale-oil industry employed 40,000 at 120 different sites. Many of these old sites can be rediscovered by following the **Paraffin Young Heritage Trail**, which starts in the town. The last shale-mine closed in 1962, shale-oil refining having been rendered uncompetitive by the crude oil gushing from wells in Arabia. Young's company still exists as part of BP, who have a huge refinery here that dominates the shore front. Incidentally Young anonymously financed David Livingstone's many expeditions to Africa.

When **Grangemouth Sports Stadium** opened on 9th July 1966 it was the first all-weather track in the United Kingdom and it continues as the heart of Scottish athletics, hosting a large number of championships and major fixtures every year, in addition to the local authority's own programme of competition. **Polmonthill Ski Centre**, just off the M9 motorway at junction 4, has a 110 metre artificial ski slope and a 15 metre starter slope, both of which are floodlit. The main run, on the historic setting of the Antonine Wall, is lubricated with a sprinkler system and is serviced by a button style ski lift.

BORROWSTOUNNESS. Downstream from Grangemouth lies Borrowstounness, better known now as the less tongue twisting **Bo'ness**. The town flourished for many years on the industrial success of the area, a story recalled in a fine museum at the nearby **Kinneil House** and estate. Another legacy of the industrial revolution admirably preserved is the **Bo'ness & Kinneil Railway**. The volunteers of the Scottish Railway Preservation Society run steam and diesel trains at weekends between April and October, and daily from mid-July to late August. Their Victorian station was painstakingly moved from Wormit

The Pineapple, Dunmore

in Fife and reassembled in Bo'ness. As well as all the paraphernalia of a working railway there are the additional attractions of a working man's home of the 1920s, in Hamilton's Cottage, opposite the station and at the other end of the line Birkhill Fireclay Mine, set in the side of Avon Gorge.

BONNYBRIDGE. Though the approach looks unpromising **Rough Castle** is the best preserved of the Roman forts along the Antonine Wall. The earthworks of the barracks, headquarters, granary and bathhouse are clearly visible, and through the centre runs the military road that the connected the forts along the wall. Started only ten years after the more famous Hadrian's Wall, it was built and originally manned by Legions recruited in Italy.

DENNY. This small manufacturing town, on the River Carron, lies to the east of the Kilsyth Hills.

Those looking for exceptional farmhouse accommodation within easy reach of the M80 and M876 trunk routes should make a point of finding **The Topps** at Denny. This luxurious chalet farmhouse is the home of Jennifer and Alistair Steel, local people who have lived in the valley for over three and a half decades and who first began offering bed and breakfast accommodation in 1982. Today, they have eight beautifully appointed guest bedrooms, all fitted with en-suite facilities, wood panelling, antique furniture and appealing tartan decoration. The Topps is also renowned for its food. Jennifer and Alistair serve delicious Scottish breakfasts at times to suit their guests and superb evening meals using fresh local ingredients wherever possible. On the day we visited, starters included gravadlax and scallops with monkfish, and main dishes included fresh River Tay trout, wild duck and Scottish lamb. The desserts too were mouthwatering, with such delicacies as summer fruit pudding, local raspberries and Glenmorangie gateaux. Scottish Tourist Board 3 Crown Commended, the Topps is RAC Highly Acclaimed and has been awarded the coveted 3 Qs by the AA and the emblem of the Taste of Scotland.

The Topps, Fintry Road, Denny
Tel: 01324 822471 Fax: 01324 823099

DUNMORE PARK. Here is a hidden gem of rare quality, one of Britain's finest follies, **The Pineapple**. Quite why, in 1761, John Murray, 4th Earl of Dunmore felt compelled to have a 53 foot stone fruit built is anyone's guess but it makes a quite unusual sight. This strange building was supposedly built as a garden retreat and must have astounded the locals who would never have seen a pineapple.

Two hundred years later The Pineapple is no longer a rare and exotic luxury but the building hasn't lost its ability to amaze the onlooker. It is not open to the public, but it can be rented! For a week in Britain's most bizarre holiday cottage call The Landmark Trust (01628 825925), who let all manner of unusual buildings all over Britain.

The Clackmannanshire

ALLOA. This strange name comes from the Celtic and means 'swift ford'. Its origin no doubt refers to the magnificent sweep of the Firth of Forth which stretches out beneath the town. Before the river silted up it had formed part of Scotland's naval dockyard in the 16th century. Here in 1511, James IV launched the great flagship of the Royal Scottish Navy, the 'Great Michael', which had reputedly taken up all of the woods of Fife to build. With 300 guns she was far ahead of other ships of the time, and was to be the pride of the King and Navy.

She spent her first two years docked for want of a better purpose, and when finally taken out, she was entrusted to the Earl of Arran, who had never actually been to sea. It is to this day a mystery as to what happened to this extravagant and costly ship. Rumour has that a wrecked hull, found years later at the port of Brest in France, was indeed all that was left of the Great Michael.

Alloa Tower, in the lower east part of the town, dates back to the 15th century as was built by the Erskine family. It was, at one time, the childhood home of James V, Mary, Queen of Scots and James VI.

AROUND ALLOA

CLACKMANNAN. This small wool manufacturing town has a 17th century stepped **Cross** and an old **Tolbooth**, built in 1592 and still with its tower, courtroom, prison and jailor's dwelling. The mysterious **Clach (Stone) of Mannan** was placed in its present position in 1833 and is sometimes said to be sacred to the pagan god, Mannan.

Clackmannan Tower, dating from the 14th and 15th centuries, is sited on a hill named King's Seat; once the residence of Malcolm IV it also has connections with Robert the Bruce.

DOLLAR. This was the scene, in AD 877, of the defeat of the Scots in battle with the Danes. **The Dollar Academy** is a fine building well worth a look, being a good example of Classical Georgian architecture built by Sir William Playfair in 1819. Sir William also designed the Academy and National Gallery in Edinburgh.

In the glen above Dollar sits **Castle Campbell**, commanding long views over the plains of the Firth. Built at the end of the 15th century, it was burned by Cromwell, although the ruin is still quite impressive. The Castle was once known as Castle Gloume, set as it is between the glens of Care and Sorrow and by the waters of Grief. It is a mystery why the area should feature so much verbal depression.

MENSTRIE. Early in the 17th century the owner of **Menstrie Castle**, Sir William Alexander suggested to James VI that creating and selling baronetcies in Nova Scotia could raise funds to develop this 'New Scotland' in Canada. Though poorly subscribed the Baronetcies were created and in the castle's Nova Scotia Room 109 baronet's shields are on display. The castle has been converted into flats and a library but is open on Wednesday, Saturday and Sunday afternoons from May to September.

Stirling

STIRLING is surely one of the most atmospheric of Scottish towns and it today retains much of the feeling and charm of days gone by. The grand and imposing **Stirling Castle** remains the most striking point on its skyline, challenged only by the Wallace Monument.

Historically, the Castle played a crucial role in the country's history, and Stirling is more closely associated with the Stuart kings than any other place. Situated at the head of the Forth on a strategic rock, it is easy to see why the Castle became so valuable. Indeed, it was the site of many a Pictish stronghold long before the Castle was actually built. It is even said to have been the Round Table upon which King Arthur trained his forces.

When James I returned from captivity in England, he held his court at Stirling and thus began a long association with the Castle for the Stuart dynasty. James II reputedly tried to curb the power of the Douglases when he persuaded William, the 8th Earl, to come to the Castle for dinner by offering him safe conduct. However, he then proceeded to kill his guest when he would not agree to break off an alliance that threatened the king.

James IV, a colourful character, made improvements to the Castle and laid out the Kings Knot, a garden still preserved in outline beneath the Castle. He also apparently dabbled in alchemy, which was what passed for science at the time. James V also spent much of his time at the Castle and did much to improve it, including rebuilding the Chapel Royal and, in 1539, building the palace. Incidentally, he was in the habit of dressing up in disguise and walking around the town incognito. His daughter Mary, Queen of Scots was crowned here in 1543. Her son,

Stirling Castle

James VI, was also crowned here but when he left for England, Stirling's importance as a Royal Seat declined.

The Royal apartments can be hired for functions. Historic Scotland (0131 2443144) can arrange everything, here and at many other historic houses and castles throughout Scotland.

Much of the city's original character has been preserved, together with a large collection of buildings from the 19th century, when the town rapidly expanded. The walk down from the Castle passes many places of interest including Mar's Wark, the Tolbooth and Mercat Cross before arriving at Stirling's street markets, which have been held since medieval times. There is so much of interest in the old town and helpfully the place abounds with plaques and notices to help visitors find their way around and not miss any of the many interesting buildings.

Stirling's antiquity and position has ensured that the town has occupied a central role in many great historical events that have shaped Scotland's history. As Scotland's historic capital, the town has more than its fair share of ghostly inhabitants. Many, like the tragic 'green lady' are known throughout Scotland, others are familiar only to local residents. This rich legacy provides the raw material which inspires the **Stirling Ghost Walk**. Guests are taken on an atmospheric exploration of the Old Town and throughout, guests are entertained with a leavened mix of comedy, drama and the occasional fright! Unique amongst this type of walk, the Stirling Ghost Walk centres on a full dramatic show using six actors, with guests touring the ancient nooks and crannies that give the Old Town such character.

The Wallace Monument also stands on this side of town and is highly recommended, not least for its unrivalled views of the town and castle. This rather strangely shaped tower commemorates the Scots' victory over the English at nearby Stirling Bridge in 1297. Sir William Wallace led the force that defeated Edward I's army of over 10,000. Though Wallace was ultimately defeated at Falkirk and met a gruesome end, being hanged, drawn and quartered, he provided the catalyst that inspired King Robert the Bruce to lead the nation to freedom in 1314 at Bannockburn. The tower itself is 220 feet high and was built in the 1850s, when a tide of nationalism swept the country. Today there is Hall of Heroes with displays that tell the story of Wallace's victory and history of the surrounding countryside, while the viewing platform, at the top of 246 steps, offers views that stretch from the Forth Bridges to Ben Lomond.

After exploring Stirling, one of Scotland's most atmospheric towns, you might feel in need of a little liquid refreshment, then look no further that **Whistlebinkies**, a traditional, olde worlde pub that is bursting with charm. This family run pub's name originates from days of old and was the name of a singing minstrel who wandered up and down the land, entertaining as he went, he was said to be a very well known sight at Stirling Castle all those years ago. The building itself was formerly a blacksmiths, solely used by Stirling Castle, and is said to have its very own ghost who pops up every now and again, usually when you least expect it!

Whistlebinkles is the home of good quality food and ale at very reasonable prices. The pub fayre is served from 12.00 pm until 2.30 pm Monday to Friday and 12.00 pm until 9.30 pm at weekends, whilst the bar itself is open all day, serving traditional ales and beers. There are facilities suitable for both children and the disabled, whilst even your pet is catered for in the expansive Beer garden, here you can sit and enjoy a quiet drink or meal in the warm summer months.

Whistlebinkles, 73-75 Mary's Stawynd, Stirling
Tel: 01786 451256

Located at the very top of Stirling town, opposite the No 39 Restaurant stands **Stirling Tours and Guiding Services**, a company that offers the visitor an in-depth insight into the local history and folklore of this beautiful part of Scotland. They can supply you with local information that is usually left unknown to most tourists. You can follow in the footsteps of the famous by enjoying STAGS Audio Walk, which is available from 24 Broad Street. Hire your own personal sound system and enjoy a gentle stroll through the centuries.

Over the years, Broad Street has been at the heart of Stirling's Old Town and has witnessed the progress of many Kings and Queens making their way to Stirling Castle. Characters from the past spring to life as you hear of their triumphs and disasters, though do allow at least an hour for this historic walk as there is so much to discover and see you will find yourself totally absorbed. In the past, Broad Street was also the setting for the weekly market and numerous local hangings, though more recently the crowds turned out to cheer Mel Gibson, who portrayed the Scots' folk hero, William Wallace in the film *Braveheart*. Also at No 24 is Fiona's Traditional Scottish Sweetie Shop, where you can choose from a mouthwatering selection such as Brandy Balls, Berwick Cockles, Soor Plooms and delicious fudge and tablet.

Stirling Tours and Guiding Services, 24 Broad Street, Stirling
Tel: 01786 446044

AROUND STIRLING

BANNOCKBURN. South of the town lies the site of the Scots' greatest victory over the English. Bannockburn saw the freeing of the nation, when Robert the Bruce led his forces in defeating a huge army of Edward I. The stirring events of June 1314 can be followed through a series of exhibitions and there is a huge statue of Bruce astride his warhorse to admire.

FINTRY. This village is hemmed in on both sides, by the Campsie Fells to the south and the Gargunnock Hills to the north. The peaks of Earl's Seat and Stronend dominating the village.

DRYMEN. On your way north from Glasgow on the Stockiemuir road with views of Loch Lomond, Ben Lomond and the Highlands you will come to Drymen, a traditional Scottish village sitting pleasantly on the foothills.

Drymen Tandoori Restaurant

Many interesting people from hidden places visited this beautiful area, Rob Roy MacGregor came often from his hideaway in Balquhidder, each time he found that the **Drymen Tandoori Restaurant** had not yet opened, so he simply stole cattle from the Duke of Mortrose, went home and made himself a kebab. In neighbouring Killearn, a monument to George Buchanan stands tall. He was an international scholar born 1506, tutor to Mary, Queen of Scots whose head was cut off by Elizabeth I, Queen of England. Revenge was sweet, when the Virgin Queen died, Mary's son, James VI of Scotland, became James I King of England.

Eric Liddell of Chariots of Fire Olympic fame became a missionary, died and was buried in a unknown place in China 1945. His parents, wife and family are buried in Drymen Parish Church.

Robert Bontine Cunninghamme Graham, born 1852, author, explorer, politician, revolutionary soldier in South America, a founder member of the Scottish National Party, a man descended from one of the noblest families in Scotland - the Grahams (Dukes of Montrose) has a plaque to his horse, which helped him explore South America, erected in the nearby Gartmore village, a real patriot.

All these interesting people above were born to early to enjoy a Drymen Tandoori Meal, Farrah Malik runs the restaurant in respect of interesting people visiting hidden places. As well as the restaurant, takeaway and bar there are also bed and breakfast facilities available. There are also seven guest rooms for your convenience.

Drymen Tandoori, Drymen Square, Drymen Tel: 01306 660103

KIPPEN. The parish title 'The Kingdom of Kippen', might seem very grand for such a small village but it was bestowed upon the village by James V. History relates that whilst residing at Stirling Castle, the King sent out his men to catch venison from the nearby hills. On returning with the venison, the men happened to cross the land of John Buchanan who ambushed them and relieved them of their bounty. When the King's men tried to reason that the venison belonged to the King, Buchanan replied that James might be the King of Scotland but he, Buchanan, was the King of Kippen. James V was amused and rode out to meet his neighbouring majesty. John Buchanan was cordial to the King and became so great a favourite that he was often invited as 'King of Kippen' to meet his brother sovereign at Stirling.

The Black Bull in Kippen is not, as one would expect, a pub but rather a nice building that has been restored through the National Trust for Scotland. The building dates back to 1729 and was once the principal hostelry in the village, standing on the back road from Stirling to Dumbarton. It retains its original style of twelve pane glazing and has scrolled skewputs on the gables.

There are still a small number of industries in Kippen which have been going for 200 years or more. The blacksmiths, for example, where the Rennie family have been shoeing horses for all that time. Andrew Rennie, the last of that long line, worked until his death in 1985, at the age of 97, at the Smiddy which is still in operation and is now owned by the National Trust for Scotland.

Sealladh Ard

The village of Kippen is situated in the Fintry Hills overlooking the Valley of Forth and commands upwards of 30 miles of landscape views. This beautiful part of Stirlingshire is home to **Sealladh Ard**, which translated means 'spectacular views' and this cannot be denied as the house has breathtaking panoramic views of the mountain scenery, which marks the start of the Scottish Highlands. The house has been owned and run by Ann McCallum for the past three years and has been awarded a 1 Crown Highly Commended from the local Tourist Board for its general excellence. There are three guest rooms available to the weary traveller, each equipped with everything that you could need for a relaxed and comfortable stay. The general atmosphere is a warm and friendly one, while the furnishings and decor are of a country style that is both homely and comfortable. Scottish breakfasts are Ann's speciality, with home-baked bread and shortbread being made on the premises, as well as a wonderful selection of Scottish preserves that are perfect especially served on freshly baked warm bread. Outside there is a large garden complete with duck pond and ducks, this is the perfect place to let your kids run free and generally let off steam before you decide to explore the extensive and beautiful countryside.

Sealladh Ard, Station Brae, Kippen Tel: 01786 870291

GARGUNNOCK. The gardens at **Gargunnock House** are a delight and well worth a visit to appreciate the blaze of colours, textures and sheer magic of narcissi, azaleas, rhododendrons and many other flowering shrubs and trees. The combination and sheer beauty of these in any season is a great pleasure, and there is also a small wood here with a charming walk. The gardens are in the grounds of an impressive house that was built between the 16th and 18th centuries and unfortunately not open to the public without prior written arrangement. Indeed the gardens themselves are something of a rare treat as they are only open on Wednesday afternoons from 1 pm until 5 pm between April and October.

BRIDGE OF ALLAN. This was a popular spa town in Victorian times as it lies at the foot of the Ochil Hills on Allan Water.

The Crooked Arm

Visitors would be well advised to call in at **The Crooked Arm**, a welcoming, traditional inn situated on Allanvale Road, a quiet backwater on the western side of the town. Unimposing from the outside, this is a cosy, old inn run by Stuart Galloway and his friendly staff and its warm, relaxed atmosphere makes it a popular venue with visitors and locals alike. The lunchtime bar menu offers a wide range of tasty home-cooked meals and there is a daily changing selection of blackboard specials which make an ideal accompaniment in the fine range of ales served here.

The Crooked Arm, Allanvale Road, Bridge of Allan
Tel: 01786 833830

DUNBLANE. This pleasant town, on the River Allan, has grown up around its historic core of buildings and, in particular, the cathedral which dates from the 13th century. The town, tragically, became the focus of the world's attention when, in March 1996, a primary school class were attacked by a gunman.

DOUNE. **Doune Castle** was built during the late 14th and early 15th centuries by the Regent Albany, who was later implicated in the murder of James I's brother David and executed in 1424. It became part of the Crown and Royalty visited from time to time; including Mary, Queen of Scots. During the '45 Rising it became a Jacobite garrison and, in fiction, Scott's hero in *Waverley* come to the Castle as well.

Interestingly, the village bridge across the River Teith was built by Robert Spital, tailor to James IV, in order to spite a ferryman who had refused him passage. The splendid **Doune Motor Museum**, about two miles north of the village off the A84, houses a marvellous collection of vintage and post-vintage cars. Collected and owned by the Earl of Moray, most of the vehicles are in running order. Other interesting local attractions to be found locally include the **Blair Drummond Safari Park**, which is a delight for youngsters - of all ages! The park can be found two miles to the south of Doune.

CALLANDER. Tucked midway between east and west coasts at the gateway to the beautiful Trossachs, Callander is an ideal base from which to begin to explore the Scottish Highlands. The town is known world-wide as 'Tannochbrae', made famous in the 1960s by the popular television series *Dr Finlay's Casebook*. Many readers will no doubt remember Arden House, the home of Drs Finlay and Cameron. Today it is a guest house that welcomes visitors from all over the world.

Callander is also home to the **Rob Roy and Trossachs Visitors Centre**. Here the visitor is taken back three centuries to rediscover the daring adventures of Scotland's most colourful folk hero and find out all about his wild and beautiful homeland.

Callander is 20 minutes driving time northwest of Stirling on the A84, which you can reach from junction 10 on the M9, head for the Callander Golf Course and 200 yards down this narrow road you will come across the superb **Dalgair Hotel**. The Dalgair Hotel and Restaurant is a small family run establishment in the heart of Callander in Central Scotland and was taken over by the McDonald family early in 1992. Jim, Jennifer and Lisa McDonald have a very clear objective, to provide their guests with good value and a very high class but personal service that will make you want to return again and again.

The Dalgair Hotel has two bars, one of which can be entered via the main street and is ideal for bar snacks which are available throughout the day, or as a social meeting place. The Cocktail bar is beside the Restaurant and is well appointed and relaxing, ideal for a pre-meal cocktail or aperitif. The spacious Restaurant offers a wide range of imaginative dishes, calculated to tempt the most jaded palate, whatever the meal, be it breakfast, lunch, tea or dinner they can guarantee something for everyone. In season the Restaurant will even serve snacks throughout the day, with all menus changing regularly to suit the time of year and the seasonal, local produce that is available. Each of the eight light and airy bedrooms have en-suite bathroom facilities and are all equipped with heating, including a heated towel rail in the bathroom. In addition the rooms each have a colour television with satellite channels, a direct dial telephone and tea and coffee making equipment.

The convenient central location of this hotel provides the visitor with a comfortable base from which to explore the many delights of the surrounding countryside. The area has everything to satisfy your needs, including deer stalking and fishing which can both be arranged by the hotel and golf (with priority teeing-off times available on weekdays). There is also hill walking, touring, historical interests, water sports, Safari and Leisure park, cycling, cruising on Loch Lomond or Loch Katrine, nature trails, forest walks and much more - now that should keep you going for a day or two! The shopping in Callander is excellent, but should you want a trip away, then Stirling, Perth, Dundee, Edinburgh and Glasgow are all within easy reach. Whatever the holiday you seek, Callander and the Dalgair experience will provide the perfect setting.

Dalgair Hotel and Restaurant, Main Street, Callander
Tel: 01877 30283

The Famous Bracklinn Falls is a delightful bar and restaurant situated on the Main Street. Its relatively plain exterior belies the beautiful surroundings inside where beamed ceilings, soft lighting and attractive furnishings provide a lovely setting in which to savour the finest traditional Scottish cuisine. Amelia Melvin is a welcoming hostess who has developed The Famous Bracklinn Falls into a first class restaurant where visitors can call in throughout the day for anything from a relaxing drink and a light snack, to a full three course dinner. Closed only on New Years Day, this really is a place for all seasons and is ideally situated for visitors exploring Callander and the picturesque surrounding countryside.

The Famous Bracklinn Falls, 63 Main Street, Callander
Tel: 01877 30622

Bridgend House Hotel rests on the River Teith in the picturesque Perthshire town of Callander. Nestling under the tree-clad slopes of Callander Crags to the north and guarded by the mighty Ben Ledi to the west, Callander is the ideal base from which to tour the Trossachs, Loch Lomond and Stirling with its beautiful Castle. The town itself has an excellent shopping centre with its touring attractions and woollen mills, potteries, local craft centres and shops. The hotel is family run and prides itself on providing personal and friendly service in a warm and relaxed atmosphere. All seven of the attractively furnished guest rooms are equipped with remote control colour televisions, including Sky channel, tea and coffee makers, radios and direct dial telephones. Named after local Lochs, bedrooms Lubnaig, Mahaick and Drunkie are three de luxe, en-suite rooms of which two have four-poster beds, with Rusky and Achray being en-suite whilst Voil and Vennacher are standard.

Fine Scottish cuisine and excellent home-cooking are a hallmark of Bridgend House. Guests can dine in style and comfort in the magnificent dining room with its outstanding outlook over the hotel gardens towards Ben Ledi. Meals can be complemented by a fine selection of wines. Alternatively, bar meals, snacks and favourites in a special children's menu are served in the newly refurbished bar which has a traditional cast iron stove at which visitors can warm themselves after a days climbing or walking. Guest can enjoy relaxing with a good book in the cosy and traditionally furnished residents' lounge with open fire, perhaps savouring a fine local malt whisky. The hotel gardens come complete with magnificent views toward Ben Ledi and are full of colour in late Spring and Summer, they prove to be a popular spot from which to enjoy a drink or a light snack whilst relaxing in the warm sun.

Bridgend House Hotel, Bridgend, Callander
Tel: 01877 330130

Standing in acres of park and farmland in the picturesque Leny Hills, close to many famous lochs and only one mile from Callander, **Leny House** is a spacious country mansion that dates from 1513. The house is listed as of special architectural and historic interest and was once a small fortress. The Gallows Hill, used in the 15th century and known as the Knoll of Justice, is still visible in the grounds. Leny House was enlarged in 1691 and again in 1845 to its present form.

Leny House

The house features in much of the history that surrounds Callander, particularly during the Jacobite Rebellion when it was used for clandestine meetings and for arms storage. Francis Buchanan, a Laird of Leny, was executed at Carlisle in 1746 for his part in the uprising when he allegedly murdered Stewart of Glenbuckie, the leader of a party of Stewarts on their way to join Bonnie Prince Charlie's army. Each changing season in Scotland has its own particular beauty and charm. The bright, varied generous splendour of the rhododendrons in spring,

221

the abundant but secretive wildlife in summer, the mellow, gentle shades of russet in autumn glens, the crisp, snow covered majesty of mountains in winter, can all be enjoyed from this ideally situated estate. The house offers its guests comfortable bed and breakfast accommodation in relaxing and tranquil surroundings. You have the choice of either twin or double rooms, some with private bathrooms and a spacious and airy family room with en-suite facilities.

Within the beautiful grounds of the Leny Estate are six solid spruce lodges that have been designed and situated on a small peaceful site to take full advantage of the view towards the Trossachs, long considered to be a particularly beautiful part of Scotland. Each of the **Leny Estate Lodges** has been appointed to luxury standard and has been awarded the highest possible Scottish Tourist Board grading of 5 Crowns de luxe. There are several self-catering establishments in Scotland that have the highest grading of 5 Crowns de luxe, however this is the only one that has this grading and been recommended by the television programme *Wish You Were Here*.

Leny House, Leny Estate, Callander
Tel & Fax: 01877 331078

STRATHYRE. Surrounded by Strathyre Forest and situated along the beautiful shores of Loch Lubnaig, Strathyre has much to offer the visitor as well as its great charm and character. The surrounding countryside is enchanting and was reputedly the inspiration behind Sir Walter Scott's *The Lady of the Lake*.

Situated in the main street of beautiful Strathyre is **The Ben Sheann Hotel**, which has been owned and personally run by Elizabeth Morton and partner for the past two years. Originally this establishment was a station hotel, as the railway used to run passed this very spot back in the late 1800s. The name was changed to Ben Sheann in the 1960s and this, roughly translated, means 'Hill of the Fairies'.

The Hotel itself is built on three floors and has a very Victorian style with a wee touch of Scottish that appeals to the sense of history and tradition that was very much order of the day when this beautiful hotel

SS Sir Walter Scott, Loch Katrine

was first built. There are nine guest rooms available, with five of these being en-suite and each one offering a very warm and friendly welcome to the weary traveller. There are two bars, one of which is a residents' only bar and the other is for everyone, locals and tourists alike, with both bars boasting large open fires that burn throughout the cold, winter months. There are extensive bar and restaurant menus available and each one offers something for everyone. On the dinner menu you can choose from such culinary delights as Woodland Pigeon wrapped in bacon and served with a rich game sauce or maybe Scallops seared and served on a potato rosti with fish essence, and if you have still got room there is Cloutie Dumpling served with a brandy sauce - positively delicious. There is also a terrific wine list that provides the diner with an excellent choice of traditional as well as New World wines.

The Ben Sheann Hotel, Main Street, Strathyre Tel: 01877 384609

Situated in the beautiful Scottish Highlands yet within easy travelling distance of many of Scotland's main towns and cities, **The Inn at Strathyre** is a 3 Crowns Inn and Hotel that offers its guests the very best. The Inn itself is over 200 years old and there is an old Scottish folk tale that says that the famous Rob Roy MacGregor had his last fight outside this very pub all those years ago.

The Inn at Strathyre

Today the Inn is run as a family concern and you are always assured of a warm and friendly welcome. There are seven guest rooms each with private bathrooms, radio/alarm clocks and tea and coffee making facilities, with a residents TV lounge situated on the same floor. The Inn at Strathyre has a reputation for offering a selection of the highest quality food from both the bar and restaurants extensive menus and is certified to use local Aberdeen Angus Beef only. The family theme is extended into the restaurant, which is named La Famiglia and has a very strong Latin influence. There are special low cost breaks available throughout the year, golfing packages from Spring to Autumn and, from November to March, there are special winter weekend breaks.

The Inn at Strathyre, Main Street, Strathyre Tel: 01877 384224

BALQUHIDDER. Here, buried in the kirk with his family, is Rob Roy MacGregor. This Robin Hood of the North, born in 1660, was apparently a decently educated man who possessed a strong physique and a masterful ability with the sword. He set out to become a cattle dealer but he lived in times of constant feuding and rivalry between clans. Faced with the poaching and pilfering rife around him, Rob Roy was forced to put together a band of men to protect his interests from other greedy landowners and landlords.

He was at one time an officer in the Old Pretender's army at the Battle of Sheriffmuir in 1715. Eventually the government set a price of £1000 on his head, though he managed to escape capture and the scaffold. He spent ten years on the run and on at least one occasion, was caught and escaped from his captors, until he was eventually pardoned in 1727 and became a convert to Catholicism. He died, peacefully, in 1734.

Visitors to Balquhidder will find there are two very good reasons for seeking out **Stronvar House** which stands on the banks of Loch Voil. As well as being a superior country house hotel, it is also the home of **Bygones Museum** and **Balquhidder Visitor Centre**, a fascinating place with a varied collection of memorabilia beautifully laid out within this splendid Laird's mansion.

To the east of the main A84 at the head of Glen Ample lies **Edinample Castle**. Once a MacGregor stronghold, its present owner is in the process of restoring it to its 16th century appearance.

Situated at Balquhidder Station stands **The Golden Larches Restaurant**. The restaurant and coffee shop was built 13 years ago and is open from April through to October, seven days a week. Owned and personally run by Lorraine Telfer and her very capable staff, Golden Larches offers its guests a range of different options, from a light snack or hot dish at lunchtime, also high teas and full à la carte menu served all day. All the food is cooked and prepared on the premises and only the freshest and finest seasonal local produce is used in the preparation of the delicious meals. If morning coffee is something that you enjoy then look no further, as all the cakes and fancies have been home-baked by Golden

Larches and offer a large selection of delicious freshly baked fayre.

Also owned by Lorraine is Tom-Na-Voil, an 18th century cottage that offers the traveller some superb self-catering accommodation. The cottage is situated in the picturesque highland village of Balquhidder, the burial place of the Scottish hero Rob Roy MacGregor. Recently renovated and refurbished to the highest standard, this lovely cottage is situated in half an acre of attractive gardens and woodland. It consists of two twin bedded rooms, one of which is en-suite, a light and airy sitting room complete with a cosy log burner, perfect for those cold winter months, and a fully fitted kitchen complete with dishwasher and microwave. There is also a utility room which has a washer/dryer for your convenience. This spacious accommodation is fully double glazed and centrally heated with all your linen provided for you. There is an initial fuel supply of a bag of coal and a bag of logs supplied free of charge by Lorraine and the electricity is operated via a coin meter. If you don't feel like cooking one evening and fancy a nice meal out, then don't forget to visit the Golden Larches Restaurant as Lorraine would love to see you.

Golden Larches Restaurant, Balquhidder Station, Lochearnhead
Tel: 01567 830262

LOCHEARNHEAD. This village lies at the west end of Loch Earn, amongst some fine mountain scenery. The road north from the village passes through **Glen Ogle**. This is a wild glen, its heathery hillsides cut by lines of rocky cliffs. A five and a half mile trail along the Glen follows riverside and woodland paths and part of the old 18th century military road before turning back along the trackbed of the Callander to Oban railway, passing the huge rock fall that provided the excuse for closing the line in the 1960s.

KILLIN. A quiet village at the west end of Loch Tay through which the enchanting **Falls of Dochart** rush. On the Island of Inchbuie on the river is the burial ground of the Clan MacNabb. Nearby, are the ruins of Finlarig Castle, which was a Campbell seat associated with the notorious Black Duncan, whose beheading pit can still be seen here.

The towering form of **Ben Lawers**, some 3984 feet above sea level, provides an impressive sight from here. Ben Lawers has long held a reputation as a botanical paradise and, from the summit, there are magnificent views stretching from the east coast to the west. The National Trust has issued a guide book, but be warned as there is a sign warning against the removal of any plants.

TYNDRUM. The area surrounding this quiet village was aptly described, in 1876, by Queen Victoria as being set in a "wild, rugged, picturesque glen surrounded by high rugged mountains". The name Tyndrum itself comes from the phrase, 'tigh an droma', which translates as 'the house on the ridge'. Small though it may be the village boasts two stations, Upper and Lower. The two lines from Crianlarich having to share the same valley as the road, only diverging beyond the village.

Situated in the picturesque village of Tyndrum, five miles northwest of Crianlarich between the summits of Beinn Odhar, Ben Lui and Ben Udlaidh, stands **Pine Trees Leisure Park**. Ideally positioned for discovering Perthshire, Pine Trees is a great place to base all your touring and sightseeing. Run by Ruaraidh and Isobel Johnston for the past four years, this well appointed country park offers its visitors 90 pitches for both tents and caravans as well as bunkhouse accommodation that is ideal for skiers and walkers alike. The caravan and camping area is very well laid out, with a children's play area, games room and a heated indoor swimming pool which also includes a sauna and showers. The on-site facilities include electric hook-ups, water points, wash-up sinks and a launderette and drying room. Also included is full toilet and shower facilities and a chemical disposal point for your convenience.

Pine Trees Leisure Park

The Bunkhouse accommodation comprises centrally heated rooms that contain two bunks and can be rented per night at a very reasonable rate indeed. Pine Trees Leisure Park also has its own fully pine-lined restaurant that is open seven days a week and offers the visitor a large and delicious selection of home-baked dishes and vegetarian meals, including the 'All Day Highland Breakfast' which is guaranteed to suffice even the heartiest of appetites! The restaurant is fully licensed to sell both beers and wines and is adjoined by a well stocked craft shop. Offering a wide range of quality gifts, the craft shop has plenty of videos, ceramics, glassware, books and some attractive hand carvings. Also on site is the all day shop that sells a good selection of groceries, camping equipment, camera films, newspapers and all those bits and pieces that we always forget to pack. So if you are lucky enough to be exploring this beautiful part of Scotland, be sure to pay a visit to Pine Trees Leisure Park, there will always be a warm welcome awaiting you.

Pine Trees Leisure Park, Tyndrum
Tel: 01838 400243 Fax: 01838 400314

CRIANLARICH. There is only one place that seems to feature on more signposts than Kincardine Bridge, way back on the Forth, and that is the tiny community of Crianlarich. Though the Caledonian Railway route, which used to travel through Doune, Strathyre and Balquhidder, is gone, Crianlarich still has a station and is the junction on the West Highland line where the routes to Fort William and Oban separate.

Peaceful and remote, Crianlarich is on the famous **West Highland Way** walking route from Glasgow to Fort William and, as such, makes an ideal base for those wishing to explore the beautiful West Highlands of Scotland. There is an abundance of wildlife and deer roam the surrounding hills; eagles and other rare birds have also been spotted.

To the south is Glen Falloch and the **Falls of Falloch**. A picnic site marks the start of a short footpath to the hidden and impressive falls where the River Falloch, striking off jagged ledges, plunges into a dark shadowy pool. Originally a cattle drovers' route, the road through the glen was improved as part of the pacification of the Highlands following the '45 Jacobite Rising. As late as 1845 there was a battle here of sorts when workers from rival railway companies set about one another, though it would be another 49 years before the North British Railway would open the route.

Whether you require a week-end break away from the city, a one night stop-over en route to remoter destinations, or a longer stay to explore and tour the beauty of Crianlarich, you will find a warm welcome at **The Ben More Lodge Hotel** and Restaurant.

Ideally located between the A82 and the A85, The Ben More is perfectly situated to provide all its visitors with a central touring point and some of the most impressive views you are ever likely to see. This family run Hotel and Restaurant backs onto the River Fillan, a tributary of the Tay, and the magnificent 3800 foot mountain **Ben More**. Offering comfortable accommodation in lodges that are set just a short step away from the restaurant and bar, this ensures that they are private and quiet when required, but still provides ready access to full hotel facilities. Each of the pine-lined lodges has a double bedroom complete with en-suite facilities with shower and some lodges have an additional room with twin bunks, which would come in handy for a family sharing. All the lodges have colour television, tea and coffee making facilities and some even have a small fridge for the guests' convenience. There is also a canopied verandah where you can sit and savour the fresh mountain air before walking over to the fully licensed restaurant that offers a variety of fare. All the dishes are cooked using only the finest and freshest local produce including game and fish, and many of the dishes have a traditional Scottish feel to them, well as they say, 'When in Rome'. The adjoining lounge bar serves a variety of draught beers and malt whiskies, with a wide range of bar meals, light snacks and coffee available throughout the day.

The Ben More Lodge Hotel and Restaurant, Crianlarich
Tel: 01838 300210 Fax: 01838 300218

Situated in an elevated position 500 yards from the roadside, between Crianlarich and Tyndrum on the A82, stands **Allt-Chaorain House Hotel**, the perfect touring centre. Built in 1912 and one of the first houses in Crianlarich to be built of concrete, Allt-Chaorain is a small residential hotel that affords its guests all the amenities, comfort and atmosphere of their own homes. The house has eight comfortable bedrooms, you can choose from double or twin beds including a large family room. All the guest rooms come complete with private facilities, direct dial telephones, TVs with remote control, tea and coffee making facilities, electric blankets, hairdryers, radios and central heating throughout. The lounge has a warming log fire that burns throughout the year and an adjoining Sunroom which offers one of the most picturesque views of the Highlands, with Ben More dominating the landscape.

Allt-Chaorain is a member of Taste for Scotland and is justly proud of its reputation for good home-cooked food which is created using only the finest and freshest local produce. The staff like to discuss their menus with all of their guests, whether it be a full Scottish breakfast or a traditional evening meal, and it is this personal touch that makes all the difference. The wood panelled dining room caters for six persons to a table, allowing most reserved guests the chance to exchange their day's experiences with others who have been fishing, walking or touring the Central Highlands. With its ideal central location and the obvious dedication and hospitality that is extended to all its guests, Allt-Chaorain House Hotel is a must for anyone travelling in the Central Highlands area.

Allt-Chaorain House Hotel, Crianlarich
Tel: 01838 300283 Fax: 01838 300238

LOCH KATRINE. At the northern edge of Loch Ard Forest is Loch Katrine, set right in the heart of the Trossachs. The loch is ten miles long and its name derives from Gaelic 'Cateran' or 'Highland robber'. Stronachlachar, which stands near the head of the Loch, is accessible by road from Aberfoyle and gives unrivalled views of the Loch and Ben Lomond. The Loch lies in Clan MacGregor country and the Clan graveyard is still to be found at the head of the Loch, as is Glengyle House, birthplace of Rob Roy MacGregor. Indeed it was Scott's colourful description of this area, in his novel *Rob Roy*, that prompted the first tourist to venture into Highland Scotland. So, fittingly, the Steamer on the Loch is named after him.

The ship itself has an interesting history. She has been taking sightseers up and down the Loch since 1900 and is the only remaining screw steamer in service in Scotland. Built on the Clyde, she was bought overland from Loch Lomond to Stronachlachar in kit form and ever since has provided leisurely pleasure cruises, to this day still using her original engines.

ABERFOYLE. Known as 'The Gateway to the Trossachs', this village is an ideal centre from which to explore this delightful area. For those keen to get out into the great wide open this is the place, the **Queen Elizabeth Forest Park** has over 60 miles of waymarked walks and cycle trails. The Visitors Centre is packed full of displays and information on the forest and its flora and fauna, as well as shop, cafeteria and toilet facilities.

It is also from here that those who prefer to take in the scenery from the comfort of their car can get details of the **Achray Forest Drive**. Using

Forestry Commission roads the drive goes right into the heart of the forest, amongst the conifers, oaks and birch. There are plenty of places to stop and picnic and an all important play area and toilets at the halfway point.

Located next door to the Church of Scotland, on the Lochard Road, you will come across **Stoneypark**, a wonderful guest house that offers visitors bed and breakfast accommodation in Aberfoyle. Built in 1889, this traditional building has been owned and personally run for the past two years by Glynis Haighton and is a non-smoking establishment. The general decor and furnishings have very much a Victorian feel to them with original open fires in all the rooms giving an air of history and tradition that makes Stoneypark so popular with all its guests.

There are three main bedrooms, one of which is a double with private toilet and shower room, one of the rooms is a twin and the other contains a king sized bed, both sharing a private guests' bathroom. There is also a very cosy guests' lounge which boasts open fires that are lit every night in the chilly winter months, and prove to be the perfect place to curl up and enjoy a good book and a warming drink. At the front of the property there is a beautiful and very large garden which is full of rhododendrons and border plants that are a real blast of colour in the long summer months.

Stoneypark, Lochard Road, Aberfoyle Tel: 01877 382208

Just two minutes walk from Aberfoyle village centre, **Crannaig House** was built around 1880 and stands handsomely in splendid grounds affording unmatched peace and seclusion. This very popular guest house is owned and personally run by Ann Anderson: three guest rooms on the first floor are traditionally decorated and furnished in an appealing way, helping to transport visitors to the best of Victorian grace and style the moment they cross the threshold.

In true style, the large building offers a cool retreat from the hottest summer days - in winter, full central heating and open log fires in the guests' reception rooms make this an ideal place away from worldly cares, whatever the season. There are large gardens to the front and rear affording stunning views and easy access to woodlands behind the

Pipe Major

property for dog walking or to take the children for nature trails. Birds are encouraged into the garden by selected planting and care of the natural habitat: seasonally, visitors may sight the rare peregrine falcon or the honey buzzard, and are likely to see the sparrow hawk, the long-tailed tit and the colourful bullfinch. Deer regularly browse the plants at the lawn edges and last year saw the birth of a fawn in the garden itself - surely there can be no higher acknowledgment of the tranquillity and peace which is the essence of staying at Crannaig House.

Crannaig House, Trossachs Road, Aberfoyle
Tel: 01877 382276

Overlooking the River Forth in the romantic Trossachs, stands **The Covenanters Inn**, a wonderful establishment that blends old fashioned charm with modern day convenience.

The Covenanters Inn

There are 53 en-suite guest rooms available, each complete with private bathroom, colour television, tea and coffee making facilities and the little touches of decor that offer you something just a little bit different. Many of the rooms look out over the splendid scenery of the magnificent Trossachs which are steeped in the history of the Highlands and the famous Rob Roy MacGregor. Legend has it that when the Stone of Destiny disappeared many years ago from Westminster Abbey, it was temporarily hidden in the Covenanters Inn, so make sure you check your wardrobes thoroughly!

Snacks and bar meals are served throughout the day in the lounge area when you just don't have time for a larger meal, but its in the dining room that the pleasure really starts. There is a variety of tempting menus available for your perusal, while the extensive wine list provides an interesting choice from the Hotel's well stocked cellar. The Covenanters Inn prides itself in arranging private functions and the grounds of the Hotel provide some spectacular opportunities for photographs. There are also dinner-dances most weekends and private suites are available for large or small parties. Whatever you wish, you'll find a friendly helpful service adding that touch of hospitality that is the hall-mark of the Covenanters Inn.

The Covenanters Inn, Hotel, Aberfoyle Tel: 01877 382347

As you explore the tranquil beauty and spectacular scenery of the Trossachs you will discover an excellent touring base at **The Inverard Hotel**. This beautifully appointed old Hunting Lodge overlooks the River Forth in Aberfoyle and was originally built by the Duke of Montrose in 1860. Owned and personally run by Caroline and Wilfred Carranza, Inverard Hotel provides excellent accommodation in 17 well equipped en-suite guest rooms. Five of these bedrooms are in the Hotel itself, whilst the other 12 are located in the individually styled modern log cabins that are situated adjacent to the Inverard Hotel.

The Inverard Hotel

At the end of a busy day's exploring, the cosy restaurant provides the perfect setting in which to savour a varied and unique menu. The emphasis is on traditional Scottish Fayre, but the unusual addition of a Filipino menu means that you will be sitting down to a real culinary experience. All the delicious food has been prepared using only the finest and freshest local produce and is accompanied by a comprehensive wine list. The bar area is very warm and welcoming and is often frequented

234

by many locals who are more than willing to offer the wayfarer some travelling advise over a glass or two of real ale. Recently refurbished, the Inverard Hotel offers the visitor the perfect base from which to explore and discover the impressive landscapes that surround this haven of peace and serenity.

Inverard Hotel, Lockmard Road, Aberfoyle
Tel: 01877 382229

PORT OF MENTEITH. Accessible by boat from Port of Menteith, **Inchmahome Priory** sits on an island in the middle of the Lake of Menteith. Founded by Augustinian monks in 1238, the house proved an ideal refuge for the infant Mary, Queen of Scots over 300 years later.

THORNHILL. Located on the outskirts of Thornhill village and with panoramic views over the Carse of Stirling to the Fintry Hills, **Mains Farm Camping** is the ideal place to pitch your tent or rent a caravan. Lying on the southern boundary of the Trossachs, which is a world famous area of lochs, glens and hills with breathtaking scenic beauty. Back in 1745, Bonnie Prince Charlie is reputed to have camped on this very land before accompanying his army to Derby before the bloody Battle of Culloden.

Mains Farm Camping

The site itself has a host of facilities to make your holiday as relaxing as possible, they include hot water, showers, shaving points, caravan electric points and a washing and drying area. Since the 1920s, Main Farm Camping has been owned and run by the Steedman family and is still as popular today as it was then. Nearby you will find a children's playground and an area for games and recreational facilities within 10 miles of the site include: fishing, golf, riding, boating, swimming, nature trails and even parachuting! A short walk takes you to the local village street which has a grocer, baker, newsagent, butcher and post office, and in the local hotels you can take advantage of the full restaurant menus and bar meals that are available throughout the day. The Steedman family offer self-catering stone built cottages too, which were originally ploughman's cottages and are fully equipped with some sleeping up to six people. There is also a selection of mobile homes to let on a weekly basis, they are of a very high quality with six berth cabins and fully equipped including a gas cooker, electric fridge and spacious lounge area, perfect for any family.

Mains Farm Camping, Kippen Road, Thornhill
Tel: 01786 850605

One mile from the village of Thornhill is **Corshill Cottage**, a luxury Guest House that offers the visitor to this beautiful area something a bit special. Built back in 1810, originally as a Blacksmith's cottage and smithy, Corshill was fully converted six years ago by your host and present owner Tona Fitches. The guest house was formed by building an additional wing on to the cottage for the visitors' requirements and there are also two self-catering units in the one acre of cottage gardens that surround this stunning building. There are three guest rooms available, each having en-suite facilities and they have been individually styled and decorated to give each bedroom a light and airy feel. The breakfasts alone are worth visiting Corshill Cottage for, as well as the full Scottish breakfast, Tona also serves smoked local salmon and fresh strawberries when they are in season, to complete a feast fit for a king, and evening meals can be arranged by prior arrangement if they are required. Corshill Cottage has been awarded a 3 Crown de luxe award by the local Tourist Board and that will come as no surprise to anyone who is lucky enough to sample some of the culinary and visual delights that this wonderful cottage accommodation has to offer.

Corshill Cottage, Thornhill Tel: 01786 850270

CHAPTER EIGHT

ARGYLL & BUTE

Castle Stalker

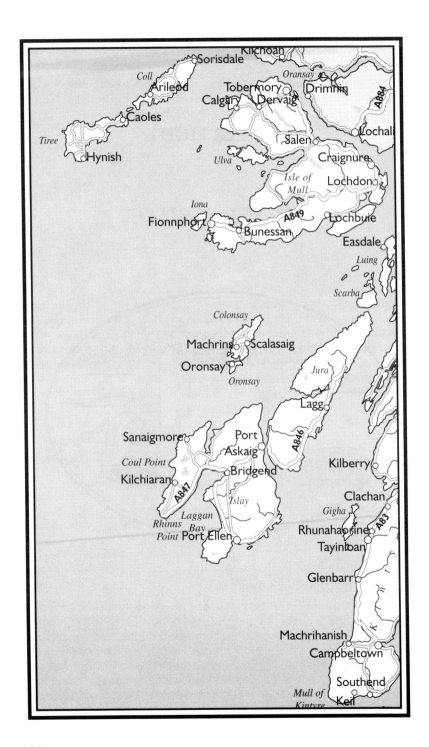

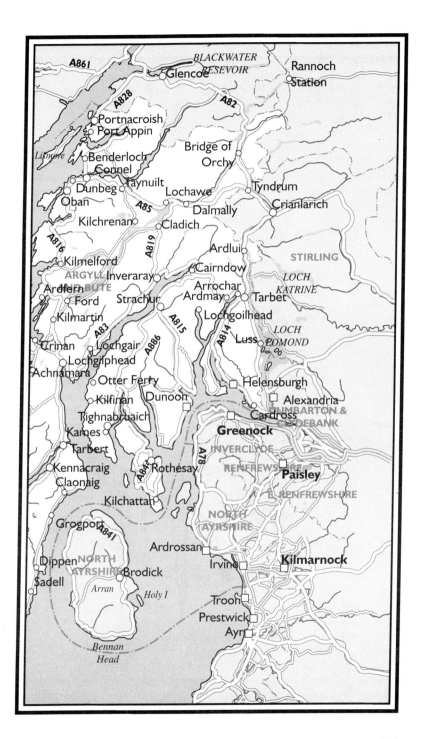

Castle Stalker, Loch Linnhe

CHAPTER EIGHT

ARGYLL & BUTE

Kintyre

CAMPBELTOWN. The township once boasted 34 distilleries but nowadays gets by with just the two. **Campbeltown Museum** displays geological, archaeological and cultural material from the whole of Kintyre. Facing the harbour, however, is perhaps Campbeltown's main focus of interest; a 15th century **Cross**, highly elaborate and with an inscription to Edward McEachern and his son Andrew.

Davaar Island, out in Campbeltown Loch, is in fact only an island at high tide. There is a life-size painting of the crucifixion in a cave on the island, done in 1887 by Archibald MacKinnon. He returned at the age of 80 to renovate the picture himself.

There are a number of interesting places to explore on foot when you visit Campbeltown, standing on the scenic harbourside **The Oystercatcher Gallery** is a family run business that is well worth a visit. The proprietors, George and Gill Stewart, have been personally running this popular business for over eight years and have two shops, the other being on the main street itself. Offering a wide range of art equipment and materials, with a picture framing service also on offer and a collection of toiletries made on the Isle of Arran using only natural products.

The Oystercatcher Gallery

George is one of the artists on display and offers a comprehensive selection of unusual gifts and artifacts, ranging from ceramics, hand-made jewellery in gold and silver and an attractive line of scented and unscented candles. The personal family service is attentive without being stifling and guarantees you an unrivalled selection of gifts and momentous.

The Oystercatcher Gallery, 2-4 Main Street, Campbeltown
Tel: 01586 551255

The Royal Hotel overlooks the harbour and Campbeltown Loch and this excellent position allows you to watch the colourful fishing boats as they come and go in the bustling harbour. This attractive Hotel has been owned and run by Jack and Jean Emmott for the past decade, this experience has given them the ability to make every guest feel welcome and allow them to obtain maximum enjoyment from their stay. There are 16 guest rooms, 12 of which have en-suite bath or shower rooms, and all have colour television and direct dial telephones. There is also tea and coffee making facilities provided in all the bedrooms, but if you should prefer you can use the comfortable coffee lounge. Breakfast is a leisurely affair, starting at 7.30 am and continuing until 9.30 am so there is no need to rise at the crack of dawn.

The Dalriada Lounge is open from 9.00 am for snacks, coffee and meals and from 11 am for bar drinks, whilst the bar offers its guests and locals alike, the chance to enjoy a game of darts or pool or just partake in some lively conversation. Dinner is the highlight of the day and is served in the attractive dining room, here you can enjoy the best of Scottish and English food from the à la carte menu, or the set meal of the day. Jack and Jean also hold Scottish evenings where you might be entertained by a folk singer, dancers or pipers from the renowned Campbeltown Pipe band. There are three golf courses in the area, one of which is classed as international standard and all welcome visitors. Also available in the area are wind-surfing, dinghy sailing, pony trekking, swimming and fishing boat hire.

The Royal Hotel, Main Street, Campbeltown Tel: 01586 552017

AROUND CAMPBELTOWN

SOUTHEND. The beach is dominated by **Dunaverty Rock**. Know locally as 'Blood Rock', it was the site of a Macdonald stronghold and, in 1647, saw about 300 people put to death by Covenanters under General Leslie, hence its name.

The island of **Sanda**, southeast of Southend, is traditionally associated with St Ninian, after whom its ruined chapel is named, and it is also said to have hidden Robert the Bruce.

KEIL. Tradition has it that St Columba's first footstep on Scottish soil were made near Southend. **Columba's Footsteps** are imprinted in a flat topped rock near the ruin of an old medieval chapel which stands on the site of the place of worship founded here by the Saint. The Mull Of Kintyre (who can forget the song) itself is deserted save for its lighthouse built in 1788 and later remodelled by Robert Stevenson. There are splendid views from here across to Ireland, just 12 miles away.

MACHRIHANISH. Located only four miles from picturesque Campbeltown, **The Beachcomber** offers its visitors superb views of the Atlantic Ocean, the Islands of Islay and Jura and the sands of Machrihanish Bay. Good food and drink is served in a friendly atmosphere by your hosts Bob and Dorothy Tait and Donald Brown, with spectacular sea views from the bar area. The menu is extremely varied, with all tastes catered for and many of the ingredients coming from only the freshest local produce. The main courses range from the light and very delicious Poached Salmon in a cream parsley sauce, to the enormous 16oz T-Bone Steak with French fries, tomato, onion rings, mushrooms, side salad, and your choice of three sauces to accompany this wonderful feast.

The Beachcomber

Machrihanish is one of the top surfing beaches in Scotland and The Beachcomber is also adjacent to a Championship Golf course with the best opening hole in the world. If you feel, after visiting this tranquil area, you would like to stay a little longer there is a self-catering holiday flat above the pub for rent throughout the year at a very reasonable rate, so surfers and golfers alike can enjoy all that Machrihanish has to offer in a relaxing environment.

The Beachcomber, Machrihanish, By Campbeltown
Tel: 01586 810355

GLENBARR. Situated on the A83, 12 miles north of Campbeltown, **Glenbarr Abbey** offers its visitors a glimpse of family living in a beautiful 18th century house. Glenbarr Abbey was formally presented to the Macalister Clan in September 1984 by its owner and present occupant, Angus C Macalister, 5th Laird of Glenbarr, to be used as a Clan Kintyre peninsula and is presently undergoing restoration to return it to its original glory. The ancestor to this earliest offshoot from the great Clan Donald was Alister MacDougalls: against Robert Bruce Alister forfeited his succession to that lordship but his descendants, inhabiting a tract of Knapdale and North Kintyre, grew strong enough to extend into Arran and Bute and they became an independent clan when the Lords of the Isles were suppressed in 1493. The first Knapdale stronghold of Castle Sweyn was assaulted by Bruce, whereafter the chief's seat became Ardpatrick and finally Loup in Kintyre. Though having lost much of its territory and strength to the Campbells, as did many other clans of this period, the clan appeared in the royalist rands with Montrose, and again at Killiecrankie.

Glenbarr Abbey Visitors Centre, Glenbarr, By Tarbert
Tel: 01583 421247 Fax: 01583 421255

TAYINLOAN. The village provides a car ferry service to **Gigha Island**. Pronounced 'gear', the name is derived from the Norse for God's island. The Island is noted for its ancient standing stones. The wooded gardens of **Achamore House**, where the collection of rhododendrons, azaleas and other exotic flowering shrubs has taken 40 years to create, is well worth a visit (owned by the National Trust for Scotland).

244

RHUNAHAORINE. Drive 16 miles south of Tarbert on the A83 and you will come across the pretty district of Rhunahaorine. Here you will find **The Baird Gallery**. This attractive building is open seven days a week and sells a unique selection of local paintings in varied mediums, including water-colour, pastels, acrylics and oils.

The Baird Gallery

As well as displaying local artists' talents, The Baird Gallery contains a range of paintings by International artists including Bill Wright, and offers a packaging facility for those wanting to ship their purchase abroad. The establishment is owned and personally run by George and Constance Baird, the artists-in-residence who display a wide range of their work for your perusal. Spend a relaxing half hour selecting that special gift from the range of beautiful antiques, collectables and objects d'art that decorate the light and airy rooms, or merely browse and enjoy the Baird's wonderful collection of paintings and prints, there is also ample off road car parking for your convenience.

The Baird Gallery, Rhunahaorine

RONACHAN BAY. Sometimes called Dunskeig Bay and also Seal Bay; this last name is particularly well deserved as the offshore rocks are a favourite with Atlantic grey seals, Britain's largest wild animal.

Nearby, **Corriechrevie Cairn** is one of the largest in Kintyre and, to the south, the **Ballochroy Stones**, comprising three standing stones, a burial cist and a boulder showing cup markings, can be reached down a small track.

CLACHAN. Located on the A83, south of Tarbert you will encounter the attractive village of Clachan and one and a half miles further south within a quarter of a mile of Seal View Layby, you will find **Ronachan Silks**. Set in some fine lawns with neatly trimmed shrubbery and bushes, this farmhouse is home to a wonderful selection of hand-painted silks all created using original and individual designs. All the items on display were produced on the premises and no two are the same with products ranging from cushion covers, ties and scarves to waist-coats, kaftans and kimonos. All of the garments are finished by hand and specialist commissions are undertaken by the owner, Mary Pollok.

Ronachan Silks, Farmhouse, Clachan, Tarbert
Tel: 01880 740242

KENNACRAIG. From Kennacraig sail the ferries to Islay, Jura, and Colonsay. These islands are reputed to receive more sunshine than anywhere else in Britain. Of course it does rain but even in bad weather they retain a dramatic beauty. The waters are incredibly clean and there are deserted golden beaches everywhere.

TARBERT is the gateway to Kintyre and the harbour to which a rather handy ferry arrives from the Cowal Peninsula, saving the long drive around Loch Fyne. Kintyre itself is all but an island: it was here that in the 11th century Magnus Barefoot, having been granted any land he could take his ship around 'with rudder in place', dragged his ships across the narrow strip of land and claimed Kintyre.

CLAONAIG. During the summer months, a ferry makes the short journey across the Sound to Arran and Lochranza.

Just along the coast lies **Skipness Castle**, which, despite an order to destroy it during the Argyll rising of 1685, stands looking out over the Isle of Arran. Built by the MacSween's in the late 1200s it ended its days as a farmstead before being taken into state care.

GROGPORT. To witness the only organic tanneries still in existence and purchase one of the best sheepskins in Scotland you have the choice of two small rural tanneries six miles apart and called **Grogport Rugs**. The first is at Carradale, you travel south from Tarbert on the Carradale road and you will then see signs four miles north of Carradale for Grogport Organic Tannery with the spotted sheep sign. The second is at Torrisdale Castle, travelling north from Campbeltown on the Carradale road, you will see signs two miles south of Carradale, go in a the Lodge gates and follow signs for the Tannery. The finished sheep-skin, deer and goatskin rugs for sale are different from those seen elsewhere, the colours are natural, specially chosen with the whites not being bleached. The length of wool varies attractively as none have been clipped and all are fully washable making them a perfect present for anyone. You will see methods that were used hundreds of years ago, although instead of old pits in the ground Molly Arthur and Mary Macalister Hall, the proprietors of this establishment, use fibreglass tanks as they can be kept clean and odour free! Methods of handling heavy skins in and out of these tanks have been evolved over the last 30 years and no chemicals are used so there is no resulting smell. It is a slow but natural method, with each rug taking four weeks to finish, but the result is quite superb and are appreciated by the discerning the world over.

Grogport Rugs at Grogport Old Manse, North of Carradale
Tel: 01583 431 255
Grogport Rugs at Torrisdale Castle, South of Carradale
Tel: 01583 431 233

CARRADALE. The Kintyre Peninsula provides some of the most beautiful and varied scenery in Scotland and it is by these beautiful heather covered hills and sandy beaches that you will find **Torrisdale Castle Holidays**. Three miles down the coast from Carradale is Torrisdale, a peaceful estate with magnificent trees and wooded walks and it is in the centre of this estate that you will find Torrisdale Castle. Built in 1815 it is now lived in by Donald and Mary Macalister Hall and their family and offers three luxury self-contained apartments for self-catering families in the ground floor of the castle. Once the kitchen and servants quarters, these extremely attractive apartments have been tastefully converted and now offer a very high standard of accommodation with fully equipped kitchens and light and airy bedrooms. There are also five cottages located within the grounds of the Torrisdale estate and all are comfortably furnished and well equipped with their own private garden area. All of the cottages have open fires with a free supply of logs and cooking is by electric cooker in the well equipped kitchen. Also included in your holiday is free all season fishing on the Carradale River and two free rounds of golf per cottage or flat at the tricky 9 hole golf course at Carradale, except in July and August. Donald and Mary personally supervise all the bookings and are always on hand to help with any problems which may arise.

Torrisdale Castle Holidays, Carradale
Tel & Fax: 01583 431233

SADDELL. Here can be found the remains of an abbey built in the 12th century by the Lord of the Isles. Though only the walls are still standing there are several carved tombstones of interest. A little to the north are the gardens of **Carradale House**. This walled garden from around 1870 has a colourful shrubbery that thrives in Kintyre's mild climate and a wild garden with laid out paths.

The Isle of Bute

Though the island is only about 15 miles long and just over a mile wide, it has an amazing wealth of scenery. The land at the northern end of the island has a wild feeling about it while the southern end is altogether more soft and gentle.

ROTHESAY. This ancient burgh was first granted a royal charter in 1401 and, three years earlier in 1398, King Robert III created his eldest son Duke of Rothesay; the title still exists today and is held by Prince Charles. Opposite Mansion House is **The Bute Museum**, which has a fascinating exhibition covering all aspects of the Isle. The Island's unusually mild climate is a result of the effect of the warm Gulf Stream. This reaches the west coast, allowing the magnificent palm trees and azaleas to thrive here.

Rothesay Castle was in existence as early as 1203. In 1230 Norsemen, led by Uspak, laid siege and having failed to storm the castle hacked their way through the wall. The breach and subsequent repairs are still visible today. Retaken in 1263, when the Norsemen were finally cleared from Scotland, the Castle was substantially strengthened with higher walls and four round towers. These improvements enabled it to withstand a siege in 1527 that saw most of the Royal Burgh destroyed. It finally succumbed to the English in 1544 and was used by both Charles I and Cromwell as a garrison. The Roundheads partially dismantled it when they left and what remained was put to the torch during the rebellion of 1685. In Victorian times the Bute family, appointed hereditary keepers in 1498, had the remains cleared and repaired.

Half a mile south of the town are the remains of **St Mary's Chapel**. A late medieval church, it contains two fine examples of recessed and canopied tombs, with effigies of a knight in full armour and lady and child.

To the north of Rothesay are the two castles of **Kames** and **Wester Kames**. Neither have any great historical significance but both are in a good state of repair. Kames is now part of a holiday home for the Scottish Council for the Care of Spastics and Wester Kames was restored in 1900 for the 3rd Marquess of Bute, after remaining a derelict for many years.

Argyll

INVERARAY. The wonder of this small town is its magnificent Castle, which is the home of the Duke of Argyll. The project of building a new castle was conceived by the 3rd Duke in 1746. By Roger Morris, with help from William Adam, **Inveraray Castle** is best known for its decor and interiors; the relics, furniture and paintings are superb and include portraits by Gainsborough, Ramsay and Raeburn. Outside, the grounds are extensive, with many pretty walks, some by waterfalls on the River Aray. Also in the grounds is the **Combined Operations Museum**, which portrays the lives and achievements of the hundreds of Commandos and assault troops that trained here during the Second World War. **Inverary Bell Tower** is 126 feet high and houses Scotland's finest ring of bells and the world's second heaviest ring of ten bells.

Inveraray Jail, Church Square, is an innovative and award winning museum, providing visitors with a vivid insight into prison life during the 1800s. Very much a 'Euro-museum', virtually all the information has been translated into French, German and Italian to help the overseas visitor. Trials in progress can be listened to in the magnificent 1820 courtroom and warders, prisoners and matron, all in period costume, can be talked to as well as the prisoners watched performing traditional tasks such as picking oakum. The Torture, Death and Damnation exhibition is not for the fainthearted, with its gruesome details of medieval punishments.

Dundarave Castle stands just a few miles north of the town on the shores of Loch Fyne. Nearly 400 years old, it is the principle seat of the

MacNachtan clan. Built in 1539 by the 12th chief of the clan MacNachtan, the Castle itself is a Grade A Listed Building: its survival only ensured when it was restored from a roofless and ruinous state by Sir Andrew Noble in 1906, who set about making the castle habitable. He retained the original character of the old tower and added two further wings which enclosed a courtyard. Today it is possible to soak up the atmosphere and views in comfort as this magnificent castle is now a luxury hotel.

Eredine Forest lies between Inveraray and Loch Awe and is a wonderful place to spend some time. The single track road through the forest ducks and weaves between the trees and passes through several tiny hamlets.

The picturesque town of Inveraray, overlooked by the fairytale castle of the Dukes of Argyll, is the home for **Fernpoint Hotel**, nestling on the very shores of Loch Fyne. This Georgian house and gardens enjoy a magnificent setting at the gateway to the Western Highlands, with superb views over the loch and the hills and mountains that surround it.

Fernpoint Hotel

All the bedrooms have a private bath or shower room, TV, tea and coffee making facilities, central heating and a beautiful view of either Loch Fyne or the attractive gardens that surround the property. In the spacious dining room, you can enjoy a dinner prepared from the freshest and finest local ingredients, or a hearty Scottish breakfast to keep you going until its time for lunch. The bar, which was formerly the stables and smithy, serves a wide range of dishes throughout the day and evening, including a good selection of malt whiskies, purely medicinal of course! Inveraray is an area of startling landscapes and dramatic scenery: tumbling rivers, wooded hills, majestic mountains, quiet lochans and secret places. Pursuits for the hardy and energetic include climbing, walking, sea and loch fishing, riding and boating, so whatever your interest you will find plenty to do at Fernpoint Hotel.

Fernpoint Hotel, Round by the Pier, Inveraray
Tel: 01499 2170

AROUND INVERARY

STRACHUR. More than 400 years ago, Mary, Queen of Scots landed at Creggans on her way through the Highlands. Today, **The Creggans Inn** stands on the same headland, looking across Loch Fyne to a tremendous prospect of hills and sea. An old Highland Inn with a tradition of hospitality, homely comfort and individual attention to the visitor, it is ideally situated amongst magnificent scenery for walks and excursions by land and sea and is within easy driving distance of the eight famous gardens of Argyll including Crarae and Langers Botanical Gardens. The Creggans Inn is owned by The Honourable Lady Maclean and Sir Charles Maclean whilst being personally managed by Mr and Mrs Findlay. The hotel has prettily decorated bedrooms with private bathrooms, a peaceful sitting room and a large and comfortable garden lounge with extensive views over the gardens and local scenery. The cheerful restaurant is split level with two attractive bars, both with open log fires where a tempting light luncheon menu includes Loch Fyne oysters, smoked salmon, freshly caught langoustines, venison, hill lamb and many other Scottish specialities. Dinner is a more formal meal served in the pretty, Victorian style restaurant. The Creggans has a well deserved reputation for excellent food and this is not surprising as Lady Maclean, who supervises the kitchens, is the authoress of several famous cookery books. It is food of a certain kind: a happy mix of her own recipes, Scottish country house cooking and French cuisine, the unifying element being the freshness and excellence of our local ingredients. Before Sir Fitzroy's death he personally selected his favourite wines from around the world which are still available today and wide range of rare old malt whiskies including one of their own, Old MacPhunn, a fine ten year old vatted malt. Because of its excellent position, The Creggans Inn is just over an hours drive from Glasgow and the fabulous Burrell Collection, the hotel is also within easy motoring distance of Inveraray, and 18th century castle and town designed by the Adam brothers for the Dukes of Argyll and many other historical and beautiful places.

The Creggans Inn, Strachur Tel: 01369 860279

251

OTTER FERRY. The tumble-down walls of the Iron Age fort of **Barr Iola** stand to the southeast while **Carn Bàn**, a chambered cairn, lies to the east.

One of the most renowned seafood restaurants in Scotland can be found on the shores of Loch Fyne at Otter Ferry. **The Oystercatcher** is a delightful pub and eating place which enjoys dramatic views across the water to the west. Diners come from miles around to sample the dishes prepared by Dorothy and Alain Miailhes and their staff. (Free moorings are available for patrons arriving by boat.) French-born Alain is an accomplished chef who specialises in cooking classic seafood dishes. His restaurant menu features such starters as local Ballimore oysters, home-made fish soup and fruit de mer, as well as such regular main dishes as Loch Fyne langoustine, scallops, mussels and salmon. Alain's fixed menu is enhanced by a constantly changing chalkboard which features a variety of mouthwatering seasonal specialities; indeed, he will attempt to cater for any special request given sufficient advance notice. For those wanting an alternative to seafood, the menu features chicken, duck, pheasant, lamb and venison dishes, as well as an impressive range of steaks and vegetarian specials.

There is also an ambitious wine list ranging from inexpensive house wines to chateau-bottled vintages. The Oystercatcher also offers an extensive bar menu with dishes cooked to the same high standard as the restaurant at surprisingly affordable prices. Children are welcome, and there is a separate room for younger patrons.

The Oystercatcher, Otter Ferry, Loch Fyne
Tel: 01700 821229

KAMES. This village was once a hive of industry but now only the striking red sandstone ironworks cottages and institute survive. Beyond the village a minor road peters out on the bleak moorland, in a hidden place that drivers should hold dear. Up here John McAdam had a tarworks, though he never thought to bind his famous gravel 'Macadam' road surface with it. A cairn was erected here in 1931 using the few stones that remained from the tar kilns.

TIGHNABRUAICH. The village overlooks the Kyles and the Isle of Bute, a 16 mile stretch of water which presents a constantly changing view of great beauty.

On reaching the seafront at Tighnabruaich, turn left, through the village and only 200 yards on the left you will come across **Susy's Tearoom**. This picturesque tearoom was purpose built as an eatery, it has garden facilities which can seat up to eighty people, which matches the capacity of the inner eating area. Owned and personally run by Amy and Brian, it is solely down to their ability to make all their visitors feel at home that this eatery is so popular with both tourists and locals alike. Susy's Tearoom serves morning coffee, afternoon tea, lunches and a range of delicious home-baked snacks throughout the day, using only the freshest local ingredients. There are ample parking facilities for cars and coaches adjacent to the tearoom, with a Gift Shop selling local Scottish gifts and crafts overlooking the Kyle of Bute.

Susy's Tearoom, Tighnabruaich, Kyles of Bute Tel: 01700 811452

CLACHAN OF GLENDARUEL. This name is an interesting one which has its origins in a battle fought in 1110 between Meckau, who was the son of Magnus Barefoot, the King of Norway, and the Scots. The Scots won and threw the bodies of their slaughtered enemies into the river, which flows through the Glen, turning the water red with their blood. The river became known as the Ruail, and the glen as Glen-daruail or glen of red blood.

DUNOON. **Holy Loch** is supposedly so named because a boat bringing consecrated soil from the Holy Land floundered in the Loch. Until recently, it contained a fleet of American nuclear submarines but today the waters are only disturbed by pleasure craft and the fish. At the mouth of Holy Loch lies Dunoon, a much favoured resort since the 18th century. The peace of the waterfront today is a far cry from the dark days of the 17th century, when the old castle was the scene of a bloody massacre. The Campbells of Argyll took advantage of a temporary truce to capture their enemies the Lamonts, and killed 200 of them, throwing the bodies into a hastily dug pit. The grave was only discovered in the

19th century when a road was being built. There is now a memorial to those who died there. The lover of Robert Burns was from Dunoon and there is a statue to 'Highland' Mary Campbell at the foot of Castle Hill.

In **Loch Eck** is the rare Powan fish that is common only to this loch and to Loch Lomond. It is a species of fresh water herring that is believed to have been trapped here and left in the loch at the end of the last Ice Age. At the southern tip of the loch is the **Younger Botanic Garden**, which has a truly wonderful display of trees and shrubs. At the northern end of the loch are the **Lauder Memorials**. For a time Sir Harry Lauder lived at nearby Glenbranter House, which has now been demolished. During his stay his only son, John, was killed in the Great War and Sir Harry erected an obelisk on a knoll a short distance from the loch. In the same enclosure is a Celtic Cross, a memorial to Lady Lauder who died in 1927.

Boasting some stunning views over the sea at Marine Parade in Dunoon, **Hunter's Quay Hotel** commands attention with its elevated position and imposing size. Dating from 1830 and still retaining original features, it was built for a Glasgow Merchant, and had many illustrious guests in times gone by; from the King of Norway to Sir Thomas Lipton, with his famous yacht Shamrock moored in front.

Today the popular hotel, sited next to the pier for Western Ferries, has a restaurant, two lounges and a friendly bar to relax over a wee refreshment. There are 12 en-suite bedrooms, some with a sea view. All meals are prepared fresh to order. For an appetizer you could try Smoked Mussels in a Cream Sauce, or Sauté Mushrooms in Garlic Butter, followed by the Fish Stew (if you are really hungry!) with scallops, salmon, etc. And to finish, Fudge Sponge with Toffee Ice-cream, totally delicious.

Hunter's Quay Hotel, Marine Parade, Dunoon
Tel: 01369 704190

Situated on Dunoon's main street, **Di Marco's Café Bar** is proving very popular with both locals and tourists alike for its terrific range of beers, spirits and wines. Owned and personally run by the Pellicci family for over 50 years, it is now the turn of Marco and Linda to take the helm, and its down to their unique ability to make all their guests feel at home

254

that makes this café bar so renowned. There is live music every Thursday, Friday and Saturday with the occasional Sunday afternoon thrown in. You are invited to listen to some of the very best in local Rock, Blues and Jazz bands while you sit back and soak up the atmosphere, not to mention the alcohol!

There is a brand new Bistro opening in the summer of 1996 called **La Cantina Bistro** which will provide Dunoon with its only Italian Bistro, serving only the most authentic pizza and pasta dishes. One of the best times to visit is during the Annual Cowal games at the end of August, the town is alive for most of the summer months and the atmosphere is second to none.

Di Marco's Café Bar, 200 Argyll Street, Dunoon Tel: 01369 705550

Affording spectacular views of the Clyde Estuary and surrounding hills of Dunoon, **The Ardtully Hotel** is set in its own extensive grounds and offers its guests award winning facilities and assured high standards. This family run, licensed hotel has been owned by James and Jan for the last five years and guarantees every visitor a warm and very friendly welcome. There are nine guest rooms, each with en-suite facilities, remote control colour TV, VCR and free movies, mini-bar and fridge, central heating and tea and coffee tray. The friendly atmosphere and stunning views from the lounge, make it the perfect setting for a relaxing drink before or after dinner.

The Ardtully Hotel

The restaurant enjoys an excellent reputation, for breakfast you can help yourself from a wide variety of cereals, fruits and juices from the buffet table and then enjoy a traditional full cooked breakfast. For dinner you can choose from the three course table d'hôte menu, which is changed daily and can include culinary delights such as Cullen Skink (a traditional Scottish soup) or Poached Salmon with Dill Sauce, delicious. James and Jan can also arrange a number of activities for you, including: golf on one of the three local courses, pony trekking, fishing, forest walks, guided tours, cruises to local islands or a trip on The Waverley, the last ocean going paddle steamer in the world. Also please note that there is a 15% discount available to those over the age of 55 when booking three days or longer.

The Ardtully Hotel, 297 Marine Parade, Hunter's Quay, Dunoon
Tel: 01369 702478

The perception of the **Esplanade Hotel** in Dunoon's West Bay is that it caters for the tourist trade. However, the Hotel, one of the most attractive in the town, has plenty to offer locals. Stroll through the archway from the West Bay, through the colourful floral gardens and into the warm and friendly atmosphere created in this long established family hotel. Since 1945 the Esplanade has been owned and run by the Watt/Togwell family and only last year they celebrated their Golden Anniversary. The Hotel was originally three separate houses and since 1945 continual refurbishment has resulted in a modern yet traditional hotel, capable of catering for the holiday maker and local alike.

The Esplanade is fully licensed and its bar, The Malt Cellar, boasts over 110 different whiskies, surely the best selection in this area? Another popular feature is the sun terrace which offers guests an unrivalled view over the Clyde and is a very popular spot on a sunny day. Your morning coffee or bar lunch can be enjoyed in the relaxing surroundings of the Garden Lounge. Clotted Cream Teas are a favourite afternoon treat and are served with home-made scones. Friday night dinner dances are a regular and popular feature in the Esplanade programme, although not a formal night, it gives you the opportunity to dress up and make it an occasion. Guests from England, Ireland, Wales, Scotland and many other parts of the world return year after year so why not pop in when you next stroll along the West Bay and see for yourself.

Esplanade Hotel, West Bay, Dunoon Tel: 01369 704070

Situated within one mile of the ancient town of Dunoon, on the main A885 north, **Cowal Bird Garden** offers visitors an unforgettable holiday experience. Stroll beneath the ancient beech trees by the ponds and see the parrots, Max and Spike, the blue and gold macaws, and Polly and Kermit, the Amazon parrots who are always ready for a chat, oh and better not forget Popeye, the Moluccan cockatoo, he's a real character. There are rheas, ornamental pheasants, peacocks, ducks, geese and much more. The children are going to enjoy playing amongst the farmyard pets and meeting Millie, Smoky and Felix the pygmy goats, Coco and Mollie the donkeys, Jock and Dumpling the pot-bellied pigs and Patch the Shetland pony.

Cowal Bird Garden

You could follow the nature trail through native woodland and watch wild birds at close quarters from the camouflaged hide, or just sit and relax with a picnic or a snack from the Garden snack shop. Cowal Bird Garden is owned and run by Annie and Phil Ratcliffe and is the culmination of a life long ambition. Cowal Bird Garden is adjacent to the Hafton Holiday Centre, in the old Hafton Estate, which offers its guests a wonderfully peaceful place to relax and enjoy the woodland and surrounding countryside.

Cowal Bird Garden, Lochan Wood, Dunoon Tel: 01369 707999

If you are looking for some good self-catering accommodation in the Dunoon area of Argyll, then look no further than the terrific selection of top class cottages and houses supplied by Colin and Angela Barnes. **Fern Cottage**, at Ardentinny, is a spacious terraced character cottage that sleeps four. Beautifully situated overlooking Loch Long with magnificent views of the sea and mountains, this tastefully modernised cottage still retains many of its original features. There is a fully fitted kitchen, modern bathroom, sun lounge, dining room, lounge and two bedrooms with all bed linen included in the rent. There is full central heating with an open fire in the lounge and all the electricity is metered and read at the end of your stay. There is also a colour TV, automatic washing machine, fridge and freezer, garden, parking for one car opposite the cottage and pets are always welcome. Fern Cottage makes a cosy and charming central base for touring the beautiful scenery and sandy beaches in this pretty county.

Fern Cottage   *Ardmun*

Ardmun, at Kilmun, is a large, detached house that sleeps up to six people. This 19th century home has been well modernised and is comfortably furnished to a high standard, with spectacular views across Holy Loch to Sandbank village and its surrounding hills and lochs. It comprises a lounge, dining room, kitchen, sun lounge, bathroom and four bedrooms with all bed linen included in the rent. There is a warming open fire in the lounge, solid fuel room heater in the dining room and electric panel heating which is run off of an electricity meter that is read at the end of your stay. There is also a colour TV, automatic washing machine, microwave, parking for two cars and a large garden that makes bringing your pets no problem at all. Within a three mile radius of Ardmun, there is golf, fishing, forest walks, botanical gardens and a bird park, and there is also a shop and pub within 500 yards of the house.

Coach House   *Glencairn*

Coach House, again at Kilmun, is a detached, converted coach house that will sleep up to six. Situated in the grounds of an early 20th century villa, this excellent conversion of a former coach house provides a good central base for touring. Downstairs you will find a lounge, fully fitted kitchen, large sun lounge with dining area, toilet with washbasin and one double bedroom. Upstairs there is another lounge, a bathroom and two more bedrooms with bed linen being included in the rent. There is a colour TV, automatic washing machine, fridge and freezer, ample parking and an adjoining garden where pets are welcome by arrangement.

Last on the list, but by no means least is **Glencairn**, at Ardentinny. Situated just yards from the shore, with superb mountain and sea views, this end terrace, character cottage sleeps up to four and has been restored to a high standard, retaining and enhancing its traditional character. With lounge/diner, fully fitted kitchen, bathroom and two bedrooms where bed linen is included in the rental price, Glencairn is centrally heated throughout with an open fire in the lounge. Again there is a colour TV, automatic washing machine, parking for two cars and a garden where pets are welcome. Electricity is charged by a meter reading.

CL Barnes, Garrachrhune, Kilmun by Dunoon
Tel: 01369 840206

FASLANE. Along the banks of Gare Loch is the Naval submarine base of Faslane. Beside the base is Faslane Cemetery and a memorial to a tragedy. In 1917 the unluckily numbered submarine K13 sank during acceptance trails. Trapped behind watertight doors 32 of the crew drowned, and it would be 55 hours before the rest of the crew were brought to safety from the bed of the loch. The memorial and the surrounding headstones form the outline of a submarine, a poignant reminder of the bravery of submariners.

HELENSBURGH. At the mouth of Gare Loch is this charming residential town and sailing centre. This was the birthplace, in 1888, of John Logie Baird, a man who some hold has a lot to answer for by inventing television. An example of his 'televisor' is displayed in the **Templeton Library**. Another famous Scot left his mark on the town, Charles Rennie Mackintosh designing **Hill House** on Upper Colquhoun Street. Considered one of his finest works it stands overlooking the Clyde from the top level of this hillside town.

Another architectural curiosity are the red painted devils on the roof of a house on William Street, the pair appear to be glaring at the church across the road.

LUSS. This pretty village has, in its church, a 14th-15th century effigy of St Kessog, a local 6th century evangelist.

From his base on the western banks of beautiful Loch Lomond, Mark Donald manages a unique business which is a boon for lovers of fine malt whisky throughout the world. At the **Ben Lomond Whisky Shop** in Luss, he not only stocks one of the most comprehensive selections of malts to be found in the Highlands, but he also operates a friendly and efficient mail order service which enables his customers to sample the fruits of the world's finest whisky distillers by direct mail. Malt lovers from London to Lagos and New York to New South Wales can choose from an interesting and informative catalogue listing the products of over 100 distilleries which are scattered throughout the length and breadth of the Highlands and Islands. In addition to the 300 whiskies on his regular list, Mark can usually obtain very rare malts or those produced in specific years. His service takes the hassle out of buying top quality malts, and he will stop at nothing to answer his customers' questions and fulfil their requests, no matter how difficult or obscure. With its unbeatable choice, knowledgeable manager and efficient service, the Ben Lomond Whisky Shop is perfect for the new enthusiast or more experienced malt collector. Visitors are very welcome to call in person and choose from one of the most extensive ranges of malt whiskies in Scotland. Those requiring a mail order catalogue should telephone Mark Donald on 01436 860208, or fax him on 01436 679409.

Ben Lomond Whisky Shop, Lodge on Loch Lomond Hotel, Luss
Tel: 01436 860208 Fax: 01436 679409

Situated in the very heart of some stunning Scottish countryside, **Doune of Glendouglas Farm** is two miles from the hamlet of Inverbeg and conveniently, only ten minutes away from the local International golf course. Built in 1750, this working farm is owned and personally run by Fay and Peter Robinson and has been Peter's family home since the day he was born.

Doune of Glendouglas offers the visitor bed and breakfast accommodation that comprises three bedrooms, one with en-suite facilities and all with those little extras that will make your stay something to remember. The generous cottage breakfast is personally made by Fay and is guaranteed to fill you up until lunchtime. This 2 Crown Highly Commended property has 2500 sheep and plenty of Highland cattle as well as a collection of family dogs who are always eager for a walk in the beautiful surrounding hills and fields.

Doune of Glendouglas Farm, Luss
Tel: 01301 702312

Mackintosh's Hill House, Helensburgh

TARBET. The name of this town is said to come from the words 'tarrain bata' or portage which stems from the time when Haakon of Norway allegedly dragged his vessels over the land separating the two waters and to have sailed into Loch Lomond to carry on his raids of pillaging and looting.

LOCH LOMOND is one of the largest expanses of water in Scotland, big enough to contain its own islands, some of which are inhabited. Many of the islands have legends or stories that surround them. **Inchlonaig** or 'Yew Island' was so named as it was supposed to have been planted with yew trees for the use of King Robert the Bruce's archers. On **Inchcailloch** the Fallow deer have been established since the 14th century and an ancient burial ground surrounds a ruined church, once the centre of a mainly landward parish. There is a ferry service to Inchcailloch from Balmaha on the eastern shore, which is also the base for the mailboat that visits the occupied islands on Monday, Thursday and Saturday mornings. Only a few people live on the islands, most of which are heavily wooded, but there are farms on some and the mailboat provides an important year-round link.

The A82 runs the full length of the west coast of the Loch from Ardlui in the north to Balloch in the south whilst much of the east side of the Loch is the sole preserve of the walker. There is also plenty of opportunity to get out on to the water with every kind of watersport catered for at centres up and down the Loch. If there is a down side to Loch Lomond it must be that, at holiday times, it can get very busy.

Loch Lomond is of course well known for that famous song about its 'Bonnie, Bonnie Banks', which has its base in an old Celtic belief that when a man dies in a foreign land his spirit returns home by the 'low road'. The song itself is said to refer to the last moments together of two Scottish soldiers captured by the English during the '45 Rebellion. One was to be set free, whilst the other was to be taken to England and executed. His spirit would thus go home by the 'low road' while his friend returned by the 'high road'.

ARROCHAR. From this village are clear views of the curious rock formations at the summit of 2991 foot **Ben Arthur** which give it its popular nickname The Cobbler.

Excellent overnight accommodation can be found at **Ravenswood**, an imposing late-Victorian stone built residence which lies at the head of Loch Long in the village of Arrochar. This handsome detached house stands within its own attractive garden in an elevated position overlooking the Loch, with magnificent views of the tree-lined 'Cobbler' beyond. Ravenswood offers the warmest of welcomes and a delicious full Scottish breakfast. The three double bedrooms all have full central heating, colour TVs and hot drinks making facilities; one has an en-suite bathroom and two have fitted vanity units and share a separate shower room and WC. There is also a comfortable guest lounge with colour TV, and a separate dining room. Conveniently situated near the junction of the A83 and A814, Ravenswood is the ideal holiday base for exploring Argyll, the Trossachs and Loch Lomond. There is also access to the scenic West Highland Railway at the nearby station, with day trips to Mallaig, including steam-hauled trains between Fort William and Mallaig during the summer months. In addition to providing overnight accommodation, Ravenswood has an attractive self-contained annexe available for those who prefer a self-catering holiday.

Ravenswood, Arrochar Tel: 01301 702489

ARDMAY. A delightful place to stay for those wanting to get away from it all can be found beside the A814 Helensburgh road, two miles southwest of Arrochar. **Ferry Cottage** stands in an elevated position overlooking Loch Long and has magnificent views over the water to the Cobbler and the Argyll Forest Park.

Ferry Cottage

Over two centuries old, this was once the home of the local ferryman who took passengers across the Loch until the service was terminated at turn of the 20th century. Now completely refurbished, the house offers three spacious and well appointed guest bedrooms, all with en-suite facilities and a number of impressive extras. The accommodation comprises one family room, one twin and one double with the added bonus of a luxurious four-poster waterbed. As well as a warm welcome, proprietors Carole and Terry Bennetton offer a delicious traditional breakfast with the option of such Scottish delicacies as porridge and Loch Fyne kipper. At certain times of the year, they also provide evening meals at special rates for guests staying a minimum of two nights. Fishing boats are available to hire locally and horse riding can also be arranged at a nearby stable. Ferry Cottage accepts all major credit cards and is a non-smoking establishment.

Ferry Cottage, Ardmay Tel: 01301 702428 Fax: 01301 702699

LOCHGOILHEAD. The narrow twisting B828 to Lochgoilhead has steeply wooded sides and is, interestingly enough, known as **Hell's Glen**. At the head of Loch Goil, visitors can take advantage of the renowned watersports facilities here, which includes boating, fishing, sub-aqua, diving and water skiing. Lochgoilhead also possesses a golf course and at **Drimsyne Leisure Centre**, between November and March, the famous sport of 'curling' is played. In this same arena, from April to October, Europe's first indoor 'sheep show' can be experienced; the event pays testament to the hill farming that has been going on here for generations and there is a collection of 19 breeds on show. The accompanying talk is impressive, highlighting the differences between the breeds and their wool and meat. Visitors are also able to see a demonstration of sheep shearing and see the dog and sheep handling that is so essential to life here.

Lochgoilhead makes an ideal centre for enjoying the benefits of the **Argyll Forest Park**. The park was created in 1933 and covers some 100 square miles, much of which is open to exploration via Forestry Commission tracks. Some of the many activities that you can enjoy in the surroundings include hill walking, climbing and pony trekking. Along the Loch from the village is **Carrick Castle** which stands right on the Loch's edge. Built in the 14th century this great rectangular keep was originally a Lamont stronghold but ended up in the hands of the Campbells (possibly as a result of the Dunoon massacre) and was used by the Scottish kings as a hunting lodge. During the Earl of Argyll's rebellion of 1685 the then owner Sir John Campbell of Carrick was called to book in Edinburgh over his small part in events. In 1715 he, perhaps wisely, came down firmly on the side of King George. Later in the century the Castle passed on to the Murrays, Earls of Dunsmore and by 1800 had been abandoned. There are plans to have it restored as a residence, if it does happen someone will awake every morning to the most wonderful view.

At the summit of Glen Croe pass is the famous **Rest and Be Thankful**. It is the highest point on the road between **Loch Long** and **Loch Fyne** and here the traveller is 803 feet above sea level. There is a small car park at the summit at which can be found a stone marker inscribed with the name of the regiment that built the military road over the pass in 1768.

CAIRNDOW. The magnificent gardens of **Strone House** contain the northernmost cork tree in Europe and the 188 foot 'Grand Fir', the tallest tree in Britain.

Castle Lachlan was first mentioned in a charter of 1314 and the ruins stand on a promontory overlooking Loch Fyne. It is the ancient home of the MacLachlan of MacLachlan. Today the clan Chief, Madam MacLachlan of MacLachlan lives in a nearby 18th century castle mansion, and if a visitor happens to be a MacLachlan she welcomes family members by appointment.

DALMALLY. From the village a small road to the south leads up to **Monument Hill** where, from the memorial rotunda to the Gaelic poet Duncan Ban MacIntyre, there is a superb panorama over Ben Cruachan, the two northern arms of Loch Awe and the wooded islets scattered around them. Beyond the village is **Kilchurn Castle**. Once surrounded by the waters of the Loch, this dramatic ruin was built by Sir Colin Campbell of Glenorchy in 1440 and abandoned during the Jacobite rebellions. From the pier beside the railway station at Lochawe village summer cruises round the islands are run by the Edwardian peat fired steam launch Lady Rowena. The **Pullman Carriage Tearoom** on the pier serves wonderful views to go with its cuppas and sticky buns.

Glenorchy Lodge at Dalmally is a first rate hotel, pub and eating place which lies on the main A85 Tyndrum to Oban road at the foot of dramatic Glen Orchy. This attractive small hotel is owned and personally run by the Whyte family, friendly and experienced hosts who provide a warm welcome, good food and drink, and comfortable accommodation.

Glenorchy Lodge

The five spacious guest bedrooms are impressively equipped with en-suite bathrooms, colour televisions, telephones and tea and coffee making facilities, and are ideally suited for those with or without children. The residents' lounge and dining room are bright and pleasantly decorated, and enjoy magnificent views of Ben Cruachan, one of Scotland's highest mountains. The Whytes serve an excellent full Scottish breakfast and an extensive range of delicious evening meals, either in the dining room or the lounge bar. Added in 1988, the Lodge Bar is a lively and popular meeting place which attracts visitors and local residents from a wide area. With its excellent connections in all directions, Glenorchy Lodge is the perfect holiday base from which to explore the beautiful mountains and coastal landscape of the West Highlands.

Glenorchy Lodge Hotel, Dalmally Tel: 01838 200312

LOCHAWE. The **Smokery and Fishery** has a detailed exhibition on curing and smoking fish in the old tradition, as well as offering the opportunity to catch some trout in the lochs. Above the **Pass of Brander** stands mighty **Ben Cruachan**, all 3695 feet of it. Hidden inside the mountain is a massive storage power station: water is pumped 1200 feet up the mountain into a vast cavern when electricity demand is low and at the push of a button released back into Loch Awe creating 400,000 kilowatts for everyone's morning coffee. The only visible evidence of all this is a dam high on the hillside.

BRIDGE OF ORCHY. At the northern end of **Glen Orchy**, this hamlet has a spectacular position overlooking Loch Tulla. There still is a bridge here, though the main road no longer crosses it, as well as a hotel, railway station and a few houses. The former coaching house still sells petrol, once a common occurrence in the Highlands in the days before self-service garages. The original road north from here passed to the east of the Loch until rebuilt in the 1930s, and a stump still runs up to the lonely and historic Inn at Inveroran and a pair of shooting lodges before petering out - the tarmac having been reclaimed by nature.

PORTNACROISH. The tall, simple tower keep of **Castle Stalker** stands on an islet in **Loch Linnhe** with the mountains of Kingairloch as a backdrop. Home to the Stuarts of Appin it was fortified after the '45 Rising and became a garrison before being abandoned to the elements. In 1965 work began to restore it and it is possible, via a boat trip, to pay a visit.

PORT APPIN. Some of the finest self-catering accommodation in this beautiful part of Argyll can be found on the shores of Loch Creran near the village of Appin. **Appin Holiday Homes** offer a range of first class accommodation, including traditional cottages, chalet-bungalows and lochside residential holiday caravans. Open all year round, the park lies beside the main A828 west coast road, midway between Oban and Fort William. Resident proprietors Mr and Mrs Weir belong to a family, now in its fifth generation, which has lived in the area since 1905. In the last three decades, they have built up an impressive holiday facility to which visitors return year after year. The accommodation includes three well-equipped brick-built cottages sleeping four to six, which enjoy breathtaking views to the south across the loch to the mountains beyond. Similarly impressive are the modern timber-built chalet bungalows which are self-contained and equipped with colour television and bed linen. The caravans feature a variety of recent models and enjoy a delightful position by the lochside. With its attractive play area containing swings, table tennis and giant chess board, and safe swimming, boating and sailing in nearby Loch Creran, Appin Holiday Homes are especially suitable as a touring base for discovering the beautiful West Highlands.

Appin Holiday Homes, Dungrianach, Appin
Tel: 01631 730287

From its elevated position overlooking Loch Linnhe, **Appin House** in north Argyll is set amongst some of the most breathtaking scenery in the Scottish West Highlands. Set in five acres of beautifully landscaped gardens, Appin House is a secluded and very private resting place for visitors who wish to escape from the hustle and bustle of every day life and just relax.

Appin House

The house was bought in 1983 by your hosts Dave and Denys Mathieson, and the old parts of the building have since been tastefully converted into six individual, self-catering apartments. Each apartment is self-contained with its own individual character and style. They vary in size from a single storey studio for a couple only, to a three bedroom cottage type for six to seven people. In 1992, in response to a demand for accommodation more suited to. Winter occupation, the Mathieson's constructed two well insulated lodges, Birch and Pine. These stand just outside the main gates, at the top of the drive, and offer the guest the ultimate in cosy comfort. Because this is not a large establishment, all guests receive personal attention at all times and because of the general aura of serenity and space, there is no feeling of overcrowding. All of the accommodation is equipped to the same high, Scottish Tourist Board inspected standard, although each apartment and lodge has its own unique feel, due to its individual design and finish. Double glazing is standard throughout and background winter heating is provided free of charge in all apartments by means of either a storage heater or radiator from the central heating system.

Appin House, Appin Tel: 01631 730207

LISMORE. The passenger ferry to Lismore out in Loch Linnhe departs from Port Appin. Only eight miles long and a mile wide, the Island was once an important religious centre. The Pictish St Moluag brought Christianity to Lismore in the 6th century and the parish church, on the site of the 13th century cathedral of the diocese of Argyll, retains his name. So does the nearby hollowed boulder known for hundreds of years a St Moluag's Chair. An Iron Age broch stands at Tirefour and the 13th century ruin of **Castle Coeffin** is perched on a headland facing the mainland of Kingairloch. North of the restored cottages of Port Ramsay, a long disused lime kiln moulders, a monument to better trading days.

CONNEL. When the railway still ran north to Ballachulish, road and rail traffic shared the bridge though it was controlled by the railway signalman and trains took priority. In 1966 the line closed but the bridge still remains, today used solely by the motor car. Below the bridge are the churning waters of the **Falls of Lora**. This is the point where a narrow channel links Loch Etive with the intersection of Loch Linnhe.

Monsters and supernatural creatures have played an important part in the Gaelic culture and Loch Etive has its very own monster, the Fachan. With 'one hand out of his chest, one leg out of his haunch and one eye out of his face', this gruesome creature is thought to represent an imperfect memory of the Celtic seers who, when they were casting spells, would stand on one leg, with one eye closed and one arm extended.

To the north lies the **Sea Life Centre**; from loveable seals to the sinister conger eels, the centre presents unique display of the native marine life in a stunning setting. The shoreline restaurant has won Taste of Scotland awards and the views could win them as well.

Only two and a half hours drive from Glasgow and Edinburgh, **The Falls of Lora Hotel** is a charming owner-run Victorian hotel that over-looks the spectacular Loch Etive. The main hotel was built in 1886, with the modern extension being added in the 1970s and is only five miles from Oban, 'The Gateway to the Highlands and Islands', making it an ideal centre for a touring, walking and sailing holiday or just relaxing in this friendly atmosphere.

There are 30 guest rooms, all of which have been individually decorated and furnished to a high standard, with private bathrooms, central heating, direct dial telephones, television and radio. The family rooms come with additional bunk-beds for the kids, who come for free if they are sharing with their parents, now that can't be bad if you are on a budget. There are also three luxury rooms, one is traditionally furnished with a luxury double bed and a stunning view of the Loch and Connel Bridge or if you want something different there is a guest room with a seven foot round bed and exotic, en-suite Jacuzzi bathroom. If you are after the ultimate in romance and style, then opt for the beautiful bay-windowed room overlooking Loch Etive, it comes complete with a six foot wide four-poster bed and a lavish en-suite bathroom with gold fittings and a king size round bath!

The Falls of Lora Hotel

The Falls of Lora Hotel also has a unique Cocktail Bar which has a centrally situated open log fire and offers its guests a choice of over 100 brands of whisky and an extensive Bistro menu featuring local produce, and on most Thursdays there is a special seven course Scottish dinner. This superb hotel can cater for all your requirements, whether on business or pleasure. You can relax in the quiet comfort of the residents lounge or hold that important meeting in the small but well appointed conference room.

The Falls of Lora Hotel, Connel Ferry
Tel: 01631 710483

Delightful bed and breakfast accommodation in this beautiful part of the country is provided by Jean Clark at her handsome detached house in Connel. Situated on the A85 Oban road overlooking the entrance to Loch Etive, **Kilchurn** is ideal for a comfortable overnight stay on the road to the isles or as a holiday base for exploring the mountains and coastline of Argyll. Mrs Clark is a friendly and experience host who provides a warm welcome and a delicious Scottish breakfast. Her three spacious and well appointed guest bedrooms are all equipped with tea and coffee making facilities, and two also have the added comfort of en-suite facilities. Scottish Tourist Board 2 Crown Commended, Kilchurn also has plenty of off-street parking.

Kilchurn Bed and Breakfast, Connel Tel: 01631 710581

TAYNUILT. On the shore of Loch Etive lies **Bonawe Iron Furnace**, the preserved remains of a charcoal furnace, or 'bloomery' for iron smelting. Established in 1753, it worked until 1876, when it was forced to close as all the forests had gone.

DUNBEG. **Dunstaffnage Castle** is a well preserved example of a 13th century castle with a massive curtain wall and round towers. Originally built by the MacDougal, Lords of Lorne, it was passed to the Earls of Argyll and held on their behalf by the hereditary captains of Dunstaffnage from the late 16th century, falling into disrepair after 1810 when the captains moved out. Angus, 20th Captain of Dunstaffnage had some of the buildings restored in the 1930s. Though successfully sieged by Robert the Bruce in 1308, Dunstaffnage was always on the side of the Government during the Civil War and Jacobite risings

OBAN. This handsome and lively Victorian port bustles with trade and tourists heading to and from the islands. From the harbour the ferries of Caledonian MacBryne criss-cross the waters around the Inner and Outer Hebrides. The town is overlooked by one of Britain's finest and most unforgettable follies. John McCaig was a local banker and adhered to the Victorian philosophy that wealth obliged the holder to better the education of the less fortunate. **McCaig's Tower** is an impressive, if ill-remembered, imitation of the Colosseum of Rome, which he'd seen on a visit to Italy. Built between 1897 and 1900, it provided unemployed masons in the area with work and was also intended to house a museum, art gallery and monument to the McCaig family. None of this came about and the hollow shell stands as a folly to his aspirations

Oban Harbour and McCaig's Folly

There is plenty to see around the town. It has its own distillery, founded in 1794, that produces the famous **Oban West Highland Malt** in Stafford Street. A trip around the distillery is available but they would appreciate a call beforehand on 01631 64262.

The mysteries of working with glass are revealed at **Oban Glass** on the Lochavullin Estate. Part of the Caithness Glass Group they take the raw materials and transform them into beautiful paperweights. Visitors are invited to see the process from start to finish and they can buy examples of what they've seen made in the factory shop.

The **Glenburnie Private Hotel** is an impressive establishment which enjoys breathtaking views across Oban Bay to the islands beyond. Conveniently situated on the Esplanade within half-a-mile of Oban town centre, railway station and ferry piers, it offers exceptional bed and breakfast accommodation in twelve twin and double and two single rooms.

Glenburnie Private Hotel

Originally built in 1897 and recently renovated, the hotel is beauti-fully furnished and finished in Sanderson decor throughout. The guest bedrooms are equipped with colour televisions, electric blankets and tea and coffee making facilities, and most also have the added comfort of an en-suite shower or bathroom. Those to the front, like the dining room and guest lounge, have magnificent views across the bay, and the superior rooms are also provided with an American-style king-size bed and a decanter of sherry. Proprietors Allyson and Graeme Strachan have owned and personally run the hotel since 1992, although the building has been in their family for over three decades. They offer a very warm welcome and a varied and delicious three course Scottish breakfast. They are also happy to recommend local eating places for the evening, as dinner is not provided at the hotel.

Glenburnie Private Hotel, Esplanade, Oban Tel: 01631 562089

The Gathering Restaurant, in Breadalbane Street, is one of the most unusual and long established eating places in the Highlands. It was founded in 1882 as an addition to the Argyllshire Gathering Hall which was built five years before as a permanent venue for the summer ball held to celebrate the annual gathering of the clans. For over 100 years it has catered for royalty and the Scottish nobility, and it remains a first class restaurant which attracts a wide cross-section of enthusiastic diners with its unique character and fine Scottish cuisine.

The Gathering Restaurant

The atmosphere is comfortable and unpretentious, with heavy traditional furniture, framed prints and antlers on the wood-panelled walls. A recommended Taste of Scotland establishment, the food is freshly prepared to traditional recipes from the finest local ingredients. Fresh fish and seafood are the house speciality, and the menu features such starters as Seil Island oysters, smoked Inverawe trout, and seafood chowder; main courses include poached Islay scallops, lobster in season and Oban Bay seafood platter - a wonderful combination of local mussels, scallops, trout and scampi flambéed in whisky. An impressive selection of steaks and game dishes is also available, including venison, and haggis with tatties and neeps, as well as a variety of lighter meals, such as lasagne, chilli con carne and seafood pasta. There is also a mouthwatering range of desserts, including the superb sounding 'Cranachan' - fresh cream, oatmeal and honey served with summer fruits - and a list of carefully chosen wines and liqueur coffees to complement the meal. The service is friendly and efficient, and the portions generous. The Argyllshire Gathering Ball continues to be held here on the last Thursday in August, the night after the Highland Games, when the restaurant is closed to the public.

The bar below the Gathering Restaurant has recently been refurbished as **O'Donnell's Irish Pub**, a lively and popular meeting place which is open each evening until 1 am. As well as a range of fine Irish beers and stouts, top quality bar meals are served until 11 pm. Live Celtic music is played most evenings, and the young at heart come here from miles around to savour the atmosphere, and perhaps even join in an impromptu ceilidh. Together, the Gathering Restaurant and O'Donnell's Irish Pub offer the complete Celtic experience, combining the best Scottish cuisine with the fun of the Irish 'Craic'.

The Gathering Restaurant and O'Donnell's Irish Pub, Breadalbane Street,
Oban Tel: 01631 564849/565421/566159

Animal lovers of all ages will enjoy a trip to **Oban Rare Breeds Farm Park**, situated only two miles from Oban, through the golf-course on the Glencruitten road. Set within 30 acres of beautiful west Highland countryside, you can meet a variety of rare breed animals seldom seen on modern farms today: like Susie and Jimmy Wong, a newly wed couple of Vietnamese pot-bellied pigs, Bruce an Anglonubian goat and Morag the Highland cow.

Oban Rare Breeds Farm Park

Winner of the 1995 Scottish Tourist Board Tourism Oscar for the best tourist attraction in Scotland and Best Established Visitors Attraction in Scotland, Oban Rare Breeds Farm Park has to be one of the best days out in Scotland. You can explore the park at your leisure, taking in the various paddocks and enclosures with their fascinating and unusual occupants. The Woodland Walk follows a meandering path, crossing and re-crossing the adjacent stream by way of numerous bridges with bracken, rowan and birch trees, ferns and colourful wildflowers on all sides. Having enjoyed your stroll, the tea-room provides a welcome resting point where you can relax with a refreshing cup of tea and a slice of cake before exploring the well stocked Souvenir Shop and Conservation Centre.

Oban Rare Breeds Farm Park, New Barran, Oban
Tel: 01631 770608

The Celtic race are renowned throughout the world for their artistic prowess. Art, music, poetry and dancing in the Celtic style are as popular today as they were centuries ago. **Tir-Nan-Og** is a testimony to that Celtic Heritage. Tir-Nan-Og, meaning Land of Youth, is the name of a new Celtic Entertainment Centre based in Oban. Located in a Grade C Listed Building in Argyll Square in the heart of the town, on the site of St Columba's church, the building has been totally restored inside and out to create a superb platform for authentic Scottish food and drink, music, art and poetry. Every day there is a new flavour of Scotland for you to savour, created by their master chef Robbie Robertson. He lovingly prepares everything from Haggis and Stovies to Scottish Salmon and Venison, not forgetting the mouthwatering Catch of the Day. The à la carte menu is extensive and suits all tastes and budgets. There is a unique selection of malt whiskies and special ales form the cask, plus all you favourite beers, lagers and wines.

Tir-Nan-Og & The Lorne Bar

The fun starts at 11 am with a delicious cup of coffee, there are four varieties to choose from, or maybe a pot of tea with a home-made buttered scone, scrumptious. If you are feeling a little more peckish you could make a choice from the extensive Snax Menu or Daily Specials. Enjoy your lunch, it can be as quick or as leisurely as you choose, with a childrens menu full of wholesome Scottish food for the weans, while dinner is really something to look forward to. Coach tours and day trippers are welcomed with open arms, quality snacks are a speciality and every cuppa comes with FREE entertainment from the resident harpist or Celtic performer. Tir-Nan-Og can cater for parties from 30 to 300 people, just book yourself prior to arrival and your away. There are live bands and contemporary musicians every Thursday, Friday, Saturday and Sunday so hurry along and experience something that is not only unique to Oban, but also to the whole of Scotland.

Also owned and run by the same establishment is **The Lorne Bar**, a very warm and welcoming family run inn that is beautifully decorated and furnished with plenty of brass, wood and marble. Children and pets are also welcome up until 9.00 pm in the lively bar area, where live bands play and freshly prepared food is served throughout the day.

Tir-Nan-Og & The Lorne Bar, Argyll Square, Oban
Tel: 01631 570505/566766

The Kings Knoll Hotel enjoys a magnificent situation, standing in its own grounds overlooking the picturesque Oban Bay it is easily located by guests when driving into Oban via the A85. Your hosts are Archie and Margaret MacDonald and this family run hotel offers a warm welcome to all, and from the moment guests arrive at the reception, they are fully aware of the genuine Highland hospitality that Scotland is so famous for.

The Kings Knoll Hotel

All fifteen guest rooms at The Kings Knoll are attractively furnished and decorated to a high standard, with the majority offering full en-suite facilities. Each light and airy room is equipped with a colour TV and complimentary tea and coffee tray, and for those special occasions there is a guest room complete with four-poster bed for that extra touch of luxury. In the Knoll restaurant, with its maritime theme, a bright and airy feel has been created by its high beamed ceilings and picture windows that boast splendid views over the town. The cuisine is outstanding and offers the guest the very best in fresh, local seafood, venison and Angus steaks, all complemented by a select and varied wine list. The elegant King's Rest lounge bar has a distinctly Highland atmosphere and a wide selection of malt whiskies for you to enjoy in this richly decorated room. For those cooler evenings there is a welcoming open fire, and entertainment is available at weekends. Upstairs you will find the comfortable residents' lounge with television, an ideal spot for some quiet relaxation before its time to explore Oban's excellent night life or local attractions.

Kings Knoll Hotel, Dunollie Road, Oban
Tel: 01631 562536

Located no more than a fifteen minute walk from the main centres of attraction in Oban, **Dungallan House Hotel** is situated high above Oban Bay with its own private drive from the shore road. Built in 1870, this Scottish Victorian house is set in its own splendid grounds and commands a magnificent panoramas over Oban Bay to the Isle of Mull, Lismore and the hills of Morvern. Under the supervision of George and Janice Stewart, the feeling of being welcomed to their private home has been continued throughout Dungallan.

Dungallan House Hotel

The moment guests arrive at the reception, they receive genuine Highland hospitality in elegant surroundings, from the rich decor and furnishings of the lounge bar to the quiet intimacy of the reading room. There are thirteen guest rooms, nine of which have en-suite facilities and all have a complimentary tea and coffee tray and colour televisions. The rooms are cosy and welcoming, each having been individually decorated and furnished to a high standard. There are traditional coal fires throughout the house for those cooler days and evenings and a wide selection of Scottish malts to warm the weary traveller.

Having gained her highly acclaimed standards and reputation from past experience at Arisaig Hotel, Janice has achieved many accolades over the years for the quality of her cuisine, prepared using only the best and freshest Scottish produce available. There is an interesting 18 hole golf course within 10 minutes drive, some superb gardens that are open to the public and a delightful Rare Breeds Park nearby, so you shouldn't be lost for things to do. George and Janice look forward to meeting old friends and to welcoming many new ones.

Dungallan House Hotel, Gallanach Road, Oban
Tel: 01631 563799

LERAGS. **Lerags House** is a superb licensed guest house which can be found at the end of Lerags Glen, four miles south of Oban. This enchanting Georgian country house stands within two acres of beautiful landscaped grounds which reach down to the edge of Loch Feochan. Resident proprietors Margaret and Norman Hill take great pride in providing the finest hospitality, food and accommodation.

Lerags Hotel

Their seven guest bedrooms are all well appointed and equipped with private en-suite bathrooms and a number of thoughtful extras; most also have fine views over the garden towards the loch and the hills beyond. The dining room and guest lounge contain many elegant features usually associated with a private home, including welcoming open fires in cooler weather.

Margaret and Norman provide a hearty Scottish breakfast and first class evening meals by prior arrangement; these are freshly prepared from the finest local ingredients, with a range of carefully selected wines available to complement the meal. Margaret, a qualified teacher of Scottish country dancing, is an invaluable source of advice for those wishing to take part in local dances. Lerags House is open between March and October, and over the Christmas and New Year period, but is unsuitable for smokers.

Lerags House, Lerags, Nr Oban Tel & Fax: 01631 563381

EASDALE. From the village on the island of **Seil**, a ferry makes the crossing to the small island of Easdale on which is a folk **Museum**.

The **Inshaig Park Hotel** is a very comfortable and intimate hotel which stands in an idyllic position overlooking the sea on the island of Seil, 16 miles southwest of Oban. Connected to the mainland by an 18th century stone bridge, this lesser known member of the Inner Hebrides is a haven for seals, otters, badgers and a wide variety of birdlife, making it a paradise for naturalists and walkers.

During Victorian and Edwardian times, the harbour at Easdale was a regular stopping place for the once frequent pleasure steamers that plied up and down the West Highland coast. Inshaig Park was originally built for the owner of the island's slate mines, but at the turn of the 20th century it was converted to a hotel to service the influx of visitors. In recent years, this handsome stone building has been completely renovated and now offers six centrally heated guest bedrooms, all with colour TVs and a number of thoughtful extras; five also have private bathrooms en-suite. Proprietors Sheila and Barrie Fletcher offer the warmest Highland hospitality and some of the finest cuisine in the area, with fresh local seafood a speciality. The beautiful private garden of An Cala stands adjacent to the hotel and is open to visitors on certain days.

Inshaig Park Hotel, Easdale, Isle of Seil
Tel & Fax: 01852 300256

FORD. In the valley at the foot of Dun Dubh (the black fort) at the crossroads between Loch Awe and Loch Ederline is the small village of Ford which is home to the beautiful **Ford Hotel**. Built on the old drovers' road, this Victorian sporting hostelry has a long tradition of offering Highland hospitality to visitors to Argyll. Ford Hotel is a family run establishment, owned by Ken and Elizabeth Hasall, and it is very important to the couple that all their guests enjoy their stay. Each of the individual eleven bedroom has en-suite facilities with facilities suitable for children. The emphasis is on a relaxed and informal ambiance coupled with comfortable surrounding, so you will leave this hotel with a general feeling of well-being and peace. Dundubh Restaurant uses plenty of local produce including Scottish beef, venison and West Coast seafood and the menus created daily are a balance between the exotic and more traditional Scottish dishes. The hotel bar is the traditional meeting place of Ford's local community, the atmosphere is warm and friendly where you can sit and enjoy a glass of malt whisky from the extensive range on offer. Surrounded by a whole host of places to visit and investigate, Ford Hotel is the perfect base from which to explore the Heartland of the Celts.

Ford Hotel, Ford, By Lochgilphead Tel: 01546 810273

KILMARTIN. This small village has the rather sorry remains of the castle that housed Rector Carsewell before he went up in the ecclesiastical world and move up the road. The rather imposing tower house that is **Carnasserie Castle** was built by John Carsewell upon his appointment as first Protestant Superintendent of the Isles, which following the Reformation of 1650. Mary, Queen of Scots later made him Bishop of the Isles, and though he was never consecrated he announced himself as Bishop from that day forth. He is perhaps best remember for publishing the first book in Gaelic, a translation of Knox's *Liturgy* in 1567. He died in 1572 and the castle passed to Campbells of Auchinleck, later the Castle was captured and partly blown up during Argyll's rebellion of 1685.

Also of interest is the churchyard which has a number of fascinating medieval carved grave slabs and large fragments of at least two 16th century crosses. The grave slabs commemorate Malcolm of Poltalloch and to this day there is a member of the family with the same name.

In the area to the southwest of the village towards the sea at Loch Crinan is the most concentrated site of prehistoric memorials in Scotland. Bronze Age burial cairns and standing stones are reached by the country roads around the Poltalloch estate. Further south, a footpath goes up to outstanding rock of Dunadd, where an Iron Age fort became the capital of the 6th century kingdom of Dalriada. The path leads to a hilltop where the earliest kings of Scotland were crowned.

CRINAN. It is certainly worthwhile visiting this tiny village at the head of the Canal, which still has a delightful character today. One of the grandest sights in Scottish sailing occurs early on the morning of Glasgow Fair Monday in July, when the second leg of the Tobermory

Race starts from Crinan. On the turn of the tide, the whole fleet of around 200 yachts races away through the maze of islands towards the Sound of Mull.

KILBERRY. As well as having a fine collection of late medieval sculptured stones, two miles north of Kilberry, stands **Stonefield Castle Hotel Gardens**. The 60 acres of shrubs and woodlands surround a baronial house, designed by Sir William Playfair in 1837, on a dramatic site beside Loch Fyne. Some of the Himalayan rhododendrons are as much as 100 years old and there are also rare trees and shrubs from as far a field as South Africa and New Zealand.

LOCHGILPHEAD. A quiet resort, it stands on the **Crinan Canal** which links Loch Fyne with the Sound of Jura via a series of 15 locks. Started in 1776 by James Watt, the canal was designed to facilitate travel for business people and locals who had previously had to sail the 130 miles around the Mull of Kintyre. The terrain proved to be difficult, skilled labour was scarce, and money ran out several times before the canal was finally opened in 1809, bringing the Western Isles and the west coast of Scotland to within easy reach of the Clyde and Glasgow.

On the outskirts of the town are **Kilmory Castle Gardens**, which were started in 1770 and include over 100 varieties of rhododendrons, some of which were supplied to Kew Gardens.

AUCHINDRAIN. One of very few West Highland villages to survive almost completely unchanged **Auchindrain Old Highland Township** gives a fascinating insight into life on a joint tenancy farm in the late 18th century. The original longhouses and barns of the period are still standing and have most of their period furnishings and equipment. It really is an informative place and there is also a useful visitors' centre, shop and lovely picnic area.

Not far north of Auchindrain the road passes close to the **Argyll Wildlife Park**. This 60 acre site has one of Europe's largest collections of wildfowl, with a large collection of owls and many rare native species.

The Western Islands

JURA is as peaceful and quiet as they come, rugged and majestic and surprisingly free of castles. It is here that George Orwell wrote *1984*, and on the very northern tip is the Gulf of Corryvreckan and its infamous whirlpool. This treacherous tide-race is very dangerous for small craft and it can be heard from a considerable distance. The Island's name is derived from the Norse for deer and today red deer remain an essential part of life here. The herds add up to some 5000 animals, mostly keeping to the trackless fastnesses of the Island's interior though they have been known to approach the sparsely populated east coast.

ISLAY. The most southerly and the largest of these Inner Hebrides, Islay is rightly famous for its fine malt whiskies, their distinctive flavour a result of the peaty water. There are several distilleries on the island and many single malts to choose from but most of this individual brew goes into blended whisky and few blends don't contain Islay malt.

Among the many Celtic and later crosses on the island, **Kildalton Cross** is held to be one of the most beautiful in all Scotland. Dating from around AD 800 and probably the work of an Ionian sculptor, the green to grey local stone carries a wealth of intricate patterns and scenes.

COLONSAY should be explored on foot, there are few roads anyway and watch out for the wild goats that were originally kept for milk. At low tide it is possible to walk across to Oronsay, off the south coast. Once a sanctuary there are the remains of a 14th century abbey on the island. It is said that any criminal who could support himself here for a year and a day would be set free, which would be a feat today let alone centuries ago.

TRESHNISH ISLES. The waters around this string of basaltic rocks that rise in terraces, are home to whales, storm petrels, puffins and seals.

STAFFA. This romantic and uninhabited small island is famous for its basaltic formations and remarkable caves, the best of which is **Fingal's Cave**. Immortalised by Mendelssohn in his celebrated *Hebrides* overture, its cluster of columns and man-made-looking symmetry gives the cave a cathedral-like majesty. Other famous visitors to the island have included Queen Victoria and Prince Albert, the artist Turner and poets and writers Keats, Wordsworth, Tennyson and Sir Walter Scott.

ISLE OF ULVA. The birthplace of General Lachlan Macquarie, Governor of New South Wales, the island is an unspoilt haven where nature can be seen at its best. The **Boathouse Visitor Centre** shows interpretive displays and is the starting point for several signed walks.

IONA. At the end of the Ross of Mull lies this historic island, reached by the passenger-only ferry from Fionnphort. In 563 St Columba with twelve followers founded a monastery here. Often sacked by Norsemen it was replaced in 1203 but, along with the Cathedral, fell into decay after first Dunkeld then St Andrews became the country's religious capital. Restoration began earlier this century and the monastery is now the home of the Iona Community (founded by Dr George Macleod in 1938). They have done much of the restoration to the Cathedral, which has a beautiful interior and interesting carvings. The oldest building on Iona is **St Oran's Chapel**, built in 1080 and now restored. The remains of the 13th century nunnery can be seen and, outside the Cathedral, is 10th century **St Martin's Cross**, 14 feet high and elaborately carved. For centuries Iona was the burial place of Scottish kings and chiefs, no less than 60 lie around the abbey and swept by the laden salt spray and winds of the Atlantic it still holds a spiritual atmosphere.

MULL. This Island may not be as dramatic as Skye or as remote as Harris and Lewis but it does have a peace and tranquility all its own. Perhaps that is why visitors find themselves drawn back here time and time again. Many parts of the rugged coast are easily seen from the main roads, but to discover the Island's 'hidden places' demands more adventure.

Much of the Island's coast consists of cliffs and those overlooking the Isle of Inch Kenneth at **Gribun** are rather unstable. Below them the ruins of an 18th century cottage still lie, crushed under a boulder which killed a young couple on their wedding night. On the roadless shoreline south of Gribun is **Mackinnon's Cave**. Tradition has it that nobody has ever reached its far end and come out again. Legend also tells of the piper sent into the cave, in the days when people could interpret the music of the pipes, and was heard to play 'woe is me without three hands - two hands for the pipes and one for a sword'. No one knows what he wanted the sword for because no one ever saw him again! It is still possible to get trapped in the cave today as it is cut off at high tide.

There is much more to be discovered along the coast but the only way to reach **MacCulloch's Tree** is on foot. **The Burg** is a massive headland that can only be reached along a track that starts off B8035 on north shore of Loch Scridain near Kilfinichen Bay. It is around five miles to the MacCulloch's Tree, a 40 foot high fossil imprint that is around 50 million years old and can only be reached at low tide.

A three mile walk from Carsaig leads to the remarkable **Carsaig Arches** tunnels formed by the sea in the towering basaltic rock cliffs, which again are only accessible at low tide. On the way is **Nun's Cave**, with its curious carvings, said to have been built by nuns driven from Iona at the time of the Reformation.

The road through **Glen More** is traditionally haunted by a headless rider and driving in the darkness on the lonely roads of Mull can take the imagination back to a far different world. Part of that world stands at the head of Loch Buie. **Moy Castle**, or Lochbuie as it was once called, was the ancient seat of the Maclaines of Buie. Abandoned in 1752, when the nearby Georgian mansion was completed, today this simple oblong tower is wreathed in ivy but still retains a dignity all its own.

AROUND MULL

TOBERMORY. The bay here forms perfect shelter for boats, something appreciated by the British Fisheries Society when they nominated Tobermory, together with Ullapool, as fishing stations in 1786. The industry flourished for nearly 200 years and though fish is still landed here today most of the boats in the harbour are pleasure craft. The harbour is an ideal base for sailing the islands and the Sound is the finishing point for the popular Tobermory Yacht Race.

One delightful feature of the harbour is its colour-washed houses on the water front. One of these house the **Mull Museum**, which has a number of displays covering local history. Out in the bay lies the wreck of a ship of the Spanish Armada. The surviving members of her crew were imprisoned in Duart Castle.

There are less than one hundred miles of roads on the island but once year, in late autumn, they are all closed for The Tour of Mull. This famous and very popular car rally sees the island reverberating to the roar of powerful rally cars for a weekend, before returning to peace and quiet. As a point of interest the rally is the only one in Britain to take place on public roads and needs an Act of Parliament, as well as the goodwill of the islanders, to take place.

DERVAIG is the venue of **Mull Little Theatre**, famous for 25 years as world's smallest professional theatre with just 43 seats housed in a converted cow byre. Shows start at 8.30 pm nightly, during the summer season, and are a continuous repertory of four varied plays featuring two or more actors.

CALGARY. The **House of Treshnish** sits on a hillside above the village and offers extensive walks through rare and beautiful shrubberies with wonderful views over Calgary bay. Calgary gave its name to the Canadian city in Alberta via the city's founder, Colonel JF Macleod, who, it is presumed, was from around this part of the island.

SALEN. The impressive **Glenforsa Hotel** at Salen enjoys an idyllic setting in six acres of secluded grounds overlooking the Sound of Mull. An attractive modern building designed in Scandinavian log-chalet style, guests are assured of a comfortable and relaxing break away from it all. Proprietors Jean and Paul Price are friendly and experienced hosts who provide first class accommodation in 16 attractively furnished and well equipped en-suite guest rooms. A fresh Scandinavian feel pervades throughout, enhanced by pine panelled walls and furniture which is apparently constructed without using a single nail.

Glenforsa Hotel

Dining at the Glenforsa is a real treat, as the Hotel's Taste of Scotland recommendation confirms. The imaginative menu incorporates both traditional Scottish and Continental dishes, all prepared using fresh local produce wherever possible. The speciality of the house is locally caught fish and seafood, accompanied by a selection of wines from a carefully chosen list. With its stylish surroundings and exceptional atmosphere, a stay at this celebrated hotel is sure to leave you refreshed and revitalised.

Glenforsa Hotel, Salen, Isle of Mull Tel: 01680 300377
Fax: 01680 300535

CRAIGNURE. Though the main ferry lands at Craignure services sail from Lochaline on the Kingairloch Peninsula to Fishnish and from Kilchoan on Ardnamurchan Peninsula to Tobermory. All carry vehicles but the Tobermory service doesn't run on Sundays.

Ferries are not the only departures from Craignure. **The Mull & West Highland Narrow Gauge Railway** runs a scheduled service between Old Pier Station and Torosay Castle; the steam and diesel-hauled trains running a mile and half through a superb sea and mountain panorama. **Torosay Castle**, whilst not strictly a castle, is certainly a prime example of Victorian Scottish Baronial architecture and is in a magnificent setting. The 12 acres of Italian terraced gardens that surround it are by Lorimer and contain a statue walk and water gardens.

DUART. Prominently positioned on a spit of land overlooking the Sound of Mull stands **Duart Castle**. The original keep was built in the 13th century, a royal charter of 1390 confirming the lands, including Duart, to the Macleans. The clan supported the Stuarts and the Castle, which had been extensively extended in 1633, was taken by the Earl of Argyll in 1674. During the 1745 Rising Sir Hector Maclean was imprisoned in the Tower of London and his estate forfeited. Garrisoned for several years it was abandoned and over the next century and a half became a ruin. It was recovered by the family in 1911, when Sir Fitzroy Maclean had it restored as the home of the clan chief

BUNESSAN. A small family-run hotel with spectacular views can be found on the southern side of the Ross of Mull, just seven miles from the ferries to Iona and Staffa. Reached from the minor road which runs south from Bunessan to Uisken, the **Ardachy House Hotel** stands in an elevated position above Ardanalish Bay, with its beautiful white sands, Iron Age hill fort and distinctive standing stones. Resident proprietors Mabs and Gordon Anderson are delightful hosts who provide the warmest hospitality, comfortable accommodation and an excellent Scottish breakfast.

Delicious home-cooked evening meals are also available by prior arrangement which are prepared to traditional recipes using fresh local ingredients wherever possible; a selection of carefully chosen wines is also available to accompany the meal. The eight guest bedrooms, seven of which have en-suite facilities, are well appointed and furnished with a number of thoughtful extras; some also have magnificent views across the Hebridean sea towards the islands of Colonsay, Jura and Islay. A wonderful base for walkers, bird-watchers and naturalists, the land in front of Ardachy House has been designated a Site of Special Scientific Interest because of its unusual rock formations.

Ardachy House Hotel, Uisken by Bunessan Tel: 01681 700505

Iona Abbey

CHAPTER NINE

TAYSIDE

RRS Discovery

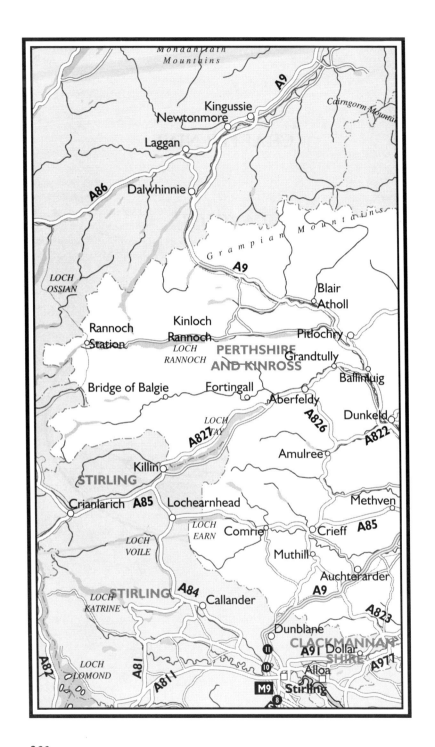

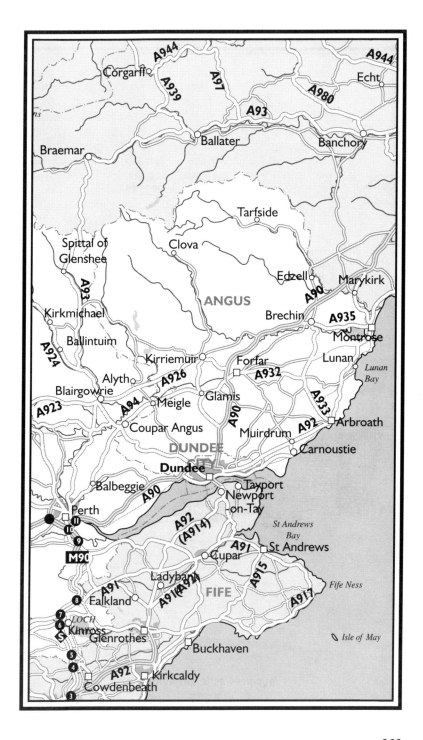

Claypotts Castle, Broughty Ferry

CHAPTER NINE

TAYSIDE

Angus

DUNDEE, Scotland's fourth city, is set against the majestic backdrop of the Sidlaw Hills and fronted by the River Tay. There is much to see and do in the city, which has a rich heritage befitting its dramatic setting.

King William the Lion made it a royal burgh in 1191 and it grew to become a major trading port. The growing wealth attracted raiders and Dundee became the subject to frequent attacks. In 1547 the forces of Henry VIII held the town for a short period, before laying waste to a greater part of it. In the 17th century the Duke of Montrose stormed the town and only the timely intervention of a relief force saved further destruction. But it was General Monk who did most damage to Dundee when, in 1657, he devastated important buildings, put many of the towns' people to the sword and looted its treasures. It would be many years before the town recovered.

The city as seen today was founded on one product - jute. At the turn of the century over half the population worked in the jute mills and the city was nicked named 'Juteopolis'. The world's largest jute works, Camperdown Works, still stand, dominated by a massive chimney known as Cox's Stack; the buildings are redeveloped into a new housing, shopping and leisure complex. The former **Verdant Works** have been taken over by Dundee Industrial Heritage to be developed as a living museum of jute and its world-wide importance.

Shipbuilding also became an important industry and the shipwrights built sleek clippers to carry the jute from India and sturdy whalers to cope with the demands of high seas, fierce winds and the ice. Their expertise led to a commission to build one of the most famous ships in the world - **RRS Discovery**, Captain Scott's Antarctic expedition vessel, launched in 1901. She now lies alongside at **Discovery Point** and is open to offer visitors a unique insight into just how tough life aboard was for the explorers and their crew. In the comfort of a special auditorium the ship's story is told.

Another piece of floating history moored at Dundee is **HM Frigate Unicorn**. She is the oldest British built ship still afloat and can be found in Victoria Dock. Built in Chatham, Kent, in 1824 this classic sailing frigate was fast and usefully armed, one of the most successful designs of her age. She still performed a useful role during the last war as a home to the naval planners covering the North Sea. Today Unicorn tells the story of the Royal Navy under sail.

Two bridges leap the Tay at Dundee and one is infamous the world over. Work on the original **Tay Railway Bridge** was started in 1871 and finished in 1878. Built to a design of Thomas Bouch it was, at 10,711 feet, the longest in the world. Queen Victoria crossed it soon after it opened, Bouch was knighted and his bridge was held up as an example British engineering supremacy.

Tragedy struck on the last Sunday of 1879 during a fearful storm, when the entire centre section of the bridge fell into the Tay, taking a train and its 75 passengers with it. Sir Thomas' career swiftly followed a similar downward turn and all work on his bridge across the Forth was stopped. It would be 1887 before trains would once more cross the Tay. The stumps of Bouch's bridge still stand out of the River alongside its replacement. What is not generally known is that much of the new bridge's iron work was taken from the old one; and that the doomed train's engine, Number 224, was pulled out of the Tay and worked east coast expresses for many years. No driver would cross the bridge with her though, until, on December 28th 1908, the 29th anniversary of the disaster, when she worked the same Dundee mail train. She was not scrapped until 1919.

One of Dundee's most famous sons was the self-styled poet, William McGonagall, whose unique approach to theatre and verse was to make him renowned, if not for the skill of his work then for its infectious delivery. The disaster inspired *Beautiful Railway Bridge of the Silvery Tay* one of his more memorable pieces and today the city is quite proud of having the world's worst poet. The city has many other famous sons and daughters: Frankenstein's creator Mary Shelley was brought up here, the inventor of marmalade, John Keiller, was a Dundee grocer and Dennis the Menace, Oor Wullie and Desperate Dan were all born here in the studios of DC Thomson, publishers of the Dandy and Beano amongst many others.

Camperdown Wildlife Centre, set right in the heart of the city the centre, has one of the finest collections of Scottish and European wildlife in the country. In addition to members of rare species that survive in Scotland they have examples of those that have not; the brown bear, wolf, Arctic fox and lynx. There is also an important collection of farm breeds that have all but disappeared. The centre is at the forefront of wildlife conservation, with captive breeding programmes aimed at bringing the capercaillie, pine marten and red squirrel back to Scotland in significant numbers.

Reform Street was constructed back in 1832 and is considered today as one of the finest neo-Classical streets in Dundee and was created by architect George Angus. **The Old Bank Bar** stands at 34 Reform Street and was originally purchased in 1833 by The Bank of Scotland and remained a bank until 1983 when it was purchased and turned into the beautiful Inn that you see before you today. The downstairs bar is flooded by light via the large and low windows that allow you to watch the world go by in the street beyond. The bar has high ceilings with half wooden panelling and contains an attractive mix of classical furniture ranging from simple wooden chairs to deep leather Chesterfields. The upstairs area is dominated by a solid wooden bar complete with a large old model sailing ship and the ceiling is an array of colourful stained glass and intricately carved plaster work. The rooms are lit by two magnificent chandeliers that are suspended above the wooden tables and chairs and give the Old Bank Bar a feeling of tradition and style. Because of its central location, the pub is frequented by a variety of people from all walks of life. After 10 am you can sit and enjoy a break from the shopping with a cup of coffee and a scone, lunchtime brings the passing trade and office staff who wish to relax with a drink and a meal. As the sun goes down, the Inn heats up, the atmosphere becomes charged and the bar becomes filled with live music and entertainment guaranteed to keep you partying until the early hours.

The Old Bank Bar, 34 Reform Street, Dundee Tel: 01382 226552

AROUND DUNDEE

BROUGHTY FERRY. Once a fishing village, Broughty Ferry is now a very individual suburb of Dundee. At the height of the jute trade it was the favoured residence of city businessmen and the huge mansions they had built were said to form 'the richest square mile in Europe'. Another example of Victorian opulence can be admired on the Monifieth road where a substantial arch stands in celebration of Queen Victoria's Jubilee.

Broughty Ferry also boasts two castles. **Claypotts Castle** stands rather incongruously next to a roundabout on the A92 in the middle of Dundee's urban sprawl and was once the home of John Graham of

Claverhouse, 'Bonnie Dundee', hero of Killiecrankie. If the word cute could ever be applied to a castle then this surely must be a candidate. Built of pink sandstone, with its modest proportions and rounded corners it looks like its on the set of a film. **Broughty Castle** is of a much more solid countenance. It stands four square on the river and was built to protect the village and guard the Firth. In later life it became a War Office gun battery and is now a local history museum.

BARRY. In continuous use from the 18th century to the early 1980s, **Barry Mill**'s water mill has rolled oats from local farms and their labourers, who received meal and oats as part of their wages, and so played an important role in the community. Now restored to working order by the National Trust for Scotland it provides a window into a way of life now long gone.

Situated on the main A92 between Dundee and Arbroath and close to Carnoustie, the **Courtyard** is an ideal meeting place for friends, business people and tourists. Built originally as a coaching inn in the 19th century it was never used as such but nearly a century and a half later it is one of the few hostelries on the A92 between Dundee and Aberdeen. The Courtyard opened as a coffee house and licensed restaurant in May 1990 and the old world charm has been retained and enhanced. Carefully chosen decor contributes to a restful and relaxing atmosphere and a woodburning stove in the original fireplace creates a cosy atmosphere. In the summer months coffee, snacks and drinks are enjoyed al fresco in the upper courtyard or the sheltered woodland garden around which runs the River Trave. It is also the ideal venue for summer barbecues.

The Courtyard has an excellent reputation for its food and carefully selected wine list. The menu is an extensive and varied one, only the finest local produce is used taking advantage of quality Angus beef, fresh fish and game. Owned and very personally run by Fraser and Norma, the welcome is a warm one with a personal service that is second to none and an atmosphere that is friendly yet not intrusive.

Courtyard, Travebank, Barry Tel: 01241 52326

Queen Victoria Jubilee Arch, Broughty Ferry

CARNOUSTIE. This famous resort is internationally famed as host to the British Open Golf Championship and many other big golfing tournaments. There are four links courses here and the championship course is widely recognized as being a major challenge. Chasing the little white ball is not all Carnoustie has to offer though. There is a magnificent beach with sailing, windsurfing and fishing facilities.

North of Carnoustie there are two Country Parks, **Crombie** and **Monikie**. Both were developed around lochs created to supply water to Dundee in the late 1800s and which had became redundant. They are now havens for wildlife and visitors alike, whatever the season. There is a host of birds and animals to see on and around the lochs and wood-lands, including woodpeckers and roe deer, and a Ranger service to help visitors spot them. There are well marked walks in both parks and Crombie has an orienteering course, whilst at Monikie there is the opportunity to get out on to the water.

ARBROATH. The home of the famous 'smokies', haddock straight from the sea cured over oak fires, Arbroath is Angus' largest town and its busy harbour area still captures the feel of the east coast's fishing heritage. On the seafront is the tall white **Signal Tower** that once guided mariners and acted as the depot for the lighthouse at Bell Rock in the North Sea. It is now the town museum with a special emphasis on fishing and the sea.

Arbroath Abbey holds a special place in Scottish history. Here in 1320, before Robert the Bruce the Scottish nobles gathered to signed a Declaration of Independence. The red sandstone Abbey was founded by King William the Lion in 1178, whose tomb lies here, and its distinctive ruins can easily be found in the town centre.

Hotel Seaforth

Hotel Seaforth stands at the centre of Arbroath's redeveloped seafront, surrounded on three sides by the Miniature World of Golf and close to other new and improved leisure facilities. In a prominent position by the A92 as you enter the town from Dundee, the hotel has its own ample grounds with parking for up to 100 cars. The Hotel is only a short walk from the picturesque fishing harbour with its many smoke houses producing traditional Arbroath Smokies (smoked haddock) and the award winning Signal Tower Museum, recording the history of this fascinating old town and its association with the Bell Rock Lighthouse.

The Hotel Seaforth has 20 en-suite bedrooms with television, tea and coffee making facilities and direct dial telephone. There is a comfortable bar and restaurant renowned for its charcoal grilled Angus steaks, and a popular Carvery is also available on certain days. For the energetic guest there is an indoor swimming pool with spa bath and a snooker room containing two full-size tables. The Seaforth is also an ideal venue for weddings, dinner dances, family celebrations and conferences. There are two function rooms, both on the first floor overlooking the sea, one comfortably accommodating 60 and the other, the ballroom for 130, with its own bar. There is also a small intimate dining room on the ground floor which can seat 12 comfortably for private meals or meetings.

Hotel Seaforth, Dundee Road, Arbroath
Tel: 01241 872232

LUNAN. Four miles of clean golden sands formed in a sheltered crescent, with a spectacular cliff backdrop, that provides an ideal escape on a sunny day. Overlooking the bay are the rather grim ruins of **Red Castle**. At the northern end of the bay is Boddin and the Elephant Rock, which does really look like one strolling into the surf.

MONTROSE. This port became notorious in the 18th century as a centre for smugglers, the numerous coves and inlets on the coast ideal for hiding from the Customs men. The port has long had a fishing fleet and still has strong connections with the sea acting as a service port for the North Sea oilfields. Montrose is also proud to be station number one for the RNIB, their first lifeboat, 'Mincing Lane', being launched in 1869. An unmissable feature of the town is the 2000 acre tidal basin behind it. It provides an ideal habitat for seabirds and waders all year round. Ornithologists literally flock to this spot and rare birds are quite often spotted, blown off their migratory course by the fierce winds of the North Sea.

On the inland edge of the basin is the splendid **House of Dun**. This fine Palladian house was designed by William Burns and has been extensively and sensitively restored. The house contains royal mementoes of the William IV period, wonderful plasterwork in the saloon by Joseph Enzer and affords outstanding views out over the estate and basin as well. In the courtyard there is a loom weaving display, a gardeners bothy and gamekeeper's room to look over too.

BRECHIN. This town is perhaps best known for the small Cathedral which today serves as a parish church. It has its origins in the founding of the Diocese of Brechin by David I in the mid 12th century.

Over the years 'improvements' and neglect have altered its appearance but the latest restoration has, as far as possible, returned it to its medieval glory. The tall thin round tower next to the Cathedral pre-dates it and was originally free standing. There are only two such towers in Scotland and it is a striking example of Celtic Culdee architecture. Built between 990 and 1012 as a refuge for the clergy in times of invasion by the Norsemen, it is all that remains of a college that once stood here. The door is some six feet above ground level making it somewhat difficult to gain entry. The Cathedral itself is actually 86 feet high, discounting the roof cap which was added a later date. The carvings inside also point to a Celtic influence, one showing a crucifixion with the legs of Christ uncrossed, in the Irish tradition. In the churchyard is a Plague Stone, built into the south gate pillar, a reminder of one of the saddest episodes of the town's history when, in 1647, some two thirds of Brechin's citizens died in just four months.

There are many historic sites and buildings in the area and **Brechin Museum** gives a penetrating insight into local history. The Mechanics Institute, centre of learning in the 1800s, has recently been restored and now makes for an impressive sight. Other mechanical marvels can be enjoyed at **Brechin Station**. The Brechin Railway Society have restored the station buildings and the magnificent glass canopy and now run both steam and diesel trains to the Bridge of Dun. The line used to run from Perth, through Forfar and on to Montrose and once carried the London and North Western Railway's crack expresses to Aberdeen. The last passenger trains ran in 1952 and the line finally closed to freight in 1981. Like many other preserved railways the staff are all volunteers and it runs on summer Sundays only, for timetable details call 01674 81318.

EDZELL. This pretty village, right on the border with Grampian Region, is the winner of several best kept village awards. Entry to the village is through the **Dalhousie Arch**, erected in 1887 by the tenants and friends, to the memory of the 13th Earl of Dalhousie and his Countess, who died within hours of each other. Just outside the village is **Edzell Castle**, which once occupied an important strategic position at the foot of Glen Esk. During various upheavals and occupations the castle survived but following the second Jacobite uprising a military detachment set about dismantling the castle to prevent further misuse. The ruination continued when the then owners became bankrupt and roof, floors and windows were removed to raise funds. Around the same time some stone work was also used in local projects, a then common occurrence. Edzell's jewel though is its Pleasance, a walled garden built by Sir David Lindsay in 1604. The heraldic and symbolic sculptures set in the walls are unique in Scotland and the flower filled recesses add to the beauty of these outstanding formal gardens.

High in the hills above Edzell is **Glenesk Folk Museum**. The building was once a shooting lodge known as 'The Retreat' and it now tells the story of everyday life in Glenesk from 1800 to present times. Further up the Glen is **Invermark Castle**, a stronghold that once guarded several hilly passes from its prominent position on the eastern edge of Loch Lee. Looking out from the castle today it is hard to believe that the area was busy with the mining of iron and silver 300 years ago, so complete is the peace and tranquillity.

FINAVON. This scattered hamlet has two interesting features that are worthy of attention. A side road to the southeast starts deceptively on the straight and level, then hairpins steeply up the Hill of Finavon. On the summit is the very peculiar vitrified fort. Clearly created by great heat, there has been much speculation how this 8th century fort and others like it became so. What is known is that the drystone walls of this type of fort were often strengthened by internal timbers, and if they caught light the lack of oxygen in the wall would cause them to burn at a very high temperature fusing the stone together. Finavon is also home to Scotland's largest Dovecote or Doocot; it now contains an exhibition on the Doocots of Angus and can clearly be seen by passing traffic on the A94.

KIRRIEMUIR is frequently described as the 'gateway to the Glens of Angus'. Most of the town retains its original 18th and 19th century character, when it was an important centre for handloom weaving. The square is dominated by an even older tolbooth dating from around 1604, a reminder of the town's connection with the Douglas, Earls of Angus. It is also the birthplace of JM Barrie, creator of Peter Pan, born at 9 Brechin Road. He gifted the cricket pavilion on Kirriemuir Hill to the townsfolk and it houses one of only three surviving camera obscura in Scotland which gives panoramic views of Strathmore and the Glens.

The fliers of the RAF are paid tribute to in a private museum in the former council offices on Bellies Brae. Richard Moss has amassed a huge selection of wartime photographs, uniforms, medals, models, newspapers and memorabilia. Open to the public everyday in summer there is no admission but donations for local charity are welcome.

The renowned **Angus Glens** are each very different; Isla, Prosen and Clova offer great beauty and are all worth exploring. The entry to Glen Prosen is dominated by the **Airlie Monument Tower**, which commemorates the 11th Earl of Airlie, who was killed during the Boer War. Keep an eye out too for the Captain Scott and Dr Wilson Memorial on the roadside. Prosen was Scott's favourite glen and he and Wilson planned their ill-fated South Pole expedition near here.

FORFAR. The administrative capital of Angus today, this ancient town has held higher station; being the site for King Malcolm Canmore's Parliament of 1057 and King William the Lion's Scottish Parliament, convened at the Castle in the early part of the 13th century. **Forfar Castle** itself was destroyed by followers of Robert the Bruce, who brought it down on the heads of its English garrison - it was never rebuilt and a modern tower marks the site. Just outside the town, on the B9113, are the ruins of Restenneth Priory.

GLAMIS. The village is famous for its **Castle**, mentioned by Shakespeare in *Macbeth*; 'Lord of Glamis' was the second of the titles which the witches foretold for Macbeth. There have been many famous visitors to this castle, including James V and his daughter, Mary, Queen of Scots. Sir Walter Scott was another guest here, and it was the childhood home of Queen Elizabeth, the Queen Mother, whose father was the 14th Earl of Strathmore. Princess Margaret was born here in 1930. The Castle with its turrets and parapets has a romantic fairy tale appeal, but above all remains a family home, much lived in and loved by the Strathmore family, who have been residents since 1372. There are extensive grounds and gardens to explore as well as the Castle and a restaurant to recover in comfort. It is open everyday from Easter through to mid October.

Perth and Kinross

PERTH. This 'fair city' has a proud, historical, tradition - it was once capital of Scotland - that has left it with a legacy of fascinating places to visit. The area was first settled over 8000 years ago and succeeding waves of Roman Centurions, Pictish peoples and Celtic missionaries established themselves here. They all enjoyed the favourable climate, fertile farmlands and an ideal defensive and trading location at the edge of the Highlands. Though few relics of the distant past survived the centuries, Perth's natural advantages remained and helped the town to become a thriving commercial, religious and cultural centre by the Middle Ages.

Perth's rise to pre-eminence was also largely due to Kenneth MacAlpine, who in AD 838 became the first King of a United Scotland. He bought to nearby Scone the legendary **Stone of Destiny** and many coronations took place atop this mystical symbol. A great abbey grew up on the site and, even after Edward I of England stole the sacred Stone in 1296, Scone (pronounced Scoon) remained at the centre of royal life.

Helped by royal and religious patronage Perth prospered. Its position on the navigable River Tay enabled the town to become an important trading port and it has retained its busy harbour to this day. Salmon, wool and other agricultural products are exported, with claret from Bordeaux a major import. Perth also established itself as a cattle trading centre, perfectly situated on the drovers route from the north and its Bull Sales are still internationally renowned. By the 16th century another of the town's products had begun to take the city's name around the world - whisky. Today Bell's, Dewar's and Famous Grouse continue to distil their fiery elixirs here.

Reminders of medieval times are plentiful. In the city centre stands the striking **St John's Kirk**, founded in 1126 and now largely restored. Perth was known for a time as St John's Toun and it was from the Kirk

THE JACOBITE REBELLIONS

The Treaty of Union, signed in 1707, brought together the parliaments of England and Scotland with Scotland receiving guarantees on the Presbyterian Established Church and on the maintenance of Scottish law and courts. However, Jacobite sentiment remained, particularly in the Highlands, and this erupted in the rebellions of 1715 and 1745.

Led by the Earl of Mar, on behalf of the Old Pretender, the 1715 Rebellion failed to gain support in the Lowlands and ended at Sheriffmuir. The end of the Stuart line; the son of James II was James Francis Edward, known as James III by the Jacobites and as the Old Pretender by the Hanoverians.

It was after this uprising that General Wade was detailed to build a network of military roads. However, this did not prevent a more serious uprising in 1745. Thirty years after his father's failure, Prince Charles Edward, better known as Bonnie Prince Charlie (or the Young Pretender) set out to claim his crown.

After initial success at Prestonpans and advancing his army as far as Derby, Bonnie Prince Charlie had to withdraw and was finally defeated, by Cumberland, at Culloden. Then began his adventurous wanderings and the Prince is said to have hidden in caves all over the Highlands and Islands. It is doubtful whether he ever shared a cave with Flora Macdonald though she did help him to escape the English and travel to Skye.

The heroine of the Rebellion, Flora was captured by the English and taken to London, where, much to her surprise she was the darling of society. After marrying a fellow countryman Flora emigrated to Carolina.

Bonnie Prince Charlie escaped to France, boarding the French frigate L'Heureux at Loch nan Umah, near Arisaig, where 14 months earlier he had landed full of expectation.

Bonnie Prince Charlie died in 1788 leaving no legitimate male heir and the death, in 1807, of his celibate brother Stuart saw the end of the Stuart male line.

that John Knox preached the inflammatory sermon which sparked the Reformation's wholesale destruction of monasteries and churches, amongst them Scone. The Church was restored in 1923 as a memorial to the fallen of the Great War.

One of the best ways to explore any town centre is on foot and the **Old Perth Trail** - leaflet available from Tourist Information Centre - is a great guide. Everywhere plaques and memorials commemorate historic events, famous visitors and notable residents; with street names such as Ropemaker Close, Horners Lane and Glover Street giving clues to the town's medieval trades. The narrow Cow Vennel was a route taken by livestock being herded to the common grazing meadows which bordered the town centre. Those parklands survive today as the North and South Inch, and are overlooked by elegant Georgian Terraces.

The North Inch was the scene of the infamous Battle of the Clans in 1396. Scores of men from the Chatten and Kay Clans were slaughtered when King Robert III attempted unsuccessfully to put an end to the feuding between Highlanders. The Battle forms the backdrop to Sir Walter Scott's novel *The Fair Maid of Perth*, which in turn inspired Bizet's opera of the same name. Nearby, one of Perth's oldest buildings, now a craft shop is known as the **Fair Maid's House**.

Incidentally, the Old Council Chambers on the High Street feature a wonderful Fair Maid stained glass window, together with other Scott characters, Queen Victoria, Prince Albert and Robert the Bruce. The building occupies a site that has, for centuries, been the hub of civic and judicial life in the city, though the present building dates from 1896. It is still used by the Leisure and Recreation Department, but visitors are welcome to this most fascinating of hidden places. Also adjacent to the North Inch is Balhousie Castle, home to the **Black Watch Museum**, which tells the story of Perthshire's famous Royal Highland Regiment.

The Fergusson Gallery in Marshall Square, near the South Inch, is a must for art lovers. Housed in Perth's first ever water works (now a Grade A Listed Building) it is the largest single collection of the works by Scotland's foremost colourist John Duncan Fergusson.

At the northern edge of the town, the **Caithness Glass Factory** and Visitors Centre, famous for its paperweights, shows the skills of glassmakers at work. Tours of **Dewar's Whisky Bottling Plant** are always popular, while those wishing to discover more about the area's rich agricultural heritage can visit the auction market or see the magnificent Clydesdales at the **Fairways Heavy Horse Centre**.

There is plenty to discover within easy striking distance of the city. To the west alongside the A85 stands the impressive **Huntingtower Castle,** formerly known as Ruthven Castle. This splendid place is a 15th century mansion that was the scene of the raid of Ruthven in 1583, when James VI found himself captive at the hands of his nobles who demanded the removal of certain royal favourites. The King tried to escape (he was 16 at the time) but found his way barred and was kept virtual prisoner for ten months, being forced to sign proclamations declaring himself a free agent. The nobles managed to hold on to some power for a few months, though the Earl of Gowrie (Lord Ruthven), who had originally invited the King to his hunting seat, was eventually beheaded in 1585. James waited a full 18 years to take revenge on the remainder of the family and the Earl's grandson and his brother were killed in mysterious circumstances, their dead bodies tried for treason and their estates forfeited to the Crown. The name of Ruthven was abolished by an Act of Parliament, and the Castle's name changed to Huntingtower. The Castle has some fine painted ceilings, murals and plasterwork, as well as unusual decorative beams in the Hall.

At the **Kinnoull Hill Woodland Park**, and the adjoining Binn and Deuchny Hills, there are well marked wooded walks which lead to fantastic views that stretch across the city, the Tay estuary and over the rolling Fife countryside to the Lomond Hills. To the north the views extend over the Highlands from Ben More in the west to Lochnagar amongst the Cairngorms in the northeast. Out to the east is **Elcho Castle**, the handsome fortified mansion of the Wemyss family which overlooks the north bank of the River Tay. Built with comfort as well as defence in mind the castle has a profusion of round and square towers and still retains the original iron grills protecting the windows.

AROUND PERTH

SCONE. Scone Palace was the crowning place of all the Scottish kings from 843 until 1296. The coronations were performed upon the Stone of Scone, which originally came from the western isle of Iona. It was stolen in 1296 and taken to Westminster Abbey. In 1951 a group of patriot Scots removed the stone and took it to Arbroath Abbey. In due course it was returned but many believe that a copy was made by a local stonemason and the stone that sits beneath the Coronation Chair in Westminster is fake. The Stone, at least the one from Westminster Abbey, was returned to Scotland in 1996. The present Palace was built in 1803 and incorporates the 16th century and earlier palaces. It contains a magnificent collection of porcelain, furniture, ivories, 18th century clocks and 16th century needlework. Home to the family of the Earl of Mansfield it is open to the public everyday between Easter and October.

ERROL. The Errol Railway Heritage Centre celebrates the golden age of the train and the station recreates a typical 1920s Scottish country station with plenty of railway artifacts and a slide show. Only open on Sundays between May and September it is worth finding for nostalgia and railway buffs alike.

Close to Errol village is **Megginch Castle Gardens**. The grounds around the 15th century castle have 1000 year old yews and feature a walled kitchen garden, 16th century rose garden and 19th century sunken garden, as well as a gothic courtyard with a pagoda-roofed dovecote. There is also a topiary with a golden yew crown. Opening times through the year vary.

COUPAR ANGUS. The network of streets and closes is this abbey town is one of the best preserved medieval patterns in Scotland, though the buildings have changed over the centuries. A Cistercian abbey was established here in 1164 and prospered well leading to the creation of the town. By the 16th century its incomes matched those of Holyrood and exceeded those of the border abbeys of Melrose and Kelso. From such heady heights the Abbey's fall was swift, its estates were disbanded following the Reformation and the Abbey fell into disuse, becoming a valuable source of quality stone for the locals. All that remains is a gateway arch.

Another building of note in the town is the **Tolbooth Tower**. This square clock tower or steeple was built by public subscription in 1762 and part of the building was once used as the town prison. Nearby on Calton Street stand **Cumberland Barracks**. The town lies at the southern end of two military roads into the Highlands and many a soldier must have spent his last night of relative comfort in the barracks, which were named after the Duke of Cumberland, who finally defeated Bonnie Prince Charlie at Culloden. The barracks were restored by the burgh council in 1974 and converted into flats.

MEIGLE. This little village has a fascinating museum dedicated entirely to ancient carved stones. The magnificent collection at **Meigle Museum** is the largest of its kind, with some 25 examples Celtic Christian sculptured monuments found in or near the old churchyard.

ALYTH. This is an attractive small town with its burn flowing through it alongside the main street. There is a charming **Folk Museum** which has interesting displays of life in the local community and in the surrounding countryside.

BLAIRGOWRIE. On the southern approach to the town stands the unique Meikleour Beech Hedge. Planted in 1746, the hedge is now over 650 yards long and nearly 100 feet tall and has earned a place in the Guinness Book of Records. Blairgowrie, Gaelic for 'field of goats', sits, with its sister community of Rattray, astride the fast flowing River Ericht, which is famed for its salmon. Blair, as it is known locally, is situated in the heart of fruit growing and farming countryside. The altitude and soil seem to combine to give just the right growing conditions for what are described as the raspberries to match any other. These raspberries are largely picked for the jam factories of Dundee.

In the centre of the town is **Keathbank Mill**. Visitors here can gaze in wonder at the huge 1862 mill steam engine, admire Scotland's largest waterwheel, enjoy watching the trains on what is thought to be Britain's largest model railway and discover all about the ancient art of heraldry.

There is a first class recreational centre in Blairgowrie with many facilities including a swimming pool, games hall, gymnasium and sunroom. There are also excellent walks in the vicinity, spring time brings the valley into true beauty, and the wildlife reserve at Loch of the Lowes welcomes many migratory visitors, including ospreys. Summer is packed with events, including Highland games and sheepdog trials. Then, of course, there is the legendary fruit picking that is available in the autumn months. The autumnal colours are quite unforgettable on the heather-clad hills and, in the winter, Blairgowrie comes alive as sports enthusiasts come up for skiing at **Glenshee**.

There are no less than 26 lifts stretching up either side of the A93 giving downhill skiers a choice of 38 pistes. Cross country enthusiasts are also catered for in the area at **Glenisla** to the east, where there are 40 miles of forest trails to explore. Apart from skiing, visitors may go pony trekking, touring, walking, fishing or play golf, tennis and squash.

BIRNAM. The village was the inspiration for Beatrix Potter's popular tales. She came here for holidays as a child and one picture-letter she sent to a friend later developed into *The Tale of Peter Rabbit*. Her timeless characters are celebrated in the **Beatrix Potter Garden**, where sculptures of Peter Rabbit and his friends can be enjoyed by fans young and old.

The Hermitage, a folly built in 1758 and restored in 1986, stands beside the River Braan.

DUNKELD is a charming little town that possesses a turbulent history. In fact, Dunkeld became the religious centre of Scotland in the 9th century and before that was the ancient capital of Caledonia (the name itself means 'fort of the Caledonians').

This small town was the home of kings and the site of at least one bloody battle in the 17th century when, after the Battle of Killiecrankie, a raw regiment of Cameronians were ordered to hold the town against the Jacobites. As the rebellious army advanced, they did great damage to the town, causing the Cameronians to retreat to the cathedral and Dunkeld House. Here, running out of ammunition, they were forced to rip the lead from the mansion's roof in desperation. Somehow they succeeded in driving the Jacobites off and even pursued them, singing hymns as they went.

Many years prior to this the Vikings attacked the town. They managed to do this by bringing with them a number of small horses aboard their ships, which enabled them to invade further inland than was previously possible. On at least one occasion, they were successful, and managed to capture and devastate Dunkeld.

Today Dunkeld is a little more tolerant of its visitors and this very attractive town has lots to offer the visitor. In a building that once was the City Hall is a unique business, **The Highland Horn and Deerskin Centre**. They make and sell a range of things in deerskin and horn that cannot be obtained anywhere else in the world. **The Little Cottages** project in the town centre, completed by the National Trust, has restored the cottages of Cathedral Street providing a glimpse of a Highland town as it would have been 200 years ago.

Close to the picturesque River Tay, is **Dunkeld Cathedral**, set in lovely grounds. Refounded in the 12th century on an ancient ecclesiastical site, much of the ruins dating from the 15th century. Only the choir is intact and it is still used as parish church. Further along the Tay, is one of Thomas Telford's finest bridges, built in 1809. A riverside path leads from here downstream to the famous Birnam Oak, which is the sole remainder of Macbeth's Birnam Beeches.

PITLOCHRY. Described as the 'jewel in Perthshire's crown', the town is certainly set amidst some magnificent scenery with plenty of first class accommodation and a wide range of activities. There are two distilleries here including, reputedly, the smallest distillery in the world. **Edradour** has been making whisky since 1825, but it was not until 1986 that the proprietors decided that the old place was worthy of greater recognition and set up the visitor centre. Come along to see the production process and take away a sample of their wares.

The other distillery is the **Blair Atholl Distillery**, owned and managed by Arthur Bell & Sons plc. This is production at the other end of the scale and there is a tour to help visitors understand the distillery process. There is also a shop here with a wide range of single malts and blended whiskies for sale. Afterwards there is the opportunity to relax over a cup of coffee.

One of Pitlochry's major attractions is the **Salmon Ladder**, at the hydro-electric power station on Loch Faskally, five minutes from the town centre. Here there is an observation chamber for visitors to watch the salmon by-passing the dam by a series of connecting pools. This is quite a feat and the fish can be seen gathering their strength for a final push up into Loch Faskally. It is best seen in May and June during the spring run and again in September, although fish can be seen most of the summer.

The **Pitlochry Festival Theatre** is set on the banks of the River Tummell and offers entertainment throughout the summer which is of a very high standard. Their resident repertory company proclaims visitors 'may stay six days and see seven plays'. It makes sense to have a look at the programme and book ahead if possible.

BLAIR ATHOLL. Blair Atholl Castle is a white turreted baronial mansion and the seat of the Duke of Atholl, chief of Clan Murray. The oldest section, the Cumming's Tower, dates from around 1269 but most of what is seen today was restored in 1869. It has had amongst its famous visitors Mary, Queen of Scots and Queen Victoria. The Castle was renowned for its generosity in the entertainment of its visitors and there is an account of Mary's visit in 1564 when 2000 clansmen were employed to drive the game from the surrounding area. The final bag included 360 deer and five wolves. This gave Blair a reputation as one of the finest hunting châteaux in Europe. It also has the distinction of being the last stronghold in Britain to be besieged, in 1746, when forces loyal to Bonnie Prince Charlie attempted to capture it and the Duke is the only British subject allowed to maintain a private army, the Atholl Highlanders. The Castle today has many fascinating collections of furniture, portraits,

Blair Castle, Blair Atholl

china, arms, armour and some exceptional Rococo style plaster ceilings. It also has extensive facilities, parklands, pony trekking and an excellent caravan park - and a piper plays outside the Castle on most days!

Almost next door to the castle is **Atholl Country Collection**, a unique little folk museum that is a real slice of Highland rural life. As well as a smiddy, crofter's stable and byre, there are displays of flax growing and spinning, once the main economy of the district. No one gets left out with road, rail and postal services, the school, the kirk, vet and gamekeeper all featured.

Blair Atholl village, which provided the setting for TV's *Strathblair*, has its own little piece of history in **The Mill**. Built in 1613 this water mill still produces traditional oatmeal and flour which can be bought in the shop, or sampled straight away in the tearoom.

Less than four miles south is **The Pass of Killiecrankie** and **Soldier's Leap**, the famous wooded gorge where, in 1689, Government troops were routed by Jacobite forces led by 'Bonnie' Viscount Dundee, who met his end in the action. Though the force was later stopped it was difficult to contain the Highlanders and the trouble that this caused ultimately led to the massacre at Glencoe four years later. Soldier's Leap was so named after Donald MacBean made his death defying leap across the gorge to evade his Highland pursuers.

CALVINE. Just off the main road are the **Falls of Bruar** which comprise three sets of which the upper is most impressive and altogether they drop over 200 feet. When Robert Burns saw the falls he remarked they were missing something so he asked the Duke of Atholl, a great arboriculturalist, to clothe the banks in trees to complete the picture. The Duke obliged Burns and now the waters cascade through pinewoods, with paths and bridges giving great views. Back on the main road is **Clan Donnachaidh Museum**. The Clan comprised the Reid, Robertson, MacConnachie, Duncan and MacInroy families and their story is told here.

KINLOCH RANNOCH. In the centre of the village, which stands at the foot of Loch Rannoch, is an obelisk erected in memory of Dugald Buchanan, the 'Rannoch schoolmaster, evangelist and sacred poet'.

FORTINGALL. In this village, at the northern end of Loch Tay, stands the **Fortingall Yew**. This great tree, in the churchyard, is claimed to be 3000 years old and is the oldest in Europe. The village is also claimed to be the birthplace of Pontius Pilate - born here during the Roman occupation. He was sent to Rome as a boy slave and rose to become Governor of Judea in AD 26. There are even suggestions that on his downfall he returned here to die. Today the village itself is very pretty having been rebuilt in 1900 with many thatched houses.

ABERFELDY will always be associated with a new era in the Highlands that began with the formation of the Black Watch. It was on this spot on the Tay in 1739, that the first of these regiments was incorporated into the British army, in an attempt to bring into line and control the warring factions and clans of the Highlands. The name Black Watch came about as the tartans worn by the men were darker in contrast with the red coats of the regular army. A memorial to the regiment was erected in Queen Victoria's Jubilee Year of 1887. The large cairn topped by a kilted soldier stands alongside General Wade's bridge over the Tay, which lies just north of the town on the B846. Built in 1733 this bridge is considered his finest, being designed by William Adam, whose work is found all over Scotland.

This area has strong connections with General Wade, who stayed in Weem Inn whilst he was directing the building of the bridge. Wade was sent to Scotland originally to assess what measures were necessary to subdue the rebellious Highlanders and his reports culminated in his appointment as Commander-in-Chief in Scotland. Whilst in office, he directed the construction of military roads, bringing the north and west of Scotland within easy reach of those south of the border. Wade eventually died in 1748 and has the fourth verse of the National Anthem dedicated to his honour.

Weem Inn, or Hotel as it is now, still stands on the B846. The history of the hotel is fascinating. Part of the building dates back to the 16th century, a time when it offered the guest a rather less comfortable nights stay, which, depending on the ability to pay, might have ranged from a heap of heather or straw to a straw mattress, with a blanket and pillow being extra. It was also the watering place of the Clan Menzies, with their ancestral home next door, who came here to drink the home-made whisky and ales. **Castle Menzies** itself is a fine example of a Z-plan castle, so called because it featured two diagonally opposite towers to cover the building's four walls. This was the Menzies' third home, the first at Comrie and earliest one on this site having been destroyed. The family line died out in 1918 and the Castle was eventually rescued from advanced decay by the Clan Menzies Society, who are slowly restoring it to former glories.

To the east of the town along the A827 is the hamlet of **Grandtully** and, at Pitcairn Farm, **St Mary's Church**. This 16th century Church has a stunning painted wooden ceiling that depicts heraldic and symbolic subjects. The Church is kept locked and the key is kept at the farm but is available at any reasonable time.

CRIEFF. A charming place, popular with visitors, the town's sign proclaim it to be 'The Holiday Town'. The Visitors Centre is certainly welcoming and gives the opportunity to tour two fascinating factories, **Thistles Pottery** and **Perthshire Paperweights** as well as having a factory shop, well stocked garden centre and restaurant, which offers Taste of Scotland specialities. At the **Stuart Crystal's Strathern Glassworks** the skills involved in decorating lead crystal wear can be watched and there is also a museum, coffee shop and the opportunity to have your purchase personally engraved.

Scotland's oldest distillery is here in Crieff; **Glenturret** was established 1775 and to this day its selection of single malt whiskies are award winners. There are guided tours, a visitors centre with displays and exhibitions telling the story of Glenturret and whisky, and two excellent restaurants, plus of course a whisky tasting bar. For those with a taste for something sweeter, in West High Street is **Gordon and Durward's**, where traditional confectionery is still being made.

The A822 north from the town runs through **Sma' Glen**, a narrow glen surrounded by towering hills awash with purple heather and with the River Almond gushing along the valley floor. This was once a strategic route from the Lowlands to the Highlands, know as far back as Roman times. General Wade chose Sma' Glen as one of the routes for his military roads, designed to allow quick access for the King's army if the Highlanders should rise again. Ironically Bonnie Prince Charlie's 1745 campaign made full use of it during his advance and retreat.

Located on the main road leading into the town of Crieff, **The Town Hotel** is a comfortable 200 year old family run hotel which boasts superb views of the Ochill hills. Built in 1792, this freehouse serves a superb selection of beers in the attractive bar area and has a superb beer garden that offers the visitor some stunning views of the local countryside. There are eight guest rooms, four of which have en-suite, the other four with private facilities, and all have colour TV, tea and coffee making facilities, telephone and full central heating. The restaurant is also open to non-residents and provides the diner with an excellent and very varied selection of dishes on the extensive menu. Just as a sample choice you could start your meal with Stilton Cheese and Walnut Paté, then follow this with Fillet of Beef Stroganoff served on a bed of rice and for dessert, why not try the gorgeous Crème Brulle with fresh raspberries and blackcurrants, a meal fit for a King. There is also a very comprehensive selection of vegetarian and seafood dishes, ranging from Queen Scallops and Smoked Bacon to the oriental tasting Sweet and Sour Vegetables.

The Towers Hotel, East High Street, Crieff
Tel: 01764 652678

Braidhaugh Caravan Park is a friendly, family run Park which stands on the banks of the River Earn amid the scenic surroundings of Crieff. Centrally situated, the park is only one hour from Glasgow, Edinburgh or Dundee and only half an hour from Perth or Stirling. Family owned and run Braidhaugh Caravan Park offers a luxurious toilet block, comfortable caravans for hire, a new shop and games room, children's play area and a boating pond

The pitches are hard standing with grass areas for awnings if necessary and most pitches have a 13 amp electric hook-up supply with water, drainage and TV points available on a selection. There is also a wide range of modern Thistle Award caravans which are totally equipped and fully serviced sleeping from between 4 and 6 people. The laundry room offers large washing and drying machines, ironing and hand-washing facilities and there is also a disabled toilet which is spacious, fully tiled and centrally heated, with its own shower and wash area.

Braidhaugh Caravan Park, South Bridgend, Crieff
Tel: 01764 652951

COMRIE. This pretty little village has the odd nickname of The Shaky Toun, due to the number of tremors the village has felt as it lies on the Highland Boundary Fault. Records go back some 400 years and to this day movement is recorded at the Earthquake House. This was built in 1869 and had its first seismometer installed in 1874; recently restored its instruments are now sensitive enough to detect earthquakes worldwide. Though the building is not open to the public it can be viewed through the door and windows and there is plenty of information on panels on the outside walls.

The village is also home to the **Museum of Scottish Tartans** in Drummond Street, which houses the largest collection of material relating to tartans and Highland dress in existence. The Tartan Room has over 450 different examples and there is a history of Highland dress exhibition. Incidentally following the failure of Bonnie Prince Charlie's Jacobite Rebellion of 1745 the kilt was banned and the bagpipes outlawed as an offensive weapon.

Comrie's other great attraction is the **Auchingarrich Wildlife Centre**. Set in 100 acres of beautiful Perthshire hill country it has a whole host of running, flying, swimming, burrowing, grunting and squawking animals and birds. In addition there is a unique wild bird hatchery, rural museum and antique farm machinery display and a spectacular 600 foot viewpoint. Then there's Rosie the pig - all 47 stone of her! All in all a full day out for everyone.

For fishermen a visit to **Drummond Fish Farm** is a real treat. In addition to being able to see and feed the thousands of trout on the farm the visitor can indulge his or her passion amongst the specially created complex of ponds. There is a pond set aside for children and all equipment can be hired on site. No need to go back empty handed either the farm shop has fresh and frozen trout; as well as other quality Highland salmon, venison and pheasant.

Westwards from Comrie is **Loch Earn**, it was here, at Ardvorlich on the southside, that Rob Roy's family, the MacGregors, reputedly beheaded a forester of the King's against whom they had a grievance and presented his head on a plate, with a crust of bread between his teeth, to his sister.

MUTHILL. Though only small the village contains some lovely examples of buildings from the mid 1700s; none survive from earlier times as the Earl of Mar burnt the all houses to the ground after the failure of the 1715 Jacobite Rising. Only the old Parish Church survived, though it too is now a ruin, worshipping having finished in about 1818. Parts of it date as far back as the early 12th century and the graveyard features some rather startling headstones that feature skulls and crossed bones, hour glass and the words 'Tempus Fugit'.

Near the village is **Drummond Castle** and its Italian style gardens. These are the largest formal gardens in Scotland and were first laid out in 1630 by the John Drummond, 2nd Earl of Perth. In around 1830 the ornamental area was Italianised and embellished with many fine figures and statues from Italy. These spectacular gardens are open from 2 pm to 6 pm between 1st May and 30th September and should undoubtedly be on the garden enthusiasts itinerary.

AUCHTERARDER. This town has a wealth of delightful antique shops as well as the **Great Scots Visitor Centre**. As well as featuring weaving displays and the last steam-driven factory engine in Scotland the centre has 'Great Scots'. This is the history of Scotland told using a huge map and computerized lighting effects. There is also the world's only **Barrs Irn Bru Bar**, which for the uninitiated is a soft drink, as well as a millshop. A little to the south of the town is **Gleneagles Hotel**; it was built by the London Midland and Scottish Railway after the Great War, which would explain why it has its own station whose platform has a telephone connected directly to the Hotel. Gleneagles is, of course, world famous for its King's and Queen's golf courses, owned by the Hotel and the scene of some of the top events in the golfing calendar.

RUMBLING BRIDGE. Here the River Devon falls through a ravine spanned by three bridges. A footpath from the north side gives good access to the spectacular gorges and falls, one of which is known as the Devil's Mill. Another, Cauldron Linn, is a mile downstream, with Vicar's Bridge, a beauty spot, a mile beyond this. The village's unusual name comes from the sound the river makes beneath the bridges.

KINROSS. Just before entering the town, adjacent to the motorway roundabout and services, is a fascinating selection of attractions clustered together. **Kin-kraft** was started by six local enthusiasts in 1990 and now has evolved into a major showcase for a huge range of crafts created all over Scotland. There are regular demonstrations of the various crafts and of course the opportunity to buy most of the wares on display.

Findlay Clark Tropical Butterfly House is one of the largest butterfly farms in the country. As British summers sadly seem to bring fewer and fewer butterflies this is a perfect antidote. Numerous tropical varieties of every size, colour and hue glide gracefully around the palms and pools. Next door to the butterflies are natures equivalent of the jet fighter - birds of prey. At the **Scottish Centre for Falconry** these elusive and magnificent creatures can be watched at really close quarters. At regular intervals displays of falconry take place, and members of the public are encouraged to join in. The Hawk Walk gives unrestricted views of the birds that the whole of Scotland once teemed with. The Centre is involved in special breeding projects and, thanks to closed circuit TV, visitors can see chicks being fed by their parents. Budding falconers might also like to ask about the expert tuition available. There is also a garden centre, golf shop and cafe on the site, so there is something for everyone.

In the Kinross town centre there is an interesting tolbooth that dates back to the 16th century and that was restored in 1771 by Robert Adam. **Kinross House** has a fine Renaissance exterior and was built for Daniel Defoe between 1685 and 1690. The gardens of the House are most interesting and are open from May to September. There is also a museum in the town that gives an interesting insight into the history of the town and the loch, with its famous castle.

It was at **Loch Leven Castle** that Mary, Queen of Scots was kept prisoner during 1567 until her daring escape 11 months later. With help from the gaoler's son she locked her guards in the Castle and made away in a boat, throwing the Castle key's into the Loch. The accidental discovery of a bunch of keys in the lock 300 years later would seem to confirm the story. A boat from Kinross takes visitors to the Island and Castle. Mary's prison was in the small round tower which is separate from the main keep.

The **Loch Leven National Nature Reserve** is the most important area for freshwater breeding and migratory wildfowl in Britain. In the winter months the loch is a favourite breeding ground for wild geese, ducks and other wild fowl.

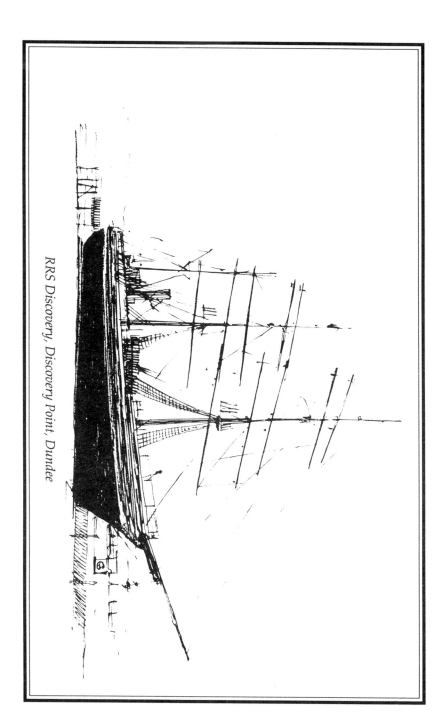

RRS Discovery, Discovery Point, Dundee

CHAPTER TEN

THE GRAMPIANS

Strathisla Distillery

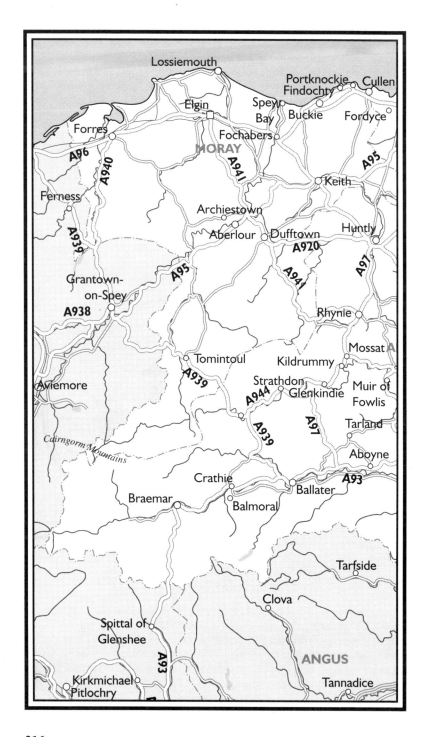

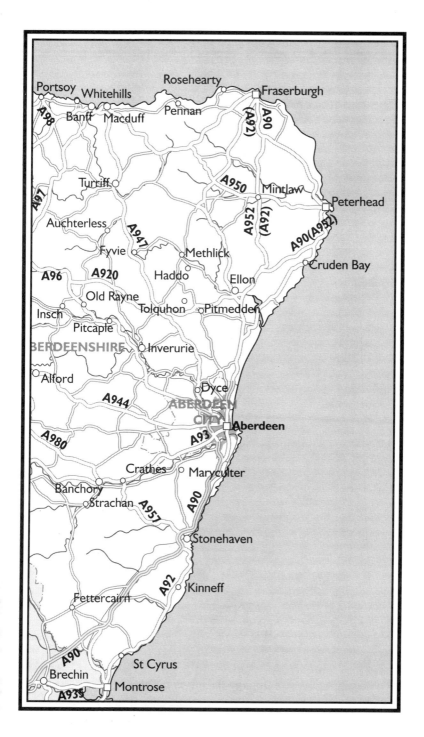

Tossing the Braemar Caber

CHAPTER TEN

THE GRAMPIANS

Royal Deeside

BALLATER. Situated on the banks of the River Dee, Ballater was a small, popular Victorian spa. **Pannanich Lodge**, the original spa, was founded in 1785 by the Jacobite Francis Farquharson of Monaltrie after hearing of a local old woman who cured herself of scrofula by bathing in the waters below Pannanich Hill.

The railway station of this pretty town was originally the station from which Queen Victoria would alight when travelling to Balmoral. **Dee Valley Confectioners**, in the Station Square, also make confectionery at the back of the shop as well as sell a wide range of sweets and candy. Many of the town's shops display the Royal Warrant.

Midway between Aboyne and Ballater is the **Muir of Dinnet National Nature Reserve**. This Area of Outstanding Natural Beauty includes the lovely Burn O'Vat and Kinord and Daven Lochs and there is an information centre, nature trails and, of course, the views of the mountains. Within the reserve is the rather magnificent **Kinord Cross** slab. The intricately carved cross covers all but one side of the slab and was probably sculpted in the 9th century. A little further north, on the A97 at Logie Coldstone, is another example of a Cross slab, the **Migvie Stone**. Rougher, taller and rather more crudely carved than the Kinord slab, it also features a horse and rider on the back.

Enjoying an enviable location near the bridge in the town, quite literally on the banks of the River Dee (noted for superb fishing), the **Monaltrie Hotel** is owned and personally run by Laddawan Anderson and is ideally situated as a touring base for the beautiful surroundings of Royal Deeside. The emphasis here is on first class service and facilities, provided in a warm relaxed atmosphere. Awarded 2 Star rating by the RAC the Monaltrie boasts two restaurants. In the elegant surroundings of the à la carte restaurant you can savour the finest Scottish cuisine prepared using fresh local produce, or if you prefer you can tantalise your taste buds with authentic spices and flavours of the Orient in the Thai Orchid restaurant. After dinner, what could be nicer than to relax with a nightcap in front of a roaring log fire before retiring to one of the 25 en-suite guest rooms, each attractively furnished and equipped for maximum comfort. The hotel welcomes non-residents and their families; children eat for just one pound between 6 - 7.30 pm. They are also welcome to enjoy the live entertainment on Friday nights. There is ample car parking space at the hotel and a beautiful riverside garden. Excellent for all the family.

Monaltrie Hotel

Monaltrie Hotel, Bridge Square, Ballater Tel: 013397 55417
Fax: 013397 55180

Royal Deeside remains one of Scotland's most popular areas for tourism and Ballater is one of its most beautiful and friendly Highland villages. Lying 42 miles west of Aberdeen, Ballater is set amid pine forests and breathtaking mountains. It's a wonderful area for indulging in outdoor pursuits and it's here you'll find **Inverdeen House**, circa 1820 and one of the original buildings in Ballater. It is the lovely home of Sandy and Heli Munroe who are happy to share it with discerning visitors requiring bed and breakfast.

Inverdeen House

The interior of Inverdeen House has been painstakingly restored to highlight the lovely original woodwork, a striking feature throughout the house. Furnished beautifully with simple antiques of the William IV and early Victorian eras, the house has three excellent double bedrooms

320

(one with double and two with king size beds) each with central heating, wash hand basins, colour TV, tea and coffee and other amenities. A period bathroom and modern shower room are located on the same floor.

Breakfasts are served in the charming 19th century dining room at a large farm kitchen table. The breakfast menu is wholesome, varied and interesting, featuring home-made preserves, pancakes and muffins along with the traditional bacon and eggs and local venison products from Ballater's 'by appointment to the Royal family' butcher. Sandy and Heli are caring and helpful hosts providing vegetarian, vegan and special dietary needs meals, packed lunches by arrangement and helpful suggestions to suit your needs. They are Scottish/Canadian and Scottish/Polish, and between them speak English, German, French and Polish offering a delightful combination of Highland hospitality and Canadian warmth. Ballater has been called the 'Gastronomic Capital of the Highlands', and even boasts its own superb Gourmet Week - the 'Taste of Royal Deeside'. Locally, there are numerous excellent restaurants and AA Rosettes and Taste of Scotland members abound. Inverdeen House is open all year round. Guests should note it is a 100% non-smoking home.

Inverdeen House, Bridge Square, Ballater Tel: 013397 55759

It seems fitting that the lovely half-timbered house built in 1902 by a Swiss Artist, has continued over many years as **The McEwan Gallery**. Peter and Dorothy McEwan, recently joined by their son Rhod, invite you to visit and browse through their display of original paintings, prints, rare books, pottery and cards.

The McEwan Gallery

Established in 1968, the Gallery specialises in fine British and Continental paintings and watercolours of the 18th, 19th and 20th centuries with particular emphasis on 17th-20th century Scottish Artists. Dr McEwan is the author of the recently published definitive *Dictionary of Scottish Art & Architecture* whilst Rhod McEwan is one of the leading dealers in golfing literature worldwide (he exhibits at the 'Open'). The

Gallery is open throughout the year and offers a full valuation, restoration, cleaning and framing service for all mediums. In addition to exhibiting at a number of the main Antique Fairs, they hold specialist Exhibitions in their own Gallery and sell to museums and public art galleries. Open seven days a week in summer until 6.00 pm and until 5.00 pm in winter. Telephone at any time for a special appointment and for details and dates of exhibitions.

The McEwan Gallery, Glengarden, Ballater Tel: 013397 55429
Fax: 013397 55995

AROUND BALLATER

BRAEMAR is famous for the 'Gathering' held here every September and attended by the Royal family. This is the largest Highland Games in Scotland, dating form 1832, and famous for the Braemar Caber, nearly 20 feet long and weighing 132 pounds. The Highland Games uphold a tradition that goes back into the mists of the past. The earliest were held more than 1000 years ago under the sponsorship of clan chiefs and kings, proving very useful for recruiting staff; race winners made good messengers and the strongest men bodyguards. Down the centuries villagers gathered once a year, perhaps their only holiday, to take part in competitions based on the tools of their trades, throwing hammers, tossing tree trunks, carrying boulders and running races, all activities now incorporated in the modern games. It also became opportunity to salute the clan chief with a march past to pipe bands and flying the clan colours. At Braemar the Queen takes the salute, a tradition begun by King Malcolm in the 11th century.

Braemar Castle was built in the early 17th century. It was the work of the 7th Earl of Mar, who held it for the Government during the Early Jacobite rising of Bonnie Dundee in 1689, falling into Jacobite hands when the Earl died. Twenty five years later the next Earl of Mar raised the Jacobite standard on the Braes of Mar starting the 1715 Rising. In 1748 following the failure of the '45 Rising the Government rented the then semi-derelict Castle from the Farquharsons of Invercauld, who had bought it off the disgraced Mar and who own it to this day. The road south of Braemar climbs the highest main road pass in the country at Cairnwell.

BALMORAL. The most famous place on the River Dee is **Balmoral Castle**, summer home of the Royal Family for over a century. The earliest reference to it, as Bouchmorale, was in 1484. Queen Victoria visited the earlier Castle in 1848 and fell in love with the location. Prince Albert bought the estate in 1852 and had the Castle rebuilt by William Smith of Aberdeen. Public access is limited to the grounds and ballroom, with it paintings and works of art, during May, June and July. Balmoral stands under 3791 foot Lochnagar mountain, which lies to the south.

Some years ago Prince Charles wrote a children's tale *The Old Man of Lochnagar*, no doubt inspired by the scenery and the myth and legends of the Highlands. The story went on to be published and was also made into an animated film with the Prince as narrator.

CRATHIE. Not far from the Balmoral Castle at Crathie village is the **Royal Lochnagar Distillery**. The Distillery was granted a Royal Warrant of Appointment by Queen Victoria in 1848 and has a visitors centre.

Crathie has a small church, built in 1895, which is attended by the Royal Family when it is in residence at Balmoral. Nearby Balmoral Bridge carries the B976 over the Dee near the castle. Commissioned by Prince Albert as part of the improvements to the Estate and designed by Isambard Kingdom Brunel, its construction took the public road away from the Castle, creating better privacy and was a more solid replacement for the original suspension bridge. Another bridge of great note is the military one upstream at Invercauld, built in 1752 by Major Edward Caulfield.

GLEN MUICK. Of scenic interest the Glen was also, in 1899, witness to a chance meeting between Queen Victoria, who was out for a drive, and a battalion of the Gordon Highlands shortly before they left for South Africa. The Queen reviewed the troops and a cairn marks the occasion.

Driving in Glen Muick, we discovered the home and business of Howard and Hilary Butterworth, known as **Paintings and Pullovers** (look out for the sign on the gate).

Paintings and Pullovers

Howard is an established artist of some 20 years or more specialising in original oils and limited edition prints. He was born in Rochdale but has lived and painted in Scotland since 1968. His main areas of activity are Royal Deeside, Scotland in general and Alicante province in Spain. He describes his work as paintings mostly in oils, representational and with emotional realism. Since 1983 signed prints have been available and, together with his greeting cards, are available from selected galleries throughout the country. Hilary, meanwhile, turns her time and talents to manufacturing knitwear - cardigans, pullovers, waistcoats and hats, using best Shetland wool and tailored in 'classic traditional styles', plain rather than patterned. Paintings and Pullovers is open all year and, since Howard and Hilary live on the premises, they are open seven days a week. If visiting from long distance, please telephone beforehand. Very professional - ideal and sensible gifts.

Paintings and Pullovers, Crofts Cottage, Glen Muick, Ballater
Tel 013397 55678

GLENGAIRN. Taking the A939 road out of Ballater puts you on route for **Gairnshiel Lodge** just six miles away. Gairnshiel is a magnificent granite dwelling used as a hunting lodge by Queen Victoria during her visits to Balmoral. It is situated in four acres on the upper reaches of the River Gairn in the foothills of the Cairngorm Mountains, between the River Dee and the River Don which offers excellent fishing and is surrounded by panoramic views. This is a wonderful location suitable for many pursuits or for people simply looking for a casual and healthy holiday. The proprietors, Monica and Martin Debremaeker provide bed, breakfast and an optional evening meal with traditional home-cooking and baking - don't get hooked on the shortbread! The bedrooms are bright and simply furnished, all having lovely open views of the hills and River Gairn. A real log fire burns in the residents' lounge on the first floor where you can relax and perhaps sample one of Martin's malt whiskies. Other facilities include a drying room, large games room and mountain bikes. Having enjoyed Monica's excellent breakfast you can leave for your day's exploring complete with a packed lunch.

Gairnshiel Lodge, Glengairn, Ballater Tel & Fax: 013397 55582

UPPER STRATHDON. Corgarff Castle is a lonely tower house that has seen plenty of history despite its location. It was built in 1537, only to be destroyed in 1571, when a party of Gordons from Auchindoun Castle fired the Castle, taking with it the Laird's wife, Margaret Forbes, and 26 others; part of an endemic rivalry between the Catholic Gordons and the Protestant Forbes. The Castle suffered a second burning in 1689 when Jacobites put a torch to it, aiming to prevent its use by forces of the King. In 1715, the Earl of Mar encamped here before raising the Jacobite standard at Braemar. After Culloden the Castle was garrisoned by Government troops having been modified in a similar style to Braemar. The final episode in the Castle's active life came in 1827-31 when a Captain, Subaltern and 56 men were stationed here to help the excisemen stamp out whisky smuggling. After then it drifted into disuse, though it has now been restored.

The road over **The Lecht** is narrow, steep, twisting and often blocked by snow in the winter. At the top of the pass are the mechanical monsters of the ski tow, skiers flocking to these hills because of that very snow. Two miles north of the summit is the Well of Lecht. Above the small natural spring a white stone plaque dated 1754 records that five companies of the 33rd Regiment built the road from here to the Spey. This marks one section of the military road that starts in Blairgowrie, passes the garrisons of Braemar and Corgarff, over the bridges of Invercauld and Gairnsheil and on to Ruthven Barracks on the banks of the Spey at Kingussie.

STRATHDON. For keen gardeners there are two gems to discover near the village. **Candacraig Gardens** is a Victorian walled garden with an 1820 Gothic style summerhouse, formal and modern rose gardens and period fountains. **Old Semeil Herb Garden**, three miles to the southeast, is a specialist herb plant nursery, with a display herb garden, plant nursery and garden centre selling garden pottery, books, seeds, gifts and unusual plants.

KILDRUMMY. Grampian is castle country and the region contains some of the finest examples of the 1200 that are spread across Scotland. **Glenbuchat Castle**, five miles south of Kildrummy, is a no nonsense Z-plan castle, which stands above the ravine through which flows the Water of Buchat. It was built in 1590 by the Gordons; Brigadier-General Gordon of Buchat supported both the '15 and '45 Jacobite Risings and avoided retribution by fleeing to France. Though he kept his head, his land and Castle were forfeited to the Earl of Fife.

Kildrummy Castle ruins, a mile or so south of the village, are the best preserved example of a 13th century castle of enclosure. Seat of the Earls of Mar, it was dismantled after the '45 Rising. There is a beautiful shrub and alpine garden in the adjacent ancient quarry below the Castle. In Kildrummy village there is an unusual rectangular bow fronted Kirk which replaced the pre-Reformation Kirk in 1805. The old Kirk still stands on a grassy mound in the kirkyard, though it has lost its font, reused in the new one.

MOSSAT. The Mossat Shop is an interesting mix between a Restaurant and Gift Shop. Situated twixt an Antique shop and Garden Centre, the view from the restaurant pleasantly overlooks the Garden Centre. The Shop is run by Ian and Liz who were both born within six miles of the village and have an extensive knowledge of the history of Mossat. Ian's speciality is pancakes whilst Liz makes superb scones and meringues. Whether you call in for a pot of tea or coffee, morning snack, light or full lunch, or afternoon tea, you will find good wholesome home-baked food and a waitress service. The restaurant is welcoming with cottage style furniture, lace tablecloths and pleasant background music. Children are very well catered for with their under 12s menu and high tea menu.

The Mossat Shop

In the Craftshop you'll find a most attractive range of gift cards, lace, pots, glass, Scottish jams, local shortbread, books and much more. Teddies and tartan items are always popular gifts and there's plenty of selection from which to choose. Open seven days a week (closed Tuesdays in April) Easter to October, weekends January to Easter. Closed late October to January. You will certainly enjoy the good food and friendly service.

The Mossat Shop, Mossat Tel: 01975 713555.

ALFORD. The scene of a battle, in 1645, between Montrose and the Convenanters, Alford is today the home of the **Grampian Transport Museum**. This houses an extensive collection of historic road vehicles in a purpose built exhibition hall and includes a huge MAC snowplough, vintage steam roller and an armoured car. There is a recreation of a 1960s transport cafe, a driving simulator and video bus featuring motorsport and road transport history. During the summer the museum is host to many events, with car and motorcycles of all ages being put through their paces on the race circuit.

The original village railway station has now become **Alford Railway Museum**. The station depicts the advent of the railway in the village and the period booking office containing a photo exhibition. The railway, the only 2 foot narrow gauge railway in Scotland, runs a passenger service to Haughton Country Park.

326

For a more unusual diversion, visit the **Montgarrie Mills** at Alford. In 1894, Angus MacDonald bought Montgarrie Mills. He named his product Alford Oatmeal as the little village of Montgarrie had no railway service - unlike its near neighbour Alford which was a terminus for the London North Eastern Railway thus ensuring that Alford always appeared on maps. Today, the railway (and Angus) have long gone, Aberdeenshire including Alford is populated by 'oil related' workers, and barley and wheat have replaced oats as the main cereal crops. Three generation on, the oats are still dried and toasted on a flat kiln floor to give the real old fashioned crispy nutty texture to the oatmeal. The various conveyors, sieves and the millstones involved in the milling of the oats are still powered by the water wheel; the latter has been in service since it was built in 1882.

Montgarrie Mills

Tours of the working mill are arranged by prior appointment and take about one hour. It's a fascinating look back into milling history and very interesting to see how the whole process works from receiving oats from the local farms and grain merchants to the finished product ready for dispatch to the retailers. There's expert advice on hand on getting the best from your cooking too. Phone for tour arrangements. Open all year.

Montgarrie Mills, Alford Tel: 019755 62209 Fax: 019755 62295

MUIR OF FOWLIS. **Craigievar Castle** is a perfect example of a fairy-tale castle, dating from 1626 and unchanged inside and out since then. Built of soft pink stone, the L-plan tower house is plain and simple up to the fourth floor, where it breaks out in a riot of conical turrets, serrated gables, chimneys and balustrades.

A masterpiece of Scottish Baronial architecture Craigievar Castle was built for William Forbes; known as 'Danzig Willie' because he made his fortune exporting fish and woollen goods to the Baltic. Home of the Forbes family until the 1960s it is now in the care of the National Trust for Scotland.

TARLAND. **Culsh Earth House** is a well preserved example of a souterrain or underground store house lying to the northeast of the village. The still air and even temperature made earth houses ideal for preserving produce for the community.

ABOYNE. A little north of Aboyne on the road to Tarland is **Tomnaverie Stone Circle**, one of many prehistoric sites scattered along the valley of the Dee. The remains of this recumbent stone circle date from around 1800-1600 BC and has yet to be excavated.

STRACHAN. Two very well equipped Thistle Award caravan homes are available for hire at **Feughside Caravan Park**, a small family run Park in the beautiful valley of the Feugh, where a warm welcome awaits from the owner, Sheila Hay.

Feughside Caravan Park

Set in the heart of Royal Deeside, the Park offers holidaymakers the chance to relax in this lovely peaceful area of Scotland. Caravaners and campers alike will find the location of this well kept Park the perfect starting point for trips to the many excellent leisure and recreation facilities in the area. Sheila will be pleased to help and advise on specific areas though her brochure already lists a vast array of possibilities. The Park offers 20 spacious pitches for tourers with hook-ups, areas for camping, well kept toilets, sheltered play area with swings and climbing frames, games hall, laundry, phone and supplies. Disabled facilities. The park is well lit and provides good car parking.

Feughside Caravan Park, Strachan Tel: 01330 850669

BANCHORY. Known as the 'Gateway to Deeside', this small town was the birthplace of the fiddler James Scott Skinner, otherwise known as the Strathspey King.

The name of **The Old Police House** conjures up a rather spartan nights' accommodation but such an idea would be totally wrong in this instance, it's a delightful private residence with a real warmth and welcome. The roomy entrance hall has a lovely antique pine balustraded staircase, flowers, plants and well chosen decorative scheme which continues throughout the house. The bedrooms have en-suite facilities, are roomy, have matching fabrics and decor, central heating and television - very inviting. It is hard to imagine this home as the local Police Station and Prison, which it was for over 50 years. Unlike those days, you will rise to a special Scottish breakfast which should keep you going well into the day. You can dine at one of several good local restaurants. Open all year except Christmas and New Year. STB - 2 Crowns Highly Commended. Very nice indeed.

The Old Police House, 3 Bridge Street, Banchory Tel: 01330 824000

CRATHES. Pronounced 'Crathess', **Crathes Castle** dates back to the 16th century and is also well known for its 18th century gardens. The painted ceilings with their accompanying rhymes and proverbs are delightful. Outside the huge yew hedges, planted in 1702, have been clipped into elaborate topiary, and the famous walled Blue garden shouldn't be missed.

MAINS OF DRUM. **Drum Castle**, a rather impressive 13th century tower house that has been added to over the centuries. The Royal Hunting forests of Drum were conferred on William de Irwin by Robert the Bruce in 1323. The family line remained unbroken until 1975 and the death of Mr Forbes-Irvine, when the castle passed into the hands of the National Trust.

KIRKTON OF MARYCUTTER. Those looking for freedom of movement, outdoor life and the convenience and facilities of the city will find **Lower Deeside Holiday Park** has a lot to offer. It is conveniently only fifteen minutes drive from Aberdeen yet is set in a tranquil landscaped area of some fourteen acres. Offering attractive six berth holiday caravans and four to six berth pinelodges for hire, the facilities also cater for touring caravans, motorhomes and tents. Briefly, the amenities include: fully equipped accommodation, tourer pitches, electric hook-ups, on-site shop with fresh bakery supplies, children's play area, games and TV room. Adjacent to the Park is an hotel and restaurant which will welcome families. Pets are welcome though must be under control at all times. Fishing permits are available for those booking accommodation. This is without doubt a well run operation with everything well presented. It is strongly recommended that you make advance booking.

Lower Deeside Holiday Park, South Deeside Road, Marycutter
Tel: 01224 733860 Fax: 01224 732490

For those readers visiting the many attractions of Aberdeen and its surrounding areas, **The Old Mill Inn** will be found to be a most convenient base offering excellent accommodation and food. This family run hotel was built in 1797 as a farmhouse with a mill on site; it became an hotel approximately 65 years ago. The white painted exterior is of an interesting and appealing design and good car parking space is available. The inn has 3 Crowns Commended rating by the STB. The bedrooms are comfortably furnished and all have en-suite facilities. Downstairs the supper menu is offered in either the spacious bar or restaurant. Lunch is served 12 - 2 pm and supper 5.30 pm until 9.30 pm. General opening hours are 11.00 am until 11.00 pm.

Old Mill Inn, South Deeside Road, Marycutter Tel: 01224 733212
Fax: 01224 732884

STONEHAVEN is a former fishing port spread around Stonehaven Bay. At the north end of the bay is Cowie village, the old fishertown quarter of the harbour. **The Tolbooth** here, situated on the quay, is a former 16th century storehouse of the Earl's Marischal. It was later used as a prison and, between 1748-49, Episcopal ministers lodged inside it, baptising children through the windows. Today it is the town museum, with displays on local history, archeology and in particular fishing.

To the north of the town is **Muchalls Castle**, just off the A92. Overlooking the sea, this tiny castle was built in 1619 by the Burnetts of Leys. Inside there are plasterwork ceilings, fine fireplaces and a hidden staircase. Only open a few days a year it is never the less a lovely place.

Storybook Glen, along the B979, is an ideal place to take younger children, with more than a hundred nursery rhyme characters spread amidst 20 acres of beautiful gardens and parklands.

KINNEFF. Part of the Old Church in the village formed the original buildings in which the crown jewels of Scotland were hidden during the Civil War. They were hidden under flag stones for nine years after being smuggled past Cromwell's besieging army at **Dunnottar Castle**. The Castle itself is an impressive ruin standing on rocky cliff 160 feet above the sea just south of Stonehaven. Known as the 'Scottish Camelot' this stronghold of the Earls Marischal was besieged in 1650 by the Roundheads. The Castle had been chosen as the safest place to keep the crown jewels during the upheavals, these were smuggled out to Kinneff before the Castle capitulated due to a lack of food. The Earl Marischal threw his lot in with the 1715 Rising and a year later Argyll rendered the Castle harmless. In recent years its spectacular position and appearance landed it a part in Mel Gibson's film *Hamlet*.

ST CYRUS. Situated on the south side of the village of St Cyrus, only four miles north of Montrose on the A92, stands **The Neuk Caravan Park**, a quiet, peaceful establishment that is owned and personally run by Ronald and Davina Dickson.

The Neuk Caravan Park

The village of St Cyrus is conveniently situated for visits to castles and many places of historic interest, there is also plenty of sea, river and loch fishing, not to mention the numerous golf courses that are available locally. Although there are cliffs at St Cyrus, an extensive sandy beach is also close at hand, and any bird watchers might be interested in the nature reserve here or at the well known Montrose Basin. The caravans are set in the very heart of the local countryside and are surrounding by peace and tranquillity, each static caravan, in addition to being fully serviced will have a fridge, gas fire and colour television. Although the bed linen and towels are not supplied, the cost of gas and electricity is already included in the original hire charge, so you won't have to put your hand in your pocket again, after the initial payment. There are mid week breaks and long or short weekends always available, in fact in many cases you can commence your week or fortnight holiday any day of the week that you choose.

The Neuk Caravan Park, Lochside Road, St Cyrus by Montrose
Tel: 01674 850389

FETTERCAIRN. A rather impressive gothic stone archway greets the visitor who approaches from the south; it was erected to commemorate a visit here by Queen Victoria and Prince Albert in 1861. The village is home to the second oldest licensed distillery in Scotland, Fettercairn. Half a mile north of the village is the magnificent **Fasque House**, one of the best preserved Victorian stately homes anywhere. Not a museum but a living house, Fasque has been the family home of the Gladstones since 1829, the sixth generation living here today. Its most famous occupant was William Gladstone, four times Prime Minister to Queen Victoria. Inside the house, especially downstairs, very little has changed since William's day. The kitchens and sculleries contain a wealth of domestic implements from a by-gone era. Above stairs there are the staterooms, drawing room, library and cantilever staircase to admire. At the front of the house red deer roam in the park. Fasque is open in the afternoons between May and September, except on Fridays, and is certainly worth the visit.

From Fettercairn the B974 road climbs passed the tiny tearoom at Clatterin' Brig and up to the **Cairn O'Mount** summit, 1493 feet above sea level. The tall poles that line the roads of the high mountains act as a guide for the ploughs when the snow is several feet deep. At the bottom of the pass is the **Bridge of Dye**. This graceful single high arch bridge was built in 1680 and is one of the earliest in the northeast. In the wall of the house nearby is what looks rather like a pill box, disguised as part of the wall no doubt at the insistence of the house owner. There are a number of pill boxes in the Grampians, part of a grid defence system against German invasion.

Aberdeenshire

ABERDEEN. Scotland's third city is also known as the 'Granite City' due to the profusion of wonderful grey granite buildings at its heart. This, at present prosperous, city offers theatre, cinema, a vast array of sports facilities, some very fine shopping and eating out to suit every palate. There is large selection of accommodation available but at certain times of the year it can be in short supply, due to the oil industry.

The present townscape that prompted the nick-name is a result of the Aberdeen New Streets Act of 1801, which inaugurated a hectic half century of civil engineering and construction. Huge town planning changes were implemented, the most dramatic being the creation of **Union Street** in 1801, which involved the removal of the sand and gravel St Katherine's Hill and the erection of a series of great arches and bridges. This undertaking very nearly bankrupted the city, a boom in trade rescuing it from financial ruin.

Here in the centre of the city the visitor is surrounded by granite, dull or sparkling according to the light, which came from the city quarries in huge quantities. Many of Aberdeen's most beautiful buildings are to be found here, and it is well worth setting aside a little time just to wander around, and wonder at, the architecture. At the western end of Union Street is **St James'**; built of pink granite the church has an odd appearance as the spire, originally planned, was never built. Behind the church, in Justice Mill Lane, is something altogether different - **Satrosphere, The Discovery Place**. A great place for kids of all ages, it is a hands on science and technology centre, exploring sound, light, energy and the environment with nearly a hundred DIY experiments.

Across Union Street at the end of Union Terrace is Rosemount Viaduct and **His Majesty's Theatre**, opened in 1906. The exquisite Edwardian interior has been restored and it is Aberdeen's main theatre, seating 1500, and hosting ballet, opera, musicals, concerts and plays. Next door are the **Church of St Mark** and the **City Library** - the three being affectionately known as 'Education, Salvation and Damnation'. In the next block is the **City Art Gallery**, which house a fine collection works from the last three centuries.

Along Schoolhill and to the right on Broad Street is **Provost Skene's House**. Erected in the 16th century, this house bears the name of its most notable owner, Sir George Skene, Provost of Aberdeen 1676-1685. (The Provost is the chief administrative official of a Scottish Burgh.) One of few remaining town houses in the city, it has remarkable painted ceilings and interesting relics. Across Broad Street is **Marischal College**, an imposing 1906 granite structure which has a soaring Tudor Gothic frontage and a quadrangle, entered by a fine archway, around which are older buildings of 1836-44, and the graceful Mitchell Tower.

St Andrew's Cathedral, on King Street, is the Cathedral Church of the Scottish Episcopal Diocese of Aberdeen and Orkney. One of few sandstone buildings in this part of Aberdeen, it contains the Seabury Memorial, which commemorates the consecration of Samuel Seabury of Connecticut, the first Bishop of the USA, in Aberdeen in 1784. There is also an exhibition showing some of the distinct features of Christian heritage of the northeast.

Aberdeen is still one of Britain's major fishing ports, and the story of this ancient port is told at the **Maritime Museum** in the **Provost Ross's House** on Shiprow. Built in 1593 and one of Aberdeen's oldest buildings, it was saved by conservationists in the 1950s with the help of the Queen Mother. The museum uses models, paintings and audio-visual displays to tell the story of local shipbuilding, the fishing industry and North Sea oil and gas developments.

Along the harbour front is **Footdee**, bound in on one side by the bustling harbour quays and protected from the elements by the sea-wall at the south end of Aberdeen Esplanade. 'Fittie' is a peninsula village with a quite separate atmosphere from the rest of the city. Its sturdy stone cottages, ranged around squares, were built early in the 19th century for fishermen and harbour pilots, the pilotage authority is still based at the Round House. Nearby **Pocra Quay** is a supply base for North Sea oil platforms and shipyards here launched many of the phenomenally fast tea-clippers, whose times were virtually unrivalled in the races to bring back the first crop of the season in Victorian times. Some small scale shipbuilding and repairs still goes on. Aberdeen is also the port from which to catch a ferry to Shetland, the voyage taking 14 hours.

To the north of the city is **Aulton**, or Old Town, which has always maintained a separate identity to the 'new' burgh and port on the River Dee. On the south bank of the River Don, it has many older buildings and a typical medieval street layout. The High Street is dominated by **King's College Chapel**. The University was founded in 1494 and this was its first building. The chapel interior has some of Scotland's finest medieval woodwork and the exterior is crowned by an imposing crown spire. In sharp contrast is Grant's Place, a row of simple single storey cottages built in 1732. Also on the High Street is the Town House, a splendidly proportioned municipal building with a small clock tower erected in 1788. A more unusual house is to be found down on the river. **Wallace Tower** is fine example of a simple towerhouse, like a castle in miniature built in 1616. Originally it stood near the harbour but redevelopment led to it being move here stone by stone in 1964.

Along the river, to the east, is **Brig o'Balgowie**. Also known as the 'Auld Brig o'Don' this massive 62 foot wide arch, that spans a deep pool of the River, was completed around 1320 and rebuilt in 1607. In 1605 Sir Alexander Hay endowed the bridge with a small property, which had so increased in value that it built the New Bridge of Don, a little down stream, in 1830 at a cost of £26,000, as well as bearing the cost of the Victoria bridge and contributed to many other public works.

Another bridge of interest crosses the Dee on the southwestern outskirts of the city. **The Bridge of Dee** was built in 1520s by Bishop

Gavin Dunbar, during the reign of James V. Its seven arches span 400 feet and the medieval solidity of the structure is enlivened by heraldic carvings.

AROUND ABERDEEN

DYCE. To the west of the village at **Old Dyce Kirk** are a pair of fine examples of Pictish symbol stones, one covered in ancient symbols including a large beast with a fine plume and muscles. The other is an intricate Cross slab. It is not completely clear what function these stones performed but at least some were involved in burial rituals, the stone commemorating an ancestor of rank, as well as providing descendants with a form of title. That many now stand in ancient churchyards may be the result of Christianization of existing Pictish burial sites.

PITMEDDEN. The **Great Gardens of Pitmedden** are formal and have been brilliantly restored to their original 1675 layout. There are huge geometric flowerbeds, marked out with box and yew hedges, as well as pavilions fountains and sundials. Three of the four parterres or flowerbeds follow designs used at Holyrood house in Edinburgh, while the fourth is the family crest of Sir Alexander Seton who started the gardens. There is also a **Museum of Farming Life**, which has an impressive selection of agricultural equipment from the last century.

In the corner of **Udny Green Churchyard**, to the south of the village, is a rather plain circular building that could easily be mistaken for a rather substantial toolstore. A second look at the strength of the walls, lack of windows and stout oak door, reveals an ingenious solution to problem of bodysnatchers. Coffins were placed in the Mort house, postponing the burial until the body was unsuitable for sale. Four separate key holders were need to unlock the door and sliding inner iron gate. Ironically it was built in 1832, when a law was passed that solved the problem of bodysnatching by ensuring a legal supply of bodies.

TOLQUHON. Once a seat of the Forbes family, **Tolquhon Castle** was originally known as Preston Tower and was a simple rectangular keep. William Forbes, the 7th Laird, was responsible for its expansion into a more spacious accommodation. Confirmation of the date of the work can be seen on one of the outer walls which shows the inscription Al this worke excep the Auld Tour was begun by William Forbes 15 April 1584 and endit be him October 1589'. Sold to the Farquharsits, the Castle passed onto the 2nd Earl of Aberdeen and was abandoned as a residence by 1800. William Forbes and his wife are laid to rest nearby in Tarves Churchyard, his fine altar-tomb showing an interesting mix of Gothic and Renaissance styles.

HADDO. Designed by William Adam for William, 2nd Earl of Aberdeen, in 1731, **Haddo House** replaced the Old House of Kellie, home of the Gordons of Methlick for centuries. When the 4th Earl, George, came into his inheritance in 1805 he found a treeless waste surrounded the neglected house, the 3rd or 'wicked' Earl having lived away with his mistresses. He set to work with a will, his 80 foresters planting trees across the estate, he made other major improvements and laid out the gardens. He was less successful in political life, having become Prime Minister in 1852 he became unhappily embroiled in the debacle of Crimea. Much of the interior is 'Adam Revival' style carried out about 1880 for John, 7th Earl and 1st Marquess of Aberdeen and his Countess, Ishbel. A large area of the 4th Earl's forest is now a country park that adjoins the house grounds.

FYVIE. The oldest part of **Fyvie Castle** dates from the 13th century, with subsequent generations adding to the grand structure over the years. Today its five towers enshrine five centuries of Scottish history and its is now a fine example of Scottish baronial architecture. Its most famous features are its 'Wheel' staircase and the important collection of fine portraits, including work by Raeburn and Gainsborough. Most of interior was created by 1st Lord Leith of Fyvie and reflects the opulence of the Edwardian era.

Three miles north of the village is the much smaller, but no less interesting, castle of **Towie Barclay**. An ancient stronghold of the Barclays dating from 1136, it has recently been reconstructed, together with its walled garden, by the present owners and has won major European restoration awards. Incidentally a descendant of the Barclay family, Prince Barclay de Toille, became a Russian Field Marshal and was immortalised in Tolstoy's *War and Peace*.

INVERURIE. Two miles south of the village, on the banks of the River Don, are the ruins of **Kinkell Church**; an early 16th century parish church, it has some fine ornate details. Within the churchyard is the graveslab of Gilbert de Greenlaw, killed in the battle of Harlaw in 1411, which bears an unusually detailed carving of an armoured knight. This slab was reused by the Forbes in 1592.

Monymusk 'Old Bakery' Tearoom

Monymusk 'Old Bakery' Tearoom was indeed built as a bakery in 1885 and was named J&K Kinghorn. Since those days it has had numerous occupants including a butcher and crafts people. The building was fully restored three years ago when it became the Tearoom. Solidly built of stone, you might easily pass by its unpretentious entrance. Once inside it will delight your eye, the centrepiece being the old granite fireplace complete with range and fittings dating from its original times as a bakery. The Tearoom is beautifully presented with cottage style furniture, polished wood floor, old mirrored dresser and pictures produced by a local artist. Irene Ellis is the owner of this lovely Tearoom and is responsible for all the home-cooking and baking. She is certainly a busy lady producing meals and light snacks every day of the week. She produces nine or ten different types of scones and her Bakery Platter is very popular. You may call early and enjoy breakfast, and at any time throughout the day there's a wide variety of food available including High Teas for all the family with a special children's menu. Enjoys a well-deserved reputation for good food and good value. Facilities for the disabled. Open 10 am - 4.30 pm Monday to Saturday and from 1 pm - 6 pm on Sundays. Same hours throughout the year.

Monymusk 'Old Bakery' Tearoom, The Village Square,
Monymusk by Inverurie Tel: 01467 651514

CHAPEL OF GARIOCH. To the south is **Easter Aquhorthies** recumbent stone circle, sign posted from the town. An impressive stone circle, the recumbent, its flankers and the circle are all of different stone, some from many miles away. Recumbent stones were Neolithic sites of communal and seasonal ritual, some later becoming cremation burial sites. The huge recumbent stones weighed any thing up to 20 tons and would have needed many men to move then even a short distance.

Within the pages of *The Hidden Places* series, we aim to offer notable places to stay, eat and visit across a wide spectrum, and it is always a pleasure to feature at the top end of the scale, houses of such classic elegance and style as **Pittodrie House**. Set on an estate of 3,000 acres in the heart of Aberdeenshire, the house is the family home of Theo Smith, who, as Chairman of the Hotel, desires that you feel an important guest the moment you walk through the door.

Pittodrie estate originally belonged to the Erskine family, a branch of the family of the Earls of Mar. It was granted to them by Robert the Bruce, for their allegiance at the battle of Bannockburn. The House was built in 1480 when nearby Maiden Castle burned down. Pittodrie House itself was burned down during the Covenanting period by the Marquis of Montrose. What was left of the house was re-built as a Z-plan castle in 1675. Substantial alterations were made to the House in 1850 by the eminent Aberdeen architect Archibald Simpson. These include the fine Drawing Room and Dining Room. George Smith bought the Estate in 1896 after selling the City Line whose ships sailed all over the world.

After making the minimum necessary changes, the House was opened as a hotel in 1977. Subsequently, an extra wing was added with bedrooms and a Ballroom and opened in 1990. The family paintings and antiques have been retained in all the reception rooms and bedrooms so as to retain the atmosphere of a Country House rather than a Hotel. The Reception rooms include the Drawing Room and Library where you can make yourself at home in front of the log fires or taste one of more than 135 malt whiskies stocked in the comfortable Bar. When dining, a true Taste of Scotland can be enjoyed; according to season, game, smoked and fresh fish and Aberdeen Angus beef are hotel specialities. Vegetables and herbs are grown in the walled garden. Completing the experience, a choice of more than 200 carefully selected wines are available.

Throughout the Hotel the air of sumptuous living is ever present, reflected also in the beautiful bedrooms with their unique decor and original features. Each room has all the luxuries you would expect of any modern hotel and your comfort is assured in every way. For those able to draw themselves away from the comfort of the Hotel, there are many diversionary interests which include the recreational facilities of the Hotel such as squash, tennis, croquet and clayshooting on the Estate, whilst a little further afield there's trout and salmon fishing, stalking, rough shooting, riding and many other sports and pursuits. We can only suggest you make your reservations early. Twenty minutes from Aberdeen Airport.

Pittodrie House, Chapel of Garioch, By Inverurie
Tel: 10467 681444 Fax: 01467 681648

HUNTLY. A once strategically important town, Huntly commanded the route from Aberdeen and Strathdon into Moray. As a result it has had an eventful history, the defensive site between the Rivers Deveron and Bogie having been fortified since the days of the Norman earls, though the two standing stones in the town square suggest much earlier occupation. From 1776 the town was expanded by the Duke of Gordon and the regular street pattern formed which is still a major feature today.

Almost in the heart of the town is **Huntly Castle**. An imposing ruin of rich golden stone, which replaced medieval Strathbogie Castle, it was, until 1544, the seat of the Gordons, the Marquesses of Huntly, and the most powerful family in the north until the mid 16th century. The Castle, now surrounded by a wooded park, was destroyed and rebuilt several times. The family's support for Charles I led to its final destruction during the Civil War in the mid 1600s.

Several miles south of the town, on the B9002, is a country seat from a different era, **Leith Hall**. The mansion house of Leith is at the centre of a 286 acre estate which was the home of the head of the Leith and Leith-Hay family from 1650. The house contains personal possessions of successive Lairds, most of whom followed a tradition of military service, a story told in the 'For Crown and Country: the Military Lairds of Leith' exhibition. The grounds contain an 18th century curved stables, not unlike the one back at Aden Country Park, as well as informal gardens and woodland walks.

To the north of Huntly, off the A97, is the fascinating **Cloverleaf Fibre Stud**. This working farm breeds llama, alpacas, guanacos, reindeer and goats bearing cashmere, cashgora and mohair, as well as rare breeds of sheep. In the farm shop everything from spinning fibre to finished garments are available.

Upon arriving at **The Forbes Arms Hotel**, you are surrounded by stunningly lovely scenery and the River Deveron on whose banks it stands. Once a coaching inn, the Hotel has recently been totally refurbished in a style and decor befitting this lovely old building which has lost none of its charm in the transition.

The Forbes Arms Hotel

The attractive, comfortable en-suite bedrooms enjoy views of the river and the tranquillity of the whole area is soothing indeed. There is a three bedroomed lodge, furnished to the same high standard with its own lounge and en-suite facilities which lies adjacent to the hotel. It can be reserved on an exclusive basis, ideal for private, business or sporting parties. In years past, The Forbes Arms was used only by fishermen but today the hotel welcomes guests from many parts who come to relax and enjoy this peaceful location. The Hotel has a private fishing beat on the river with salmon and sea trout pools, available exclusively for residents. Fishing on beats adjacent to the Hotel can also be arranged. Bar lunches and restaurant suppers are served daily and the hotel's traditional five course dinner created by the Hotel chef from fine local produce, is also available on request. Salmon, caught in the river, is smoked locally and served fresh at your table. A large residents' lounge with television and superb views of the river is an ideal place to relax after your days activities. In the surrounding local area there are several championship golf courses, pony trekking, birdwatching, sea angling, curling, bowls or you can follow the Castle, Whisky or Fishing Heritage Trails.

The Forbes Arms Hotel, Miltown of Rothiemay, Huntly
Tel: 01466 711248

At the roundabout on the A96 Huntly Ring Road, you would be well advised to call in at the **King George V Garden Centre and Restaurant**. Apart from having obvious appeal to the gardening enthusiast, this is much more than just a garden centre and has something to offer the whole family. As you browse, looking round the vast selection of shrubs and trees, many varieties of pot plants, planters, pots and hanging baskets and other garden accessories, the children can run off energy in the adventure playground, complete with dodgem cars.

The floral department offers a complete florist service and has the largest selection of real and silk flowers in the area, while the gift shop will provide you with a wealth of ideas for that perfect present or memento. There is also a well-stocked book shop and a super restaurant which offers traditional Scottish fare, ranging from teas and snacks to freshly cooked main meals and the Centre's excellent modern facilities include toilets for the disabled and a unit for nursing mothers, ensuring everyone's needs are catered for. Open seven days, throughout the year.

King George V Garden Centre, Huntly Tel: 01466 793908
Fax: 01466 794577

Enjoying a central location on Gordon Street in Huntly, just a stones throw from the castle and the golf course, **Greenmount** is a welcoming 3 Crown Commended guest house run by George and Evelyn Manson. This impressive Georgian building dates back some 150 years and since 1973 has been providing passing travellers with very comfortable accommodation and warm, Scottish hospitality. The dining room provides a cosy setting for a substantial breakfast each morning as well as a wholesome evening meal, by prior arrangement. Four of the eight guest rooms are en-suite and each is attractively furnished, with the useful addition of a comprehensive information pack to help you plan your stay in this beautiful part of Scotland.

Greenmount, Gordon Street, Huntly Tel: 01466 792482

TURRIFF. In 1913 Turriff became known throughout Great Britain when a local farmer, Robert Paterson, refused to join Lloyd George's new National Health Insurance Scheme. One of his cows was impounded and Sheriff's Officers tried to auction it to cover the payments, a riot ensued and they were chased out of town. Similar attempts in Aberdeen met with little more success and eventually his neighbours bought the cow and after parading through the streets presented it back to Paterson. The 'Turra Coo' as it was known made front page news and there was a healthy souvenir industry of 'coo' postcards, mugs, plates and the like. Today the two day Turriff Show is one of Europe's major agricultural events attracting 50,000 visitors.

Two miles east of the town is **Delgatie Castle**. A stout tower house, home of the Hays of Delgatie, dating back to the 11th century and featuring a magnificent turnpike stair of 97 steps. Mary, Queen of Scots stayed here for three days in 1562, a portrait hanging in the room she used. The beautiful colour ceilings were installed in 1590 and amongst the interesting contents are many pictures and arms.

MINTLAW. **Aden Country Park** covers some 220 acres of an estate that once covered 10,000. Footpaths explore broadleaf and conifer woodland, pass a wildfowl lake which used to hold a head of water for the mill and crosses a footbridge over the winding South Ugie Water.

This mixture of habitats attracts many kinds of birds and small mammals; and visitors early or late in the day may catch sight of the roe deer feeding on the open ground. Aden's beautifully restored semi-circular range of farm buildings house a series of displays illustrating the lives of the estate workers. The 18th century mansion house is now a gaunt ruin, but it is easy to imagine how opulent it must once have been. There is also an interesting ice-house, this underground store would be packed with tons of snow and ice that would see the estate through to the next winter. Part of the park is now a 20 acre working farm where northeast farming in the 1950s is brought to life.

To the north of the village is **Mormond Hill**, a prominent Buchan landmark with an RAF signal station on its summit. A large white horse and white stag were cut into is flanks in the 18th century by Captain Fraser of Strichen.

PETERHEAD. Europe's busiest fishing port, dozens of boats a day land their catches here and there is a very busy fishmarket early every weekday morning. The history of the town's long connection with the sea is told at the **Arbuthnot Museum and Art Gallery** in St Peter Street. There are displays on the development of the fishing and whaling industries, with special Arctic exhibits, a section on local history, and photograph and coin exhibitions. On Golf Road, at the mouth of the River Ugie, is the oldest salmon fish house in Scotland. **Ugie Salmon Fish House**, was built in 1585 for George Keith, 5th Earl Marischal of Scotland, and still supplies tasty fresh and smoked salmon today.

On the coast south of Peterhead is **Cruden Bay**, with its rocky cliffs and the Bullers of Buchan as its masterpiece. This is a vast sea chasm 200 feet deep, where the sea rushes in through a natural archway open to the sky. Standing on the cliffs above the bay are the extensive ruins of **Slains Castle**; built in 1597 and remodelled in the Gothic style in the 19th century, only to fall into disuse. Once home of the Dukes of Erroll, Johnson and Boswell stayed here on their Highland journey, as did Bram Stoker, who got inspiration for his gothic horror masterpiece *Dracula* here. Cruden Bay is famous in golfing circles for its course, so popular late last century that the Great North of Scotland Railway Company built a 140 room hotel. Both it and the railway are now distant memories.

FRASERBURGH. Unlikely as it may seem today the fishing port of Fraserburgh, once had a university. Built in 1595, with a grant from the Scottish Parliament, it soon withered away when the principal was flung in jail by James VI for defying his ecclesiastical policy. The only remnant is the Moses Stone, a carved stone, that now stands at South Church. At **Kinnaird Head**, north of the harbour, is an interesting lighthouse. When an Act of 1786 demanded a light at the most northerly part of Aberdeenshire the tower house built in the 16th century by Sir Alexander Fraser, 8th Laird of Philorth, was ideally placed and provided a ready made platform for the light. It was first lit on 1st December 1787, becoming the first lighthouse in Scotland. Originally the light was fixed and used whale-oil lamps, but even so on a clear night its beam could be seen up to 14 miles away. Though much modified it is still in use today.

On the rocks below the lighthouse is the **Wine Tower**, a mysterious building that is thought to have been a private chapel. Built in the 1400s, the tower features in many local legends and is reputed to be haunted. South of the harbour the sandy town beach stretches for three miles and has won international awards for cleanliness.

ROSEHEARTY. Ruined **Pitsligo Castle** dates from 1424 and passed through various families on to the 4th and last Lord Pitsligo, an ardent Jacobite, who is remembered for his generosity to the poor and successful attempts to evade capture following the '45 Rising. It was purchased by an American descendant of the Lord, Malcolm Forbes the multi-millionaire publisher, who had the buildings structure secured prior to his death in 1990.

PENNAN. This beautiful old smugglers haunt stands at the foot of mighty cliffs, hidden by the overhang. Pennan was the location for the film *Local Hero* which told the topical tale of how a small Scottish community hoodwinked a giant American oil company. Interestingly enough the village's public phone box is a listed historic monument. The cliffs nearby are full of caves and secret bays that made life very hard for the excisemen chasing the smugglers.

MACDUFF. A bustling fishing port on the eastern bank of the River Deveron, the harbour is overlooked by the imposing War Memorial, a 70 foot high octagonal tower erected in 1923. **Doune Church** is unusual in that it has a clock tower with four faces, one of which is blank. This faces across the river to Banff and marks the indignation felt by the folk of Macduff to those of Banff when they advanced their clocks to bring forward the execution of local outlaw James MacPherson to ensure he could not be pardoned. The empty clockface is meant to ensure that Banffers never again know the time.

BANFF. This royal and ancient burgh contains a great number of 17th and 18th century buildings; The Banff Preservation Society have helpfully placed information plaques on many of them. In the centre of the historic quarter of the town is the **Plainstones**, or market place. Here is well preserved Mercat Cross from the 16th century, the very ornate Biggar fountain and a cannon captured at Sevastopol during the Crimean War; these are all overlooked by the strangely conical-shaped tolbooth steeple. It is only a short walk from here to Sandyhill Road and something rather different. **The Sculpture Garden** features a number wondrous and unique garden sculptures, carved from huge pieces of tree trunk, that really fire the imagination.

Nearby **Duff House** is very different again but still does its best to overpower the senses. Although incomplete, William Adam's splendid and richly detailed mansion is amongst the finest works of Georgian baroque architecture in Britain. Started in 1730, of all William Adam's

Coastline at Pennan

Fordyce Castle

creations this is the most assertive, most brash, specially when compared with the relative restraint of Haddo, which he was building at the same time. The explanation lies in Adam's ability to interpret a client's demands. In William Braco he had one that was determined to impress, if not daunt, his visitors.

Braco was one of the richest men in Aberdeenshire, thanks to his father's banking interests; he became Lord Braco in 1735 and Earl of Fife in 1759. Adam responded to his clients wishes to the letter and work began in 1730 though only half the intended pile was ever built. A dispute between architect and customer in 1736 left the house without its pair of intended pavilions and the sweeping colonnades that would have joined them to the main house. The dispute remained unresolved at the time of Adam's death in 1748 and, such was Braco's bitterness, he could never bring himself to live in it, drawing the blinds of his carriage whenever he passed it. Eventually occupied by the 2nd Earl and his descendants, it has since been a hotel, nursing home and army billet before being rescued by Historic Scotland, who intended to house works of art from the national collection here.

PORTSOY. This beautifully preserved town is built around a picturesque small harbour. Many of the houses of the town were skilfully restored in the 1960s, among them the **Old Star Inn** of 1727 and the oldest, **Soy House**, built in the 1690s. Much of the town is now designated an outstanding conservation area. **Portsoy Marble**, taken from a vein that runs across the braes to the west of the town, has been greatly appreciated for its beauty, some finding its way into The Palace of Versailles. These days Portsoy Marble Workshop, housed in a renovated building overlooking harbour, continues the tradition of crafting the local marble.

FORDYCE. This secluded village nestling under Drum Hill, though small, has its own castle, which sits right in the centre of the village. Built in 1592 by Sir Thomas Menzies of Drum, this four storey L-plan tower house in pink sandstone is a diminutive model of a 16th century Scottish baronial architecture. Today Fordyce is a fine conservation village, its narrow streets flanked by lovingly restored cottages; it really is one of the undiscovered gems of the region.

SANDEND, as its name suggests, stands at the end of a broad sandy bay that is one of the most popular beaches in the area. The row of old fishermen's cottages on the shorefront are all lovingly looked after, and are unusually painted; the edges of the rough hewn stones painted black and the mortar lines painted white to give a regular block pattern appearance. Along the cliffs to the west of Sandend is **Findlater Castle**. This spectacular ruin is built into the rock-face, its empty windows look out over a sheer drop of 50 feet. The heavily fortified castle was built by the Oglivies in 1455. Unsuccessfully besieged by Mary, Queen of Scots in 1563, it was abandoned in the 16th century and today its crumbling remains cling on to a windlashed rock, overlooked by the taller cliffs.

Moray

DUFFTOWN. In 1817 James Duff, 4th Earl of Fife, founded Dufftown, or Balvenie as it was initially named, to create employment after the Napoleonic wars. Like other new villages of the period, Dufftown has spacious streets laid out in a regular plan. The four main streets converge on **The Clocktower**, which was completed in 1839. It was originally the town jail, then the burgh chambers and now it houses the Tourist Information Centre and a small museum. The clock comes from Banff and is the very one that was put forward an hour to ensure that James MacPherson was hanged, and is known locally as 'the clock that hanged MacPherson'. Dufftown is at the centre of the whisky distilling industry, being surrounded by seven distilleries, the most famous probably being **Glenfiddich**, which is on the whisky trail and open to the public.

Not far from the distillery is **Balvenie Castle**, this picturesque 13th century moated stronghold was originally owned by the Comyns. During a turbulent history it was visited by Edward I in 1304, by Mary, Queen of Scots in 1562, during her campaign against the Gordons. It gave refuge to Montrose in 1644 and was stormed by Royalists 1649, occupied by victorious Jacobites after the Battle of Killiecrankie in 1689 and, finally, held by Government troops in 1746.

Also within walking distance of the town square is **Mortlach Church**, founded in around AD 566 by St Moluag. Undoubtedly one of the oldest places of Christian worship in Scotland, it has been in use ever since. Parts of the present building date from 11th and 12th centuries, though it has been substantially reconstructed in 1876 and again in 1931. Legend has it that in 1016 it was lengthened by 3 spears length on the command of King Malcolm II, in thanksgiving for his victory over the Danes. Inside the church has some very fine stained glass and, in the graveyard, is a weathered Pictish cross, one side depicting two fish monsters, a relief cross and a grotesque beast, the other a serpent, bull's head and a horseman. In the vestibule of the church is an even earlier Pictish symbol stone, the 'Elephant Stone'. Later monuments around the graveyard include a fine heraldic gravestone dated 1417 and a recumbent effigy of Alexander Leslie of Kininvie in full armour dated 1549, as well as lots of distillers' tombs. There is also a watch-house, used to guard against bodysnatchers.

To the southeast, in Glen Fiddich, is **Auchindoun Castle**. A massive ruin that stands on an isolated hillside, and can be seen from miles around. The keep, encircled by Pictish earthworks, was built by Robert Cochran, a favourite of King James III. It went on to become a stronghold of the Ogilvies and later the Gordons and met its end in 1592, burned in a feud with the MacIntoshes. The only access to these rather dangerous ruins is a walk up a rough track from the A941.

Dufftown Clocktower

AROUND DUFFTOWN

CHARLESTOWN OF ABERLOUR. The old village general store has all the original fittings, records and stock dating back to the 1920s and is a window into the past. North of the village on the A941 is **Craigellachie Bridge**. One of Thomas Telford's most graceful designs, the 152 foot single span iron bridge carried the main road until 1973 and is probably the oldest iron bridge to survive in Scotland.

TOMINTOUL. **Tomintoul Museum** features displays on local history, wild life and the changing environment. There are also reconstructions of a farmhouse kitchen and a blacksmith's shop. A day out with a difference can be arranged at Tomintoul Tourist Information Centre where visitors can book to take a safari around a working Highland estate. These Ranger guided tours of the **Glenlivet Estate** by Land Rover cover its history, landscape, wildlife and work.

KEITH. Though much of the town owes its existence to the fashion for developing planned towns, Keith's history goes back to at least AD 700. It was here, in 1700, that the outlaw James MacPherson was captured and sent to be hanged back at Banff. Forty six years later the last successful action of the Jacobite army took place here, when a section of the Government forces were take by surprised and routed. The great development of Keith seen today began in 1750, when the Earl of Findlater laid out New Keith.

The town is on the famous **Speyside Malt Whisky Trail**, which takes those fond of a tot on a 70 mile journey around the beautiful countryside, visiting eight distilleries and a cooperage. Speyside is covered in distilleries, many open to the public. There are 56 in and around the Moray District, out of the 116 in Scotland. The four in Keith include **Strathisla**, which is on the trail, and is famous for its Chivas Regal blended scotch which is exported all over the world.

CULLEN. When the original village of Cullen got a little too close to the Laird of Seafield's planned house extensions his solution was to pull down the existing village and build a new one some distance from the big house. Work started in 1821 and everything was to be provided; Town Hall, library and hotel, all centred around a town square. The original village's Mercat Cross was transported to the square and mounted on an ornate octagonal base.

The most striking thing about Cullen is the series of towering railway bridges that snake between the town and Seatown, the existing fishing village on the shoreline. Built in 1886 by the Great North of Scotland Railway Company, they by-pass the grounds of Cullen House. The biggest is nearly 100 feet high and has eight arches, while the eastern one is a prominent feature of the centre of the new town. The line eventually closed in 1967 and much of it is now a footpath. Out in Cullen Bay are the Three Kings, a triumvirate of isolated sea-stacks.

Strathisla Distillery, Keith

PORTKNOCKIE. Unlike its near neighbours, Portknockie is not on the shoreline, there being no room between the foot of the cliffs and the sea, but along the clifftops overlooking the harbour, which is the only one in the area accessible regardless of the tide. A walk along the cliffs from the village gives fine views of the **Bow Fiddle Rock**, which look not unlike its namesake.

FINDOCHTY. The village's brightly painted cottages cluster around its pretty tidal harbour. The custom of decorating the houses arose from the need to use oil paints to keep the weather out, the vivid colours becoming now an established tradition, with each household vying with its neighbours to keep the paint fresh and neat.

BUCKIE. Once the largest town in the old county of Banff, Buckie is still one of the largest in Moray District. Still a fishing harbour, the market takes place daily between 8.30 and 10.00 am. Buckie's two boatyards still build and repair traditional wooden boats. **Buckie Maritime Museum**, in Cluny Place, has displays of fishing methods, cooperage, lifeboats, navigation and local history, and the **Peter Anson Gallery** houses watercolours showing the development of fishing in Scotland. Nearby is the **Seamen's Memorial**, a small chapel with beautiful stained glass windows, dedicated to local fishermen who have lost their lives at sea since 1946. Opened by the Queen in 1982 access can be gained by collecting the key from 6 New Street. Keep an eye out for the town's war memorial, which is held to be one of the finest in northeast Scotland.

SPEY BAY. **Tugnet Ice House** stands near the B9104 south of the village. Its permanent exhibition tells the story of the River Spey, its salmon fishing and wildlife. This historic ice house is possibly the largest in Scotland, dates from 1830 and was the centre of a complex salmon fishing station. During the netting season salmon would be packed in ice prior to their journey south, initially by sea and later by rail. At its height, in the late 1800s, 150 people were employed here and it would have been an important part of the local economy.

A little to the south off the same road is **Speymouth Railway Viaduct**. Built in 1886 and stretching over the Spey, this awe inspiring iron structure is almost 330 yards long. Now part of the Speyside Way, walkers on the bridge can the admire this cathedral of girders, as well as cross the river with ease.

BRIDGE OF TYNET. **St Ninian's Chapel** is the oldest post-Reformation Catholic Church still in use in Scotland. This unassuming place of worship was originally a sheep-cote and was given by the Laird to the local Catholic Community in 1755 for use as a clandestine church during the anti-Catholic period.

FOCHABERS. An old church has been converted to house a **Folk Museum** with its large collection of horse drawn carts on the top floor and, on the ground floor, a varied collection of items that tell the history of Fochabers over the past 200 years.

Nearby is the famous **Baxter's Foods Factory** and visitors centre. George Baxter set up his grocery store in the village 125 years ago and now the family's tinned soups are famous the world over.

LOSSIEMOUTH. On a calm sunny day walkers on the coast between here and Cullen can be almost sure of seeing a group of 20 or so bottle-nosed dolphins leaping and playing, sometimes quite close to the shore.

To the southeast of Lossiemouth is **Duffus Castle**. The massive ruins of a fine motte and bailey castle are surrounded by a moat, still complete and water-filled. The 14th century tower that crowns the Norman motte, has caused subsidence of the motte fracturing it in an impressive fashion.

Nearby RAF Kinloss is the base for the long range Nimrod reconnaissance aircraft that patrol the Northern Atlantic and often help guide the air-sea rescue helicopters from Lossiemouth to ships in distress.

ELGIN. The medieval street plan of this administrative and commercial centre is well preserved. The main street widens to the old cobbled market place, now known as the Plainstones, and is dominated by **St Giles Church** of 1825. Its position on an island site means both ends are equally prominent, one all Greek and columned, the other an eclectic round tower. A few buildings still retain the arched façades which were typical of early 18th century Elgin. One of the best examples is **Braco's Banking House** on the High Street. Built in 1694, the building takes its name from William Duff of Dipple and Braco, an ancestor of the Earl of Fife, who built Duff House in Banff.

Elgin's most famous old building is undoubtedly the **Cathedral** on North College Street. When it was complete it was perhaps the most beautiful of Scottish cathedrals, known as the Lantern of the North. It was founded in 1224, damaged by a fire in 1270, but in 1390 it was burned by the 'Wolf of Badenoch', Earl of Buchan, together with the towns of Elgin and Forres. Rebuilt it did not finally fall into ruin until after the Reformation. The lead was stripped from the roof in 1667, and on Easter Sunday 1711, the great central tower fell in. The ruins were used as a 'common quarry' until 1807, when steps were taken to preserve what is now see today.

Elgin is also well known for the fine fabrics from **Johnstons of Elgin Mill**. Here visitors can watch the process that, using only the purest Cashmere from Mongolia and China and the finest lambs' wool from Australia, sees fibres dyed, spun, woven and finished at Newmill. Established nearly 200 years they are now the only British mill to convert natural raw cashmere into finished garments. In addition to the mill tours there is a shop where these high quality garments can be bought.

Pluscarden Abbey, to the southwest of Elgin, was originally founded in 1230 and, in 1390, the church was burned, probably by the 'Wolf of Badenoch', who burned Elgin. It became a dependant priory of the Benedictine Abbey at Dunfermline in 1454 until the suppression of monastic life in Scotland in 1560. Thereafter it fell into ruin, until 1948, when a group of Benedictine monks from Prinknish Abbey, Gloucester, began its restoration. The surrounding countryside is certainly a suitably serene location for that most rare of modern ecclesiastical sights a working abbey, a status it regained in 1974. Visitors will find the Monastic services are open to the public.

Out from Elgin on the road to Lossiemouth is **Moray Motor Museum**, a unique collection of over 40 cars and motorcycles, housed in an old mill building, that should keep any transport buff engrossed for a few hours.

FORRES. The name of Forres has been made famous by Shakespeare, who set the opening scenes of *Macbeth* here. Entering the town from the east visitors are met by **Sueno's Stone**. This, the tallest and most complex piece of early medieval sculpture in Scotland, most probably commemorates an heroic battle campaign, possibly against the Norse settlers of Orkney. The elaborate carvings tell the story of a great victory, the stone being a sort of war report. Discovered buried in 1726, it is now housed in a glass structure to protect it from the ravages of the weather.

West of the town is **Brodie Castle and Gardens**, just off the A96. There have been Brodies at Brodie for 800 years, 25 lairds in all and this structure being the work of the 12th Laird, Alexander. The Castle was largely rebuilt after the earlier structure was burned in 1645. Based on a 16th century Z-plan house, with additions in 17th and 19th centuries, it remains, outside, stout, simple and uncluttered. Inside the story is a little different. The house contains fine French furniture, English, Continental and Chinese porcelain, and a major collection of paintings. The plasterwork of the Dining Room is exceptionally intricate, in each corner dusky brown maidens and vines spill from a blue background, appearing to represent the elements: earth, air, fire and water. Back outside a woodland walk has been laid out in the gardens by edge of 3 acre pond, which was intended to be the centre piece of a much grander scheme, until the money ran out.

ARCHIESTOWN. Named after its founder, Sir Archibald Grant of Monymusk, Archiestown preserves the feel of a small planned settlement of the 18th century. Close to the village is **Ladycroft Agricultural Museum**, a museum dedicated to the time when all the farm implements were worked by horses.

Elgin Cathedral

CHAPTER ELEVEN

THE HIGHLANDS

Tioram Castle

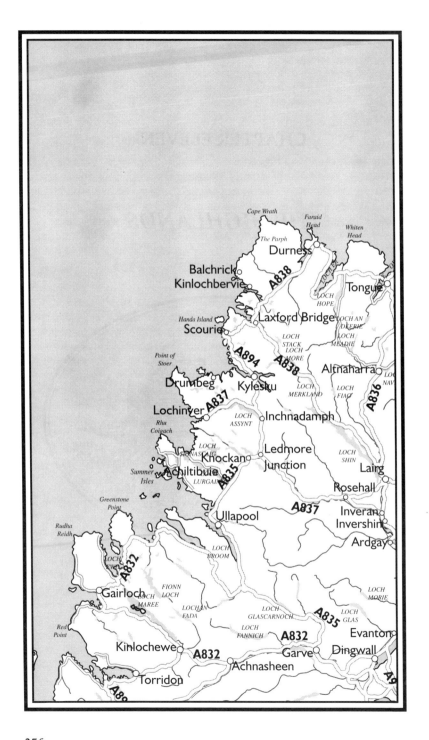

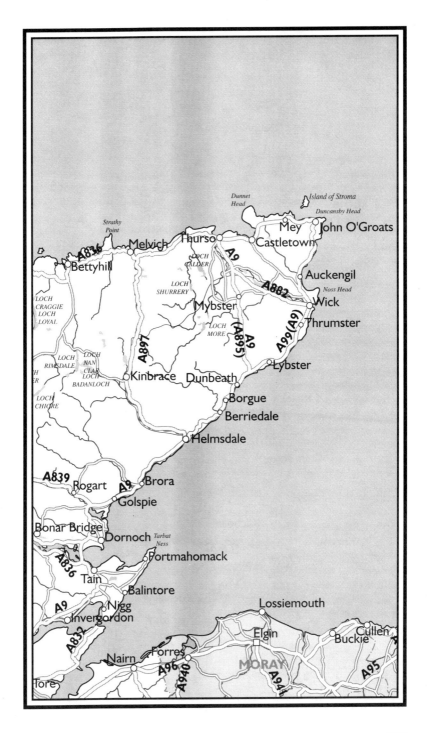

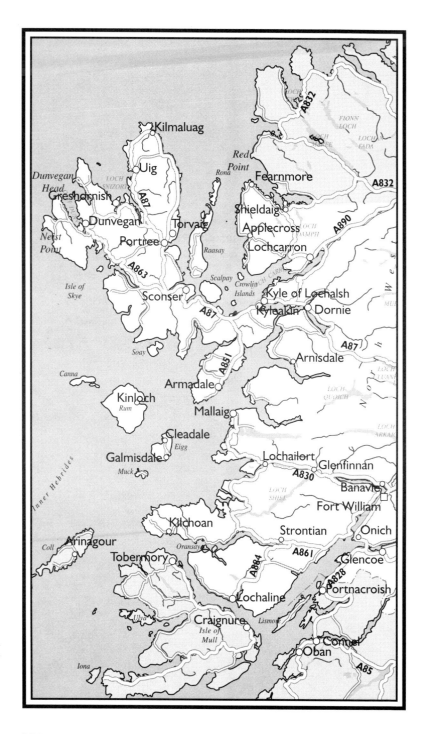

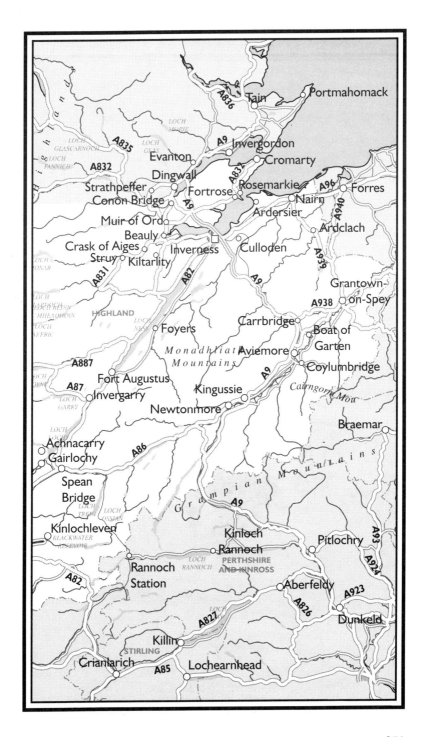

Monarch of the Glen

CHAPTER ELEVEN

THE HIGHLANDS

Eastern Highlands and the Moray Firth

INVERNESS. The 'capital of the Highlands', Inverness is the administrative, commercial and service centre of the vast Highland Region. Situated at the junction of the Beauly and Moray Firths, with the River Ness flowing through its centre, the town grew up as a trading port from the 6th century. Many of the town's most interesting features are clustered along its banks. Dominating the town today is **Inverness Castle**, a fine red sandstone building which still serves as courthouse and council offices and stands on the same site as the castle where Macbeth murdered Duncan in The Play.

The **Town House** is ornamented Victorian Gothic and is where Lloyd George called the first cabinet meeting outside London. In front of the House stands a restored cross on a base which encloses the Clach-na-Cuddain (Stone of the Tubs), a rough block on which women carrying water from the river rested their tubs. Many tales surround the origin of the stone, one that it was used as a coronation stone and another that the prosperity of Inverness depends upon its remaining where it is. Across the road is the impressive corinthian columned Royal Bank of Scotland building, **Aberdaff House**.

On Huntly Street is **Balnain House**, the home of Highland music. The Balnain Trust is dedicated to preserving every aspect of Highland music and the exhibitions present a huge selection covering everything from heroic warrior songs to Gaelic rock 'n' roll. There are a dozen listening stations and also the opportunity for visitors to try the instruments for themselves. The house itself has quite a history. Built for a merchant in 1726, it was used as a government field hospital following Culloden. In the 1880s it was the base for Royal Ordnance making the first survey map of the Highlands.

Getting away from the hustle of a busy town centre is easy in Inverness. Just a few minutes walk from the bustle are a series of footbridges that link up the wooded Ness Islands where anglers can be watched casting for salmon in the fast running water. Another beautiful place is more unexpected. A local boast is that Inverness has the best-placed burial ground in the world. **Tomnahurich Cemetery** occupies a wooded hilltop above the Caledonian Canal and a favourite local walk is to the viewpoint at the summit.

An exhibition in Falcon Square 'correlates the fossil evidence of the Plesiosauridae with advanced studies of the morphology of the biomass' or, more simply, presents the research into the Loch Ness monster.

There are roads down both sides of **Loch Ness** and so the opportunity for an excellent round trip. The vast loch, 24 miles long, as much as a mile wide and up to 900 feet deep, can also be seen from the water and there are plenty of cruises from which to choose. The greatest expanse of fresh water in Europe, its water are clouded by peat hiding anything that may lurk in its depths. One hidden 'monster' the loch has give up recently is a World War II Wellington bomber, the last of its type, that had crash landed on the surface in 1941. It is now being restored at Brookland in Surrey, where it was originally built. The **Loch Ness Monster Video Show** covers, amongst other items of interest, the search for the illusive monster.

In the bustling city centre of Inverness you will find a haven of peace and tranquillity, it is called **Chimes Tea Room** and has been run by Mary Donaldson for the past seven months. The building was built over 100 years ago as a dwelling, then 60 years later it became a bookmakers and last year it was fully converted into an attractive tea room. The walls are half woodpanelled with an original tiled fireplace adding character to this warm and friendly establishment. Open six days a week, from 10 am until 5 pm there is a wide selection of home-made soups, sandwiches and cakes, with speciality teas proving very popular with Mary's clients. The decor and furnishings are traditional with a definite farmhouse feel and both children and pets are always welcome.

Chimes Tea Room, 8 Stevens Brae, Inverness Tel: 01463 719181

Pleasantly situated on the banks of the River Ness, close to the centre of Inverness, **Riverside Gallery** is the perfect place to browse through the work of local artists. This old stone property was built in the early 1900s and is only 50 yards from the Greig Street Suspension Bridge so you should have very little trouble finding this beautiful establishment. Owned and run by Hugh Nicol for the passed ten years, Riverside Gallery has established itself locally as a specialist in Scottish landscapes and wildlife. Situated on two floors, the Gallery exhibits hundreds of paintings covering a wide range of subjects including Highland landscapes, sporting, natural history and wildlife in a variety of mediums. The Gallery is open from 9.30 am until 5.30 pm daily except Sundays, and in addition there is a full packing and shipping facility available on request as well as an on-the-premises framing service, with commission work being undertaken if required. With his deep love and extensive knowledge of the Highlands, Hugh can also advise those who are touring further of many varied and interesting places to visit.

Riverside Gallery, 11 Bank Street, Inverness
Tel: 01463 224781

Standing next to the oldest house in Inverness, Aberdaff House home to the National Trust, you will find the **Dickens Restaurant**. This charming eatery was established back in 1979, when it was first opened. George Kong and Marie Clair took over in 1985, making them a very formidable team. The decor is superb Rennie Mackintosh, with full air conditioning and a friendly atmosphere that makes you feel comfortable and at ease.

Dickens Restaurant

The menu is quite staggering in its variety, with dishes from

363

Scotland and France and especially China, it gives the diner a truly International choice. I shall give you a brief taster of some of the delicious cuisine that is available at this wonderful restaurant. For appetiser you could try Yau-Pao Oysters which are quick fried with ginger, garlic, spring onions and oyster sauce, or you could try a traditional French favourite Moule Marinière. There is then a vast choice of hors d'oeuvres, soups, seafood, grills, steaks, chicken, beef, pork, duck, curries and many more. The specialities are quite delicious and include such delicacies as Sizzled Cantonese Steak and the Dickens Sizzler Plate which comprises steak, chicken and prawns served with onions, baked potato, mushrooms, tomatoes and sauce... and if you still have room there is also an extensive sweet menu! George and Marie Clair also cater for small private parties of up to 30 people as well as business lunches, Sunday lunch and a wide selection of daily specials. So if you want to try something a bit different then Dickens International Restaurant is definitely the place to go.

Dickens Restaurant, 77-79 Church Street, Inverness Tel: 01463 713111

Take time to unwind and enjoy a **Jacobite Cruise** on the beautiful Caledonian Canal and on to majestic Loch Ness. These cruises have been running ever since 1974 and have been organized by Rod Michie since 1983. Enjoy the freedom of sailing through the open spaces of the Scottish Highlands, where waterways are still unspoiled and uncrowded, see spectacular views among some of the most memorable scenic beauty in Britain.

Jacobite Cruise

The round trip is to Urquhart Castle and back and takes, on average, three and a half hours, though you can travel up to the Castle by coach and return via the boat, or visa versa. Take part in the sport of Nessie Spotting, you may even get a sighting. There are light refreshments available on board or you can enjoy a drink at the fully licensed bar and if you mention that you saw this advertisement in the Hidden Places you can have a free cup of tea! Why not consider a private charter for your office party, wedding reception or business meeting, and of special interest to organisers of school trips, take you pupils on a cruise which is both enjoyable and educational, the basis for a project with a difference. Access to the vessel is not a problem for wheelchairs or disabled people, however toilets are down eight steps from the saloon deck level, so don't drink too much tea! The tours run from Easter until the last Saturday in October, seven days a week, though booking is advisable in the high season as Jacobite Cruises are very popular with all visitors to this beautiful area.

Jacobite Cruises, Tomnahurich Bridge, Glenurquhart Road,
Inverness Tel: 01463 233999

Nestling in the pretty village of Lentran, **Northern Lights** is a small and very personal establishment that creates varied and unusual hand-made candles. Owned and run by Tal Glikman, Northern Lights offers the visitor an in-depth insight into how candles are made and the incredible shapes and forms they can be created if the maker is experienced enough. This isn't a problem for Tal, he has been making candles for over 13 years and started his business on the Isle of Arran, but moved to his present workshop eight years ago.

Northern Lights

The building was once a crofter's cowshed and is made out of old railway sleepers, but it does enjoy some spectacular views of Moray Firth, Black Isle and the Ben Wry mountains. You can visit throughout the day and sit and watch as Tal creates fruit candles, perfumed candles, and candles and other realistic shapes and designs, all of which are for sale at very reasonable prices and a mail order service is available on request. Because of its very nature, the workshop is on ground level and offers good access for disabled visitors as well as children and pets, there is also a small car park available for up to six cars.

Northern Lights, Firthside, Lentran, Inverness
Tel: 01463 831332

CULLODEN. This bleak moor was the site for the last land battle on mainland Britain and saw the final demise of the Jacobites' attempts to regain the throne of Britain and the end of the Highland tribal system.

In April 1746 1500 clansmen lost their lives fighting at Bonnie Prince Charlie's last stand. The actions of the victors has gone down as one of the most shameful events in the long proud history of the British army. After the battle orders were given to kill every Highland survivor, starting with the wounded. The English army carried out its orders with ruthless efficiency. Men were shot, bayoneted and burnt alive, then the army went on the rampage through the Highland camp slaughtering the women and children. The killings spread across the Highlands as Clan chiefs loyal to the crown exterminated hereditary enemies. The King extracted his revenge on the Jacobites in thorough fashion; lands were forfeited, the kilt was banned and the bagpipes deemed an offensive weapon.

The story of the battle and the Prince's flight are told in an exciting audio-visual show at the visitors centre. Whilst outside visitors can wander the battlefield and see the many graves of the clans. This melancholy moor seems a desperately inglorious place for such high dreams to have died.

ARDERSIER. The **Gun Lodge Hotel** at Ardersier is an outstanding establishment which was a finalist in the 1996 Scottish Pub of the Year awards. Originally built to house the commander at Fort George on the headland a mile away to the north, this traditional hotel, pub and eating place is personally run by the Mason family. The menu offers some of the finest Scottish cuisine in the area, including haggis, venison, salmon steaks and shellfish, as well as vegetarian dishes and a special choice for children. A good range of draught beers and over 20 malt whiskies is served in the bar, and for those looking for overnight accommodation, there are ten comfortable guest rooms equipped with washbasins and colour TVs; three also have en-suite facilities. Karen, the youngest member of the family, takes great delight in welcoming young visitors and showing them her pet pigs and goats.

Gun Lodge Hotel, High Street, Ardersier Tel: 01667 462734

FORT GEORGE. Built out into the Moray Firth on a promontory, the Fort was built in 1748 as a result of the '45 Rebellion. It is an imposing sight, with massive ramparts and solid walls. Inside there is **Regimental Museum of the Queen's Own Highlanders**, who are still barracked here, as well as displays on the Seaforth Highlanders, Queen's Own Cameron Highlanders and the Lovat Scouts. The surrounding area is used for manoeuvres, so don't be at all surprised if a clump of bushes stands up and walks off!

NAIRN. An attractive county town and holiday resort, Nairn has long been regarded as marking the boundary between the Lowlands and the Highlands. In Laing Hall, on King Street, is the **Nairn Fishertown Museum**; it houses a collection of photographs and articles connected with the Moray Firth and herring fishing industry during the days of steam drifters. The remains of an industry of a very different nature stands just up the coast at Whiteness Head. The giant skeleton of the oil platform construction yard stands idle as testament to the boom years of the North Sea oil exploration.

A fascinating and surprising visitor attraction can be found beside the A96 Forres Road on the eastern edge of Nairn. Opened in 1994, the **Invernairn Mill Visitor Centre** incorporates a museum of rural history, craft centre, restaurant and shops, and provides an interesting and enjoyable day out for all the family. Owned and personally run by Chic and Ellen Henderson, Invernairn Mill is housed in a building which was originally constructed for the motor trade in the 1980s. Its conversion involved over eighteen months of dedicated labour by all the members of the family, assisted by two welders and a painter/panel beater. The result creates the impression of a covered village, complete with street market, shops, mill house and water wheel. The giant wheel was kindly donated by the Walkers of Gallantry Farm and had to be completely restored, having lain unused for over half a century.

Invernairn Mill Visitor Centre

The centrepiece of the visitor centre is a fascinating museum containing a series of displays and room settings which create an authentic impression of life in this beautiful part of Scotland in the early part of the 20th century. Exhibits include a Harris tweed loom, early equipment for commercial jam-making and the interior of an Edwardian farmhouse complete with furniture, ornaments and ephemera of the time. There is also a small motor museum containing the car in which Chic competed in the Monte Carlo rally, an unusual collection of antique farm implements and a forge with a working blacksmith who gives regular demonstrations of wrought iron-making. A series of life-size model birds and animals is scattered throughout the premises, some hidden, and some, like the replica Clydesdale horses, not so hidden; these can be searched for and recorded by children on a special sheet. The centre also incorporates a series of attractive small shops, including a craft shop, woollen shop, delicatessen and traditional sweet shop, as well as the delightful Oasis Restaurant which offers everything from a home-baked scone to a delicious four course meal which can be eaten whilst enjoying the view of the Lethen Hills. Invernairn Mill not only provides a highly enjoyable and educational experience, but it is also the ideal place to find that special gift, delicacy or item for the home. Open daily (except Mondays in winter), 10 am to 6 pm, all year round.

Invernairn Mill, Forres Road, Nairn Tel: 01667 455273

Sunny Brae is a charming private hotel which stands in a magnificent position on Nairn seafront. Set within its own extensive garden, this purpose built establishment enjoys breathtaking views over the Moray Firth and the Black Isle. Resident proprietors Sylvia and Ian Bochel are friendly hosts who provide a warm welcome, first rate hospitality and excellent food prepared from fresh local produce. Each of their ten guest bedrooms is well appointed and fitted with en-suite facilities; six are situated on the ground floor. The guest lounge, with its floor to ceiling picture windows, enjoys a panoramic vista of the garden with the Links and sea views beyond. On a good day there may be the opportunity to watch the dolphins swimming.

The sporting facilities in the immediate area include public tennis courts (situated within two minutes' walk of the house), swimming, bowling, watersports, and two championship golf courses, one of which will host the 1999 Walker Cup; bicycle hire and baby-sitting for guests can also be arranged. There is also a well equipped self-catering chalet available within the grounds which sleeps up to five.

Sunny Brae Hotel, Marine Road, Nairn
Tel: 01667 452309 Fax: 01667 454860
e-mail: sunnybrae@easynet.co.uk

CAWDOR. The old central tower of **Cawdor Castle** dates back to 1372 and is surrounded by 16th century additions. Shakespeare's Macbeth was Thane of Cawdor and the Castle is one of several traditional settings for the murder of Duncan at the hands of the real Macbeth; Shakespeare's 'Scottish Play', being loosely based on real events.

ARDCLACH. Here stands a lone bell-tower; the parish church was set so low down on the river bank that the peel of its bell would never carry; so the tower was built, in 1655, calling the locals to worship or warning of attack. Near the junction of the A939 with the A940 an unclassified road heads west to Lochindorb. On a small island stands the ruined **Lochindorb Castle**, once seat of the Comyns. In 1371 it became the stronghold of the Earl of Buchan, the vicious 'Wolf of Badenoch', who terrorised the area. James II ordered its destruction in 1458 to prevent any further misuse.

GRANTOWN-ON-SPEY. One of Queen Victoria's favourite villages, Grantown-on-Spey was originally laid out in the 18th century around a central square. This traditional Highland resort grew in stature when Victorian doctors recommended it for its healthy air. A little way out of the village, on the A95, at Dulnain Bridge is the **Speyside Heather Garden Centre**. Here the Heather Heritage Centre houses an exhibition on the historical uses for heather. It was made into weaving ropes, doormats, baskets and used in thatching as well as in medicine, drinks and dyeing wool. Outside the landscaped show garden has approximately 300 varieties on show. There is also the opportunity to buy heather or gifts from the heather craft shop.

CARRBRIDGE. The stone bridge that gave the village its name in 1717 still survives, an elegant single high-arched span. The imaginative **Landmark Visitors Centre** here includes a sophisticated audiovisual history of the Highlands. Outdoors there is a boardwalk maze and even, securely raised on timber stilts, a tree-top-level trail and a 65 foot tall observation tower.

BOAT OF GARTEN was originally named after the ferry here across the Spey. Today it is the northern terminus of the **Strathspey Steam Railway** and the magic of steam on the old Perth to Inverness line between here and Aviemore Speyside can be discovered. The line was originally closed in 1965, but in 1978 trains started running once more thanks to the help of a mainly volunteer team of enthusiasts who also have plans to expand the route through to Grantown-on-Spey. In the restored station buildings at Boat of Garten there is a small display of railway relics and rolling stock. From outside the station a vintage coach trip can be taken up to the RSPB's **Loch Garten Reserve**. Ospreys nest here every year and visitors can watch the from the well equipped visitor centre.

AVIEMORE. At the southern end of the Strathspey railway and the main year round holiday resort in the Spey Valley, Aviemore is dominated from the west by the birchwood cliffs of the Craigellachie and the huge bulk of the Cairngorms fills the southeastern skyline. Much of the village was built during the 1960s to provide facilities for the growing number skiers. On the way out of the village to the mountains the road passes the steam railway station and its engine shed full of burnished locomotives. The shed itself is original but the station buildings came from Dalnaspidal, and the turntable from Kyle of Lochalsh.

COYLUMBRIDGE. At Loch Morlich and the **Cairngorm Reindeer Centre**, visitors may accompany the guide to see Scotland's only reindeer herd free-ranging in their natural surroundings. Beyond the Loch, the road bends south and becomes the 'ski road', climbing steadily above the forest to the high level car parks which in winter and early spring service the Cairngorm ski-lifts. The whole year round a chair-lift operates to the Ptarmigan Restaurant, which at 3600 feet, is the highest building in Britain.

KINGUSSIE. Based at an 18th century shooting lodge much of the **Highland Folk Museum** is open air and features a 'black house' from Lewis and a wide variety of farming equipment. Indoors the farming museum has fine displays of all manner of articles, as well as a exhibition on Highland tinkers. The **Highland Wildlife Park**, owned and run by the Royal Zoological Society of Scotland, has breeding groups of Scottish mammals past and present in a beautiful natural setting. The drive through the reserve has red deer, bison and Highland cattle roaming free, whilst the walk around area has capercaillie, eagles, wolves and wildcats. In the visitors centre there is an exhibition on 'Man and Fauna in the Highlands'.

South of the village on the B970 are the substantial ruins of **Ruthven Barracks**. Standing on a site originally occupied by a fortress of the 'Wolf of Badenoch', the barracks were first built in 1716 to keep the Highlanders in check following the 1715 Rising and were added to by General Wade in 1734. After the debacle of Culloden some Jacobite forces rallied here hoping Bonnie Prince Charlie might once again take the field. When they realized the cause was hopeless they destroyed the barracks.

NEWTONMORE. The unique **Waltzing Water Show** is an unusual and stunning combination of water, lights and music which provides great all weather entertainment for all the family.

FOYERS. Here, in 1891, Britain's first aluminium smelter opened but the main attraction of the location remains the **Falls of Foyers** and the hydro-electric power they once supplied. The smelter closed in 1967 and the falls have never really recovered.

DRUMNADROCHIT. The **Loch Ness Monster Centre** here displays photographs, drawings, sonar scans, and some rather speculative claims about one of the world's greatest mystery phenomenons. Expeditions from all over the world have searched high and low for the vital piece of evidence that something lurks in the Loch and their endeavours are also recorded here.

To the east of Drumnadrochit and on the lochside stands **Urquhart Castle**. These dramatic ruins were once one of the largest castles in Scotland. Its strategic position led to it changing hands several times until, finally, it was blown up in 1692 to prevent its being occupied by Jacobites. Not far beyond is a memorial to John Cobb, the land speed record holder who was killed on the water near here in 1952, attempting to set a new water speed record in his jet-engined craft Crusader. The A82 is a very pleasant road on this part of the lochside, with the Forestry Commission spruce plantations on the hillsides and the ancient birch, rowan and alder fringing the loch.

STRUY. Owned and personally run by Bill Sanderman for the past three years, **Struy Inn** is situated in the picturesque village of Struy, only a few miles from Beauly. This freehouse was originally built in 1865 as a coaching inn for the weary traveller's who journeyed to and from Inverness-shire.

Struy Inn

The bar is filled with ambiance and Bill has the knack of making every guest feel right at home, this coupled with the great atmosphere from the locals, you will soon feel very welcome. All the food served in the wooden beamed restaurant is home-made using only the freshest local ingredients and even Bill has been known to pick up the apron and give it a go! The menu is changed daily and includes such delicacies as Angus steaks, venison and salmon, with seven starters, ten main courses and seven different sweets at any one time and all at very affordable prices. There is a large beer garden at the rear of the premises which proves very popular with children and dogs alike, here you will find a terrific play area for the kids and plenty of tables and chairs for you to sit and enjoy a meal or drink. All told the Struy Inn is the perfect place to stop for a while and catch your breath, enjoy the typical Scottish hospitality and the warming atmosphere.

Struy Inn, Struy, By Beauly Tel: 01463 761219

Glen Strathfarrar, the most northerly of three glens which drain eastwards into Strathglass and the Beauly River, is one of the finest glens in the Highlands of Scotland. Situated in the lower half of this glen on Culligran Estate are the **Culligran Cottages**, comprising a traditional cottage and four Norwegian chalets within a naturally wooded area stand. The cottage has a separate entrance hall, a light and airy sitting room, large and well equipped kitchen, three double bedrooms and a bathroom. The chalets have a roomy open plan living room with a combined dining and kitchen area, two or three double bedrooms and a bathroom. The cottage can sleep up to seven persons and the chalets from five to seven if the sofa bed in the living room is used. Both the cottage and chalets have been furnished very comfortably and decorated to a high standard with double glazing and electric heaters. There are fitted carpets or linoleum throughout each property and an electric cooker and fridge in all kitchens.

Your hosts are Frank and Juliet Spencer-Nairn, who will do their utmost to ensure that your stay at Culligran is both enjoyable and relaxing. It is with this in mind that they regularly offer guided tours by Land Rover of Culligran Deer Farm, here you can watch and even feed the red deer at close quarters from May until October. Also available is a good selection of salmon and trout fishing, fly only, with a daily permit that allows you to fish on the Rivers Farrar and Glass, tributaries of the famous Beauly. If you prefer something a bit more energetic then may we recommend that you hire one of the Culligran bicycles and explore the 15 miles of private road in the glen and enjoy the breathtaking scenery protected under a National Nature Reserve agreement.

Culligran Cottages, Glen Strathfarrar, Struy, Beauly
Tel & Fax: 01463 761285
(Open Mid March - Mid November)

KILTARLITY. Located 12 miles west of Inverness on the A833, Beauly to Drumnadrochit road, **Highland Liliums** is a nursery and garden centre that stocks a wide range of plants with the emphasis on hardy perennials. Highland Liliums began in 1974 when Calum and

Nancy MacRitchie moved north from Windsor to start a nursery in the Highlands growing Lilium bulbs. Now over 20 years on, the Liliums are still grown, but the overall production side of the nursery has changed markedly. It is still very much a family business with son Neil and daughter-in-law Frances having joined Calum and Nancy in the running of the business. The production area now spans an area of 10 acres and includes a range of over 30 different Liliums, with the original five varieties being totally unique to this nursery and can be found no where else in the world. The wholesale part of the operation services retail outlets throughout Scotland and the north of England on a regular basis. For local customers there is a plant centre on site at Kiltarlity, stocking a wide selection of all types of plant material with a small shop catering for every gardener's need in terms of garden sundries. Open six days a week from 9 am until 5 pm, Highland Liliums welcomes you one and all to browse awhile round these wonderfully stocked gardens and choose at your leisure.

Highland Liliums, Kiltarlity, Beauly
Tel & Fax: 01463 741365

CRASK OF AIGAS. Set in the picturesque gorge of the River Beauly, the dam at Aigas is opened daily to allow fish to continue their journey upstream. Visitors are admitted to a viewing chamber at the dam.

Aigas Golf Course is situated at the foot of Strathglass, an area renowned for its outstanding natural beauty and great wealth of wildlife. Designed as a family course by Bill Mitchell of Grantown-on-Spey, it features large, quality greens subtly blending into the landscape. Every care has been taken to make full use of the undulating parkland that lies snugly between the fine Aigas Forest and the peaceful River Beauly immediately before it plunges through the gorge at An Druim. The sweeping first fairway introduces the visitor to the gentle delights of this scenic course. Playing over the dyke onto the secluded second green requires accuracy to keep out of trouble. The sixth tee overlooking the river refreshes the mind and spirit before facing the challenge of this swinging fairway to the dramatic gorge green. The long hitter may be tempted to take a short cut over the bend of the river, but a sliced shot here will end with a splash! The Aigas Forest offers pleasant walks with plenty of opportunity for the nature lover to enjoy the abundant wildlife.

Self-catering accommodation is available at Mains of Aigas, an old home farm in the most beautiful setting beside the River Beauly on the A831, 5 miles from Beauly village. The farm and surrounding area have much to offer to the country and nature lover as it is extremely rich in wildlife. All accommodation is supplied with water immersion heaters, electric cooker, colour TV, refrigerator and electric meter. The kitchen is fully equipped with all the utensils and crockery that you will need and the bed linen is provided free of charge, though guests are requested to bring their own towels.

Aigas Golf Course, Aigas, Beauly
Tel & Fax: 01463 782942

BEAULY. The town's name is derived from the French 'beau lieu' which in turn refers to the now ruined priory, once the 'Monasterium de bello loco'. Founded in around 1230 by Sir John Bisset of the Aird for French Valliscaulian monks, the most striking features seen today are the three 13th century triangular windows in the south wall, the window-arcading in the chancel and the 13th century west door to the south transept.

Set in the attractive Highland town of Beauly, just 12 miles north of Inverness, **Chrialdon House Hotel** is a superb Victorian villa offering a friendly and informal atmosphere in elegant surroundings. Originally built in 1908, Chrialdon became a hotel in the mid 60s and over the years has been updated and modernised to the high standard that you see today. Owned and personally run by Nicoll and Val Reid, there are nine guest rooms, mostly with en-suite facilities, and all with colour television and tea and coffee makers. All of the rooms are attractively and comfortably furnished, including easy chairs or sofas and have those little extra touches which anticipate guests' requirements. The dining room offers either a robust full Scottish breakfast suitable for a day on the

374

hills or a Continental style meal with fresh fruit, yoghurt and muesli. Dinner is prepared by the family using only the best local produce and can include soups, patés, trout, fresh wild salmon, venison and, of course, fine Angus beef and lamb. A choice of menu is always available and a selection from the extensive wine list will complement the evening meal. Chrialdon has a residential license and guests are invited to enjoy a wee dram, or several, from the selection of fine malt whiskies and spirits that Nicoll and Val keep in stock. Beauly is a centre for all the Highlands, so whether touring, cycling, rambling, fishing or golfing, Chrialdon House Hotel has all of the facilities you may require.

Chrialdon House Hotel, Beauly
Tel: 01463 782336

Situated in the picturesque High Street of Beauly near Inverness, **Lynda Usher Knitwear** is a small shop that sells probably the widest range of quality knitwear outside Edinburgh. Lynda has been designer and hand-knitter for over 15 years and two years ago opened this shop by demand of her many customers.

Lynda Usher Knitwear

Offering a wide variety of textiles, hats, gloves and scarves, she is also the only retail shop to stock an inspiring rang of natural yarns and pure Shetland Wool for hand-knitting within a hundred miles. The knitwear displayed in the shop is by many different designers from both Scotland and England, with a lot of the clothes being individual, one-off designs. Open six days a week, many of the items in Lynda's shop have been produced locally and, with a mailing service that will deliver to anywhere in the world, you are guaranteed not to run out of woolly sweaters this winter!

Lynda Usher Knitwear, 50 High Street, Beauly
Tel: 01463 783017

Located only a few miles from the centre of Beauly, **Cluanie Park** has a superb Highland setting where you can marvel at the unique relationship between Birds of Prey and man. Cluanie Park was set up over three years ago by Andy Williams and has increased in popularity as each year has passed. Falconry is the art of hunting wild quarry with a trained hawk or falcon and has it origins in remote antiquity. It has had many romantic and mythological associations but it is still widely practised today. At Cluanie you can see these magnificent birds at close quarters and there are regular talks and flying demonstrations throughout the day.

Cluanie Park

You can explore the Nature Trail that winds its way through the surrounding countryside, here you should see the red deer stags and hinds and other types of deer including the roe and fallow. You will be able to learn more about these and other animals, and the environment in which they live, by watching the video show and display that is available for all. Children will love Cuddle Corner where they can come in and make friends with some of the smaller animals, and while they enjoy the playground, you could visit the attractive tearoom and gift shop that offers lots of crafts, gifts and books.

Cluanie Park, Beauly
Tel: 01463 782415

HIGHLAND LIFE

The Highlands have not always been as deserted as they are today. The evidence of long-ruined villages and the once-cultivated land around them can still be seen though much has reverted to a wild state. The causes for the depopulation in the 18th and 19th centuries are numerous; too many people for the land, a potato famine and emigration to the New World but there are also the deliberate policy of **Clearance**.

At the time many of the landowners and their agents began looking for ways of obtaining more income from their vast estates than they were raising from the subsistence-level smallholders. Renting the land for sheep-farming and, later, the development of deer-stalking and other gaming pursuits led to many evictions. The most brutal of the evictions took place in Sutherland and Knoydart where men, women and children along with the sick and the elderly were thrown out of their homes and had no option but to emigrate or move to the cities. By the time the first Crofters Act was passed, in 1886, many of the glens and straths were already deserted and the legal protection was too late for many crofters.

Although much of the land in Scotland is still taken up with large estates, over two million acres are occupied by **Crofts** (or smallholdings). Generally of several parts, there is arable land near the croft house with grazing on the hills for sheep and cattle and, in some area, a share in a peat moss. Common grazing around the village is arranged by an elected grazing committee and, during busy times, neighbour helps neighbour with the work. It is not uncommon for a crofter to have a full or part time job elsewhere in the community and a hospitable croft provides ideal holiday accommodation off the beaten track.

The Highland clansmen of old were part of individual great families that lived in the same area and were loyal to the same clan chief. The word **Clan** is Gaelic for children and the chief would be responsible for the welfare of his clan. This quasi-feudal system survived for many years, with bouts of interclan feuding, until the intervention of the British monarchs following the Act of Union. It was the Battle of Culloden in 1746, however that finally put pay to the ancient system. The Clans united and backed Bonnie Prince

Charlie and the 1745 Jacobite Rebellion which was defeated at Culloden by George II who then went on to destroy the power of the chiefs once and for all. There are now large clan associations which maintain the romance and tradition of the kinship but descendants of the clan chiefs have little or no powers today.

The word **Tartan** actually comes from the French word tartaine, a particular kind of cloth which has nothing to do with colour at all. It is generally excepted that the origins of tartans lie back in the 7th century when invading Irish introduced striped linen shirts to Scotland. The striped shirts, over the years, became criss-crossed with coloured threads and by the end of the 16th century had developed into tartan are it is recognised today. Originally used to identify an area, each tartan became associated with the clan in that area and also with the clan name. Today, there are hundreds of tartans and many are still attached to a particular clan. Though legally anyone may wear any tartan, with so many to choose from and with a little research it is possible that everyone can find a tartan with which he or she has a tenuous kinship claim.

The Gatherings, or **Highland Games**, were originally local fairs organised by the clan chiefs. Sometimes with a military undertone, such as the Gathering following Bannockburn, which claims to have been held annually since then, the Games became an important feature of the Scottish social calendar with Queen Victoria's patronage of Braemar. They remain so today, where the main features include competitions in Highland dancing, caber tossing, putting the stone, hammer throwing and all manner of piping events.

The **Bagpipes**, considered by many to be the unofficial symbol of Scotland, can in fact be traced back to ancient Persia, Greece and Egypt. Introduced into Britain by the Romans, the pipes became popular in Scotland (and Ireland) and, by the 16th century, there were something of a status symbol with clan chiefs having their own hereditary pipers. Used extensively by the military they became an essential ingredient in the armoury of the Highlanders, so much so that the pipes were banned at Culloden. The piobaireachd (pronounced peebroch) is the ancient classical music of the pipes passed down from generation to generation and, as well as slow-time strathspeys, there are jigs, reels and, of course, marches.

MUIR OF ORD. The Glen Ord Distillery was established here in 1838 and visitors can take a tour around the works.

Muir of Ord has its very own British Rail station only a couple of stops from Inverness and it is here that you will find **Ord House**. Originally built in 1637, this country house was designed and constructed as the Laird's house and has been cleverly converted into a hotel without losing any of its elegance. It is run by the owners John and Eliza Allen whose main objective is to ensure you are enjoying your holiday in a relaxed atmosphere. There are 11 bedrooms all with their own bathrooms. One guest room has a four poster bed, two are ground floor rooms and all are individually decorated and furnished to a high standard. The grounds consist of 40 acres of walled, formal and vegetable gardens, park and woodland, and guests are encouraged to walk and enjoy the peace and tranquillity. The vegetable garden provides the hotel with some of its fruit and vegetables and the herbs grown around the house are all used in the cooking. Food is a speciality of Ord, fresh local produce is put to good effect to produce delicious and mouth-watering dishes. Game, fish and local beef and lamb are all featured on the menu and à la carte, so there will always be something for everyone to enjoy.

Ord House

The sportsman is ideally suited to Ord House. The Conon and Beauly rivers for salmon fishing are only a couple of miles away. There are 12 golf courses all within 30 minutes drive including the championship courses of Nairn and Royal Dornoch. Muir of Ord has it own 18 hole golf course which can be enjoyed at a special rate. Stalking for deer and grouse can be arranged and pony trekking, trout fishing and hill walking are all available locally.

Ord House, Muir of Ord Tel: 01463 870492

Built over 100 years ago as a coaching inn, **The Ord Arms Hotel** was originally built on what was once the old A9, but is now more commonly known as the A862. The accommodation comprises ten individually styled guest rooms, eight of which are en-suite, and all come with a colour television, direct dial telephone and tea and coffee making facilities. The Ord Arms has two bars, a public bar and the lounge bar, both of which are comfortably decorated and extend a warm and friendly welcome to all visitors.

The Restaurant is also open to non-residents and has a non-smoking policy. The food is of an excellent quality and produced using only the freshest local produce available, with the delicious selection of steaks and sauces being the Hotel's speciality, but be prepared to book, as the food at The Ord Arms is much sought after. If eating al fresco appeals to you in the summer months, then the large beer garden at the side of the property is perfect for enjoying a glass of wine or a meal. Both children and pets are always welcome at the Hotel, and even though there are no facilities for the disabled, the patio area at the front of the establishment has plenty of room to enjoy a drink in the sun.

The Ord Arms Hotel, Great North Road, Muir of Ord
Tel: 01463 870286

FORTROSE. Where there was once the ferry across Beauly Firth now stands the magnificent Kessock Bridge carrying the A9 north on to the **Black Isle** - which is neither black nor an island. This ancient burgh and resort has many fine examples of attractively colour-washed vernacular houses and, in particular, the magnificent remains of a 14th-15th century Cathedral. It was from this Cathedral that Cromwell used stone to construct his fort in Inverness.

From the centre of the town a road runs out, across the golf links, to **Chanoney Point** and its lighthouse; the point opposite Fort George where the Moray Firth narrows. It was here, traditionally, the Coinneach Odhar, the Seer of Brahan, met his painful death. When asked by the Countess of Seaforth to tell her what her absent husband was doing, the Seer rashly told the truth; that he was in the arms of a beautiful French woman. Furious, the Countess ordered Coinneach to be burnt to death in a barrel of tar. A stone records this gruesome incident.

ROSEMARKIE. The village claims to have been the forerunner of Fortrose as a bishopric and is said to have been evangelised by St

Boniface. The **Groam House Museum** has a fine collection of Pictish artefacts including 'The Soul of Rosemarkie', a decorated cross slab dating from the 8th century.

The **Plough Inn** is a fine old pub and eating place which stands at the northern end of the village of Rosemarkie. It is thought to be the oldest inn on the Black Isle, and a marriage stone dated 1691 set above the fireplace in the public bar confirms the building to be over three centuries old. A handsome detached structure built of warm red stone, it was refurbished in 1907 when the upper storey and turreted windows were added. Proprietors Kate and John Lamond are delighted to discuss the history of the building with visitors, and will attempt answer any questions put to them. Since taking over in 1989, they have built up a thriving business which is a popular meeting place for visitors and locals alike. The atmosphere inside is warm and welcoming, with comfortable traditional furnishings and an open fire in winter. The bar has wood-panelled walls, a panelled ceiling and a handsome solid wood bar built to a standard rarely seen today. Excellent food is served throughout the day between 12 noon and 9 pm, seven days a week. Dishes on offer include steaks, gammon, chicken and scampi, along with a fine selection of vegetarian dishes, such as spring vegetables in cheese sauce, or mushroom and nut fettucini. One of the specialities of the house is fresh salmon caught in the nearby river by local fishermen. A wide variety of snacks is also available, including ploughman's lunches, pizzas and a range of meals suitable for younger diners. In fine weather, customers can sit outside in the attractive garden, which is also ideal for children.

Plough Inn

The Plough Inn lies within easy reach of Rosemarkie's safe sandy beach, with its rock pools, prehistoric fossils and magnificent views across the Moray Firth. At low tide, it is possible to reach a series of caves, including **Caird's Cave** which was once inhabited by Neolithic man, although care should be taken as the way back may be cut off at high tide. Another local attraction is the **Fairý Glen**, once the haunt of witches and water sprites, whose deep pools and sparkling cascades lie beneath great cliffs of rare red boulder clay. A good place to visit in bad weather is nearby Groam House, an award winning local museum where visitors can learn about the mysterious Pictish people and hear the prophecies of the famous Brahan Seer who was burnt at the stake near Chanonry Point in the 17th century.

Plough Inn, Mill Road, Rosemarkie Tel: 01381 620164

CROMARTY. Situated on the northern tip of the Black Isle, this small town is a real gem and an almost perfect example of an 18th century Scottish seaport. The failure of the fishing in Moray Firth and the coming of the railway saw the port go into decline. The decay and neglect that threatened it for so long has now been reversed and restoration of the rope works, brewery, fisher-cottages, civic buildings and merchants' houses is well under way. Another piece of history is the car ferry that still crosses the Firth to Nigg during the summer, the last ferry in the area. Hugh Miller, the famous geologist, stonemason and writer was born here (in 1711) and his cottage which is open to visitors is run by the National Trust for Scotland.

Cromarty Courthouse

The acclaimed **Cromarty Courthouse** is a fascinating museum which has won over a dozen awards and commendations since it opened in 1990. Among its many distinguished patrons has been Prince Charles, who visited in 1994. The Museum's curator is David Alston, a local historian who has become an expert on the history of this ancient port and market town. Founded in early 13th century, Cromarty's renaissance came in the 1770s when the owner of the Cromarty estate, George Ross, invested a fortune in rebuilding the town in the elegant vernacular style that can be seen today. The Museum uses the latest technology to explore over eight centuries of history. Visitors can experience a lively reconstruction of an 18th century court trial complete with moving figures, and there is also a video room, a cellblock complete with prison cells, and a talking model of Sir Thomas Urquhart, the first person to translate the work of Rabelais into English. The admission price includes an interesting 45 minute taped walk around the streets of old Cromarty, 'led' by Hugh Miller, an early 19th century collector of Scottish folklore. Visitors to Cromarty Courthouse can try on 18th century costume and visit the Museum shop, with its display of work by local craftspeople.

Cromarty Courthouse, Church Street, Cromarty Tel: 01381 600418

CONON BRIDGE. Situated, as its name suggests, on the River Conon, there are several stories of animals with supernatural powers that lived around the village. There are tales of a fearsome water horse that lived in the River and also of otters. Anyone catching a King Otter, easily distinguished by their lighter colour and their large size, would be granted a wish it they set the otter free. If, on the other hand, the catcher killed the otter and wore its pelt, he would be rendered immune from bullets and swords.

The popular village of Conon Bridge, which lies only seven miles from Inverness and some two miles from Dingwall, is the home of **The Conon Hotel**, a long time favourite haunt for fisherman from all parts of the UK. Originally built in 1720, it served as a coaching house for the people who departed from the River Ferry and was state owned up until 1973, but is know owned and run by the Jack family. This newly refurbished hotel has thirteen guest rooms, each having been individually decorated and furnished to a high standard, with full en-suite facilities and a complimentary tea and coffee tray.

The Conon Hotel

The Regency style restaurant is very spacious and offers a wide range of meals, whether you prefer to lunch or dine from the table d'hôte or à la carte menu or take a less formal snack or meal in the bar. The range of dishes on the menus are very comprehensive, with a few surprise dishes for those who are a bit more adventurous in their eating habits. There is Pork Holstein, an escalope of pork, breadcrumbed, pan-fried and topped with a fried egg and anchovies, or you could try Cabbie Claw, a traditional northeastern dish of cod cooked in a white wine sauce enriched with horseradish and chopped boiled egg. Whilst in the Hotel guests can enjoy a quiet drink in the cosy cocktail bar, relax in the residents' TV lounge or visit the public bar and enjoy a game of pool or darts. The Royal Dornoch Golf Club is only 45 minutes away by car and a reduced daily and weekly green fees can be arranged through the Hotel provided at least seven days notice is given. Whether you wish a quiet, relaxing holiday or prefer something a bit more energetic, then the Conon Hotel is the ideal centre.

The Conon Hotel, Conon Bridge Tel: 01349 61500

STRATHPEFFER. This Victorian spa town is full of genteel villas and grand houses and is a marked contrast to the wild hills and moors nearby. The waters can still be taken at the restored pump room in the village square. Sulphurous and pungent with a lingering aftertaste, the waters were held to be a fine restorative.

Legend has it that the hot, sulphurous springs smelling of brimstone and the iron springs that abound in this once volcanic area are actually caused by the Devil, taking a bath. Wherever the waters from the two types of springs meet, the water turns black and this is accounted for by the Devil washing his filthy black clothes.

Outside the village is the **Eagle Stone**, a Pictish stone that has eagle and horseshoe shapes etched on it. Across the road from the stone is the long closed Strathpeffer Station. Though the trains are gone the building is still very much alive, full of craft shops and a superb museum.

Highland Museum of Childhood

The **Highland Museum of Childhood** is a fascinating all-weather attraction suitable for visitors of all ages. Housed in Strathpeffer's restored railway station, it tells the story of childhood in the Scottish Highlands through a series of beautifully presented displays, incorporating such topics as education, health, homelife, folklore and recreation. Items on show include toys, games, puppets, cradles, a school desk, slate and strap, plus a number of rare dolls from the Angela Kellie Collection.

Hands-on exhibits include a dressing-up box and a toy train for children of all ages. There is also a series of original illustrations by Christopher Fry and a unique collection of historic photographs showing Highland children at work and play since Victorian times. The Museum has its own attractive café offering delicious freshly brewed coffee and a mouthwatering selection of home-baked scones, cakes and pastries; in fine weather, tables are set out on the old railway platform. There is also a shop stocking an unusual range of traditional toys, games, children's books and cards, and a number of interesting craft workshops, including a wood carvers. The site incorporates an attractive picnic area and is open daily between mid-March and end-October, and at other times by appointment.

Highland Museum of Childhood, Old Railway Station, Strathpeffer
Tel: 01997 421031

Owned and personally run since 1970 by the Kennedy family, the **Strathpeffer Hotel** has been a popular hotel and eating place since Victorian times when this was one of Europe's premier spa towns with a daily train service from London. Scottish Tourist Board 3 Crown Commended, its 35 guest bedrooms are comfortable and well equipped with en-suite bathrooms, colour televisions, tea and coffee making facilities and a number of thoughtful extras. The large residents' lounge contains an interesting selection of books and the atmosphere throughout the hotel is relaxed and homely.

Strathpeffer Hotel

The restaurant, which is also open to non-residents, serves a good selection of traditional Scottish fayre, including fresh local fish and prime steaks, as well as vegetarian and Continental specialities. Excellent bar meals are served in the lounge bar, an impressive room with a conservatory and dance floor which also provides evening entertainment several nights a week. The Hotel even has a friendly resident ghost - the Grey Lady - who is thought to be the jilted lover of the local blacksmith who hanged herself in one of the back rooms. The Strathpeffer Hotel lies within easy reach of superb facilities for golfing and angling, and is ideally situated for day-trips to John O' Groats, the Cairngorms and the West Highland Coast.

Strathpeffer Hotel, Strathpeffer Tel: 01997 421200 Fax: 01997 421110

DINGWALL. A traditional bustling market town, Dingwall is the administrative centre for the large district of Ross and Cromarty. The town's history stretches back over 1000 years and its name is derived from the Norse for 'Place of the Council'. From being a southern outpost of the great Norse Earldom of Orkney, it became a strategic fortress of the Celtic Kings, a stronghold against the Vikings to the north and the wild and rebellious Highlanders all around. The visitor can't miss the tall monument tower, which stands in Mitchell Hill cemetery, overlooking the town. It was erected in memory of General Sir Hector MacDonald, an outstanding soldier who served with the Gordon Highlanders and was known as 'Fighting Mac'.

Above the town on the Heights of Brae is the **Neil Gunn Memorial**, which overlooks the Cromarty Firth and the Black Isle, the inspirations for his Highland novels.

EVANTON. The village lies at the foot of **Black Rock Ravine**, a remarkable cleft, over two miles in length, through which the River Glass surges.

The **Wheel Inn Motel** is a first rate pub, restaurant and place to stay which stands beside the old A9 at Evanton, a pleasant community lying at the foot of Glen Glass, half a mile inland from the Cromarty Firth. This unusual single storey building was constructed in the 1950s as a transport café to serve the busy main road north from Inverness.

Wheel Inn Motel

Today, it is owned and personally run by Sue and Gordon Parsonson, friendly and experienced hosts who provide a warm welcome, excellent food and drink, and comfortable overnight or weekly accommodation. The bar serves an impressive choice of whiskies and draught beers, and

Sir Hector MacDonald's Monument, Dingwall

the dining room offers an extensive range of home-cooked dishes, from simple toasties and bar snacks to steaks and Continental specialities. There is also a lively games room with a pool table and a selection of toys and activities for children. Accommodation is in four modern and well-equipped A-frame chalets, two of which have been fitted with self-catering facilities. These are set within their own attractive grounds and are available by the night or week. As an added attraction, live country and western music is played in the bar on Wednesday evenings.

Wheel Inn Motel, Novar Toll, Evanton Tel: 01349 830763

INVERGORDON. Planned as a model village to encourage local trades, today the town is the centre for the repair and refitting of North Sea oil rigs. There are often as many as a dozen scattered around the Firth and they are best seen by driving along the front.

To the east is **Tarbet Ness**. There are several Pictish stones on the Ness, and indeed all over Ross-shire, each intricately carved. Perhaps the most impressive here are at Shandwick and Nigg.

HILL OF FEARN. **Fearn Abbey**, built in the 13th century, was converted into a Parish church but, in 1742, the roof collapsed killing 42 of the congregation. The nave and choir of the Abbey were restored and are still used as the parish church, whilst the north and south chapels remain roofless.

TAIN. The attractive **Tolbooth**, with its conical spire and small angle turrets, was originally built in the 16th century and then rebuilt in 1707. Back in the 19th century, Tain, however, was a notorious centre of the ruthless Clearances scheme and if the crofters resisted the orders of dispossession they were imprisoned in the Tolbooth.

The history of this sturdy town, however, goes back much further, to the times of the Norsemen, in fact, and its name is a corruption of Norse 'Thing' which means council. Close to the Tolbooth, **Tain Through Time** tells the story of the town's past: as the birthplace, in around 1000, of St Duthus, who went on to become Bishop of Ross; its days as a sanctuary; and to James IV, who made over 15 pilgrimages to Tain in expiation for his part in the death of his father.

St Duthus Church, built around the 1360s, stands on the site of an earlier building, traces of which can still be seen. **St Duthus Chapel**, now a ruin standing in a cemetery near the shore, dates from the 13th century and was built as a prayer cell with accommodation for a resident hermit. It is said to have been built on the site of the cottage in which Duthus was born and the Chapel, traditionally, housed the saint's bones.

Just to the north of the town is the **Glenmorangie Distillery**; it was an illegal distillery until 1843, when it was licensed, and is well worth a visit.

WHISKY

A characteristic feature of the Highland landscape, particularly in Speyside, Glenlivet and Perthshire, are the whitewashed buildings of the whisky distilleries with the pagoda-like roofs of the barley-drying kilns.

There are, chiefly, two types of whisky: blended and malt whisky. Blended whisky contains mainly grain whisky made without allowing the barley grain to form shoots (or maltings) and then smoking them. However, connoisseurs prefer single malt whisky. Each coming from one particular distillery and with very distinctive flavours, the maltings are smoked and the special character of each malt whisky lies very much in the combination of local climate, peat and soft burn water used. The malt whisky is then left to mature in oak casks, never metal, where the flavour develops and the whisky matures.

The first record of whisky distilling in Scotland is dated 1494 though there is little doubt that the Highland crofters were distilling spirits from barley long before this. The art of distillation was probably brought to Scotland in the Dark Ages by Irish missionaries.

Following the imposition of excise duty in 1644 and further confusion after the Act of Union in 1707, illicit distilling and smuggling were rife. It was not until 1823 that an Act of Parliament clarified the issues and the business of whisky distilling settled down into the form it is today.

There are more than 100 whisky distilleries in the Highlands and Islands today, many of which offer guided tours which demonstrate the careful process of making uisge-beatha - the water of life. As well as the more well known distilleries such as Glenmorangie and Glenlivet, there are many much smaller operations to be found. The variation in taste and colour between two whiskies, even those produced just a few miles apart, is a constant source of discussion and fascination somewhat akin to the wine industry in regions of France.

It is also worth noting that this is the only case in which the adjective Scotch is used instead of Scottish.

Western Highlands

FORT WILLIAM. Situated on the shores of Loch Linnhe and at the southern end of the Great Glen, Fort William is the capital of the Western Highlands and business centre for the whole region. The **West Highland Museum** holds many displays of great historical interest. Be sure not to miss the 'secret portrait' of Bonnie Prince Charlie, a meaningless smudge of colour until viewed in a cylindrical mirror. It dates from a time when anyone caught possessing his image would receive the death sentence.

Fort William's story began in 1655 when General Monk built an earthwork here. Later, rebuilt in stone during the reign of William III, the town, firstly called Maryburgh, became known by its present name. The fort, now demolished had the distinction of holding out during both the '15 and '45 Jacobite Risings. The coming of the railway has turned the town into a prosperous centre and a key place for tourists visiting the West Highlands.

The town stands at the foot of **Ben Nevis**, the highest mountain in Britain at 4406 feet. Thousands who have never climbed a mountain before, or since, have struggled up to the summit, their personal Everest. The easiest route is up the bridle path from Achintee in Glen Nevis, though it has challenges for every level of mountaineering competence. It goes without saying that on the few and far between clear days the views are wonderful. **Glen Nevis**, below the western and southern flanks of the mountain, is an interesting drive and the **Glen Nevis Visitor Centre** has exhibitions covering the ben and the glen.

Milton Hotel and Leisure Club

In 1645, the Marquis of Montrose routed the Campbells right on the site of the **Milton Hotel and Leisure Club**. There is a monument to commemorate the Highland battle and the ruins of the old castle stand nearby. Happily, times are now more tranquil and patrons will find this a great place to stay and relax. There's plenty to do close at hand, and the hotel can arrange every kind of activity: wonderful shopping, great golf, exhibitions, historic sites, mountain biking, fishing and pony trekking. The area boasts some of the finest scenery in the world for walking, with Ben Nevis only a stone's throw away from the front door. Fort William truly is an all-year-round holiday destination, with winter mountaineering and the newest Scottish ski resort - the Nevis Range - only ten minutes drive from the Hotel. The Milton lies within easy reach of the town centre - less than a mile on the north road - and has ample private parking facilities. After a £1.3 million refurbishment, its appearance is very different from days gone by. It now boasts a magnificent fully equipped leisure club, a beautiful arched covered walkway, an upgraded lounge, restaurant and foyer, along with redesigned front-facing bedrooms. Three hundred and fifty years ago they were fighting to get in here, now they only pitch in to great Scottish hospitality!

Milton Hotel and Leisure Club, North Road, Fort William
Tel: 01397 701177 Fax: 01397 703695

One of the finest establishments in Fort William, the **Alexandra Hotel** is the ideal holiday base whatever the time of year. Conveniently located near the town centre, this handsome gabled building has been part of the fabric of this famous resort since 1876. Now fully modernised, the Hotel has all the facilities one would expect from a top Scottish Tourist Board 4 Crown Commended Hotel.

Alexandra Hotel

All the guest bedrooms are appointed to a very high standard, with private en-suite bathrooms, colour televisions, direct dial telephones, radios and complimentary tea and coffee making facilities; several also have magnificent views of Ben Nevis and the surrounding countryside. Children are very welcome, and a number of rooms are available for guests with young families. Each morning, diners are treated to a full Scottish buffet breakfast and, at lunchtimes and in the evening, the Hotel's two restaurants offer a superb choice of top class international cuisine. The lounge bar, with its impressive selection of real ales and malt whiskies, is the ideal environment in which to enjoy a relaxing aperitif or after dinner drink. A programme of live entertainment is presented every evening, and free use of the superb leisure facilities at the Milton Hotel is also available to guests at all times.

Alexandra Hotel, The Parade, Fort William
Tel: 01397 701177 Fax: 01397 703695

The following story is an interesting dated history of the **Ben Nevis Distillery**, a Highland distillery that was first established back in 1825 and has been producing matured whisky ever since.

22nd October 1825. This day I left my home at Torgulbin in the valley of the Spean River and came the short journey to Lochy Bridge, a few miles to the north of the town of Fort William. I had been charged by those men of substance and authority within the district of Lochaber to assist in the extirpation of a plague of illicit stills and unlawful brewers of spirits, and to undertake the establishment here of a legitimised still house. I endeavor to search out a place compatible with the production of Uisge Beatha, 'The Water of Life', and have come to the lee of that Ben Nevis. Here I do hope to find a constant and regular source of pure, clear water. It is not for nothing that I am known as 'Long John', my size being of no small deterrent to those who would challenge the legitimisation and regulation of whisky manufacture.

I was born into an ancient Highland family, a branch of the Macdonalds of Keppoch in the year 1798. The fortunes of my family ebbed and flowed, reaching their lowest point after the 1745 Jacobite Rebellion when 2000 of our men marched against Bonny Prince Charlie. The Jacobite defeat at the Battle of Culloden in 1746 was hard on my family and many good men died. Fifty-three years after this tragedy I was born, one of seven sons, into a farming family at Torgulbin, by the side of the River Gulbin, in my beloved Lochaber.

14th June 1827. Many believe that there exists a divine secret, a miraculous ingredient or genius behind the manufacture of Scotch whisky. I, however acknowledge no miracle other than that which is worked when science and nature combine. The principal ingredients are three, notably, water, barley and yeast, with a measure of peat smoke or 'reek'. The barley must be clean and plump, fully rounded and quite dry, containing exactly the right amount of protein. Special distiller's yeast has the texture of dough or putty and is vital to the process of fermentation. The peat comes to the whisky through its water passed over peat bogs on its way down the mountain, and from the reek from the fire lit during the manufacturing process. We are fully fortunate in that nature in her magnificence, has created on the hill behind us, an ample supply of peat in our own banks to fuel the fires drying the barley.

26th April 1848. I find mention of myself in the pages of the *Illustrated London News* which records the recent visit of Her Royal Highness, Queen Victoria, to my distillery. It seemed appropriate to mark this great occasion and I took the opportunity of presenting a cask of whisky to Her Majesty. An order has been sent to the Treasury permitting the spirits to be removed to the cellars of Buckingham Palace free of duty.

5th October 1877. The Distillery currently employs some 51 people with a total wage bill of £32 22d weekly. Duncan Cameron, a carter, earned 16s 3d for five days work and his son, Duncan Junior, went away with 15s 5d.

15th March 1878. In order to meet the demand for the Dew of Ben Nevis whisky I have committed myself towards the opening of a second distillery, the Nevis Distillery, on the banks of the River Nevis at Fort William.

21st December 1885. The annual output of the Dew of Ben Nevis Distillery in the year past was 152,798 gallons of pure Highland malt whisky.

4th August 1887. The business of distilling whisky here in Lochaber is going well. Fifty years ago the Ben Nevis Distillery was producing 200 gallons per week in full production and now our output is more than ten times that amount. The Distillery now incorporates a smithy, engineer's shop, cooperage, joiner's shop and sawmill, cart sheds, stables, stores and housing for the workmen. There are ten warehouses which together currently hold 8161 casks containing 523,722 gallons of whisky.

1st November 1891. The death occurred today, at the age of 56, of Donald P Macdonald. Mr Macdonald, who died from a cerebral haemorrhage and who left the considerable estate of £110,311 9s 8d, was greatly respected throughout Lochaber.

28th November 1891. Following the death of DP Macdonald the stewardship of the distilleries was undertaken by his two sons, John and Archibald Macdonald, later Colonel AW Macdonald of the Lovat Scouts.

1941-1955. After more that 100 years and three generations of the Macdonald family the Dew of Ben Nevis Distillery has been sold to Joseph Hobbs. In 1955 Mr Hobbs added a coffey still to the four existing pot stills making the Dew of Ben Nevis one of the first distilleries in Scotland which could produce both malt and grain whiskies under the same roof.

18th April 1984. In 1978 the Distillery went out of production and three years later Long John International, the Spirits Division of Whitbread, acquired the premises mainly for storage purposes, from Joseph Hobbs Jnr, proprietor of Inverlochy Castle Hotel. In 1984, however, following an upturn in their share of the whisky export market, Long John International decided to reopen the Distillery for production. After extensive modernisation and renovation it was opened by Sir Donald Cameron of Locheil, Lord Lieutenant of Inverness-shire.

18th April 1989. Today, the Nikka Whisky Distilling Company Ltd of Japan acquired the Ben Nevis Distillery from Whitbreads Spirit Division. This ensures the future of distilling in Fort William which had been in doubt, with the closure of Glenlochy Distillery in 1984 and production having ceased here at Ben Nevis in May 1986.

28th September 1990. Today, the Distillery was officially opened again as a production unit. Since the beginning of the year engineers and tradesmen have installed and fitted a new boiler, mash tun and associated pipeworks, controls and new fermentation room.

Today. Many decades have passed since Long John last walked the Distillery yards, and he might find it difficult today to recognise his old Distillery, but not everything has changed. They still take the water from Coire Leis and Coire Na Ciste, drawing it off from the Allt A Mhuilin Burn at a point about 750 feet above sea level.

The malt is ground in a traditional roller mill and transferred into a grist hopper. The grist is then mixed with hot water in a mash tun, in which malt sugars are extracted in a solution called wort. From each mash, 42,000 litres of wort are collected and the process of fermentation takes place when the yeast slurry is added. The mixture is allowed to ferment for two days, during which time the sugar is converted into crude alcohol or wash. The wash is pumped to a 25,000 litre wash still where it is heated until it boils, the resulting steam is passed along the swan necks of the pot stills and into a condenser where it reverts to a liquid known as low wines. Since low wines contain impurities they must be distilled once more, this time in a spirit still, to create the actual whisky. It is here that the skill of the stillman comes to the fore. He passes the distillate through a spirit safe which separates the first and last runs from the spirit still (the foreshots and feints) which are not satisfactory; the middle cut is then taken to a 50,000 litre spirits receiver in the warehouse or filling store. The actual production capacity of the Distillery is some 3 million litres of alcohol per year with more than 1.5 million litres being produced in 1992.

Today there are seven warehouses which, together, have the capacity to mature up to 6.5 million litres of alcohol. It is here in the cool, silent darkness, that the whisky is stored in oaken casks, slowly becoming imbued, over many years, with its character, colour and bouquet. If it is true that Long John Macdonald might not now recognise much of his original distillery, it is also true that he would still know his Dew of Ben Nevis. It would please him to learn that his fine golden Water of Life is still being made; that his spirit still resides at the foot of his beloved Ben Nevis; and that his dream and his dram are still alive.

Ben Nevis Distillery, Lochy Bridge, Fort William Tel: 01397 700200

AROUND FORT WILLIAM

KINLOCHLEVEN. For over 80 years aluminium has been smelted in this seemingly unlikely place. It was cheap electricity that brought industry here, using the water pouring off the hills to generate the huge amounts needed for the process. **Loch Leven** also provided access to the sea, essential once for the raw materials coming in and the finished product going out to destinations all over the world. The story of the smelter and the community that grew around it is told at **Kinlochleven Visitors Centre** on Linnhe Road in the town.

Those choosing to cross **Ballachulish Bridge** may spot the James Stewart Monument overlooking its southern end. James of the Glen had his story immortalized in Robert Louis Stevenson's book *Kidnapped*.

A delightful refuge for walkers and touring visitors alike can be found on the edge of Kinlochleven, just off the B863, and within five minutes walk of the West Highland Way. **Edencoille** is a charming small guest house which stands in an elevated position with the dramatic peaks of Glen Coe and the Mamore Forest all around. The building was originally constructed in Edwardian times to house a manager of British Aluminium, then in the mid 1980s it was acquired by Mrs Elsie Robertson, who completely refurbished the property to bring it up to the standard of a comfortable modern guest house. Now Scottish Tourist Board 1 Crown Commended, it offers five well appointed guest bedrooms, all immaculately decorated in attractive country style. Each room is equipped with a colour television and tea and coffee making facilities, and has the use of a shared bath or shower-room. Mrs Robertson is renowned for her full Scottish breakfasts, a meal which is guaranteed to provide a hearty start for the most enthusiastic walkers, climbers and anglers. She also provides delicious evening meals by prior arrangement, using fresh local produce wherever possible. The speciality of the house is her home-made fish soup, a delicacy for which guests have returned again and again.

Edencoille, Garbhein Road, Kinlochleven Tel: 01855 831358

Perched 600 feet above sea level on the slopes of Am Bodach, and with spectacular views over Loch Leven and the surrounding Highland scenery, stands **Mamore Lodge Hotel**. Built at the turn of the century for Captain Frank Bibby, whose family were one of Liverpool's great shipping families and owned Bibbys' Shipping Line, the Lodge was used for hunting and as a holiday retreat. The family were great hosts and enjoyed amongst their notable guests Sir Henry Fairfax-Lucy, Viscount Churchill and King Edward VII. The wild beauty of Mamore has not changed since then, deer still roam the estate and the spectacular landscape provides unforgettable views and walks for present day guests. Mamore Lodge Hotel has retained much of its original character which provides 17 comfortably appointed rooms, nearly all with en-suite facilities, magnificent views and with original Scottish pinewood panelling. The restaurant and dining room where traditional Scottish meals are served, as well as the lounge, have fine views over the Loch and village to the mountains north of Glen Coe. The Mamore Forest covers over 45,000 acres, and miles of stalking tracks and pony paths provide access to all parts of the region with a choice of easier low-level walks, or of breathtaking and more strenuous high-ridge walks, all from the Lodge itself. Reached by private road off the B863 near Kinlochleven.

Mamore Lodge Hotel, Kinlochleven Tel: 01855 831213.

GLENCOE is know the world over for the infamous massacre that took place here in 1692. The story has been told and retold until it has become a legendary tale of treachery. The reality is rather different. King William III and his government realized that to contain the Highland clans by force would be impractical and so was tempted into using a single act of severity to frighten the clan chiefs. All the clans were ordered to sign an oath of allegiance to the King, MacDonald of Glencoe had been late in giving his, due partly to truculence and partly because of bad weather. Government troops billeted with the clan and, led by Captain Robert Campbell of Glenlyon, were ordered to make an example of them. It was a botch job: at dawn, on 13 February 1692, 38 MacDonalds were slaughtered but 300 escaped. Though there is no excuse for such a bloody act this small clan had an ill-name for thieving and were hated by those on whom it preyed. There have been far worse atrocities committed between the clans yet Glencoe still offend. Even today the sign on the **Clachaig Inn**'s door proclaims 'Nae Campbells'. The **Signal Rock**, near the inn, marks the spot where it all began.

ONICH. Inchree Chalets is an established family run, self-catering holiday centre situated eight miles south of Fort William in the heart of the West Highlands - an Area of Outstanding Natural Beauty. The Inchree Centre is a group of nine, comfortable, well equipped holiday homes situated on a five acre, naturally wooded hillside. The comfortable chalets are of traditional, permanent construction in two

396

and three bedroom styles, fully insulated with electric heating and full cooking facilities, on site is the **Four Seasons Bistro and Bar** with its unusual and relaxing interior and log fire. Emphasis is placed on serving freshly prepared quality food at reasonable prices. The à la carte menu, offering a variety of tempting dishes prepared with a very imaginative flair, regularly features prime Aberdeen Angus steaks and fresh local Scottish fish and game. The wine list provides a pleasing choice of wines from around the world at sensible prices. Enjoy too, real ales, bottled beers, and a fine selection of malt whiskies. From the Inchree Centre there are extensive views down Loch Linnhe to the Isle of Mull and the Morvern Hills. Located off the A82 on the north side of the village of Onich it is easily accessible from all major centres. Graded and Commended by the Scottish Tourist Board.

Inchree Centre, Onich Tel & Fax: 01855 821287

STRONTIAN. The village may seem familiar as it lent its name to the radioactive isotope Strontium, discovered here in 1790. Before the discovery, this pleasant village was well known for its lead mines and provided, during the Napoleonic Wars, lead for the bullets and the mines were worked by some of the French prisoners of war.

KILCHOAN. The ruined **Mingary Castle**, a 13th century stronghold of a branch clan of the Macdonald Lords of the Isles, stands on a rocky promontory guarding the entrances to both Loch Sunart and the Sound of Mull. The Castle also saw the downfall of the Lords of the Isles when, in 1495, James IV received their submission. During the 17th century the Castle was taken by the Campbells, besieged by Argyll and seized for Montrose.

TIORAM. Reached by a north bound unclassified road, **Tioram Castle** stands in an islet in Loch Moidart and is one of Scotland's best hidden castles. Once the seat of the MacDonalds of Clan Ranald; it was burned on the orders of the then chief when he joined the 1715 Jacobite Rising, fearing it might fall into the hands of his enemies the Campbells. Accessible at low tide it offers fine views along the Loch.

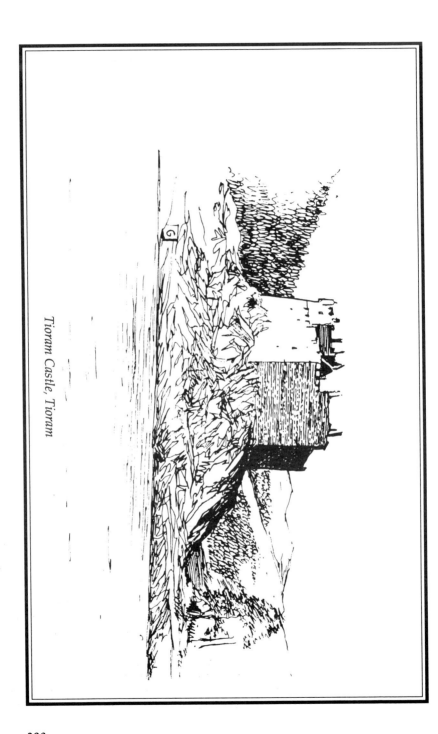

Tioram Castle, Tioram

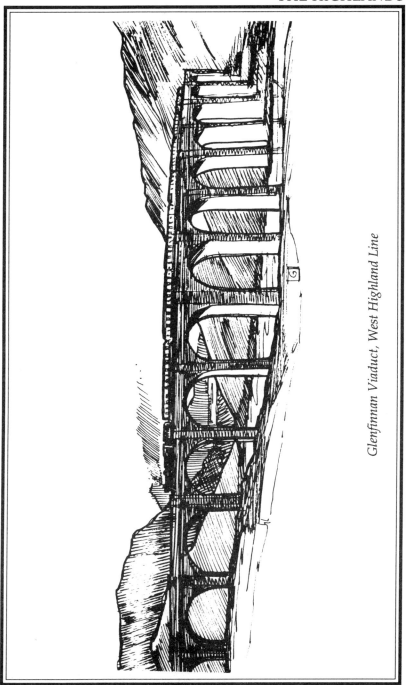

Glenfinnan Viaduct, West Highland Line

MALLAIG. The terminal of the West Highland Line, Mallaig was once one of the remotest communities in the West Highlands, only accessible by 40 miles of rough track. It has, however, become a major ferry and fishing port and from here the traveller can cross to the Inner Hebridean islands of Rum, Eigg, Canna and Muck, as well as, in the summer, to Skye over the Kyle of Lochalsh.

In the harbour, **Mallaig Marine World** is devoted to the work of the town's fishing boats and local species, whilst, the **Mallaig Heritage Centre** tells the story of the town and surrounding area through old photographs and clips of film.

GLENFINNAN. There is much to see and admire in this quiet and remote place: **Glenfinnan Viaduct** carries the West Highland railway extension from Fort William to Mallaig. The line was built by Sir Robert MacAlpine between 1897 and 1901 and was the first to use concrete in its construction. The 21 arches stand as tribute to 'Concrete Bob' who pioneered its use. **Glenfinnan Station Museum** uses the redundant station buildings to tell the story of the line. The introduction of radio signalling in 1988 swept away three quarters of a centuries working practices and the museum aims to preserve atmosphere of the railway from those times.

South of the station at the head of Loch Sheil stands the impressive **Glenfinnan Monument**. It was at this point that Bonnie Prince Charlie raised his standard in August 1745 and began rallying the clans to support his rebellion. A visitors centre tells the story of the Prince's endeavour, which reached as far south as Derby and ended at Culloden.

LOCH NAN UAMH. Here is a memorial cairn that marks the spot from which Bonnie Prince Charlie sailed for France in September 1746, having wandered the Highlands as a fugitive with a price of £30,000 on his head. He escaped, with the help of two French frigates who, if they had arrived earlier with their supplies of men and money, might have changed the course of history. The Prince died in 1788, a forlorn drunk.

BANAVIE. Here is the delightfully named **Neptune's Staircase**, a series of eight locks that raise the Caledonian Canal some 64 feet. The Canal itself was designed by Thomas Telford and completed in 1822. The **Old Sawpit**, next to the staircase, tells the story of the canal's construction and displays the tools and equipment in use at that time.

TORLUNDY. Climbing, walking, skiing and riding are just some of the many activities you can enjoy based at **Torlundy Farm** with **Great Glen Holidays** in Scandinavian Lodges. The eight lodges are sited amongst Scots pine and silver birch with spectacular views of the north face of Ben Nevis and the Great Glen. This is definitely a holiday area with many exciting things to do - take a day to go riding with Torlundy Farm Riding Centre where both novices and experienced riders are catered for with escorted rides through an unspoiled landscape of mountains, woods, rivers and lochs. Skiing is near at hand on Aonach

Mor, which boasts the longest ski run in Britain or take the gondola lift 1800 feet up to the Nevis Range just for the pleasure of it. You are perfectly situated at Torlundy farm to experience the beauty of the Highlands with the convenience of the shops, swimming pool and amenities in Fort William three miles away.

Great Glen Holidays

The Lodges sleep four in two bedrooms and two extra persons can be accommodated in the spacious living room. Each lodge has heating, colour television and pine panelling throughout providing a cosy atmosphere, while three full-length windows give plenty of internal light. A high standard of furnishings and equipment is maintained and your comfort is clearly the prime consideration here. Awarded 4 Crown Commended by Scottish Tourist Board.

Great Glen Holidays, Torlundy Farm, Torlundy
Tel: 01397 703015 Fax: 01397 703304

SPEAN BRIDGE. Standing above the town, the **Commando Memorial** is an inspiring sculpture erected in 1952 to commemorate the Commandos who trained in these mountains and gave their lives in the struggle for freedom. There can be few more worthy spots to contemplate the brave deeds of others. A **Museum**, at the Spean Bridge Hotel, tells the story of the soldiers and also of the local incident, 200 years earlier, when a dozen of MacDonald of Keppoch's Highlanders routed two companies of government troops.

It is always nice to find a family run restaurant where great care is taken in the selection and preparation of food. **The Coach House** is just such a place and is found just beyond Spean Bridge on the A82 at Glenfintaig. Iain MacDonald extends a warm invitation for you to visit his licensed restaurant and enjoy some modern Scottish food in his converted 18th century coaching inn. All meals are prepared to order, made from local produce including game, seafood and vegetarian, the dishes are imaginatively presented and the quality first class. Iain also has a fine selection of wines, spirits and real ales. On a sunny day you can sit outside and enjoy a beer or glass of wine in the garden, whilst for colder days there's a woodburning stove to warm yourself by. The restaurant is open from 12 noon until 4 pm for lunches and afternoon tea. Dinners are served from 6 pm with last orders at 9 pm.

Coach House Restaurant, Spean Bridge Tel: 01397 712680
Fax: 01397 712100 e-mail: cram_tara@bigfoot.com

GAIRLOCHY. This small hamlet sits on the Caledonian Canal and is a great place to relax and watch the boats as they negotiate the lochs down to the sea at Corpach.

ACHNACARRY. The fascinating **Clan Cameron Museum** can be found in Achnacarry, a tiny settlement lying between Loch Lochy and Loch Arkaig which can be reached from Spean Bridge via the B8004 and B8005. This remote yet beautiful spot is the ancestral home of the chiefs of Clan Cameron, the present Achnacarry House having been constructed in the early 19th century to replace an earlier timber structure burnt down after the '45 Rebellion. The Museum is housed in a listed cottage on the estate which was completely refurbished in the late 1980s in a project backed by members of the clan worldwide. Its contents trace the history of Clan Cameron from medieval times to the present day, highlighting the roles played by such chiefs as Sir Ewen Dubh Cameron (1629-1719) and Donald Cameron (1695-1748), the 'Gentle Lochiel' who supported Bonnie Prince Charlie's Jacobite Rising of 1745. The Prince is known to have spent a few nights close to Achnacarry when on the run after Culloden, and the museum contains a room setting depicting him holding a reward poster placing a bounty of £30,000 on his head. Also on show is a scarlet waistcoat belonging to the Prince and a ring incorporating his hidden portrait.

After 1745, the only way a Highlander could legally wear the kilt and carry arms was to join one of the newly-formed Highland regiments. One of these was the 79th Cameron Highlanders (later the Queen's Own Cameron Highlanders) and the Museum contains a section chronicling the history of this famous regiment from the Napoleonic Wars to the 20th century. There are also a number of photographs and exhibits relating to the important commando training centre which was located nearby during the Second World War. The Clan Cameron Museum is open all day in July and August and afternoons only during the rest of the season.

Clan Cameron Museum, Achnacarry, Spean Bridge Tel: 01397 712052

INVERGARRY. **Invergarry Castle**, ruined and standing in the grounds of Glengarry Castle Hotel, was a successor to earlier castles and was, for many years, the seat of the MacDonells of Glengarry.

The **Invergarry Hotel** in Invergarry village is an impressive Victorian hotel which provides a tranquil holiday haven for visitors to this dramatic part of the Highlands.

Invergarry Hotel

Run by proprietor Robert MacCallum and his friendly team of staff, this Scottish Tourist Board 3 Crown Commended establishment offers superb accommodation in ten beautifully furnished and well equipped en-suite guest rooms. The bar is a popular meeting place where guests and locals mix easily, exchanging tales of the day's activities over a relaxing drink. A selection of over 40 malt whiskies is on offer, along with perhaps the finest choice of Scottish cask-conditioned ales in the area, including those from the Isle of Skye. A wide range of meals is available in the bar at lunchtimes and in the evening, or for more formal dining, the hotel's à la carte restaurant offers an extensive menu incorporating the finest Scottish produce freshly prepared to the highest standards. There is also a popular self-service restaurant which is open to guests and non-residents between Easter and October. A wide variety of meals and snacks is served here throughout the day, making this an ideal stopping-off point for those exploring the breathtaking landscape of the Great Glen.

Invergarry Hotel, Invergarry Tel: 01809 501206

FORT AUGUSTUS. A flight of lochs here lifts the Caledonian Canal up from the level of Loch Ness as it travels south. Close at hand is the **Great Glen Exhibition**, which illustrates the story of the canal, as well as the local history. The village grew up around the site of a barracks, constructed after the Jacobite Rising of 1745 and it was named after George II's son, the infamous Duke of Cumberland who had commanded troops at the Battle of Culloden.

Fort Augustus Abbey was built around General Wade's barracks and fort and is, theologically, the successor to two other abbeys. Now in the hands of the Benedictine order, the visitors centre displays material telling the story of both the Fort and the Abbey as well as monastic life in the Highlands from early times to present day.

DORNIE. Along the A87 at the confluence of Loch Alsh, Loch Long and Loch Duich stands the Castle that is the image of Scotland, **Eilean Donan**. Its picture postcard appeal should perhaps be tempered by the bloody truth of its history, but regardless of its past it remains the most photographed and most painted - irresistible to all who pass this way for the first time. Originally the chief stronghold of the MacKenzies of Kintail, who became Earls of Seaforth, it was later looked after by their bodyguards the MacCraes. In 1331 Randolph, Earl of Moray, decorated the walls with the corpses of 15 men executed in a 'territorial' dispute. Twice besieged, in 1304 and 1579, it met its end during the abortive Jacobite Rising of 1719. Garrisoned by Spanish troops under William MacKenzie, 5th Earl of Seaforth, it succumbed to gun fire from three English warships. It remained a ruin until Colonel MacCrae-Gilstrap had it restored as the MacCrae family seat in the 1930s.

Described as 'the loveliest glen in the west Highlands' **Glen Sheil** certainly has a bigger landscape than even Glencoe and, though blood was shed here aplenty, it shares none of Glencoe's perpetual melancholy nor its infamy. Below the mountains, at Sheilbridge, there is a narrow road into Glenelg built by General Wade which takes the road into the land that inspired Gavin Maxwell's book *Ring of Bright Water*, the wonderful story of his life with the otters. He had a house on the coast which burned down in 1968 claiming the life of his otter Edal. Within a year Maxwell was dead and his ashes scattered over the site of his home near Sandaig.

404

LOCHCARRON. Once known as Jeantown, this is a lovely little village laid out in typical 18th century style. Along an unclassified road to the west stands **Strome Castle**, on the narrow neck of Loch Carron. A small and muddled ruin, managed by the National Trust for Scotland, its demise was reputedly caused by the stupidity of the castle women. In 1602, Kenneth Mackenzie of Kintail laid siege to the Castle and succeeded in capturing it and blowing it up because the women of Strome, having drawn water from a nearby well, had emptied their containers into a vat of gunpowder and not the water tub, and so had rendered the defenders helpless.

SHIELDAIG. A drive around the **Applecross Peninsula** is one of the last great motoring adventures of Britain. In good weather, often in short supply, the gradients, hairpins and the 2000 foot summit of Bealach na Ba will still leave vivid memories. In winter the road can become a game of Russian roulette. Those who live in Applecross were grateful for the opening of the new road to Shieldaig in 1970, a long diversion but at least an escape route.

TORRIDON. The **Torridon Countryside Centre**, with an audio-visual display, describes the wildlife of the Torridon Estate, whilst nearby is a static display on the life of the red deer.

KINLOCHEWE, at the inland end of Loch Maree, was, during the clan wars, one of the most dangerous places in Europe. It lies on the northeast edge of the **Beinn Eighe National Nature Reserve**, the home of the red deer, golden eagle, pine marten and the very rare and shy Scottish wild cat.

Loch Maree, one of Scotland's best loved lochs, is thought to have been named after St Maree or Maelrubha, the monk who, it is claimed, founded the monastery at Applecross. The Loch's banks are swathed in ancient Caledonian pinewoods of the sort that once covered much of Scotland. Queen Victoria visited the area in 1870 and at Slattadale the falls were renamed in honour of her visit. The eastern end of the Loch is dominated by the mighty Slioch; 3215 feet to the summit.

GAIRLOCH is very popular with those who love the great outdoors; attractions include golfing, angling, windsurfing, canoeing and boating. **Gairloch Heritage Museum** has won awards for its displays on the past life of a typical West Highland area from prehistoric times right up to the present day.

LOCH EWE. In the 1940s supply convoys to Russia gathered here and the sides of the Loch are scattered with the remains of concrete bunkers, pill boxes and anti-aircraft platforms, the castles of the 20th century. There is still a NATO refuelling jetty in the Loch. On the surrounding hillside are **Inverewe Gardens**. Plants from many countries flourish in this garden created by Osgood MacKenzie over 120 years ago. They feature eucalyptus from Australia, giant forget-me-nots from South America and Himalayan lilies, giving an almost continuous display of colour. There are also guided walks with the gardening staff and a caravan and camping park, restaurant, petrol and plant sales.

GURINARD BAY. During the last war the island in this sandy bay was used for biological warfare experiments and landing on it was prohibited until the 1980s, when it was cleaned up at great expense.

Skye

There is little subtlety about the scenery of Skye, it is dramatic and beautiful whatever the season. Above all it is a paradise for the serious walker and climber. The peaks of the **Black Cuillin** are unlike any other in the land, a landscape from another planet, with towering summits. In winter they offer a special challenge held to be more difficult than any in the Alps and even admiring them from the safety of a road side lay-by it is easy to see why they demand and gain respect from everyone who ventures up their flanks.

PORTREE, the capital and the touring centre of Skye, is built around a harbour and bay sheltered by the bulk of Raasay. There are many hotels and guest houses to choose from, offering that special Highland hospitality and plenty of shoreline, clifftop and hill walks starting from here to work off all that hospitality. The oldest building is **Meall House**, which once served as the jail and it is now the local visitors information centre. The tourist information officer working from the condemned cell!

North of Portree even reluctant walkers can get a taste of the Island's flamboyant rock architecture by taking the 45 minute walk up to the hollow beneath the Trotternish Ridge. Here stands the **Old Man of Storr**, a 160 foot rock pinnacle that looks as if one shove would have it over. The area has the makings of a giants' adventure playground, with its colossal boulders, high pinnacles and dramatic overhanging cliffs. The Royal Hotel now stands on the site of **MacNab's Inn** where Bonnie Prince Charlie took leave of Flora Macdonald and fled to France.

If you are travelling through the pretty town of Portree on the Isle of Skye and are travelling on a budget, then make a bee line for **Portree Backpackers Hostel**. This family run hostel is centrally located just 10 minutes walk from the town centre, but if you are feeling a little foot sore then jump on to the FREE courtesy bus that runs daily to and from the hostel. Sleeping up to 30 people, the Portree Backpackers Hostel offers the independent traveller first class accommodation complete with some excellent shower and laundry facilities. The kitchen is fully equipped with everything you should need when self-catering, including FREE tea and coffee and a bright and friendly atmosphere. The comfortable lounge area comes complete with an open coal fire for those colder evenings and a television so that you won't miss your favourite soaps! In the attractive gardens you will find plenty of picnic benches and tables, here you can sit and enjoy your meals al fresco served hot from the barbecue facilities that are available throughout the long summer months. You can also book yourself and friends on our minibus tour, setting off from the hostel the minibus will take you past all the local beauty spots, castles and places of historical interest, in warmth and comfort. Owned and personally run by Mairi Murdo and Angus Gordon, the Portree Backpackers Hostel has also proved very popular amongst schools, colleges and universities throughout the country.

Portree Backpackers Hostel, Woodpark, Dunvegan Road, Portree
Tel: 01478 613641 Fax: 01478 613643

AROUND PORTREE

TORVAIG. If you are travelling north of Portree on the A855 Staffin Road and need to immerse yourself in some traditional Scottish hospitality, then make sure you stop at **The Shielings Guest House**.

The Shielings Guest House

Your hosts are Sara and Paul Bates, who have owned and run this attractively converted croft house for over eight years and offer their

407

guests a quiet and peaceful retreat in a warm and friendly atmosphere. The view from the reception area is spectacular and takes in the magnificent Cuillin Hills and Macleod's Tables. All of the guest rooms are pine-cladded and furnished to a high standard with private facilities and a complimentary tea and coffee tray. There are two lounge areas, one for smokers and one for non-smokers, and the generous breakfasts are served in the spacious dining room, with evening meals being supplied if you book on arrival. Stroll in the pretty gardens to the rear of the property or maybe explore further afield on one of the many local walks that take you through the picturesque countryside that surrounds this haven of peace.

The Shielings, 7 Torvaig, Portree Tel: 01478 613024

KILMUIR. Around the head of the peninsula at Kilmuir there is a cluster of thatched dwellings that make up the **Skye Cottage Museum**; of particular interest here is the collection of old photographs and documents. Nearby is the graveyard that contains **Flora Macdonald's Celtic Cross Memorial Grave**. She was the Jacobite heroine who, in the words of the song which recalls a most daring escapade, brought Bonnie Prince Charlie disguised as her maid 'over the sea to Skye'.

UIG. This neat village, in its sheltered bay, is important and well known for its car ferries to Harris and North Uist. Adventurous motoring can be had by taking the hill road from the village across the Trotternish Peninsula towards Staffin.

GRESHORNISH. On visiting the Isle of Skye you will find all the ingredients for a perfect holiday, peace, tranquillity and some delightful places to stay including the historic **Greshornish House Hotel**.

Greshnornish House Hotel

Once an 18th century Scottish Highland mansion, Greshornish has been tastefully converted into a private country house hotel secluded in its own 12 acres of picturesque grounds. This 3 Crown Commended

Flora MacDonald's Memorial Grave, Kilmuir

establishment offers its guests a real escape from the busy outside world, immerse yourself in the gracious olde worlde charm that still lingers in these elegant surroundings. Each guest room has been individually tailored to meet your every need; complete with central heating and private facilities there is even a four poster bedroom for those special occasions. Your hosts for your stay are Campbell and Sandra Dickson, a couple who offer their guests true Scottish hospitality, right down to Campbell's kilt and his tradition of piping all his visitors to dinner in the evening! All the food is freshly prepared using only the best local ingredients and is served in an elegant atmosphere with crystal glasses, mahogany tables, silver candelabra and silver tableware. The dining room is spacious and comes complete with open log fires that burn brightly in the colder months, they are also the main feature in the drawing room and attractive cocktail bar which is the prefect place to relax with a warming glass of whisky after that superb meal.

Greshornish House Hotel, Greshornish
Tel: 01470 582326 Fax: 01470 582345

DUNVEGAN. The famous **Dunvegan Castle** has been the home of the Macleods for at least 700 years. It is full of fascinating and bizarre relics, ranging from the 'Fairy Flag' to letters from Dr Johnson; there are also many items from Jacobite times including a lock of Bonnie Prince Charlie's hair. Legend says the 'Fairy Flag' brings luck in battle and photographs of it were carried by members of the family serving with the RAF during World War II.

Orbost House is situated in a truly magnificent position, offering its guests superb panoramic views of Varcasaig Bay to the south. On a clear day, the islands of Rum and Canna and the Cuillin Mountains can be observed in all their majesty.

Orbost House

This beautiful establishment offers the traveller two centrally heated self-catering apartments, each with a touch of elegance and style. Surviving graffiti scratched on a chamber window pane, "MD 1765" and "17611111", date the house better than any historian could, and the House itself has been divided into several building periods with the core of the building being a mid 18th century tack house. Both of the self-catering apartments are situated in the west wing, built between 1790 and 1880 and recently modernised to offer spacious, comfortable accommodation. The ground floor apartment sleeps up to five or six people and has a large, stone-flagged sitting room with an original 19th century hearth. The first floor accommodation has two double bedrooms and a large lounge area that can sleep another two people if needed. Both apartments come complete with all the facilities you will need including a washing machine and a fully equipped kitchen with electric cooker and refrigerator.

Because of the House's excellent position it offers a focal point from which many activities can be pursued, such as bird-watching, fishing, sailing and sub-aqua diving. There are some excellent restaurants and interesting art and craft shops close by. There are also plenty of lovely places to walk and explore including the famous Dunvegan Castle and some superb seal colonies and archeological sites can be easily reached on foot or by car.

Orbost House, Dunvegan Tel: 01470 521389
Fax: 01470 521719

SCONSER. Between 1913 and 1919 an ironstone mine was in operation here, worked for a time by German prisoners during World War I. The abandoned workings were never tidied up but slowly nature is hiding them again. **Sligachan Hotel** is perhaps the most famous hotel on Skye, standing at the junction of the A850 and A863, it has long been a favourite base for climbers, standing as it does on the doorstep of the Cuillins.

KYLEAKIN. Most visitors land at the small town of Kyleakin after a five minute journey across Loch Alsh; taking the ferry gives a real sense of travel that the new bridge has sadly taken away. Near the pier are the forlorn remains of Dunakin Castle, once a stronghold of the MacKinnons of Strath it is now called Castle Moil - 'the roofless castle'.

The village is named after the Norse King Haadon, who sailed through the narrow straits on his way to defeat at the Battle of Largs in 1263. The ruins of **Castle Moil**, once known as Dun Akin and built as a defence against marauding Norsemen, overlook the strait. Legend has it that a local, enterprising chatelaine, known as Saucy Mary, stretched a chain across the strait and levied a toll from passing ships.

Open to the public from May to August, **Kyle House Gardens** are noted for their flowering shrubs and splendid coastal views. Whilst, just offshore, Kyleakin Island was home in 1968-9 of author Gavin Maxwell, after his home on the mainland was burned down.

Along the A850 from Kyleakin is **Luib Folk Museum**. The theme here is the crofting life of Skye early this century. Skye still has hundreds of crofts - smallholdings which usually have some arable land, a share of the hill grazings and the use of communally held peat banks where fuel can be cut for free, except for the labour involved.

ARMADALE. Just as members of the Macleod clan head for Dunvegan, members of the Clan Donald head for Armadale, in the southeast of the Island. Here the award winning **Clan Donald Centre** is set in 40 acres of restored 19th century exotic gardens. The story of the Macdonalds and the Lord of the Isles is told in a restored section of the Castle. From Armadale it is possible during the summer to take the ferry to Mallaig.

The Far North

DORNOCH. At the mouth of the Dornoch Firth, this attractive seaside town has miles of excellent and deserted beaches and there is also the famous Royal Dornoch golf course, ranked among the top 12 in the world. **Dornoch Cathedral** dominates the town; dating from 1224 a fire in 1570 left only the tower and its spire unscathed, the rest was roofless. The choir, transepts and nave were restored in the 17th century but major restoration had to wait until 1835 and the sponsorship of the Duchess of Sutherland. Restoration earlier this century, as part of the Cathedral's 700th anniversary celebrations, revealed the beautiful 13th century stonework that had lain behind plaster for centuries.

As well as the Cathedral to admire there is the 16th century **Bishop's Palace**, now a hotel and the **Old Jail**, now a craft centre. Dornoch was also the site of the last witch burning in Scotland in 1722, the poor woman being tarred, feathered and then roasted alive. Just north of the town is **Skelbo Castle**, on the shore of Loch Fleet. Originally built in 1259, it is now a rather dangerous ruin best seen from the roadside. **Loch Fleet** itself is a massive salt water basin at the mouth of the River Fleet, home to seals, ducks, waders and a Scottish Wildlife Trust Reserve.

Next to the beautiful Cathedral in the ancient and charming town of Dornoch is **The Mercat**, a craft shop that has been owned and run by Alice and Elaine Hook for the past three years. They have strong connections with Dornoch as the family has lived there for generations. Indeed, one of the Cathedral's magnificent stained glass windows was donated by the owner's aunt. Situated in the High Street, The Mercat is packed full of interesting crafts and paintings with about 70% of the stock produced locally. There is a lovely collection of knitwear, most of it designed and knitted by one of the owners, often using wool from a mill in the district. They also sew tartan rag dolls and hats and even find time to paint the occasional picture! The original paintings are by local artists; many depict local scenery and come mounted only or completely framed.

The stock is too varied to mention in detail, but I will have a quick go at remembering a few of the things that I noticed. There were handmade leather goods, a wide selection of jewellery including silver and pewter Celtic designs and stained glass, doughcraft, silk scarves and a colourful selection of children's wear.

Open six days a week from 10 am until 5.30 pm, The Mercat is a must for anyone wanting to purchase an original gift that really has been individually created.

The Mercat, 8A High Street, Dornoch Tel: 01862 811180

The Eagle Hotel is situated on the left hand side of the main street into Dornoch, within short walking distance of the Cathedral and approximately half a mile from the famous Royal Dornoch Golf Course. This stone built property was constructed around 1850, but was purchased by the present proprietors in January 1996. They have refurbished the building and succeeded in creating a friendly pub atmosphere. Your resident proprietors, Paul and Irene are both keen golfers and proudly offer you their unique blend of hospitality and attention to detail that ensures your visit will be a memorable one.

The Eagle Hotel

There are nine individual guest rooms, all with en-suite facilities,

413

colour TV, a complimentary tea and coffee tray - and breakfast is served until 10 am. The spacious comfortable lounge bar is the perfect place to enjoy local gossip and the small lounge area is great for relaxing and watching some TV. Home-cooked bar meals are served with fresh local vegetables and salads and are available to non-residents all day. Fresh local haddock dipped in Murphy's Irish stout batter and deep fried to a golden crisp texture sounds like heaven.

If you wish to tour the Highlands and base yourself in Dornoch you can reach the north, east and west coasts in a day. On the other hand, if you are a golfer you can enjoy a wide variety of delightful and uncrowded golf, from classic links to superb inland and upland fairways, which are set against the ever changing backdrop of mountain, sea and sky - truly a golfers paradise.

The Eagle Hotel, Castle Street, Dornoch Tel: 01862 810008

AROUND DORNOCH

GOLSPIE. **Beinn a'Bhragaidh** (Ben Vraggie), which overlooks the village, is crowned by a monument to the 1st Duke of Sutherland and reached by a steep climb from the town. The Big Burn Walk at the north end of the village is well recommended as is a visit to the Orcadian Stone Company's workshops and geological exhibition.

On the outskirts of the Golspie is **Dunrobin Castle**, the ancient seat of the Earls and Dukes of Sutherland. Parts of the Castle date back to the 1200s, although most was built in the 19th century in the style of a French chateau. The Sutherland family have a rather colourful history, full of treachery and intrigue, presiding over many of the Highland clearances of last century amongst many other earlier misdeeds. There are fine gardens to explore and a museum that houses a collection of archaeological remains and hunting trophies from the world over. The Castle has one of the most exclusive railway halts in Scotland. Rustic **Dunrobin Castle Station** was built as a private stop and last regularly used in the 1960s. Though it no longer appears in the timetable during the summer British Rail organises excursion trains from Inverness.

HELMSDALE stands on one of the great salmon rivers of the north and the village owes its origin to the herring boom of the last century. Boats still land fish here but the boom days are sadly gone. Surrounded by steep hillsides and crofts it also has a rocky shoreline where fossils and gemstones have been discovered. Helmsdale is also home to **Timespan**, which uses the latest in audio-visual technology to tell the dramatic story of the Highlands. A short drive up the Strath of Kildonan leads to Baille an Or and Suisgill, scenes of the Sutherland gold rush of 1869.

North of Helmsdale the A9 climbs to the **Ord of Caithness**, 1300 feet above the nearby sea. From this high point there are wonderful views north to the Caithness coastline, south over east Sutherland and, on a clear day, across the Firth to the Moray coast and the Grampian Highlands beyond.

A little north at **Ousdale** a footpath leads from a lay-by to the ruined crofts of Badbea, perched above the cliffs. This lonely settlement was founded by tenants evicted from the inland straths during the infamous Clearances. Tradition has it that the livestock and children of the village had to be tethered to prevent them being blown over the cliffs.

LAIRG. Situated at the southern end of Loch Shin, Lairg is at the centre of Sutherland's road network. The Lairg lamb sales are the biggest one-day sales in Europe, a reflection on the importance of sheep farming in the north to this day. Not far from the village are the picturesque Falls of Shin. The water crashes through a rock gorge that is famous for its leaping salmon. Also nearby is **Carbisdale Castle**, Scotland's most impressive Youth Hostel. Overlooking the Kyle of Sutherland it was commissioned by the Dowager Duchess of Sutherland and completed in 1914, two years after her death, and was gifted to the Scottish Youth Hostel Association in 1945.

BONAR BRIDGE. The town lies near a bridge spanning the channel that links the head of Dornoch Firth with the loch known as the Kyle of Sutherland. Originally built in 1812 by Thomas Telford, the bridge was rebuilt in 1892 after a flood.

WICK was once the busiest herring port in Europe, and today there is plenty to see in this friendly town. The award winning **Wick Heritage Centre** includes a cooperage, blacksmith's shop, kippering kilns and an outstanding collection of photographs. Wick has its fair share of castles too. **Oldwick Castle**, to the south of the town, is one of the earliest stone castles in Scotland and there are also the three castles of **Sinclair's Bay** nearby. **Girnigoe** and its once Siamese twin **Sinclair** stand together, clinging on to the cliff edge above the southern end of the bay. One time strongholds of the Earls of Caithness, Girnigoe is the older, dating from the end of the 15th century, and Sinclair was built in 1606. Attacked by a force from Keiss in 1679 both were abandoned and within 20 years were ruins. At the northern end of the bay stands the third castle, **Keiss**. As with its southerly brothers it is built on a rocky promontory in typical Caithness style defending against attack from land or sea. Another fortress of the Sinclairs, they abandoned it, in 1755, for Keiss House and it is now a sorry if impressive ruin.

At the end of the 17th century, when Campbell attempted to take land he thought was his from the unwilling Sinclairs, he deliberately let a shipment of whisky go aground near Wick. The Sinclairs found the ship and spent the night drinking the cargo. The next day, suffering from hangovers, the Sinclairs were unable to put up much of a fight against Campbell. However, the story is discredited locally since a single cargo could never have affected Caithnessmen so badly!

DUNBEATH. The **Dunbeath Heritage Centre** has interesting displays on the natural and social history of the area and a fine audio-visual presentation. The village is the birthplace of the author Neil Gunn, the surrounding area and its people providing this renowned Highland storyteller with the inspiration for many of his tales. A mile north of the village is **Lhaidhay Croft Museum**, an original longhouse dating from around 1842 which contains many examples of implements and furniture used by 19th century crofters.

LYBSTER. This village boasts a fine harbour and an interesting Celtic Cross, now protected from the elements with a cover, standing on the south side of the churchyard. Just north of the village a minor road leads to the Neolithic **Grey Cairns of Camster**, chambered burial cairns dating back to the 2nd and 3rd millennia BC. North of the village, near Halberry Head, is further evidence of ancient civilization in the area. At the **Hill O'Many Stones**, early Bronze Age stone rows in an array of 22 rows, with an average eight stones each, can be seen.

ULBSTER. The **Cairn of Get**, which measures over 80 feet in length and nearly 50 feet wide, lies opposite the **Whaligoe Steps**, which descend the spectacular cliffs to a small harbour where boats used to land their catches. In the middle of the last century over 150 fishermen lived on the cliff tops and the womenfolk would climb the 300 steps from the harbour with the full herring-baskets and then walk the six miles to the fishmarket at Wick. The harbour is long abandoned but the steps have been repaired, though they can be precarious in wet and windy weather.

AUCKENGILL. The **Northlands Viking Centre**, previously called the John Nicolson Museum, has displays telling the archaeological history of Caithness, concentrating on the unique Iron Age brochs of the county, and on John Nicolson, a Victorian antiquarian. Of special interest is a 4000 year old beaker which would have contained food or drink to sustain the dead person on his or her journey to the afterlife.

JOHN O'GROATS. This is not, as is often supposed, the northernmost part on the mainland of Britain (that is Dunnet Head), it is though the opposite of Cornwall's Lands End, some 876 miles away. This scattered village, overlooking the Pentland Firth, is named after a Dutchman, John de Groot, who settled here in around 1500. Legend has it that the Dutchman, who ran the Orkney ferry, had eight sons who cared so much about precedence that John built an octagonal house, with eight doors and containing an eight-sided table. Then, each son could enter by his own door and sit at the head of the table. The site of the house is marked by a mound and a flagpole.

DUNCANSBY HEAD. The lighthouse on Duncansby Head commands a fine view of Orkney, the Pentland Skerries and the headlands of the east coast. A little to the south are the three Duncansby Stacks, huge stone 'needles' in the sea. The high sandstone cliffs are severed by great deep gashes running inland, one of which is bridged by a natural arch. Seabirds wheel between the rock faces and the seals sunbathing far below. Though much of Caithness is relatively flat much of the county is still hundreds of feet above sea level.

MEY. The **Castle of Mey** in the village of the same name is Queen Elizabeth, the Queen Mother's holiday home. The Royal Gallery in the Castle Arms Hotel has a unique collection of photographs of the Queen Mother and the Royal family in Caithness. The locals would have visitors believe that she has been known to pop in for a drink when holidaying at the Castle. Once known as Barrogill Castle, the Castle of Mey has its very own ghost. Legend has it that the daughter of the 5th Earl of Caithness fell in love with a ploughman. Imprisoned by her father in the tower, one of the windows in her room was bricked up so that she would not see the man at work. The unhappy girl threw herself out of another window. Known as the Green Lady, the girl is said to drift around the Castle to this day.

DUNNET HEAD. This is the most northerly point on the mainland of Britain but, unlike its pretender to the east, it is not as well remembered. From here it is nearer to the Arctic Circle than London. Above the lighthouse, amongst the remains of the wartime radar station, is a viewfinder table. This identifies the far distant mountains of Ben Loyal and Ben Hope, visible on a clear day, the Old Man of Hoy off Orkney, and the other landmarks around. It is also an excellent place to watch the ships in the busy shipping lanes of the Pentland Firth.

THURSO. Dating back to Viking times, the entrance to Thurso is guarded by the bizarre **Thurso Castle Lodge**. It is a wild piece of Gothic architecture, a folly if ever there was one, with over-sized battlements and towers and a top heavy gateway that looks set to topple in the slightest breeze. The town itself has an excellent **Heritage Museum**, amongst the exhibits are a reconstruction of a crofter's kitchen, a runic cross discovered at St Peter's Kirk and a collection of the plant and fossil specimens gathered by the 19th century naturalist, Robert Dick.

Old **St Peter's Kirk** itself is situated down near the harbour, in the now restored old town and some of its ruins date as far back as the 12th century. The **Meadow Well** stands nearby; it was once the main water supply for the town and is now covered by an unusual round building. On the western edge of the town is Pennyland Farm, the birthplace of Sir William Smith, the founder of the Boys' Brigade.

On the banks of Thurso River grows a rare grass, known as Holy Grass. How it comes to be growing here is put down to an old local story. The plant was so named because it used to be strewn before the doors of some Continental churches and it is said that the floor of the chapel which once stood here was covered with Holy Grass cut in Norway. The church floor was damp and the seeds in the grass began to take root and grow.

DOUNREAY. The Atomic Energy Authority's Dounreay site houses Britain's oldest nuclear reactor, built in 1955. It is to be closed, part of the move away from nuclear power, but in the meantime visitors can discover all about atomic energy in a free exhibition and in the afternoons everyone over the age of 12 can join a guide tour around the reactor.

MELVICH. Lying at the mouth of the River Halladale, which drains much of Sutherland's interior, the village has a beautiful beach surrounded by massive cliffs. Nearby is the **Split Stone**: legend has it the Devil split the rock in a fit of temper, having chased an old woman round and round it.

BETTYHILL. One of north Sutherland's biggest villages, Bettyhill was named after Elizabeth, 1st Duchess of Sutherland. It is a crofting community situated beside the striking Farr Beach and, as with many coastal settlements, it owes its existence to the notorious Highland Clearances of the last century. The history of those troubled times is well told in **Strathnaver Museum** in the village. To the south of Bettyhill is a witness of the clearances, **Achanlochy** village, now just bare outlines in the turf.

The story of the Clearances is very sad; greed overcoming the traditions of the Highlands. The clans had lived happily in settlements like Achanlochy for centuries. Their chief was the clan 'father' responsible for administering justice, receiving no rent but able to rely upon the young men to serve him in times of trouble. Culloden changed everything. Lands were handed over to loyal chiefs, who lost most of their powers and simply became landlords. The rents that their new tenants could raise were not enough though, to maintain their new lifestyles.

An easier means of raising the money to live in comfort did appear; the Cheviot sheep, which was hardy enough to withstand the winters and gave better quantities of quality meat and wool. The draw back was that they needed the land the clansmen lived on. With their new found position in society to maintain many chiefs turned their backs on the clans, ignoring their ancient obligations to look after them in times of hardship and simply evicting them to make way for the sheep. The people left passively, bewildered and unable to understand why their protectors would cause them such misery, sent to poor coastal lands or forcibly emigrated to America.

The single largest land owner in the area was Lord Stafford, later 1st Duke of Sutherland. He was English and his wife had inherited the chieftainship of the people of Sutherland. In his name the factors (Scottish land agents) organized clearances with increasing ruthlessness and brutality. Many thousands were displaced between 1800 and 1841. Even as late as 1853 Mrs MacDonell, widow of the 16th chief of Glengarry, oversaw the burning of her people's cottages, a ship standing by to take them to America. Those who resisted were left without shelter to die in the hills. It wasn't until the 1880s that laws were introduced to put a stop to the Clearances.

TONGUE. Standing above the Kyle of Tongue, in the centre of Sutherland's north coast, the village has a fine church with a laird's loft, or private gallery, and close by are the ruins of **Caistail Bharraich (Castle Varrich)**, a MacKay stronghold that may date back to Viking times. The village also boasts what is possibly the world's most northerly palm tree, a reflection on the mild weather the coast enjoys. The Kyle itself is crossed by a long causeway that offers panoramic views of Ben Loyal and Ben Hope.

ULLAPOOL. In all the 140 miles of coast between Thurso and Fort William there is only one other town, Ullapool. Today the main port for the Northern Hebrides, it is the focal point for the sparse and wide spread communities of Wester Ross and was purpose-built as a fishing centre in 1788 by the British Fishery Society to a plan by Thomas Telford. Now a major tourist centre it still retains a real frontier town feel, specially during the autumn fishing season, when Loch Broom is full of fish factory ships from Eastern Europe and the streets ring with strange tongues from faraway places. The town has a fine hostelry, the **Ferry Boat Inn**, which stands on waterfront. As well as offering meals and bed and breakfast, for the real ale enthusiast it offers hand-pulled ales, very much a rare commodity in the Highlands. Directly across Loch Broom is the Altnaharrie Hotel, which is only accessible by private launch from Ullapool and has an international reputation for its cuisine.

Only a few minute drive out of the town, on the A835, is the **Leckmelm Shrubbery and Arboretum**. This ten acre arboretum and two and a half acre walled garden was originally laid out in the 1870s. It lay unattended for 45 years until 1985 and is now gradually being restored. A few miles further along the road is **Corrieshalloch Gorge**, one of the most accessible spectacular sights in this area of the Highlands. A mile long, many rare plants cling to the side of out of harms, and the sheep's, way. The **Falls of Measach** tumble 150 feet into the gorge and the best viewpoint is from the Victorian suspension bridge which dangles over the falls. Not for the vertigo sufferer, the bridge has a sign recommending that no more than two people go on it at a time!

AROUND ULLAPOOL

SUMMER ISLES. Across Badentarbat Bay are the Summer Isles. The biggest, **Tanera Mor**, has been busy for a 1000 years and more. The Anchorage, a sheltered bay, has been used since Viking times; they called the island Hawrarymoir - the island of the Haven. Cruises from Ullapool tour the islands, seeking the seabird colonies and seals, and boats cross from Achiltibuie. It is even possible for the fully equipped camper to stay on the island.

ACHILTIBUIE. Inverpolly has few settlements and the largest is Achiltibuie, reached by the winding road that passes right beneath Stac

Stac Pollaidh, Inverpolly

Pollaidh and through the empty Coigach mountains. Here is one of the most unusual hidden places of Scotland, **The Hydroponicum**. Robert Irvine built this prophetic 'garden of the future'; a garden without soil. With its three distinct climates - Hampshire, Bordeaux and the Canaries - and the spectacle of strawberries hanging overhead, ripening bananas, passion fruit, lemons, figs, vines, flowers and vegetables growing in the far northwest it is an astounding place. The gift shop stocks special growing kits, so you can have a go yourself. Food of a different and more traditional kind is on offer at The Smokehouse. Discover the secrets of smoking and curing of salmon, fish, meat and game at this purpose built smokery, with its viewing gallery and well stocked shop, that has a mail-order service.

LOCHINVER. A major herring port since the 17th century, Lochinver is now the largest village in west Sutherland and investment in recent years has seen the construction of a new quay and the port is, together with Kinlochbervie and Ullapool, a major white and shell fish centre. The twisting narrow road to the south demands the driver's complete attention, so undoubtedly the best way to enjoy the glorious scenery is to get out into it on foot.

INCHNADAMPH. At the eastern end of Loch Assynt is Inchnadamph and its hotel, which still sells petrol as once did many of the roadside resting places of the Highlands years ago.

ELPHIN. Children will love the **Scottish Farm Animals Visitors Centre** where they can meet many of the traditional breeds of Scottish farm animals, including the seaweed-eating Soay sheep, hairy Highland cattle and 30 other breeds. Almost next door is Knockan and its spectacular cliff. **The Cliff Visitors Centre** offers two very different trails along and up the cliff, one looking at flora and the other at the local geology.

The land between Loch Inver and Loch Broom is a remote and almost uninhabited area of bog, moorland, woodland, cliffs and towering summits. A desolate but beautiful wilderness. At its heart is the **Inverpolly Nature Reserve**, home to many rare plants and animals. The coastline is a shambolic riot of lochs and tiny islands, the work of the last Ice Age, some 10,000 years ago. The area is as much water as land, over 300 lochs and lochans scattered amongst the magnificent mountains. Described by renown Scottish writer Jim Crumley, as 'a glimpse into Valhalla'.

KYLESKU. In this landscape of old rock the idea of a concrete bridge blending in seems highly improbable and yet the bridge that takes the A894 across the lochs at Kylesku achieves just that. A graceful design, it has won many awards since being opened by the Queen in the mid 1980s when it replaced one of the few mainland-to-mainland ferries left in Britain. There is a lay-by next to the northern end of the bridge which offers an ideal spot to pause and take in the view of the bridge and beyond. In one corner of the lay-by there is a Memorial Cairn, erected in 1993, to commemorate the men of the XIIth Submarine Flottila who gave their lives in action. The top secret midget submarine flotilla trained in the local waters and perhaps their best remembered feat was to seriously damage the German Battleship Tirpitz in a Norwegian fjord.

From Kylesku village pleasure boats take visitors up the lochs to see the seal colonies and **Eas Coul Aulin**, Britain's highest waterfall with a drop of 658 feet. It is possible to reach them on foot but be prepared for a walk that will take half a day. Back in the village there is a little inn well worth finding.

SCOURIE.
A picturesque crofting community with a safe bathing beach in the bay, keen fishermen may like to pause here as Scourie is at the heart of a famous Brown Trout fishing area. The village also has a notable war memorial; it is a sad fact that even the smallest and most remote communities in these Highlands and Islands have need of a memorial to the war dead. Scourie's is a fine example, its 17 names guarded over by a kilted soldier.

HANDA ISLAND.
To the north of Scourie Bay is Handa Island. Until as recently as the first half of the 19th century the 12 families that inhabited the Island upheld the eldest widow as their leader, the Queen of Handa. They survived on the numerous seabirds, providing meat, eggs and feathers, which they bartered for wool. On the northern coast is **The Great Stack**, an isolated pillar in a U-shaped inlet. The bird-catchers reached its flat grassy top by rope - going hand over hand 300 feet above the waves! The only inhabitants today are the Scottish Wildlife Trust warden and the thousands of puffins, fulmars, shags, gulls, kitti-wakes, skuas and auks. Day trips to this 'twitchers' paradise can be arranged with local fishermen in Scourie and nearby Tarbet. RSPB members can stay a little longer as the island has a well-equipped bothy accommodation available to them.

LAXFORD BRIDGE.
One of few road junctions in this area, the traveller has a choice of returning southeast passed Loch Shin towards Lairg and Dornoch; going right up to the north coast; or travelling down the west coast. To the west of Laxford Bridge are the two white mountains of Arkle and Foinaven. **Arkle** is build like a rampart, a brutal pile of a mountain. Directly across the glen is **Ben Stack**, a total contrast, with its tall spire of a peak, looking just as a mountain should look. At **Achfary**, beneath the Ben, is Britain's only black and white telephone box. Achfary Estate have been given special permission by British Telecom to paint the local kiosk in keeping with the estate's colour scheme.

KINLOCHBERVIE.
Lying at the mouth of Loch Inchard, Kinlochbervie is the most northwesterly of the mainlands great white-fish landing ports. It is worth the detour to see the fish being landed and the boats tied up at the jetty alone, but what is more amazing is the sight

of the huge articulated lorries that collect the fish. The road to the village from the south is a typical Highland single track road, narrow, twisting and full of brows. It must take skill and great patience to guide these leviathans of the highway safely. To the west of the village are the crofting townships of Oldshoremore, Oldshorebeg and Sheigra, which have beautiful sandy beaches and wonderful opportunities for pleasant walks. It is another five miles on foot to the spectacular **Sandwood Bay** and its sea stack, possibly Britain's remotest beach, but worth the effort.

CAPE WRATH is only accessible by the small, summer only, passenger ferry across the Kyle of Durness. One of the loneliest roads in Europe it is then 11 miles by mini-bus to this the northwestern tip of the British mainland. Even on a clear bright day it is easy to imagine that the Cape is more than capable of living up to its foreboding name. The lighthouse here was built in 1827 and on a clear day Orkney to the east and Lewis to the west are visible. To the south of the Cape the **Clo More Cliffs** reach up 920 feet and, teeming with seabirds, they are the highest mainland cliffs in Britain. Much of the wild moorland inland is used as an army firing range.

BALNAKEIL. The remains of the village's 17th century church, which has a monument to Rob Donn, a famous Celtic bard, still stand here. **Balnakeil Craft Village** is housed in buildings that were once a Cold War early warning station, and visitors are welcome to watch the wide variety of crafts being made. On nearby Balnakeil Beach the grave of a Viking warrior was recently discovered.

To the north is Faraid Head, noted for its cliffs and seabirds and, to the east, is **Smoo Cave**, three vast caverns at the end of a deep cleft in the limestone cliffs with waterfall. The entrance to the first resembles a Gothic arch and the second can be viewed from a platform. A boat is needed to enter the third chamber and see the 80 foot waterfall. For information about trips enquire at Durness Tourist Office.

DURNESS. Rather than a compact village, Durness is a number of scattered settlements and is the most northerly settlement on the British mainland.

ALTNAHARRA. This tiny settlement sits in the heart of Sutherland, in the true wilderness of the Flow Country. This type of wetland country is rare in world terms and anyone passing through the area cannot help but be impressed with the scale of it all.

Highland Cattle

CHAPTER TWELVE

THE ISLANDS

Uig Chessmen

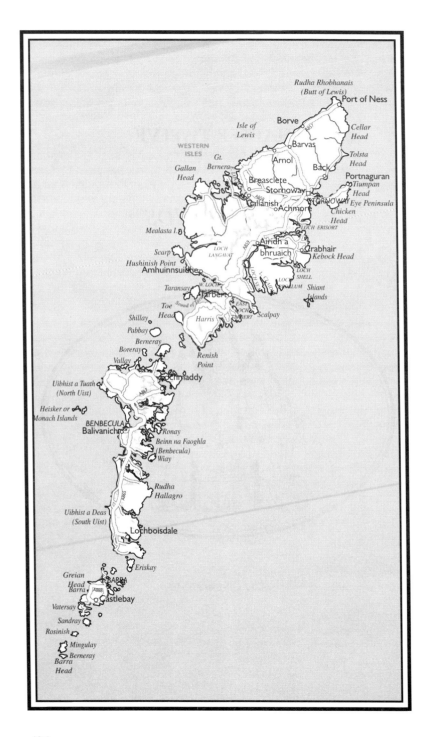

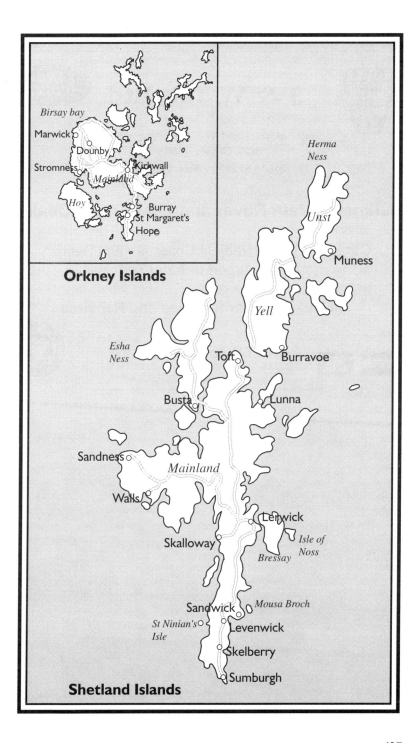

Orkney Islands

Birsay bay

Marwick

Dounby

Stromness

Mainland

Kirkwall

Hoy

Burray

St Margaret's

Hope

Shetland Islands

Herma Ness

Unst

Muness

Yell

Burravoe

Esha Ness

Toft

Busta

Lunna

Sandness

Mainland

Walls

Lerwick

Isle of Noss

Skalloway

Bressay

Sandwick

Mousa Broch

St Ninian's Isle

Levenwick

Skelberry

Sumburgh

CHAPTER TWELVE

THE ISLANDS

Orkney Islands

The Orkney and Shetland Archipelagos were governed by The Norse for some 400 years. It was not until 1468 that the Islands were ceded to Scotland as part of a marriage settlement. The Norse influence has remained strong and today the local accent is still as much Scandinavian as anything else. Many of the place names are pure Norse and, as late as the last century, the ancient Norse language of Norn was still in use on Shetland. The Orcadias and Shetlanders are a very independent folk, both seeing the Scots as being as foreign as the English.

The Orkney group of islands and islets numbers, in total, 70 of which some 17 are inhabited. By far the largest is called Mainland and, with Kirkwall as its capital, it is some 20 miles long. Inhabited for some 5000 years, the Islands have Northern Europe's greatest concentration of prehistoric monuments including burial cairns, chambered tombs ad stone circles.

Whaling and fishing have been the most important industry of the Islands and the Orcadians were, at one time, recruited by the Canadian Hudson's Bay Company. Today, the oil industry provides much of the employment and during both world wars the Scapa Flow naval base brought prosperity. The flat and treeless but fertile land provides an abundance of wildflowers in the summer and along with magnificent coastal scenery, the towering cliffs support a huge bird population during the breeding season.

KIRKWALL is the capital of Orkney (never 'the Orkneys') and the ferry to Shetland docks here. The town is most famous for its great **Cathedral of St Magnus**, founded in 1127. At the time of the Reformation the protestations of the people of Kirkwall saved it from destruction. In 1911, a skull and some bones were found concealed in one of the Cathedral's pillars. The skill was cleft as if by an axe; exactly the way Magnus was said to have met his death in around 1117. A mere 100 yards away is **Earl Patrick's Palace** which has been described as one of the finest pieces of Renaissance architecture left in Scotland. Built in 1607, by the tyrannical Earl Patrick Stewart, it is a fine looking ruin and must have looked magnificent in all its glory.

To the south of the town is the **Highland Park Distillery** which dates from 1798 and welcomes visitors to tour the distillery, taste the whisky and take a look round the Visitor Centre and shop.

To the northwest of Kirkwall, on the road to Finstown, is **Rennibister Earth-house**. Discovered in 1926, when a tractor fell through its roof, this is a particularly fine example of an earth-house and there were several human skulls and bones found here.

There are two crofts lying about seven miles apart in the open countryside of Orkney, the first of these is **Kirbuster Farm and Folk Museum**. Lying close to a small loch, Kirbuster, in its day, was one of the more substantial farmhouses of its kind. The visitor enters through a room now used for showing the construction and history of the farmhouse, which then leads into the oldest part of the building, the heart of the museum and the prime reason for Tankerness House in Kirkwall to have acquired the croft. This part is the last surviving example of the old firehooses, as they were called. Here were the living quarters for the family and for some of the animals. The date 1723 on an old re-used lintel may be the date of this building but a parish record of 1595 already refers to a firehoose on this site. This is what the Orkney firehooses looked like until the early 19th century and when you go there, you are likely to find a peat fire burning, an essential ingredient in what it felt like, and smelt like, too.

A particular feature of Orkney houses was the roof made of Orkney stone flags, used like slates as they were plentiful and split readily into even layers. A good deal of the smoke from the fire finds its way out eventually, and used to pass across meat and fish hung in the roof space for smoking. Kirbuster Farm was only taken over in 1986 and although it was still lived in until 1961, a great deal of restoration work remains to be done. Apart from later additions to the buildings there is a round kiln typical of Orkney, which is very beautiful to look at inside. Also a vivid reminder of the self-sufficiency that was required of these crofts is a diminutive smithy behind the pig sty. Visitors are likely to find a pig as well as other animals in residence when they come and the caretaker is herself a mine of first-hand information about the way of life on their crofts.

Both Kirbuster and Corrigall Farm and Folk Museums are administered from Tankerness House in Kirkwall and admission is by a common entrance ticket. What the visitor sees at **Corrigall Farm and Folk Museum** is a later development from around the middle of the 19th century. The living quarters with the kiln at one end and the single building serving as byre and barn were built parallel to each other with a flagged passageway six feet wide in between. The byre preserves its flagged floor and the stone stalls for cattle. The family living area known as the 'in-bye' has a regular hearth and is separated from the 'oot-bye', which is the fireback, with another room for box beds beyond. On the far side of the oot-bye was the byre, the cattle coming in through the same door as the family. This was later converted for use as the best parlour or to sleep a farm servant and is now used for museum display, including an 18th century loom.

The nearby barn has a kiln of the circular type not uncommon in Orkney. Information bats are provided in both crofts and are designed to be held in the hand, elegantly hand-written with simple drawings to help identify objects, and the objects are introduced in an order that makes an understanding of their functions in the life of the croft easy to follow: for instance things used in brewing the 'platting tub' in which a pig was scalded after it was killed to remove the bristles, or the 'klibber', a wooden pack saddle with straw panniers for carrying peat on the horse.

The **Tankerness House Museum** is a fine 16th century town house standing in its own courtyard opposite St Magnus' Cathedral, with an ornamental garden behind. It was considerably altered and enlarged in the early part of the 18th century and was lived in by the Baikies, a distinguished Orkney family. It was fully restored in 1968. The Museum is the headquarters of the historical museums in Orkney, since Corrigall and Kirbuster are branch museums, and Stromness Museum, although run by an independent trust, also relies on the services of the curator in Kirkwall.

The most recently arranged display is on the ground floor, opened in 1985. Called 'The First Settlers', it aims to tell the story of the Neolithic and Bronze Ages in Orkney, that is the story of the settlers from 5000 years ago. The way it is told is unusual; the plan of the exhibition is intelligently thought out and the presentation is clear, although in places visually unattractive. Visitors are appealed to directly to think for themselves what it was like being the first people to settle on the island: what could be found to eat, or for shelter, or for making dwellings or clothes. The section on ritual, the area about which we want to know most, but know least, is very good. Among the artifacts is the Neolithic stone from Westray and its strangely beautiful design of spirals, which is perhaps the finest of its kind found in the UK. There is also an account of the chambered tomb, the 'Tomb of the Eagles', excavated at Isbister. This is accompanied by an impressive array of skulls and bones set out to give an impression of the remains of over 300 early settlers that were found there. And finally there is a display showing the ancient monuments that are to be seen in Orkney.

The **Stromness Museum** is administered by the Orkney Natural History Society, and this gives the clue to its origins and original purpose. The Society was founded in 1837, with the object of promoting natural science and collecting specimens of natural history and antiquities in Orkney. One of the early members was the geologist Hugh Miller, and among the fossils in the Museum is his so-called petrified nail, or more properly the Homosteus milleri, which he found in 1843 and gave to the museum. The building itself was put up in 1858 to house the Museum on the upper floor and the Stromness Town Hall below. In 1929 it was taken over entirely by the Museum. The first floor is devoted to the natural history of Orkney. This is perhaps more valuable to the tourist than in many places, for even a townsman cannot spend long on the island without becoming curious about its wildlife, the birds in particular: the fulmars, puffins and cormorants, and the osprey and the golden eagle are both occasional visitors. There are also specimens of the rocks found on the Islands and a group of fossil fish, a number of them found in the Stromness flagstones. There are models of boats, including the Orkney version of the yole. Relics salvaged from wrecks, like the 'Svecia' of 1740 which was being dredged from 1975 and are now on full display.

The Stromness Museum

There is the terrible history of Eliza Fraser who was ship-wrecked on the Great Barrier Reef to see her husband the ship's captain murdered whilst she herself was enslaved by the Aborigines until her rescue in 1836. Another display concerns Arctic explorers. One of them, Sir John Franklin (1786-1847), sought a passage to the Pacific via the Arctic, the North West Passage that had been sought for so long, but his ship disappeared after leaving via Stromness for the Arctic in 1846. Finally eight years later Dr John Rae (1813-93) led the expedition that finally discovered what happened to Franklin, you will have to visit this wonderful Museum to find out for yourself.

Orkney Island Council, Tankerness House Museum, Broad Street, Kirkwall
Tel: 01856 873191

The delightful **Trenabies Café** is situated in the heart of old Kirkwall, midway between the harbour and St Magnus' Cathedral. This exceptionally pleasant café and eating place occupies a handsome 18th century building which was once the residence of the local tax collector, the keyholder of the King's Girnel. It first became a restaurant in the 1900s and, in 1990, was acquired by its present owners, Elma and Alex Mair, two very welcoming hosts who believe in providing good food, friendly service and excellent value for money. The atmosphere is lively and informal, with timber tables and chairs, cheerful tablecloths, tasteful decoration and unobtrusive background music. The wide-ranging menu contains an excellent choice of light meals and snacks, including freshly made pizzas, baked potatoes and toasted sandwiches. It also offers a marvellous all-day breakfast and an appetising selection of home-made cakes, pastries and delicious Orkney ice cream. Drinks include genuine espresso and cappuccino coffee, as well as a range of soft drinks, teas and herbal infusions. Trenabies Café is open seven days a week until 6 pm, opening at 8 am on Mondays to Fridays, 9 am on Saturdays and 10 am on Sundays.

Trenabies Café, 16 Albert Street, Kirkwall Tel: 01856 874336

The **West End Hotel** is situated in Main Street, Kirkwall within five minutes walking distance of the town centre and the 12th century Viking Cathedral of St Magnus. This impressive family run establishment is housed in an imposing Georgian residence which served as Orkney's first hospital between 1845 and 1926. In recent years, it has undergone a complete refurbishment and is now Scottish Tourist Board 3 Crown Commended.

West End Hotel

The West End Hotel has ten comfortable guest bedrooms in the main building and six in the annexe, all beautifully appointed and equipped with en-suite shower-rooms, colour TVs, direct dial telephones and tea and coffee making facilities. The West End is owned and personally run by Jimmy and Isobel Currie, excellent hosts who create a friendly and homely atmosphere throughout the Hotel. The lounge bar is popular with visitors and locals alike and there is also a pleasant dining room which serves the finest Orkney cuisine using fresh local ingredients wherever possible. First-rate meals are also served at lunchtimes and in the evening in the lounge bar; on the day we visited, main courses included Orkney salmon steak cooked in Highland Park whisky and orange butter, char-grilled steaks and vegetarian dishes.

West End Hotel, Main Street, Kirkwall Tel: 01856 872368
Fax: 01856 876181

The **Lynnfield Hotel** is an impressive family run establishment lying in its own secluded grounds within easy walking distance of Kirkwall town centre. The Hotel adjoins Highland Park, home of the famous whisky distillery around which visitors can take a guided tour. Originally constructed to house the distillery manager, the Hotel's extensive garden contains a tennis court, children's play area and large private car park. The ten centrally heated guest bedrooms all have private en-suite bathrooms, colour televisions, radio-alarms and tea and coffee making facilities; two rooms are fitted with four-poster beds and several also have panoramic views over Scapa Bay. The dining room is renowned for its seafood and steaks and also enjoys a fine view over the bay and nearby Wideford Hill. With its open log fire and oak panelling, the lounge bar is the perfect place to spend a relaxing few hour, and there is also a second bar for that pre-lunch or dinner drink. Proprietor George Currie is a very welcoming and able host who does everything in his power to ensure his guests have an enjoyable stay. He offers the finest hospitality and is happy to organise fishing trips and tours around the Islands for his guests.

Lynnfield Hotel, Holm Road, Kirkwall Tel: 01856 872505

Those looking for a store with an outstanding range of Orkney food products under one roof should make a point of finding **Cumming and Spence** in Albert Street, Kirkwall. Founded in 1885, this long established traditional grocery shop stocks a mouth-watering variety of items from the Islands, including famous Orkney cheese, butter, herrings, oatcakes, shortbread and fudge. The store has a delightful old fashioned feel which is very appealing to visitors more used to battling their way around the supermarket on Saturday afternoon. Fresh bread and bakery products are made on the premises each day, along with hot soup and fresh sandwiches, and there is also a good selection of vegetarian and delicatessen products on offer. Cumming and Spence offer a free delivery service throughout Kirkwall and specialise in supplying pleasure boats and working vessels putting in at the harbour, as well as visitors staying in the area in self-catering accommodation. Visiting crews and new arrivals should telephone for further details. The store is part of Scarth Orkney Ltd, a long established group of businesses led by Tom Laird which has wide ranging interests, encompassing retailing, wholesaling, engineering and vehicle hire.

*Cumming and Spence, 17 Albert Street, Kirkwall Tel: 01856 872034
Fax: 01856 872750*

The handsome **St Ola Hotel** is set in the heart of old Kirkwall along its recently revitalised harbour front. Popular with business people in winter and holidaymakers in summer, this pleasant family run Hotel is Scottish Tourist Board 3 Crowns Commended. The six guest bedrooms are all spacious and well appointed, with full en-suite facilities, colour televisions, direct dial telephones, radio alarms, hair dryers, trouser presses and ironing boards; two also have magnificent views over the boat-filled harbour. The central heating, mellow wood furniture and continental quilts help to create an atmosphere which is warm and comfortable. The hotel is owned and personally run by Vina and Smith Foubister, two very welcoming hosts who provide the finest Orkney hospitality.

The St Ola also has two ground floor bars overlooking the harbour area which are popular with visitors and locals alike. The smaller, with its traditional wood panelling, comfortable seating and lively atmosphere, tends to be frequented by younger people, especially at weekends. The larger, with its open fire in winter, dart boards and fine collection of nautical photographs, is a traditional seafaring pub which attracts a colourful clientele from all walks of life. Here, the atmosphere is enhanced by a number of unusual fittings, including a large propeller hanging from the ceiling, a row of wooden barrels behind the bar, and a giant 7 foot by 4 foot mirror on the wall. The ferry terminals for the islands of Shapinsay, Stronsay, Eday, Sanday and Westray lie within two minutes' walk of the Hotel, and buses connecting with the ferries from Houton and Tingwall leave from just around the corner. Kirkwall Airport is only a short distance away by taxi and air services from here connect with the Outer Isles, Shetland and the Scottish mainland. Coach tours leave regularly from the nearby terminus for Orkney's many wildlife reserves and archeological sites, or for those seeking peace and tranquillity, there is some attractive walking within easy reach. The surrounding countryside holds many attractions for the more seasoned outdoor enthusiast, including hill and coastal walking, trout and sea fishing, or diving on the wrecks of the old German battleships that were scuttled in Scapa Flow at the end of the First World War. The St Ola Hotel is open all year round and welcomes all major credit cards.

St Ola Hotel, Harbour Street, Kirkwall Tel & Fax: 01856 875090

Vina and Smith Foubister, proprietors of the St Ola Hotel, also own and personally run the **Queens Hotel**, another fine establishment on Kirkwall's lively waterfront. Situated within a 100 yards of its sister hotel, the Queens is an imposing Victorian structure which looks out over the bustling lights of the port. Its nine brightly furnished guest bedrooms all have private en-suite bathrooms, radio alarms, colour TVs, direct dial telephones, trouser presses, hair dryers and ironing boards; some also have lovely views over the harbour. There is also a television lounge for guests and a separate residents' breakfast room which sometimes doubles as a function room.

However, the Queens is perhaps best known as a first-class eating place. Its Buckingham Restaurant has an enviable reputation for serving the finest home-cooked cuisine in an atmosphere which is comfortable and stylish. The surroundings are tastefully decorated in blue and enhanced with soft lighting and arrangements of dried flowers. Wherever possible, the chef uses fresh Orkney ingredients, most notably fish, seafood, vegetables and cheese. On the evening we visited, the wide-ranging menu included starters such as crab mousse, deep-fried Orkney cheese, and marinated herring rolled in oatmeal and served with a seaweed dip. Main courses featured beef stroganoff, duck glazed with a plum and rhubarb sauce, and a choice of steaks, including Highland steak topped with haggis and served with a creamy whisky sauce. There was also a special vegetarian dish, a pasta dish and the 'catch of the day' - fresh fish or seafood brought straight from the harbour-side. Excellent bar lunches and suppers are also served in the hotel's Windsor Lounge, a lively room which has an impressive wooden bar with attractive leaded glass at the back. Here, the menu included starters such as deep-fried spicy coated prawns, and main courses such as chicken and leek lasagne, and for vegetarians, cheese and lentil loaf served on a tomato and tarragon sauce. A mouthwatering selection of desserts included fresh fruit pavlova, along with such traditional specialities as knickerbocker glory and home-made spotted dick served with custard or cream. The Windsor Lounge has a children's certificate and, like the restaurant, is open to non-residents.

Queens Hotel, Shore Street, Kirkwall Tel: 01856 872200
Fax: 01856 873871

With its 44 guest bedrooms, the **Kirkwall Hotel** in Harbour Street, Kirkwall is Orkney's largest hotel. This impressive Victorian structure was purpose-built in 1890 on a superb site overlooking the harbour which was purchased two years before for £1525. In its time, it has been visited by several crown heads of Europe, including the King of Norway and several members of the present British Royal family. As Orkney's premiere hotel, it draws a wide clientele from all over the world who come on business or to enjoy the many natural and historical attractions of this beautiful northern archipelago.

The public rooms of this Scottish Tourist Board 3 Crown Commended Hotel are spacious and elegant. The Tudor lounge bar provides a pleasant setting for a relaxing drink or light meal. It is stocked with an impressive range of real ales and whiskies, and also offers a good selection of dishes, both at lunchtimes and in the evening. Or for those preferring a taste of local colour, the Georgian Bar has an atmosphere brimming with traditional character. With its relaxing pink and brown decoration, the Kirkwall Hotel's spacious air-conditioned restaurant offers top quality cuisine in surroundings which are comfortable and elegant.

Don't forget. !
There is a list of
Tourist Information Centres
at the back of the book.

Kirkwall Hotel

The restaurant overlooks the harbour and diners can look out at the returning fishing boats, knowing that their catch might appear on their plates in just a few hours' time. Fresh local fish and seafood is the speciality of the house, including oysters, crab and lobster when available. On the day we visited, the imaginative à la carte menu included such delicacies as seafood crepe, fresh Orkney scallops, and salmon steak, along with such non-marine specialities as wild Orkney duck, Highland Park steak, noisettes of Orkney lamb and deep-fried Orkney cheese. There was also an appetising selection of desserts, cheeses and special coffees to round off the meal. Thirty-six of the Kirkwall's 44 beautifully appointed guest bedrooms have private bath or shower-rooms en-suite and all have satellite TV, direct dial telephones and tea and coffee making facilities; several also have breathtaking views of the harbour with the Northern Isles beyond. The hotel is also ideally equipped for business customers and offers a choice of suites for confidential meetings or private dining, as well as larger rooms for banqueting and conferences.

The Kirkwall Hotel, Harbour Street, Kirkwall Tel: 01856 872232
Fax: 01856 872812

Anjo and Paddy Casey, proprietors of the Kirkwall Hotel, also own and personally run the **Albert Hotel** in Mounthoolie Lane. Delightfully situated in the heart of old Kirkwall, this friendly family-based Hotel lies within easy reach of the main shops, Cathedral and harbour. Scottish Tourist Board 3 Crown Commended, it has 19 beautifully appointed guest bedrooms, all with private bath or shower-room en-suite, colour television, direct-dial telephone and tea and coffee making facilities. However, it is for its food that the Albert is perhaps most renowned.

The Stables Restaurant has a well deserved reputation for providing the finest Orkney cuisine, using fresh local ingredients, including prime Orkney beef, Gaitnip lamb and seafood from the waters around the Islands. On the evening we called, main courses included halibut steak, whole lemon sole, noisettes of lamb, a choice of steaks, and the speciality of the house, 'Albert's Surf and Turf' - fillet of Orkney beef layered with local scallops and bound in a creamy white wine sauce. There was also a good selection of starters, including crab pancakes, and a mouthwatering range of desserts. The restaurant has a very pleasant atmosphere, with old beams, mellow wooden fittings, hanging baskets, and a part-timbered floor. It is also a proud and enthusiastic member of the Taste of Scotland scheme for promoting and developing Scottish cuisine. Excellent lunches and suppers are also served in the Albert's attractive bars. The surprisingly extensive evening menu included starters such as whitebait and goujons of sole, and main courses such as scallops, seafood kebab, sirloin steak sizzler, and the famous 'Orkney Fondue' - a selection of Orcadian produce served with deep-fried vegetables and an Orkney cheese sauce. The prices represented very good value, and at lunchtimes, children's half portions were available on request.

Albert Hotel

The Bothy Bar has a cosy peat fire and a bright traditional atmosphere. Live music can be heard here at certain times and beers on offer include Raven Ale and Dark Island from the local brewery. Some of the black seawormed beams originated from the galleon Loch Madie which sank in Inganess Bay just outside Kirkwall. Matchmakers is a larger bar with mirrors, high stools and a lively stylish atmosphere. The Albert Hotel is very child friendly, and families are welcome to enjoy a quiet meal together in the lounge bars.

The Albert Hotel, Mounthoolie Lane, Kirkwall Tel: 01856 876000
Fax: 01856 875397

Anyone with an interest in the traditional handicrafts of Orkney will be fascinated by **Robert Towers' Workshop** in St Ola, a mile-and-a-half from Kirkwall on the A964 Orphir road. Robert is a skilled wood-worker who specialises in making Orkney Chairs; these distinctive pieces of furniture are made to a design unique to the Islands which was born out of the local people's need for a simple piece of furniture which they could make for themselves using materials that were readily available.

In its early stages of development, the Orkney Chair was little more than a round stool covered with straw; this evolved into a low chair thanks to the addition of a woven straw back. The next development was the inclusion of a hood, which was probably added to give the occupant shelter from biting winter draughts. Most of these early Orkney Chairs were made on a one-off basis with no two having exactly the same specifications, the shape and dimensions depending instead on the skill and materials the maker had available. During the late Victorian era, an attempt was made to produce standardised chairs on a commercial basis, with the frames and backs being made separately and joined together at a later date. However, this practice led to a poor quality end-product as the makers found it impossible to make the back fit sufficiently tightly onto the ready-made frame.

Since setting up his workshop in 1977, Robert Towers has established a reputation for the finest handiwork. All his chairs are made to traditional designs, with the backs and hoods being woven directly onto a pine or walnut frame. All are fitted with a seagrass seat and have the option of a drawer. Robert's chairs have appeared on numerous occasions in interior design magazines and have proved to be particularly popular in the United States. Indeed, the King and Queen of Norway were presented with a pair in 1995 to commemorate their state visit to Orkney. Robert welcomes visitors and gives demonstrations daily; his workshop is open Monday to Friday, 8.30 am to 1 pm and 2 pm to 5 pm

Robert H Towers, Orkney Chairmaker, Rosegarth House, St Ola, Kirkwall, Tel & Fax: 01856 873521

AROUND KIRKWALL

CLESTRAIN ORPHIR. All that survives of the 11th or 12th century circular church at Orphir is a small apse. Though to have been modelled on the Church of the Holy Sepulchre, it was probably built by a crusader or pilgrim, possibly Earl Haakon who made a pilgrimage to Jerusalem as penance for his murder of Magnus.

Two hundred and fifty years ago, there were three inns at Orphir, one of which is rumoured to have been a house of ill repute. Today, there is only one, the very fine **Scorrabrae Inn** at Scorradale. The present building was constructed in 1982 on a site which has magnificent views over Scapa Flow. It lies within easy reach of the ferry terminal at Houton and the RSPB reserves of Hobbister and Kirbister Loch, making it a welcome haven for travellers, bird-watchers, anglers and walkers. Proprietors Iain and Ingrid Macleod provide a warm welcome for visitors and locals alike. They serve an excellent pint of beer and delicious pub food, including jacket potatoes, burgers, chicken, salmon, salads and vegetarian specials from the chalkboard. They also offer a special children's menu and an appetising range of desserts. Diners can eat in the non-smoking restaurant area or on the pleasant patio at the front of the building. The Inn has a cheerful atmosphere, with bare brick walls and cottage-style furnishings, and there is also a lively games area with a stone floor. Iain and Ingrid also have a limited range of local crafts available for sale.

Scorrabrae Inn, Scorradale, Orphir Tel: 01856 811262

Those looking for exceptional bed and breakfast accommodation within easy reach of the Houton ferry should make a point of finding **Westrow Lodge** at Orphir, midway between Kirkwall and Stromness. This delightful timber-built residence is constructed in attractive Norwegian style and enjoys spectacular views over Scapa Flow and the surrounding coastline. Completed in the spring of 1995, the interior is warm, bright and luxurious, with attractive wood furniture and stylish modern furnishings. There is a lovely south-facing sun lounge for the use of guests, and three beautifully appointed guest bedrooms, two of which have private en-suite bathrooms. Proprietors Kathy and Keith Bichan offer their guests the warmest of welcomes and a delicious Orkney breakfast. Alternatively, special diets can be catered for by prior arrangement. Kathy hails from Seattle in the northwest United States and since arriving in 1994, she has built up an enviable reputation for her excellent hospitality. Keith is a native Orcadian and can direct visitors to various sites of interest. Evening meals are not available but can be enjoyed at the nearby inn. Westrow Lodge is unsuitable for smokers and pets.

Westrow Lodge, Orphir Tel: 01856 811360

STROMNESS. The Old Man of Hoy, an inspiring 450 foot stack (not climbed until 1966), stands off the high cliffs of Hoy and guards the approaches to the little port of Stromness. A safe harbour since Viking days, through the centuries it has played host to whaling, herring and battle fleets. Now little more than a car ferry port, Stromness has, in the past, enjoyed several periods of prosperity, during which times it was one of the principal ports on the northern sailing routes and a base for the Hudson Bay Company ships.

The **Pier Arts Centre**, housed in an 18th century house and warehouse, combines a permanent exhibition of 20th century British art with temporary exhibitions.

Smuggling and piracy have long been a part of life in the Islands and one particularly notorious pirate, John Fullarton, an 18th century captain, became known as 'The Pirate of Orkney'. Utterly ruthless, as his nickname suggests, Fullarton killed all those who stood in his way, even his own cousin. His death, however, was as violent as his life. He captured a Scottish merchant vessel, The Isabella, and after boarding her, murdered her captain. Mary Jones, the captain's wife, took hold of a pistol and, holding it to Fullarton's head, killed him.

To the east of the port is **Maes Howe**, a vast Neolithic tomb that is accepted as the finest chambered tomb in Europe. Built with huge stones, some weighing up to 3 tons, it is 25 feet high and 115 feet in diameter. Originally filled with treasure, in 1150 it was looted by a group of

Norsemen, who left runic graffiti recording their act of vandalism. There are also 14 personal names, an animated dragon, a walrus and a knot of serpents. Closer to Stromness lies the **Unstan Cairn**, which, though not as impressive to look at as Maes Howe or the Standing Stones of Stenness, is of great archaeological interest. During its excavation in 1844, the cairn gave up the largest collection of Stone Age pottery ever found on any Scottish site (now in Edinburgh's Museum of Antiquities) as well as two human skeletons. Also well worth a visit is **Stromness Museum** detailed on page 431.

A real find in Stromness is **The Dairy**, a delightful white-painted shop with a distinctive green sign which can be found in Graham Place. This charming family run grocers, delicatessen and wholefoods store is the ideal place for those looking for a comprehensive range of Orkney-made food products under one roof. Some of the renowned products available include Island herring, cheese, biscuits, cakes and the speciality of the house, fabulous Orkney ice cream. The Dairy also stocks a wide selection of wholefoods and vegetarian products, including dried fruits, nuts, cereals and pulses, as well as fresh bread and a range of fresh fruit and vegetables in season.

Heather and Callum MacInnes, helped by their children Fraser, Rhona and Isla, offer a friendly helpful service and will pull out all the stops to help their customers find that special gift. They also make special hampers to order composed of Orkney products packed in charming traditional baskets, which can be collected or forwarded by mail order. For walkers, anglers and bird-watchers they provide delicious packed lunches, and well as a selection of fresh sandwiches for regular customers and visitors to Stromness.

The Dairy, 23 Graham Place, Stromness Tel: 01856 850551

Overlooking the colourful and ever-changing harbour at Stromness from the patio, **The Cafe** is the perfect spot to enjoy a full breakfast, light lunch or a splendid evening meal. Open 7 days a week from 9 am until late, The Cafe offers its guests a full and very comprehensive menu as well as a special kids menu for those with smaller appetites. All the food is freshly produced using local Orkney produce and the restaurant is also licensed and carries a good selection of alcoholic beverages. Daily specials are displayed all day and are guaranteed to be both varied and delicious. You can choose from a wonderful selection of main courses, for example, Fresh Salmon Steak in white wine, American Cheeseburger with chips, Southern Fried Chicken, or traditionally home-cooked Mince and Tatties. Also available on the menu is The Latin Quarter which comprises a selection of the best meals from Italy and Mexico including Beef and Bean Burritos and Spaghetti Bolognaise, delicious. If you arrive early and are looking for a substantial breakfast, then The Cafe is the place to come, with one egg, two sausages, two slices of bacon, fried bread and tomato at a very reasonable price indeed. There is also a terrific selection of toasted sandwiches, pizzas and baked potatoes for those who only want a light lunch.

The Cafe, 22 Victoria Street, Stromness

The recently modernised **Ferry Inn** is pleasantly situated in the harbour area in the heart of old Stromness. This delightful modernised inn, restaurant and hotel is surrounded by narrow cobbled lanes and stands overlooking the attractive bustle of yachts and motor craft in the harbour, with Scapa Flow, the famous naval base of two world wars, beyond.

Ferry Inn

The inn has strong maritime atmosphere throughout. The lounge bar resembles the interior of a schooner, being fitted out entirely in mahogany and decorated with charts, pictures and a variety of nautical memorabilia. In 1995, the Inn was named Orkney Pub of the Year, having been runner-up the year before. Excellent bar meals are served here daily, both at lunchtimes and in the evening, including such local specialities as Westray haddock and Orkney salmon. The Inn's famous restaurant offers an even wider menu, including Orkney steaks, locally caught fish, meat and vegetarian dishes, along with an imaginative choice of starters, desserts and carefully selected wines. The inn also has seventeen spacious and well-appointed guest bedrooms available; most have private baths or showers, and some also have beautiful views of the harbour.

Ferry Inn, Stromness Tel: 01856 850280

STENNESS. The **Standing Stones of Stenness**, though now only four stones, are contemporary with Maes Howe and there is evidence that there were other stones and a ditch, now silted up, around the site. Couples in the parish of Stenness once made their betrothal vows among the stone circles.

The impressive **Standing Stones Hotel** stands in a magnificent position overlooking the Loch of Stenness, midway between Kirkwall and Stromness. An ideal base from which to explore the many attractions of Orkney, the hotel attracts bird-watchers, anglers, archeologists and sightseers from all over the world. The present building rose from the ashes of a 19th century timber-built structure which was destroyed by fire in 1989.

Standing Stone Hotel

Reopened in 1991, this comfortable modern hotel now has 17 beautifully appointed guest bedrooms, all with en-suite facilities, colour TVs, telephones, radios, hair dryers and tea and coffee making facilities. The Brodgar Restaurant is renowned for its breathtaking views across the Loch of Stenness towards the Ring of Brodgar, the standing stones from which the hotel takes its name. It also serves an imaginative table d'hôte menu which, on the evening we visited, included smoked salmon and prawn coronets, and supreme of chicken stuffed with date and banana, as well as an appetising choice of desserts and Orkney cheeses. The Hotel also has two relaxing guest lounges, and an attractive lounge bar offering a good selection of bar meals to residents and non-residents alike.

Standing Stones Hotel, Stenness Tel: 01856 850449 Fax: 01856 851262

The **Mill of Eyrland** offers exceptional accommodation in a delightful rural setting at Stenness. Built in the 1860s as a flour mill for the Balfour Estate, this lovely old stone building still retains its original water-wheel and milling machinery. The house is full of antiques and pieces from the old mill and the three guest bedrooms are spacious and equally full of character. Proprietors Morag and Ken Robertson offer a warm welcome, a hearty Orkney breakfast and delicious evening meals prepared from fresh local ingredients. The house and garden are filled with pieces of wrought-iron furniture made by Ken, some of which are for sale.

Mill of Eyrland, Stenness Tel & Fax: 01856 850136

HARRAY. To the west of Harray, on the coast, lies **Skara Brae**, one of Orkney's most exciting and oldest sites. Dating from as far back as 3000 BC this Stone Age settlement is well preserved, perhaps because it became buried in sand and remained there for some 4000 years until a particularly violent storm revealed the buildings in 1850. The passages that linked the individual rooms can still be made out and all the personal touches can be seen including hearthstones, fish larder pools, stone beds and other primitive furniture.

A good place to stop on the road between Stromness and Birsay is **Wylie's Tearoom and Stores**, at Harray. Set in beautiful rural surroundings, this pleasant family run restaurant, filling station and general store has been owned by the Wylie family for over two decades. The wood-panelled tearoom has an agreeable atmosphere, with simple wooden

446

tables and chairs and offers a good selection home-made cakes, pastries and main meals, including fresh Orkney herring cooked in oatmeal. The general store stocks a variety of locally produced items, along with a range of basic provisions. Open 9 am to 6.30 pm, seven days a week.

Wylie's Tearoom and Harray Stores, Harray

DOUNBY. To the east of the village lies **Click Mill**, the last surviving example on the Island of an old horizontal watermill. Built in 1800 and still retaining its turf-roof, the style of the mill is much older in origin.

Excellent accommodation in the centre of Orkney's Mainland can be found in the village of Dounby. **Dounby House** is a friendly 2 Crown Commended guesthouse which occupies a handsome former doctor's residence dating from the 1890s. Indeed, the house remained in the possession of the local doctor until 1990 when it was acquired by Yvonne and Dennis Paice, two very welcoming hosts who moved here from Lancashire.

Dounby House

The three guest bedrooms all have wash-hand basins and tea and coffee making facilities and one also has an en-suite bathroom. There is also a warm and comfortable guest lounge with colour TV. Yvonne and Dennis provide a delicious Scottish breakfast and evening meals, by arrangement. Vegetarians are catered for and children and well-behaved pets are welcome. Dennis also organises tailor-made tours of Orkney throughout the year. Ideal for bird-watchers, botanists and anglers, these take in the RSPB reserves on the Mainland, a selection of Orkney's prehistoric sites and, weather permitting, a visit to the island of Hoy with its towering cliffs and magnificent 450 foot high Old Man. If required, Yvonne and Dennis are happy to pick up guests from the airport or ferry.

Dounby House, Dounby Tel: 01856 771535

MARWICK. At **Marwick Head**, on the clifftop, is a memorial to Lord Kitchener, the World War I leader, who died off these shores in 1916 when the HMS Hampshire, on which he was travelling to Russia, was mined.

BIRSAY. The nearly tidal island of **Brough of Birsay**, reached on foot via the causeway at low water, is home to an interesting early Christian and Norse complex. Built on the landward side of the tiny island, the Brough of Birsay is most associated with Earl Thorfinn (who lived in the 11th century) and the site includes the remains of Christ Church which was built on the remains of an earlier Celtic church. The Earl's church was promoted to a cathedral at one time and to the north of its ruins lie the remains of the bishop' palace.

SCAPA FLOW. This huge natural harbour was used in both world wars as a major naval base. Under the cliffs of Gaitnip, in eastern Scapa, lies the battleship Royal Oak, sunk within five weeks of the outbreak of the Second World War in an audacious submarine attack. The grave of 800 men, her position is marked by a buoy and the traces of fuel oil on the sea surface, still seeping from her bunkers. Royal Oak is not the only battleship in Scapa Flow. After the Great War the German High Seas Fleet was interned here. Their skeleton crews carried out one last defiant and dramatic act and scuttled the entire fleet. Many were raised for scrap but battleships, cruisers and destroyers still lie where they finally came to rest in 1919.

BURRAY. The **Italian Chapel**, just across the water from Burray, it is a beautiful chapel built inside two old army Nissen huts and was constructed out of scrap metal in 1943 by Italian prisoners of war. The chapel was rededicated in 1960 when it was also restored by its original designer, Domenico Choicchetti.

A very interesting and rewarding place to visit can be found on Burray, the small island lying between the Mainland and South Ronaldsay which is connected to both by the famous Churchill anti-submarine barriers. The **Orkney Fossil and Vintage Centre** at Viewforth is owned and personally run by Leslie Firth and Heather Bain, two genuine enthusiasts who have spent many years amassing their unique collection of fossils and historical artefacts from Orkney and beyond. A fascinating place to spend a few hours, the Centre consists of a series of rooms with specific themes. The first, the Devonian Room, is devoted to fossils found on Orkney itself. Originally laid down in the sediment of Lake Orcadie around 380 million years ago, they were re-discovered in northwest Mainland in an area now known as the Sandwick fish beds. The second section is devoted to fossils from all over the world and includes a giant ammonite from northeast England and a remarkable fossilised fish shoal from the Green River Formation, Wyoming. There is also a special hands-on area where visitors are encouraged to touch the exhibits. In the darkroom, certain light-sensitive rocks minerals can be seen to glow dramatically under ultraviolet light.

Orkney Fossil and Vintage Centre

Upstairs, the centre takes on the flavour of a museum of local history, with a series displays dedicated to the social history of the Islands. Exhibits include furniture, toys, tools and kitchen implements, many of them displayed in room settings. There are also special exhibits dedicated to the two World Wars and displays by the Orkney Vintage Club. The archive room contains a fascinating collection of early photographs, books and magazines through which visitors are welcome to browse. The Centre also has a coffee shop serving snacks, lunches and high teas in pleasant relaxed surroundings. The menu includes chicken, fish, lasagne, baked potatoes, filled rolls and home-made cakes and pastries, along with a selection of hot and cold beverages. Finally, there is a well laid-out gift shop which stocks an imaginative range of fossils, minerals, semi-precious gemstones, paperweights and books, some of which originate on the Islands; there is also a frequently changing exhibition of paintings by Orkney artists. The centre is open 10 am to 6 pm, seven days a week between April and September and 10.30 am to 6 pm Wednesdays to Sundays during October.

Orkney Fossil and Vintage Centre, Viewforth, Burray
Tel: 01856 731255

The Shetland Islands

The sea is a part of everyday life in Shetland, Britain's northernmost islands, and such was the reputation of Shetlander's sea faring skills that nearly 3000 were serving with Nelson's fleet during his great victories. The Islands are so far north that during the summer there is scarcely any night, just the dimming of the sky around midnight, know locally as simmer dim.

Like the Orkneys, some 60 miles to the south, Shetland's principal island is called Mainland, with Lerwick as the capital. The name Shetland is derived from the Norse word 'Hjaltland' which means high land and, for the most part, the island is upland peat bog and grass or heath moor with countless small lochs. Some 50 miles long, Mainland is so indented that it varies in width from 20 miles to just a few yards and no where on the island is more than 3 miles from the sea.

Shetland is, of course, the home of the hardy ponies and the distinctive black and brown native sheep, said to be descended from a Siberian breed, are everywhere. Until the 1970s most Shetlanders were either fishermen, crofters or serving the local needs, but since the development of the oil industry this has changed. However, most of the development has been contained within the Sullom Voe area of the Mainland and those seeking spectacular scenery, peace and quiet will not be disappointed.

LERWICK. The skies above Shetland's capital light up on the last Tuesday of January when the islanders celebrate **Up Helly Aa**. The men of the town dress as Vikings and parade through the streets with a replica Norse Galley, which is put to the torch in a flaming declaration of Viking ancestry.

In 1653 Cromwell's fleet of 93 ships arrived in the town and built **Fort Charlotte**, probably Lerwick's first permanent building. In 1781, the Fort was repaired after being burned by the Dutch some hundred years before and a large barrack block was added. Today it is the only Cromwellian building remaining in tact in Scotland.

The town's most memorable sight must be **Clickimin Broch**. Forming an island at the end of a causeway out into the loch, the Broch, some 65 feet in diameter and with 18 foot thick walls, was part of a larger settlement dating from 6th century BC and probably was occupied until the 6th century AD.

The very luckiest of visitors to Shetland many be treated to the most spectacular light show on earth - Aurora Borealis - the Northern Lights. This amazing natural phenomenon comes from the polar horizon and once seen is never forgotten.

The Shetland Museums Service, part of the Shetland Islands Council, is responsible for running three fascinating museums: the **Shetland Museum** in the centre of Lerwick, the **Croft House Museum** at Voe, Dunrossness, and the **Böd of Gremista Museum** on the outskirts of

Lerwick, the birthplace of the co-founder of the P&O shipping line, Arthur Anderson.

Opened in 1966, the **Shetland Museum** shares its premises in Lower Hillhead with the Shetland Library. The most northerly museum of its kind in the UK, it was founded after many years of struggle to establish a permanent place for the display and safe storage of the Islands' historic relics. Prior to this many unique artefacts, particularly those from the major archeological sites of Jarlshof, Clickimin and Staneydale, were removed from Shetland to mainland Britain.

The public expenditure involved in setting up the Museum required the approval of the Islands' population. At the time, public feeling about the export of indigenous relics had been running high thanks to two important archeological finds: the remains of an 18th century traveller at Gunnister, whose clothes and trappings were in a remarkable state of preservation and the St Ninian's Isle Treasure. This spectacular cache of Celtic silver artefacts was unearthed at the site of the ancient church on the Island and is still reckoned to be one of the most important single discoveries of its kind ever made in Scotland. When a plebiscite was held, the result was an overwhelming vote in favour of the formation of an institution which would keep such items on Shetland.

The underlying aim of the Museum is to document and present the history of humankind on the Islands from the earliest times to the present day. It is thought that the Islands were first inhabited by nomadic hunter-fishermen who settled here in family groups early in the Neolithic era (3500-1800 BC). These early Shetlanders lived in small houses built of stone and turf; however, the most spectacular relics of this era are the chambered cairns, some as big as 12 metres across, in which they buried their tribal chieftains. During the Bronze Age (1800-600 BC), the climate on Shetland began to worsen, and families who had previously lived in scattered isolated farmsteads now concentrated themselves in small townships around the coast, the most spectacular of which are Jarlshof near Sumburgh and Clickimin near Lerwick, two fascinating places to visit today. The Iron Age (600 BC-600 AD) seems to have been a troubled time, forcing the construction of a series of defensive fortifications. At first, these were simply blockaded promontories or small islands in sheltered lochs and sea inlets, but in time these were replaced by round stone towers, or brochs, the best examples of which can be found at Clickimin and Mousa. Towards the end of the Iron Age, the Picts, a fierce tribal people with a hierarchical upper order, took over and left behind a number of symbolic carved stones, including the Lunnasting Stone and the Mail Stone.

The next important influence on Shetland was the Celtic priesthood who founded a number of important Christian centres, the most notable of which were at St Ninian's Isle and Papil, Burra. Then, at the end of the 8th century, the Islands became the target for settlers from Norway who brought with them their own customs and language. So dominant was the Nordic culture that it remained a major influence on the islands well into the medieval period. Indeed, some present day Shetlanders would openly declare to having a greater affinity with Scandinavia than mainland Britain.

The main collections at the Shetland Museum are organised in a series of galleries. Gallery 1 is devoted to seafaring and shipping and contains a unique collection of model ships, figureheads and other nautical relics. Two poignant items commemorate the Hull whaler, Diana, which reached Shetland after being trapped in pack ice in the Davis Straits over the winter of 1866/7. The ship eventually made landfall the following April, by which time almost her entire crew, nine of whom were Shetlanders, had either perished or were in the final throes of scurvy and starvation.

Gallery 2 contains a collection of archeological artefacts which chronicle the development of Shetland society from its earliest occupation to the modern era. Among the objects from the Viking period is the priceless Gulberwick Brooch, a 9th century silver cloak pin which, according to local legend, was about to be melted down by a young boy when his father intervened. Gallery 3 is a lecture room and art gallery for a continually changing display of local contemporary art and Gallery 4 contains a fascinating collection of folk material, mostly from the last three centuries, which vividly illustrates the traditional lifestyle of the islanders.

The Croft House

The **Croft House Museum** at Voe, Dunrossness was opened in 1971 thanks to a generous donation from the Shetland Homefarers, a group of expatriates who visited their homeland in 1960. The museum consists of a house, barn and byre which are typical of mid-19th century working croft. This type of farmstead had evolved over many centuries and was extremely well adapted to local conditions. The intercommunicating layout allowed a light to be carried between the units during even the most severe storm conditions. The croft also incorporates a small water-powered grinding mill of a type believed to have been introduced into these parts by Norse settlers. The croft house is furnished in the period 1870-80 and contains many indigenous items. Self-reliance and ingenuity were vital qualities of the crofters, as evidenced by the clever use of driftwood, both structurally and for making furniture.

The **Böd of Gremista** was first opened as a museum in 1987 after the building had been extensively restored. The building is a typical 18th century booth, providing family accommodation as well as a working store for the nearby fish-drying beach. Almost two-thirds of the ground floor was used as a store, mainly for salt used in the fish curing process, with the kitchen at the south end serving as the main living area for the family. Its open fire, with its crook and links from which pots and kettles were hung to boil, is in the traditional style for the period.

The building's main claim to fame, however, is as the birthplace of Arthur Anderson, co-founder of the P&O shipping line, who was born here in 1792. Anderson's father had risen to become the manager of a fish curing operation at Gremista and as a consequence was able to send his son to a private school in Lerwick, an experience which set him apart from most his contemporaries and sowed the seeds of an extraordinary career which eventually led to him founding the famous shipping company. His three storey former home contains many mementos of his life of times. The main room on the first floor is filled with model ships, portraits and memorabilia associated with the early years of the company, and a second floor room was established to acknowledge Anderson's valuable philanthropic work. The bedroom containing the cradle in which he was rocked as an infant is on the first floor, and there is also a room devoted to the people and skills that were involved in the recent restoration of the building.

Shetland Museums Service, Lower Hillhead, Lerwick Tel: 01595 695057

Lerwick is a very beautiful area of Shetland and offers the perfect location for **Puffins**, the local coffee shop that offers you much more than just a cup of coffee. Owned and run by Ian and Elizabeth Whitham, Puffins had its very first foundation stone laid on 29th July 1823 by William Gordon McCrae Esq. The local controller of customs, Mr Gordon had a rather unsavoury hobby of collecting heads! His favourite was that of an unfortunate New Zealand Chief, whose head had been preserved perfectly, with hair, beard, teeth and gums all entire and the skin as black and hard as a billiard ball. The building was originally a chapel but, in 1960, it was purchased for use as an entertainment centre and dance hall and was known as Planets Ballroom. After passing through several hands since then, it was finally purchased in 1989 and renamed Puffins, where it has been trading ever since.

Puffins

The Craft Shop stocks all kinds of wonderful and interesting items, from crystal and candles to fabrics and wallpapers. There are locally made jams, mustards and fudge which sit alongside beautiful hand-made cushions and traditional Shetland gifts. You can wander to your hearts content in this Aladdin's Cave of gifts, with the soft music playing in the background and the gorgeous smell of freshly baked cakes wafting from the Coffee Shop. The Coffee Shop itself is very comfortably furnished with traditional pine furniture and a warm and cosy atmosphere. There is a pretty terrace outside where you can sit in the warm summer months and enjoy your coffee or tea. The home-made cakes are available all year round, with their apple pie being a speciality and always on the menu due to popular demand. There is also a children's menu, as well as a full range of sandwiches, either plain or toasted, for you to enjoy at your leisure in these lovely surroundings.

Puffins, Puffin House, Mounthooley Street, Lerwick
Tel: 01595 695060

One of the most pleasant eating places in the Shetland Islands can be found in Commercial Road, Lerwick, home of David Wood's **Candlestick Maker Bistro**. This lively café-restaurant is housed in premises which were previously a butchers and then a bakers, hence its curious and appealing name. The attractive tiled floors, white-painted walls and brightly coloured table covers create a very relaxed and stylish atmosphere which attracts a cheerful clientele, with much background laughter being heard on the day we visited. The lunchtime menu features a good selection of steaks and delicious freshly-made pizzas (the only in Lerwick that are made-to-order) as well as a choice of daily specials. This is extended in the evening to a full à la carte menu which incorporates a range of special fish and seafood dishes, including fresh Shetland crab and shellfish. The bistro is open for lunch every day except Sunday, and for dinner seven nights a week, with last orders being taken at 10 pm. Advance booking is advisable, especially at weekends. Children are welcome, and there are both smoking and non-smoking sections. Pizzas, lasagne and certain other dishes can also be purchased to take-away.

Candlestick Maker Bistro, 33 Commercial Road, Lerwick

The famous **Queens Hotel** stands in the heart of Lerwick in a magnificent waterfront position overlooking Bains Beach. This handsome building was constructed in the 1840s on the site of three traditional Shetland storehouses, or lodberries, dating from the late 18th century. Prior to the construction of the esplanade at the end of the 19th century, the rear of the Hotel stood above a natural inlet and cave known as Murray's Hol. As well as being a marketplace for buying and selling whelks, this was a notorious landing place for smugglers which the local revenue men had to keep under constant surveillance.

Today, the Queens Hotel is one of Lerwick's best known landmarks. Despite being severely damaged by fire in September 1987, it rose from the ashes and was completely refurbished in time for the summer season the following year. It is now a pleasant and comfortable establishment which has been awarded 3 Crowns by Scottish Tourist Board. Its 26 spacious bedrooms all have private en-suite facilities, colour televisions, direct dial telephones and tea and coffee making facilities, and the hotel also has an attractive café-bar and an elegant restaurant serving the finest Shetland cuisine. The chef takes pride in using the best local produce available and, in the evening, offers both an excellent value table d'hôte menu and extensive choice of à la carte dishes. Alternatively, both guests and non-residents can watch the boats go by as they enjoy their lunch or supper in the café-bar which looks out over Lerwick's busy waterfront.

Queens Hotel, Commercial Street, Lerwick Tel: 01595 692826
Fax: 01595 694048

The **Grand Hotel** lies further along Commercial Street to the north of Lerwick's Market Cross and information centre. This first rate establishment was built in the 1860s on the site of a grand 18th century house which once belonged to Orcadian, John Kelday. The distinctive turret was added at a later date to improve the appearance of the building from the road. For many years, the southern end of the Hotel was used by a shipping contractor who hired the hardy breed of local sailors known as 'Greenland Men' for seal and whale hunting in the stormy north Atlantic.

Today, the Grand Hotel has 23 comfortably appointed guest bedrooms, all with private en-suite bath or shower, colour television, direct dial telephone, radio and tea and coffee making facilities. The Hotel also has two welcoming bars and a spacious dining room serving delicious Shetland breakfasts, lunches and dinners which are prepared using the finest locally sourced ingredients. The evening menu features an extensive selection of à la carte dishes, as well as an excellent value table d'hôte menu. The Grand is also the proud location of the only permanent nightclub on Shetland. Posers Nightclub is an exciting venue offering the latest dance sounds in surroundings which are lively and stylish. The Hotel has recently undergone a comprehensive refurbishment and has been awarded 3 Crowns by the Scottish Tourist Board. The staff are happy to tailor holidays to their guests' individual requirements, including all air and ferry travel. They also offer special inclusive breaks for guests wanting half-board accommodation. Please note that the Grand is not located on ground level and may not be suitable for patrons who have difficulty climbing stairs.

Grand Hotel, Commercial Street, Lerwick Tel: 01595 692826
Fax: 01595 694048

First opened in 1969, the recently refurbished **Kveldsro Hotel** is now one of the most luxurious hotels on Shetland. It can be found at the southern end of Lerwick in Greenfield Place, within easy walking distance of the information centre. Kveldsro means 'evening peace' in Norse, and the Hotel is aptly decorated in warm and restful style. The bar is the perfect place to relax and watch the world go by whilst enjoying a drink, a light lunch or supper. Alternatively, the elegant restaurant offers top class table d'hôte and à la carte menus, along with an extensive list of carefully selected wines. The cuisine is prepared using the finest local ingredients which the chef purchases on a daily basis. On the day we visited, the menu included partridge, duck, local crab and home-cured gravadlax, as well as a mouthwatering range of starters and desserts. The restaurant also welcomes private parties of up to 20 diners.

The Kveldsro's guest bedrooms are all stylishly decorated and appointed to a very high standard, and there are also a number of private suites for that special occasion. The staff throughout the Hotel provide a high level of attentive yet discreet service and are delighted to accommodate business meetings and small conferences. Indeed, the hotel prides itself in tailoring individual packages, including all travel arrangements, for guests from any destination in Britain.

Kveldsro House Hotel, Greenfield Place, Lerwick
Tel: 01595 692195 Fax: 01595 696595

Nestling in the picturesque area of Lerwick, you will come across a hidden gem, **The Solheim Guest House**. Victorian, built back in 1885, Solheim Guest House still offers you the traditional warmth of welcome that is all too scarce these days. This bed and breakfast accommodation has been owned by Valerie and Stephen Farnworth for the past four years, helped of course by their two children Danny and Katie.

The Solheim Guest House

Solheim offers four light and airy bedrooms and, although the rooms are not en-suite, there is a large bathroom on each of the three floors of the property and a wash basin, TV and tea and coffee making facilities in every bedroom. Children and pets are very welcome, with a large and very comfortable shared lounge with open fire for the dog and Sky TV for the kids, you can be sure they will have plenty to keep themselves occupied. The charming hall way is decorated in the original pitch pine and all the rooms are big and airy, with high ceilings and a warm and cosy atmosphere. There is a separate dining room where you can sit and enjoy your vegetarian or full traditional Scottish breakfast, complete with porridge; it is guaranteed to keep you going until lunch.

Valerie was born on this beautiful Island and so would make the perfect guide if you need to get around. Imagine it, rolling hills and rugged open moorland interlaced with lochs and streams. A profusion of wild plants and flowers and abundance of birdlife, all this and of course a thriving local craft industry famous for its knitwear, tweed and jewellery, Solheim Guest House is the perfect place from which to explore.

Solheim Guest House, 34 King Harald Street, Lerwick
Tel: 01595 695275

Boasting impressive views over Bressay Sound and located in a conservation area, you will find **The Old Manse**. Lerwick's oldest inhabited house, the Old Manse was built in 1685 to house the first minister of the parish, Reverend James Milne. James Milne was ordained in 1704 and died in 1718, but there was never any evidence that Reverend Milne ever lived in the house! Reverend Thomas Waldie was his successor and did live in the property until his death, aged 44, in 1739. There is evidence which suggests that the Lerwick merchant, James Craigie of Stebbigrind in Whiteness and his wife, Margaret Ross, were living in the house in 1788 and it passed down through the family until 1836.

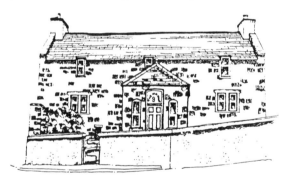

The Old Manse

Today The Old Manse is owned by Marcia and Les Irving who like to keep it running very much in the traditional family way, with a warm greeting awaiting every guest. There are three bedrooms, one of which is en-suite with the other two having a shared bathroom, all have tea and coffee making facilities and are tastefully decorated and furnished throughout. This lovely old house has a large, yet cosy kitchen that still contains a huge cooking range and a separate lounge and dining room, with the original exposed beams, which guests can use throughout the day. Evening meals can be provided if required and are served between 6 and 8 pm with special diets catered for if necessary. Marcia and Les have a great love for old motorbikes and make any would be bikers very welcome, also Marcia demonstrates the traditional art of spinning to any guest that may be interested. In the summer the large Patio area comes in very useful to soak up the sun and to sit and enjoy the occasional barbecues that the guest house throws in those long summer months.

The Old Manse, 9 Commercial Street, Lerwick Tel: 01595 696301

Joan and Trevor Howarth, and their dog Sûilean Dubh (meaning black eyes), offer a very warm welcome at their superb guest house in Knab Road, Lerwick. Originally a chapel dating from 1904, **Glen Orchy House** is an imposing stone-built structure which has recently been extensively refurbished to a remarkably high standard. Scottish Tourist Board 3 Crowns Highly Commended, the establishment has recently been awarded the coveted 3Q listing by the AA. The 14 beautifully appointed guest bedrooms all have en-suite bathrooms, trouser presses, and satellite television with teletext, as well as underfloor heating, double glazing, an air filtration system and full sound proofing. Video cassette recorders and ironing boards are also available on request. One room has also been equipped for disabled guests.

Glen Orchy House

Trevor, an ex-RAF chef, and Joan offer a delicious full Scottish breakfast, as well as home-cooked evening meals by arrangement. The breakfast menu offers a choice of cereals and fruit juices, then a main dish featuring a selection of fresh locally sourced produce, including sausage, bacon, mushrooms, black pudding, tomato, and either poached, fried, scrambled or boiled egg, all washed down with lashings of tea or coffee. Porridge and kippers are also available on request. The evening table d'hôte menu is changed daily; on the day we visited, it featured Joan's appetising mushroom soup and Trevor's equally delicious treacle pudding. The dining room is decorated with attractive fisherman's floats and, along with several of the bedrooms, has a wonderful view of the sea. The delightfully decorated public rooms include an elegant guest lounge, a games room and a smoking room (smoking is not permitted in the dining room). There is also a good selection of books available for guests to enjoy and a fully licensed bar in the lounge which operates on an honesty basis when unattended. Joan and Trevor offer the finest Shetland hospitality and provide a full range of backup services for their guests, including tourist information and laundry facilities. Glen Orchy House has its own private car park and stands adjacent to a scenic 9-hole golf course. Open all year round, children are very welcome, as are well-behaved pets.

Glen Orchy House, 20 Knab Road, Lerwick Tel: 01595 692031

You will find much to marvel at in this collection of peaceful islands that are situated midway between Norway and Scotland, and in Lerwick you will find another of these marvels, **Hjaltasteyn**. This workshop sells some of the most beautiful jewellery you will ever see, all of which has been designed and entirely hand-made in the Shetland Islands. Owned and run by Rosalyn Thompson and her two daughters Eloise and Sian, Hjaltasteyn (which means Shetland Stone) has been established for nearly four years and offers a large selection of jewellery, inspired by original Nordic designs. The business was originally started back in 1968 by a local geologist and Rosalyn worked there as a part-time employee until eventually she took the workshop over and now runs it as her own.

Hjaltasteyn

From start to finish, quality is the word best used to describe Rosalyn's work. Only Sterling silver and gold are used in the production of ear-rings, necklaces, pendants, brooches and bracelets with prices ranging from as little as £8 to as much as £300, depending on the size and material of the item. All the original drawings, soldering, crushing of enamel and shaping are done by Rosalyn herself, so when the jewellery is described as hand-made, you can guarantee that every individual piece is unique in its own right. Visits to the workshop can be arranged by phoning 01595 696224 and Hjaltasteyn is open from Monday to Saturday, 9 am until 5 pm.

Also definitely worth a visit is **The Norseman Inn** where Rosalyn has a small workshop and can be found demonstrating many of her skills to the public. There is a gift shop which sells much of her jewellery as well as a selection of local Shetland gifts such as wool, sweaters and produce. If you are feeling a little peckish then you have come to the right place, there is a large bar and restaurant which serves some delicious food. Why not try the 8 oz Sirloin Steak with a Pepper Sauce or maybe Roast Pork with Apple Sauce and all the trimmings. If you are after something lighter, then morning coffee and afternoon tea are served throughout the day, seven days a week, including a wonderful selection of home-made desserts. Every year a local Viking Festival is held and Rosalyn is greatly sought after to create the Viking shields and axes that are used in the re-enactment's performed by the local community.

Hjaltasteyn, 161 Commercial Street, Lerwick
Tel: 01595 696224

David Anderson is the fourth generation of his family to have produced fine knitted garments on Shetland from pure Shetland Island wool. The family firm, **Andersons of Shetland**, was established in the 1870s by his great-grandfather and David has already been personally involved in the business for over three decades. Founded in its present location in 1873, visitors can view the three storey showroom with its superb selection of traditional 100% Shetland wool knitwear in over a hundred different styles.

Andersons of Shetland

Items on display include a wide selection of baby and nursery-wear, as well as clothing to fit boys up to the age of eight years and girls up to the age of twelve. Other special articles include babies' knitted christening shawls. Perhaps the most celebrated items on offer, however, are the famous Everest sweaters, a range of knitwear made to the same specification as those supplied to the expedition which first conquered Mount Everest in 1953. These garments were required to be as lightweight as possible and made solely from the highest grade pure Shetland wool. This is because wool produced in Shetland by purebred Island sheep has unique heat retaining properties. It is also incredibly

461

light, soft and comfortable to wear, a valuable natural characteristic which is best demonstrated when the yarn is knitted fairly loosely into loose-fitting body shapes. The sweaters also had to be very strong and hard wearing, a quality which was achieved by knitting them without seams on a hand frame in a time-honoured procedure which is followed to this day. Everest sweaters are very special garments which are in limited supply, thanks to the restricted availability of top grade real Shetland wool, and because there are only a few knitters on the Islands with sufficient skills to operate a hand frame to the exacting standards required. They come in nine colours and are incredibly popular all over the world, especially in Japan. Andersons of Shetland provide a world-wide mail order service and offer special terms to trade customers. The showroom is open daily, except Sundays, from 9 am to 5 pm, and has plenty of easy parking and wheelchair access. A full range of knitting patterns and yarn is stocked and the staff are happy to give free advice and assistance.

Andersons of Shetland, Lerwick Tel: 01595 693714

AROUND LERWICK

CUNNINGSBURGH. Located in the pretty village of Cunningsburgh, you will find the new workshop premises of **Barbara Isbister Knitwear**. The Knitwear business has been running for over six years, though Barbara herself has been knitting for 20 years and is an expert in her field.

Barbara Isbister Knitwear

They specialise in classic Fair Isle sweaters using traditional patterns and colours so that you can take home a genuine memento from Shetland. All her garments are hand-frame knitted and hand finished in Shetland yarns, with the opportunity to take advantage of Barbara's mail order facility by selecting your choice from the full colour brochure or even have an original piece commissioned. You can choose from

462

childrenswear, menswear and womenswear, in classic, traditional or even designer styles that are guaranteed to suit every taste. The workshop is signposted on the main road through Cunningsburgh and is open from 9 am until 9 pm seven days a week, so why not drop by and watch this classic knitwear being produced in this warm and friendly atmosphere.

Barbara Isbister, Meadows, Cunningsburgh
Tel: 01950 477241

Situated in the charming village of Swarthoull, amidst the stunning scenery of Cunningsburgh, you will find the workshop of **Shetland Designer**. Owned and run by Wilma Malcolmson, this business first started up 14 years ago. Wilma, who had been knitting all her life, decided to turn her hobby into a full time occupation and Shetland Designer was born. They produce Classic knitwear for men and women including sweaters, cardigans and matching gloves, hats and scarves. Inspired by traditional patterns and colours, each garment has been individually knitted in Shetland using the best quality natural yarns.

Shetland Designer

Shetland Designer believe in individuality and attention to detail, and will even adapt styles to fit in with your individual requirements on a commission work basis. The patterns range from traditional to some very colourful and modern designs with plenty of samples of their work available so that you can decide on exactly what you are looking for. There is a small showroom with a busy workshop where you can watch the sweaters actually being produced using age old methods, all offering disabled facilities and children are welcome. Shetland Designer is open from 10 am until 4 pm Monday to Saturday or by appointment if you ring 01950 477257. Wilma also offers a full mail order service worldwide and regularly exports her work to her many customers all over the world.

Shetland Designer, Swarthoull, Cunningsburgh
Tel: 01950 477257

MOUSA BROCH stands on the small island of the same name. It is the best preserved of the brochs or forts unique to the northern tip of Scotland and the northern and western islands. It stands over 40 feet high, its inner and outer walls containing a rough staircase the can be climbed to the parapet. Little is known of this broch's inhabitants but it is believed that local Picts successfully sought refuse here from Roman slave hunters and, many years later, in 1150 it is said that a Norse nobleman hid here with a famous beauty with whom he was eloping.

SANDWICK. Boat trips to the beautiful uninhabited island of Mousa are operated during the summer months by **Tom Jamieson**, a fireman at Sumburgh Airport who doubles as the skipper of the MB Solan III. This handsome Department of Trade-approved Class VI boat has a capacity for 30 passengers and plies the 15 minute journey between Sandwick and Mousa between mid-April and the end of September.

As well as being known for its seals, seabirds and occasional sea otters, the Island is renowned for its remarkable Pictish Broch, an unusually well preserved double-skinned cylindrical stone tower which was erected for defensive purposes in the 1st century AD. These towers are among the most impressive military works of Iron Age society and are unique to Scotland. Inhabited until 1830, the Island is now without houses, roads or marked paths, and is a fascinating place to spend a few hours exploring, bird-watching and picnicking. Tom has been operating his boat service for 25 years and even runs special evening trips for twitchers to catch a glimpse of the rare stormy petrel. The service varies according to Tom's pattern of work; please phone to confirm times and book places.

Tom Jamieson, Leebitton, Sandwick Tel: 01950 431367

SKELBERRY. Perfect for those of you who wish for some action on your break away, and nestling in the charming village of Skelberry, you will find **Broothom Ponies**. Owned and run by Helen and Rhona Thomson, Broothom Ponies offers riding and trekking to all. From children of all ages through to adults, this well appointed riding stable offers facilities for the disabled on carefully selected horses and ponies.

464

even Shetland ponies for the very small! You can go for a simple walk or trek among the heathery hills, with rides along the long, sandy beaches and into the waves for those who are more adventurous. Riding hats are provided, but booking is advisable as Broothom Ponies proves very popular at any time of year, seven days a week. So why not come along, no matter what your age, and enjoy the beautiful countryside from horseback.

Broothom Ponies, Skelberry, Dunrossness Tel: 01950 460556

LEVENWICK. A good place to camp at the southern end of Shetland's mainland is the **Levenwick Camp Site** at Levenwick, between Sandwick and Sumburgh Head. This scenic spot has pitches for 12 tents and a standing caravan registered for four occupants. With hot water, showers, toilets and a chemical disposal point, the site is well-equipped for those staying for long as well as short periods.

The site is run by John Jamieson on behalf of the local community to support the village hall, and is attended each evening between 7 pm and 8 pm. Campers turning up at other times are welcome to choose their own pitches on arrival. The camp site lies within half a mile of a beautiful clean sandy beach which is known for its seals, sea otters and birdlife. With access by road as well as on foot, this sheltered beach is also ideal for canoeists. A second, even more secluded beach lies a dramatic miles walk away along the clifftops. Another unusual feature lying within walking distance is an old copper mine whose entrance shaft can be explored with care to a depth of around 200 yards (entrance at own risk). A local shop which stocks a good range of essentials and is open all hours lies within 500 yards of the camp site.

Levenwick Camp Site, Taingview, Levenwick

SUMBURGH HEAD. As well as the total peace and tranquillity there are plenty of things to discover on the islands. **Jarlshof** at Sumburgh Head is a remarkable site, where seven distinct layers of civilization can be identified amongst its ancient dwellings. One of the most remarkable archaeological sites in Europe, its oldest, Iron age, dwellings are very similar to Skarabrae on Orkney. The Norse name, a fanciful invention of Sir Walter Scott's, is rather misleading as the site dates from at least the Bronze Age. From that period can be seen evidence of farming as well as a metal worker's shop and the Iron Age is represented by two earth-houses, a broch and by later (probably 3rd-8th century) wheelhouses. The small museum is well worth a visit too; particularly for the imaginative illustrations of how Jarlshof might have looked at various stages of its occupation.

ST NINIAN'S ISLE. Today the Island is only occupied by ponies and sheep but at one time it was the site of an early Christian settlement. Named after the British bishop and, though St Ninian made Pictish Scotland his missionary area, there is no evidence that he visited Shetland. All that remains of the 12th century chapel are its lower courses and excavations in 1958 revealed not only the remains of a pre-Norse church but also a magnificent hoard of 8th century Celtic silver.

SCALLOWAY. Situated on the west coast of Mainland, opposite Lerwick, this village was, until 200 years ago, the capital of Shetland. The stark ruin of **Scalloway Castle**, built in 1600 by the Earl Patrick Stewart is the village's most prominent feature. Constructed in the medieval style, it was old-fashioned before it was finished and fell into disuse just 15 years later when the notorious Earl was executed. He had paid for its construction, and that of Earl's Palace on Orkney, by the simple means of extracting free materials and labour from his tenants on pain of forfeiture of their own lands and properties.

During the last war, Scalloway was used as a base by the Norwegians carrying out clandestine operations: to 'take the Shetland bus' meant to escape from Norway to Shetland. The **Scalloway Museum** tells the story of those desperate times as well as going back through the ages to prehistoric times.

Shetland Pottery

Thought to be the only pottery currently operating on the islands, the **Shetland Pottery** at Braehead, Scalloway is a fascinating place to

466

The Old House of Sumburgh, Jarlshof

spend an hour. Situated in a handsome 200 year old building which is partially constructed of stone taken from the nearby Castle, the workshop overlooks the sea at the eastern end of Scalloway harbour. Proprietor Linda Armstrong has lived on Shetland for two decades and has over ten years experience as a potter. All her stoneware is hand-thrown, individually glazed using local materials, and fired to a hard ovenproof finish. She specialises in making individual pieces which can be personalised and so make ideal wedding presents or gifts for that special occasion. Linda is happy to accept one-off commissions and operates a worldwide postal service for her customers. She also welcomes children to her workshop and often lets them feed the chickens in her garden. She sometimes even lets them have a go at making their own pots, subject to the pressure of work. In 1996, she installed a new kiln and opened a new showroom. The Shetland Pottery is signposted from the Castle and is open 10 am to 8 pm daily, including Sundays.

Shetland Pottery, Smidday Closs, Braehead, Scalloway
Tel: 01595 880808

Lying at the western end of Scalloway Harbour, Port Arthur was built in the early part of the 20th century as a herring curing station with its own large kippering kiln. The area is now dominated by the magnificent North Atlantic Fisheries College where visitors are made welcome and where, not surprisingly, seafood is served as a speciality in the restaurant. Port Arthur is also the location of the impressive **Scalloway Boating Club**, a thriving haven for boating enthusiasts from all over Shetland and beyond.

Scalloway Boating Club

Formed in 1975 with a remit to develop the social side of this fast growing leisure activity, the Club evolved from a yacht club which had been established almost a century before. Its first clubhouse was a prefabricated building which had previously been used as a canteen for contractors building a North Sea oil supply base at Lerwick. Since then, the members have made a great many improvements both to the building, which has been extended and converted into a permanent weatherproof structure, and to the site, which now has a large boat park, car park and a 200 foot floating pontoon which had previously been used on a Shetland salmon farm. The Club's resourcefulness at making use of existing materials was shown when they constructed a new sea wall from concrete anchor blocks which had previously been used to secure an oil pipeline to the seabed across Yell Sound.

Today, the Clubhouse provides a first-class amenity for its 400 members as well as visiting boat crews. An extension at the north end of the building incorporates showers and toilets, with external access so that they can be used 24 hours a day. Commodore James Ward and his wife Ismay have been involved with the Club for many years. Ismay manages the Clubhouse which has a very relaxed and friendly atmosphere and is open seven days a week to non-members. The facilities include a fully licensed bar with a wide-screen TV and games area, and a lounge/function room with a dance floor. Live music is a regular attraction here on Saturday evenings. There is also a large patio area at the front of the building offering wonderful views across the harbour. The Club also organises regular fishing and sailing competitions which are open to visitors.

Scalloway Boating Club, Port Arthur, Scalloway

One of the most comfortable places to stay on Shetland can be found within ten minutes drive of Lerwick at Upper Scalloway. **Hildasay Guest House** is an imposing modern residence built in Scandinavian style which welcomed its first guests in 1994. Born and bred on Shetland, mother and daughter Anne Robertson and Elaine Watt offer delightful hospitality and first-rate accommodation. Their well appointed guest bedrooms (three twin and one family) are all furnished with attractive pine furniture and equipped with en-suite bathrooms, colour televisions, shaving sockets and tea and coffee making facilities. All are on the ground floor and one is impressively equipped for disabled guests.

Hildasay Guest House

Anne and Elaine are renowned for their home cooking and serve delicious Scottish breakfasts and, if required, evening meals. (Anne's mouthwatering oatcakes and Elaine's home-made lasagne are worth the visit alone.) Fresh trout is also a regular feature on the menu as both their husbands are experienced anglers who have a wide knowledge of the local lochs. Indeed, trout fishing trips can be arranged for those with an interest. Outside, there is an attractive patio and garden with panoramic views which is ideal for summer barbecues.

Hildasay Guest House, Upper Scalloway Tel: 01595 880822

WALLS. The impressive **Burrastow House** Hotel and restaurant stands in splendid isolation on the remote western edge of Shetland's Mainland. Originally built as a landowner's house in the mid 18th century, it stands on a promontory overlooking Vaila Sound and looks out towards the island of Vaila. The Hotel provides the perfect base for exploring the dramatic surrounding coastline which is known for its seals, otters and beautiful wild orchids. Proprietor Bo Simmons has created an unusually relaxed and informal establishment which has the atmosphere of a stylish country house, with timber floors, antique furniture, original fireplaces and oil paintings on the walls. Guests are welcomed on their return from a day in the elements with open peat fires, a restful library and superb home-cooked food which is among the finest on Shetland. The beautifully decorated lounges are perfect places to relax and the five luxuriously appointed guest bedrooms all have their own en-suite bathrooms. One is specially equipped for disabled guests, and another is a particularly spacious family room. A remarkably complete series of photographs shows the development of the house between 1890 and the outbreak of the Second World War; these can be viewed in the library by arrangement with the proprietor.

Burrastow House

Bo Simmons is an able and enthusiastic cook who produces out-standing cuisine using fresh local ingredients wherever possible. Lunch and afternoon tea are served informally in the conservatory and library, and dinner is served in the magnificent panelled dining room. The four course table d'hôte evening menu features the choice of a fish, meat or vegetarian main course, along with a mouthwatering range of starters and desserts. The restaurant welcomes non-resident diners every day except on Sunday evenings and Mondays.

The Hotel has its own boat which residents can use to explore Vaila Sound. The surrounding area also has excellent facilities for windsurfing, riding and sea angling, and there is shop, post office and swimming pool two miles away in Walls village. A bus service runs each day except Sunday between Walls and Lerwick, 27 miles away. Burrastow House is a perfect place for a holiday during Shetland's brilliant summer, or for a dramatic out-of-season break. Children and well behaved pets very welcome. Closed January and February.

Burrastow House, Walls Tel: 01595 809307
Fax: 01595 809213

SANDNESS. A fascinating place to visit on the western tip of the mainland is **Jamieson's Knitwear** at Sandness. Established over a century ago, this impressive small woollen mill produces an exclusive range of yarn from the undyed wool of native Shetland Island sheep. This hardy breed grows a fleece which has long been renowned for its unusual warmth, light weight, softness and wide range of natural colours.

Jamieson's Knitwear

The business was founded in Sandness by Robert Jamieson in 1893 and has passed through four generations of the family to the present owner, Peter Jamieson, who established the first ever spinning mill on the Islands in 1980, thus making it possible to produce yarn in sufficient quantities to satisfy demand for pure Shetland wool garments. All items are produced locally on small hand-operated machines, and are hand-finished and completely seam-free. Visitors are welcome to tour the mill and purchase items bearing the much sought after Jamieson's label. The family also own and operate a shop in Commercial Street, Lerwick which stocks an even wider range of knitwear. Jamieson's are also the main UK mail order supplier of exclusive Alice Starmore knitting patterns.

Jamieson's Knitwear, Sandness Industrial Estate, Sandness
Tel: 01595 870285

BUSTA. In Shetland there is a total absence of noise and rush, you begin to relax, to feel totally at peace with yourself and the world. To make the most of this unique experience you stay at **The Busta House Hotel**. This is the kind of Hotel that you don't come across very often on your travels and it comes as a pleasant surprise to find it somewhere as peaceful and secluded as Shetland.

The Busta House Hotel

It was built in 1714 by the Gifford family, who were lairds of Busta and prominent figures in Shetland society. The history of the Giffords of Busta House is a strange, sad tale of superstition, tragedy and a long, pointless feud which brought ruin to the most prosperous estate in Shetland and gain to no-one. The House is now one of the few listed buildings in Shetland and it is reputed to be the oldest continuously inhabited house in the Islands. American guests, particularly, are intrigued to learn that the Queen and her family have also taken tea in the Long Room, when they came ashore from the Royal yacht Britannia as the guests of the Lord Lieutenant.

Peter and Judith Jones have run Busta House for the past seven years, very much on the traditional family lines. They take a natural, personal pride in what is their home as well as their hotel, and welcome you very much in that spirit. You'll dine on delicious traditional food prepared from the finest and freshest of local produce. The Restaurant was featured in Taste of Scotland and offers a very extensive menu. You can choose from such culinary delights as Braised Pigeon Breast with Whisky and Bacon or Grilled Shetland Salmon with a Wholegrain Mustard Crust followed by home-made Baileys Irish Cream and Chocolate Chip Ice Cream, delicious. When your meal is finished, then settle down with coffee and a superb selection of malt whiskies to follow in the warmth and scent of a traditional peat fire. When it's time to retire to one of 20 bedrooms, each being a happy blend of tasteful elegance and modern day convenience, with en-suite facilities to ensure you're fully rested and almost entirely self-sufficient. To ensure that your stay is totally restful, Peter and Judith will book your air or sea passage, lay on a car for you and even line up any number of outdoor activities. Choose from fishing, diving, sailing, pony trekking or walks along the 3,000 miles of unspoilt coastline which is peppered with isolated beaches, majestic cliffs and rolling hills. All there is left for you to do is enjoy yourself, now that shouldn't be too hard, should it.

Busta House Hotel, Busta, Brae Tel: 01806 522506

ESHA NESS. Esha Ness Lighthouse stands close to the precipitous cliff edge from which can be seen the magnificent length of eroded cliffs, stacks and clefts known as **Grind of the Navir** (Gateway of the Giants).

VOE. Situated on the sea front at Voe, you will come across the very charming **Pierhead Restaurant and Bar**. Built in the early 1900s as a local grocery shop by Thomas Mountford Adie, the family business soon grew and developed into fish curing. When the cod and ling fishing grew in size, the shop purchased and chartered smacks, which sailed to Faroe, Rockall and Iceland, bringing their catches back to Voe. Drying beaches were made and premises built but, as the fishing industry started to decline with the coming of steam drifters, the firm's interest turned to woollens. The business stayed in the family through many generations until 1991, when it was turned into the Restaurant and Bar that you see today. Your host is Margaret Kirk, who is originally from New Zealand, but moved to Shetland nearly three years ago.

Pierhead Restaurant and Bar

The restaurant area is lovely, with wood panelled walls, lots of fresh green foliage and stunning sea views, you really couldn't ask for a nicer spot to indulge yourself. The menu is a full and comprehensive one, offering seafood specialities every day that are cooked by Margaret herself and to the highest standard. You can choose from such delicacies as Smoked Salmon Pasta or Deep fried Scallops with home-made tartare sauce and a wonderful selection of mouth-watering desserts. The fish has been brought only 20 yards from the fishing boats and is freshly caught the same day it is cooked, there is also a Seafood Buffet on Wednesday nights throughout the summer months. Separate from the restaurant, you will find the very comfortable and friendly bar area, also filled with beautiful wood furniture, the bar is open for a drink or light snack every day of the week.

Pierhead Restaurant & Bar, Voe

LUNNA. **Lunna House Hotel** is situated amid quiet, peaceful walking country where you can stroll around the seashore and watch the seals and otters play in the waves. During World War II, Lunna was the headquarters of the Norwegian resistance movement, and the 'Shetland Bus' was established, transporting arms and Allied agents into German occupied Norway. The property had been derelict when it was bought by Ruby Lindsay 31 years ago, and after extensive conversion it is now a comfortable guest house that still retains its original old world charm.

Lunna House Hotel

Today Lunna House is still run by Ruby, with help from her son James, and between them they have turned this Hotel into a real home from home. Visitors can relax in one of two spacious lounges with their traditional open peat fires and admire the breathtaking views from the large, picturesque windows. There are six bedrooms, two twin, two single and two double, which all have full use of two large public bathrooms. Ruby still prepares all the food, which is served in the comfortable dining room, and is famous on the island for her home-made cakes and afternoon teas. The oldest church in use in Shetland is at Lunna and is open to visitors all week. **Lunna Kirk** is perhaps best known for its two leper holes (whereby lepers could listen to church services) at the back of the Church. The views from Lunna Church are magnificent, taking in a wide sweep of sea, cliffs and hills, the perfect place to explore the numerous lochs nearby for fishing. In the early summer the days are long and the sunsets glorious, and the Lunna House Hotel is the perfect location from which to sit and watch the sun drop below the horizon in this friendly little community.

Lunna House Hotel, Lunna, Vidlin Tel: 018067 237

BRESSAY. This island may be visited from Lerwick and, for many, the interest lies not on this island but on **Noss**, the small island 200 yards off its eastern shores. With cliffs alive with seabirds, visitors are taken across, only in good weather, in inflatable boats by Scottish Natural Heritage.

Maryfield House Hotel

The sea is part of everyday life in Shetland, Britain's northernmost islands, some 100 in all and it is at Bressay that you will find the renowned **Maryfield House Hotel** which is owned and run by David and Linda Wood. Despite its location, Maryfield House Hotel has created quite a reputation for its superb seafood menu and has had guests travelling from as far as Japan to sample their superb dishes, all of which have been prepared and created by Linda.

The Hotel specialises in banquet meals that are so magnificent, they take up to four hours to consume and include a whole host of unusual dishes and speciality foods. The menu changes daily, according the fresh local produce that has been caught that day and the Restaurant boasts some stunning views over the sea and surrounding landscapes.

The three guest rooms are individually styled in classic Victorian decor, but offer all the usual modern conveniences that you will have come to expect when travelling. So if you wish to sample some of the very best in fish cuisine whilst enjoying some traditional Scottish hospitality, we recommend that you look no further that Maryfield House Hotel.

Maryfield House Hotel, Bressay Tel: 01595 820207

YELL. The island is reach by ferry from **Toft** on Mainland, and is, in large part, made up of rolling peat moor. The oldest building on the island, **Old Haa** at **Burravoe**, is a large white crowstepped building dating from 1637 and it is now home to the local museum as well as being an arts and crafts centre.

At the northern end of the island, on the shores of Kirk Loch, is roofless **Kirk of Ness**. Dedicated to St Olaf, this medieval Church was abondoned in 1750. Lying between the Church and the shore, half lost in the sand and grass, are many stone fragments which are though to represent thousands of years of prehistoric and later occupation of the area. Overlooking Gloup Voe stands the **Fishermen's Memorial** which tells of the devastation of the fishing community in the voe during a great storm in 1881 when six boats and 58 men were lost

UNST. This is Britain's northernmost inhabited island and it is known for its spectacular cliff scenery, its ponies and its fine knitted work which is now, sadly declining. On the eastern shore, at **Mu Ness**, is the ruin of **Muness Castle**. It was built by Lawrence Bruce, the designer of Scalloway's castle, in 1598 and was burnt down, possibly be French privateers.

The magnificent cliffs on the northern tip of Unst are one of Scotland's most important seabird sanctuaries. Conservation began at **Hermaness National Nature Reserve** in 1831 when the laird Dr L Edmondston protected a few breeding bonxies or great skuas. In 1891, the Edmondston family employed a keeper to protected the site and this role was taken over by the RSPB in 1907. Declared a National Nature Reserve in 1955, it is now managed by Scottish Natural Heritage and is home to bonxie, puffin, fulmar and gannet - Britain's largest seabird. As well as being a haven for seabirds, the land back from the cliff edge is home to many rare and special varieties of plant.

Fair Isle

Lying half-way between Shetland and Orkney, Fair Isle is famous for its intricately pattern knitwear whose history has been traced back to the Spaniards who were shipwrecked here during the Armada in 1588. A staging post for many migrating birds, the **Lodge and Bird Observatory** was founded in 1948 by the late Dr George Waterston, the then owner of the Island. There is a twice weekly mailboat and scheduled flights, both from Shetland, but the weather can easily leave the Island isolated for weeks.

Hermaness Coastline

Outer Hebrides

The ferry from Ullapool takes three and a half hours to reach Stornoway, on the Hebridean island of Lewis. The Outer Hebrides stretch for 130 miles, a string of islands that in most places rise no more than a few hundred feet and are battered by the full force of the Atlantic. To the west the first land reached is the coast of Labrador. It sounds desolate but there are miles upon miles of empty beaches with dazzling white sand, unbelievably clear water and breathtaking sunsets. There is also a fascinating range of flora and fauna here, with most islands having at least one nature reserve. The Islands have been inhabited for over 6000 years and today some 31,000 people live on the 12 populated Islands. The people are Gaels and guardians of a rich culture, perhaps most accessible to visitors in its music. There are rich Scandinavia influences here as well since the Vikings ruled the Islands from the 9th century until 1280 and many placenames are of Norse origin, especially in the north.

It is important to remember that Sundays are treated with a degree of reverence on these Islands that has long since vanished in England and are one of the features that makes life here different. Some ferries do not run on the Sabbath, most hotel bars and pubs are closed and some bed and breakfast establishments would prefer if you book a Sunday night stay on Saturday.

Lewis and **Harris** are actually one Island, a pair of Siamese twins. Although solidly joined they are very different lands. Lewis is largely moorland, flat and boggy and scattered with a thousand tiny lochs that offer some of the finest and most expensive fishing in Europe. Harris is mountainous, one of the peaks rising to 2622 feet. Its western coast has spectacular beaches, the work of the crashing Atlantic waves, whilst the east shelters several small fishing villages.

STORNOWAY, founded by James VI, is the capital and the biggest town in the Outer Hebrides. With the exception of this town Gaelic is the first language of all these islands. It is many years, however, since the death of the last islander to speak no English at all.

The **Museum Nan Eilean** is devoted to telling the story of the Island's history, culture and tradition and, of particular interest, are the **Uig Chessmen**, seen here during the summer under an agreement with the British Museum. At **St Peter's Church** can be seen David Livingstone's prayer book, whilst another famous explorer, Alexander Mackenzie, was born here and is remembered by a tablet on Martin's Memorial Church.

On the western side of the harbour is **Lews Castle**, now a technical college. Built between 1856-63, it was presented to the town by Lord Leverhulme who, in 1918, had acquired Lewis and Harris and tried, unsuccessfully, to modernise the farming methods used here.

A small shop with an astonishing selection of crafts and unusual gift ideas can be found in Point Street in the heart of Stornoway's main shopping area. **This 'n' That** is the place to go for that special present or souvenir. Norwegian-born proprietor Anne-Lise Engebretsen has assembled a breathtaking selection of cards, jewellery, glassware, fragrant oils and candles, chimes, soft toys, handbags, picture frames, woollen scarves, designer knitwear and Harris tweed, all crammed in to create a wonderful Aladdin's Cave atmosphere. She also stocks an attractive range of Celtic silver jewellery and a variety of items based on the designs of the famous Glasgow Art Nouveau designer, Charles Rennie Mackintosh.

This 'n' That, 36 Point Street, Stornoway Tel & Fax: 01851 702202

Captions, the first Internet café in the Western Isles and the fourth to open in Scotland, can be found in Church Street in the heart of old Stornoway. Here, visitors have a unique opportunity to connect to the Information Superhighway in a friendly and informal atmosphere which also offers delicious home-cooked food, coffee and soft drinks. For a small hourly charge, customers can have access to the World Wide Web with its vast international library covering a range of subjects from sport and education, to hobbies and travel, all presented in a way which is easy and fun to use. They can also send electronic mail to their friends around the world, or advertise on the Internet to reach a potential audience of over 50 million. As well as a stimulating environment, proprietors Mairi and Angus Mackenzie provide a comprehensive range of light meals, including soup, sandwiches, baked potatoes, burgers and home-baked scones and cakes. They also offer a fax and photocopying facility, and stock a wide range of tapes, CD singles and sports videos. Open Mondays to Saturdays 10 am till late, those wanting more information can visit Captions' web site at http://www.captions.co.uk/ or send an e-mail to bayble@captions.co.uk.

Captions Internet Café, 27 Church Street, Stornoway
Tel: 01851 702238 Fax: 01851 706782

Conveniently situated in the centre of Stornoway, this 200 year old grain store houses the superbly hidden gem, the **Lewis Loom Centre**. Owned and run for the past two and a half years by Ronnie McKenzie, this wonderful step back in time offers you a guided tour of the history of Harris tweed and a terrific, well stocked gift shop. The tour itself takes 45 minutes and will give you a full demonstration of traditional wooden Harris tweed looms, a Hattersley Harris tweed loom, warping and waulking the tweed by hand listening to Gaelic songs, hand spinning and hand carding with the full history behind this trade explained to you as you travel round the Centre. There are displays of many of the traditional patterns once used by designers with all the different coloured yarns, charts and pictures that depict the fascinating history of the world renowned Harris tweed. The gift shop has a wonderful selection of tweed, traditional Island knitwear and knitting yarns all in the beautiful Harris tweed colours, as well as some smaller gifts and keepsakes of your memorable visit to the Lewis Loom Centre.

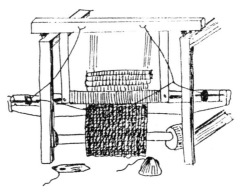

Lewis Loom Centre, 3 Bayhead, Stornoway Tel: 01851 703117

Those looking for excellent bed and breakfast accommodation in Stornoway should make a point of finding **Primrose Villa** in Lewis Street. This handsome residence was built by a sea captain, Captain McIntyre, in 1896 as his family home.

Primrose Villa

An imposing stone-built structure, in places its walls are over two feet thick. Inside, the atmosphere is comfortable and very welcoming. Sandra and Hamish Afrin are friendly and experienced hosts who have run a guesthouse for over 20 years. They provide a hearty full Scottish breakfast which is large enough to last throughout the day and delicious evening meals which include a choice suitable for vegetarians. Children are very welcome and smaller portions can be provided if required. The four guest bedrooms are spacious and comfortable and equipped with wash hand basins and first-rate facilities. The motto at Primrose Villa is *Ceud Mile Failte* - 'one hundred thousand welcomes' - making this the ideal holiday base for exploring the Isles of Lewis and Harris, or for delightful shorter stays when arriving or departing from Stornoway by ferry or plane.

Primrose Villa, 31 Lewis Street, Stornoway Tel: 01851 703387

AROUND STORNOWAY

BACK. The fascinating **Coll Pottery** can be found in the township of Coll, six miles northeast of Stornoway on the B895 Tolsta road. Originally founded in 1970 by Marjorie MacLennan, a potter who hand-modelled earthenware figures reflecting traditional island life, it is now under the ownership of Carol and Barry Edwards, two accomplished craftspeople who trade under the name Fear an eich, the Gaelic term for 'horseman', whose form is reflected in the company logo. When she retired in 1987, Marjorie left a series of designs for hand-cast figures, including the famous Hebridean peat lady, which has been added to over the years. This has been enhanced by a second, more functional range of hand-made marbled slipware whose glazes are inspired by the colours of the Hebridean landscape.

Coll Pottery

In recent years, a range of ceramic brooches and badges has been introduced, with designs including the seal, salmon and blackface ram, along with a range of beautiful hand-modelled figures representing the birds and animals of the Islands. Visitors are welcome to call at the pottery to watch Carol and Barry at work. A range of finished items is available for sale, along with a variety of other Hebridean crafts, and there is also an attractive tearoom serving teas, coffees, soft drinks and home-made cakes, scones and shortbread.

Coll Pottery, Back Tel: 01851 820219 Fax: 01851 820565

NESS. The **Butt of Lewis**, with a lighthouse, is a confusion of cliffs and rock pinnacles jutting out into the sea that are alive with a wide variety of seabirds.

Visitors to Joan and Murdo MacLean's weaving studio at Ness have a wonderful opportunity to view Harris tweed being woven using traditional Hebridean methods. When their firm, **Nesstex**, was established here in 1986, Murdo had already been a producer of hand-woven material for over three decades.

Nesstex

Whilst he specialises in fabric design and weaving, Joan concentrates on commissions for bespoke items and finished garments. Highly skilled craftspeople in their own right, they still use pedal power to weave on a loom built in 1947. Quality assurance is very important and both take steps to ensure that every article and piece of material is made to the very highest standard. Their studio shop stocks an extensive range of hand-woven fabric which is available to purchase by the metre, along with a selection of ready-made items, including tartan rugs, scarves and shawls. Joan and Murdo also give fascinating weaving demonstrations, and visitors are very welcome to call at the studio to watch them at work or browse through the display of genuine Harris tweed fabric and finished items.

Nesstex, 24 Swainbost, Ness Tel: 01851 810534

BORGH. A fascinating place to visit on the A857 Butt of Lewis road is the **Borgh Pottery** at Borgh (Borve), the studio of Sue and Alex Blair. Sue and Alex began potting in Stornoway in 1974 before moving to their present premises four years later. All their pots are individually hand-thrown or hand-built in a variety of materials, including porcelain, stoneware and frost-resistant terracotta, which gives them scope to explore new shapes, textures and glazes.

Borgh Pottery

As well as an attractive range of smaller items, they specialise in larger pieces of studio pottery. Commissions are accepted for one-off pieces and such items as dinner sets. Their work has been exhibited in galleries throughout Scotland and is much acclaimed for the way it reflects the flavour of the Hebridean landscape. An attractive showroom stocked with a range of their pots, plus a small selection of other carefully-chosen crafts, is open Mondays to Saturdays, 9.30 am to 6 pm, all year round. Visitors are most welcome and at certain times may be able to view the pots being made.

Borgh Pottery, Fivepenny House, Borgh Tel: 01851 850345

GALSON. **Galson Farm Guest House** is centrally located, just off the A857 Stornoway to Port of Ness main road. This fully restored and modernised 18th century farmhouse is situated on an 18 acre croft on the west coast of Lewis overlooking the Atlantic Ocean. Your hosts are Dorothy and John Russell and of course their dog, Gypsy, who all endeavour to make your stay at Galson Farmhouse a happy and relaxing one. The large and roomy double/family room and the two twin bedded rooms all have en-suite facilities, central heating, tea and coffee making equipment and hairdryers. There are two residents' lounges that are open all day with tea and coffee always available and the open peat fires add a warming glow in those colder months. The dining room is welcoming and cosy with everyone enjoying their meal round the large, wooden table. All the food served at Galson is traditionally cooked on an Aga cooker by Dorothy using only the freshest local ingredients. Dorothy offers her guests a good, hearty breakfast to start your day and a four or five course evening meal which is complemented by the full liquor license that is held by the Farmhouse. Also available is a Bunkhouse that offers people the opportunity to share their thoughts as well as their accommodation in a large and comfortable room that is equipped with eight bunk beds and a separate showering facility, all at a very reasonable price.

Galson Farm Guest House, Galson Tel & Fax: 01851 850492

BARVAS. An enchanting place to visit when exploring northern Lewis is the **Morven Gallery** at Barvas. Beautifully fitted with timber floors, this elegant art gallery and coffee shop is housed in a handsome former farm steading which was constructed over a century ago. Proprietor Janis Scott opened the Gallery in 1994 and since then has built up an impressive reputation for showing the finest original work by contemporary artists from the Western Isles and beyond. Pieces on show include paintings, sculpture, ceramics, woodcarvings and photographs, as well as textiles, tapestries, embroidery, knitwear and Harris tweed. The work is of the highest quality, and the majority of pieces are for sale. Janis organises a series of constantly changing exhibitions throughout the spring and summer months and also arranges adults' one-day recreational workshops and children's activity classes. There is also a charming coffee shop offering delicious teas, coffees, cakes and pastries. The Morven Gallery offers a unique opportunity to view the finest in Hebridean art and is open on Mondays to Saturdays from 10 am to 5 pm from March to October.

Morven Gallery, Barvas Tel: 01851 840216

BREASCLETE. **Boreas Knitwear** at Breasclete is an enchanting cottage industry which lies on the western side of Lewis overlooking East Loch Roag. Proprietors Sheila and Barry Leigh produce traditionally knitted hand-framed items from 100% pure Harris wool. This beautiful yarn is renowned for its warmth and durability and is also used to make world famous Harris tweed which, of course, is only obtainable from the Island. Visitors calling at the workshop can see demonstrations of work in progress and browse through the display of finished sweaters, waistcoats and other garments. They will also find a selection of beautiful hand-knitted garments, including a range of baby clothes. Items in a choice of over 500 colours can also be specially commissioned and forwarded by mail.

Boreas Knitwear, 29a Breasclete Tel: 01851 621241

The Isle of Lewis and Harris is an island of great natural beauty and provides interest for fisherman, birdwatchers, walkers and climbers, who all visit to enjoy the peace and tranquility that emanates from this beautiful Isle. Situated on a small croft in Breasclete, a small weaving village on the western coast of the Island of Lewis, **Eshcol Guest House** is a superb example of the warm hospitality that is extended to every visitor to the Island.

Eshcol Guest House

Neil and Isobel are your hosts and have been in business for nearly a decade and, armed with this knowledge, they have the ability to make all their guests feel immediately at home. There are two light and airy twin rooms, both with en-suite facilities and a double room with its own private bathroom and, as all these bedrooms are located on the ground floor, they are perfect for those visitors who have problems with stairs. The bedrooms also have a colour television, radio alarm, superb views and tea and coffee is always available throughout the day. The guest lounge is very large and offers some absolutely spectacular views of Loch Roag, the beautiful island of Great Bernera and the surrounding hills of Uig and Harris.

The food at Eshcol is cooked and prepared by Isobel's own fair hand, using only the freshest local produce and Neil is rumoured to make the best porridge in Scotland! All meals are served in the attractive dining room which is filled with traditional Regency furniture and a terrific collection of past family photographs adorn the walls. I am sure that if you do decide to visit this lovely example of Scottish hospitality, you will leave feeling completely rested, refreshed and totally at ease.

Eshcol Guest House, Breasclete, Isle of Lewis
Tel: 01851 621357

CALLANAISH. Another sight not to be missed are the famous **Standing Stones of Callanish**. This great stone circle, with its avenues radiating from it, is one of the best preserved sites in Europe. Legend has it that the stones are giants turned to stone for refusing to be baptized by St Kieran. Just a few miles away is **Dun Carloway**, an Iron Age Broch similar to those on Orkney and Shetland.

The delightful **Callanish Blackhouse Tea Room** is situated off the A858 Stornoway to Carloway road at the head of East Loch Roag (watch out for the signpost). The closest building to the famous Callanish Standing Stones, this 150 year old former crofter's house has a distinctive thatched roof and is full of Hebridean character and charm, with beamed ceilings and rustic furnishings. It was converted to a tearoom in 1980 by the present proprietress Beatrice Schulz, a friendly and experienced hostess who provides a warm welcome and some of the finest home-baking on the Isle of Lewis. As well as teas, coffees and soft drinks, she serves delicious light lunches, including soup, sandwiches and home-made specialities. She also stocks a carefully chosen range of crafts and gifts, many of which are made on the Islands. However, her personal speciality is the unique and charming family of teddy bears known as the 'Macbears' which are lovingly made by hand using predominantly Harris tweed. The Callanish Blackhouse Tea Room is open on Mondays to Saturdays, 9.30 am to 5.30 pm between early May and the end of September (larger groups preferably by appointment).

Callanish Blackhouse Tea Room, 18 Callanish
Tel: 01851 621373/621306

AIRD UIG. One of the most unusual enterprises in Britain can be found on a remote clifftop near Gallan Head in an area of Lewis known as the 'Jewel of the Isles'. **Smugglers** is a unique restaurant, bed and breakfast and self-catering establishment which occupies a deserted RAF base built at the most northwesterly point of the British Isles during the Cold War. Opened in 1954 and abandoned nine years later, it lay disused for almost three decades before being acquired and completely remodelled by the present owners, Catherine and Alan Farquharson. They began by converting the former guardhouse to a family home, the fire station to a two-bedroom cottage, and the administration building to a first-class restaurant and are now able to offer exceptional food and accommodation in one of the most dramatic locations in Europe.

Smugglers

Smugglers' Restaurant, for which evening booking is essential, specialises in seafood dishes, including lobster, crab and shellfish in season, and there is also an attractive lounge, a dance hall which hosts regular ceilidhs, and a small craft shop stocked with a range of local gifts, including the famous Lewis chess sets. Excellent value bed and breakfast accommodation is also available, along with two well-equipped self-catering apartments which sleep up to six.

Smugglers, Aird Uig, Timsgarry Tel: 01851 672351

TARBERT. Throughout the Islands men and women can be found hard at work weaving the Harris tweed; the Harris Tweed Association, formed in 1909, prevents imitations. It is a real cottage industry, most houses having a loom on which to work in odd moments. Moves to allow the use of power looms were smartly stopped by the weavers in 1975. Located in the pretty village of West Tarbert in the beautiful Isle of Harris, **Soay Studio** is a craft studio with a difference. Owned and run by Margaret McKay, this studio is the workstation and exhibition area for Margaret's skill of natural dying and knitting. She has been skilled in this traditional craft for over 16 years and offers her visitors an insight into this ancient and time consuming skill. Margaret uses only traditional dyes in her woollen creations, they include such ingredients as peat-soot, heather, iris root and willow bark and the dying takes place in a large iron pot over a peat fire. The demonstrations of this craft are given daily and the items produced include waistcoats, hats, sweaters, gloves and socks, though because of the natural element in their production some pieces can take several weeks to complete. Each piece produced by Margaret is totally unique, as no colour can be copied exactly and even the water used for the dying comes from the stream that runs through the studio's grounds. There is a full mail order facility available and commission work is taken on regularly, though be prepared to wait as Margaret's wonderful creations are much sought after. The Soay Studio is open from May until September, Monday through to Friday from 9 am until 4 pm.

Margaret also offers visitors to the Island a self-catering cottage on the lower slopes of Gillaval, overlooking the West Loch Tarbert and Ben Luskentyre. Soay Cottage will sleep up to six people, with a double bedroom with extra single bed, a twin bedded room and a ground floor single bedroom. There is a bathroom with bath and shower and a comfortable sitting room that comes complete with a colour TV and a warming open fire that burns coal and peat, which is supplied free of charge. The fully equipped kitchen has a four ring electric cooker, a microwave and fridge/freezer, and there is also a washing machine and tumble dryer for your convenience. Both the house and gardens face southwest and catch any sun that is going and there are garden chairs and a table if you fancy eating your meals al fresco. Soay Cottage really is a home from home, and Harris offers its guests some of the most spectacular scenery in the world, from breathtaking mountains and lochs, to silvery beaches and flower speckled machair.

Soay Studio, West Tarbert, Isle of Harris Tel: 01859 502361

Standing virtually adjacent to the Harris car ferry terminal from which the Hebridean Isles sails to and from Uig on the Isle of Skye, **The Harris Hotel** is the ideal centre from which to tour Lewis and Harris. This old established hotel has been owned by the same family since 1904 and offers all its guests a friendly welcome and a stay that guarantees you both peace and tranquillity.

Built in 1865 as an Inn, it was originally named Tarbert New Inn. It was a popular stopping off point for traveller's who had just departed the ferry and wanted somewhere to stay overnight, before they visited Amhuinnsuidhe Castle, which was built by the Earl of Dunmore in 1868. It changed its name in the 1930s and has been run by John Murdo and Helen Morrison for the past 25 years, having been handed down to them by Helen's Grandparents. The Harris Hotel has 25 bedrooms, all with either en-suite facilities or a private guests' bathroom, and there are also two large family rooms available. The restaurant, which is named My Grandfather's House, is open seven days a week from 11 am until 10 pm and can serve up to 90 people per sitting. The food is freshly cooked using only the finest local produce and you can sample such delights as Medallions of Pork Fillet served with a Creamy Pear and Brandy Sauce or Roast Sirloin of Scottish Beef with Yorkshire Pudding and Roast Potatoes, now that should get your tastebuds watering. In the dining room window can still be seen the etched initials of well known novelist JM Barrie, the man who wrote *Peter Pan*, a high accolade indeed for this fine Hotel. There is also a small and intimate residents' bar where you will find probably one of the largest selections of malt whiskies in the north (over 100 at the last count!) and there is also a choice of over 60 different wines on the wine list.

The Harris Hotel, Tarbert, Isle of Harris Tel: 01859 502154

North Uist

A vaguely circular island, North Uist is connected to Benbecula and South Uist by causeways. The chief community is **Lochmaddy**, on the east coast, which takes its name (Loch of the Dogs) from the three basalt islets at the harbour entrance. An Island of high moorland on the eastside, the west is fairly fertile. In such a place, years ago, the cow was a valuable possession and the crime of stealing milk was very serious. At **Vallay**, on the northwest coast, there is a pit that can never be filled in, it is said, as a witch was once buried alive. Caught with stealing milk, the chief had ordered her to be buried up to her neck at the entrance to the cattle-fold and there she remained, as the cattle passed over her, until she was dead.

Benbecula

Lying between North and South Uist, this is the smallest of the main Outer Hebridean islands and the principal village, **Balivanich**, lies in the northwest. It was from the Rossinish area of the Island that Bonnie Prince Charlie made his famous escape aided by Flora Macdonald. She had, at first, been unwilling to help him, but was eventually persuaded by his famous charm. A cairn stands at the site of her birthplace on South Uist.

In 1830, women gathering seaweed on the shore, saw a mermaid out at sea. Evading capture the creature, so the story goes, was however hurt when a boy threw stones at her. A few days later, the tiny creature's body (the top half that of a child and the lower like a salmon without the scales) was found washed up on the shore. The local sheriff thought the body sufficiently human enough to warrant a shroud and coffin and the creature lies buried above the high water mark along the shore.

South Uist

The island is, historically, associated with the meeting between Flora Macdonald and Bonnie Prince Charlie. Flora, born on the Island, met the Prince when he was in hiding and being looked after her brother, Neil MacEachain Macdonald. It was Neil who suggested that Flora take the Young Pretender, dressed as a servant girl, back to Skye with her. At first she could not be persuaded but, on meeting the Prince in person, her objections crumbled.

Today **Flora Macdonald's Birthplace** is a simple memorial cairn surrounded by a low-walled ruin. **Ormaclete Castle** is also a ruin and now stands surrounded by a farm. Built in the early 1700s for the chief of Clan Ranald, the Castle had a short life as, in 1715, it was gutted by fire during celebration of what turned out to be premature reports of a Jacobite victory at Sheriffmuir.

Eriskay

It was here, in 1941, that the SS Politician was wrecked with a cargo of 20,000 cases of whisky. This was the raw material for Sir Compton

Mackenzie's hilarious novel, *Whisky Galore*, and the wonderful Ealing comedy of the same name. Those bottles are now collector's items and can be worth several thousand pounds. As an aside Sir Compton owned the Shiant Islands off the coast of Lewis.

Barra

The southernmost of the larger Hebridean islands, Barra has the only airfield in Britain that is under water twice a day - the scheduled flights landing on the beach at Castlebay. **Kisimul Castle** stands on a small island in the bay. This was the home of the MacNeils, once notorious for their piracy and vanity. It is said that a servant was employed to stand on the battlements everyday and announce 'MacNeil has dined; Kings, Princes and the rest of earth may now dine!' After decades of neglect an American descendant of the MacNeils has now restored the castle to its former glory.

St Kilda

The islands of St Kilda can safely lay claim to being Britain's most hidden place. The three islands, Hirta, Soay and Boreway lie 50 miles west of Harris, open to the full force of the Atlantic. The main island **Hirta** has a majesty and power all its own, surrounded on the most part by towering cliffs a 1000 feet high; those at Conachair, at 1397 feet, are the highest in Britain. Incredibly the Island was inhabited for centuries by a community of around 200, who clung to life on this barren rock. They finally left in 1930 when their numbers had dropped to an unsustainable 72. The Island is now home to a National Trust for Scotland warden and the military, who arrived in the 1950s, building a radar station to monitor the missile test firings from Benbecula. Trust organized summer working parties are the only way for the public to land on Hirta. Britain does have a more remote spot than Hirta, but **Rockall**, 230 miles out in the Atlantic, is a pinhead of rock surrounded by the endless ocean.

TOURIST INFORMATION CENTRES

Centres in **bold** are open all year round.

Aberdeen, St Nicholas House,
 Broad Street 01224 632727
Aberfeldy, The Square
 01887 820276
Aberfoyle, Main Street
 01877 382352
Abington, Welcome Break
 Service Area, Junction 13, M74
 01864 502436
Aboyne, The Square
 013398 86060
Alford, Railway Museum, Station
 Yard 019755 62052
Alva, Mill Trail Visitor Centre
 01259 769696
Anstruther, Scottish Fisheries
 Museum 01333 311073
Arbroath, Market Place
 01241 872609
Ardgarten, Arrochar
 01301 702432
Auchterarder, 90 High Street
 01764 663450
Aviemore, Grampian Road
 01479 810363
Ayr, Burns House, Burn Statue
 Square 01292 288688

Ballachulish 01855 811296
Ballater, Station Square
 013397 55306
Balloch, Balloch Road
 01389 753533
Banchory, Bridge Street
 01330 822000
Banff, Collie Lodge 01261 812419
Bettyhill, Clachan 01641 521342
Biggar, 155 High Street
 01899 22106

Blairgowrie, 26 Wellmeadow
 01250 872960
Bo'ness, Seaview Car Park
 01506 826626
Bowmore, Isle of Islay
 01496 810254
Braemar, The Mews, Mar Road
 013397 41600
Brechin, St Ninians Place
 01356 623050
Broadford, Isle of Skye
 01471 822361
Brodick, The Pier, Isle of Arran
 01770 302140/302401
Burntisland, 4 Kirkgate
 01592 872667

Callander, Rob Roy & Trossachs
 Visitor Centre, Ancaster Square
 01877 330342
Campbeltown, Mackinnon
 House, The Pier 01586 552056
Carnoustie, 1b High Street
 01241 852258
Carrbridge, Main Street
 01479 841630
Castlebay, Main Street, Isle of
 Barra 01871 810336
Castle Douglas, Markethill Car
 Park 01556 502611
Coatbridge, The Time Capsule,
 Buchanan Street 01236 431133
Coldstream, High Street
 01890 882607
Craignure, Isle of Mull
 01680 812377
Crail, Museum & Heritage
 Centre, Marketgate
 01333 450869

Crathie, Car Park, Balmoral
Castle 013397 42414
Crieff, Town Hall, High Street
01764 652578
Cupar, The Granary, Coal Road
01334 652874

Dalbeattie, Town Hall
01556 610117
Dalkeith, The Library, White
Hart Street 0131 660 6818
Daviot Wood, A9 by Inverness
01463 772203
Dornoch, The Square
01862 810400
Drymen, Drymen Library, The
Square 01360 660068
Dufftown, Clock Tower, The
Square 01340 820501
Dumbarton, Milton, A82 North-
bound 01389 7423065
Dumfries, Whitesands
01387 253862
Dunbar, 143 High Street
01368 863353
Dunblane, Stirling Road
01786 824428
Dundee, 4 City Square
01382 434664
Dunfermline, 13/15 Maygate
01383 720999
Dunkeld, The Cross
01350 727688
Dunoon, 7 Alexandra Parade
01369 703785
Durness, Sango 01971 511259

Edinburgh, Edinburgh & Scotland Information Centre, 3
Princes Street 0131 557 1700
Edinburgh Airport
0131 333 2167
Elgin, 17 High Street
01343 542666

Eyemouth, Auld Kirk, Manse
Road 018907 50678

Falkirk, 2-4 Glebe Street
01324 620244
Forfar, 40 East High Street
01307 467876
Forres, 116 High Street
01309 672938
Fort Augustus, Car Park
01320 366367
Fort William, Cameron Square
01397 703781
Forth Road Bridge, by North
Queensferry 01383 417759
Fraserburgh, Saltoun Square
01346 518315

Gairloch, Auchtercairn
01445 712130
Galashiels, St Johns Street
01896 755551
Gatehouse of Fleet, Car Park
01557 814212
Girvan, Bridge Street
01465 714950
Glasgow, 11 George Square
0141 204 4400
Glasgow Airport 0141 848 4440
Glenrothes, Rothes Square,
Kingdom Centre
01592 754954/610784
Gourock, Pierhead 01475 639467
Grantown-on-Spey, High Street
01479 872773
Gretna, Gateway to Scotland,
M74 Service Area 01461 338500
Gretna Green, Old Blacksmith's
Shop 01461 337834

Hamilton, Road Chef Services,
M74 Northbound 01698 285590
Hawick, Drumlanrig's Tower
01450 372547

Helensburgh, The Clock Tower
01436 672642
Helmsdale, Coupar Park
01431 821640
Huntly, 9a The Square
01466 792255

Inveraray, Front Street
01499 302063
Inverness, Castle Wynd
01463 234353
Inverurie, Town Hall, Market
Place 01467 620600
Irvine, New Street 01294 313886

Jedburgh, Murray's Green
01835 863435/863688
John O'Groats, County Road
01955 611373

Kelso, Town House, The Square
01573 223464
Kilchoan 01972 510222
Killin, Breadalbane Folklore
Centre 01567 820254
Kilmarnock, 62 Bank Street
01563 539090
Kincardine Bridge, Pine 'n' Oak,
Kincardine Bridge Road, Airth
01324 831422
Kingussie, King Street
01540 661297
Kinross, Kinross Service Area,
off Junction 6, M90
01577 863680
Kincaldy, 19 Whytecauseway
01592 267775
Kirkcudbright, Harbour Square
01557 330494
Kirkwall, 6 Broad Street
01856 872856
Kirriemuir, Cumberland Close
01575 574097

Kyle of Lochalsh, Car Park
01599 534276

Lairg 01549 402160
Lanark, Horsemarket, Ladyacre
Road 01555 661661
Langholm, High Street
01387 380976
Largs, Promenade 01475 673765
Lerwick, The Market Cross
01595 693434
Leven, The Beehive, Durie Street
01333 429464
Linlithgow, Burgh Halls, The
Cross 01506 844600
Lochboisdale, Pier Road
01878 700286
Lochcarron, Main Street
01520 722357
Lochgilphead, Lochnell Street
01546 602344
Lochinver, Main Street
01571 844330
Lochmaddy, Pier Road
01876 500321

Mallaig 01687 462170
Melrose, Abbey House
01896 822555
Millport, 28 Stuart Street
01475 530753
Moffat, Churchgate
01683 220620
Montrose, Bridge Street
01674 672000

Nairn, 62 King Street
01667 452753
Newtongrange, Scottish Mining
Museum, Lady Victoria Col-
liery 0131 663 262
Newton Stewart, Dashwood
Square 01671 402431

North Berwick, Quality Street
01620 892197
North Kessock 01463 731505

Oban, Argyll Square
01631 563122
Oldcraighall, Granada Service
Area, A1 Musselburgh
0131 653 6172

Paisley, Town Hall, Abbey Close
0141 889 0711
Peebles, High Street
01721 720138
Pencraig, A1 by East Linton
01620 860063
Penicuik, Edinburgh Crystal
Visitor Centre, Eastfield
01968 673846
Perth, 45 High Street
01738 638353
Perth, Inveralmond, A9 Western
City Bypass 01738 638481
Pitlochry, 22 Atholl Road
01796 472215/472751
Portree, Meall House
01478 612137

Ralia, A9 North by Newtonmore
01540 673253
Rothesay, 15 Victoria Street
01700 502151

St Andrews, 70 Market Street
01334 472021
Sanquhar, Tolbooth, High Street
01659 50185
Selkirk, Halliwell's House
01750 20054
Shiel Bridge 01599 511264
Spean Bridge 01397 712576
Stirling, Dumbarton Road
01786 475019

Stirling, Royal Burgh of Stirling
Visitor Centre 01786 479901
Stirling, Pirnhall Motorway
Service Area, Junction 9, M9
01786 814111
Stonehaven, 66 Allardice Street
01569 762806
Stornoway, 26 Cromwell Street
01851 703088
Stranraer, 1 Bridge Street
01776 702595
Strathpeffer, The Square
01997 421415
Stromness, Ferry Terminal
Building, The Pier Head
01856 850716
Strontian 01967 402131

Tarbert, Pier Road, Isle of Harris
01859 502011
Tarbert, Harbour Street, Argyll
01880 820429
Tarbert (Loch Lomond), Main
Street 01301 702260
Thurso, Riverside 01847 892371
Tobermory 01688 302182
Tomintoul, The Square
01807 580285
Troon, Municipal Buildings,
South Beach 01292 317696
Tyndrum, Main Street
01838 400246

Uig, Ferry Terminal
01470 542404
Ullapool, Argyle Street
01854 612135

Wick, Whitechapel Road
01955 602596

Index

THE HIDDEN PLACES SERIES

To order more copies of this title or any of the others in this
series please complete the order form below and send to ;
M & M Publishing Ltd.
118 Ashley Rd. Hale, Altrincham, Cheshire. WA14 2UN.

TITLE		QUANTITY
Scotland	£8.99	....
Ireland	£8.99	....
Wales	£8.99	....
Lake District	£5.99	....
Northumberland & Durham	£5.99	....
Yorkshire	£5.99	....
Lancashire, Cheshire, & I.O.M	£5.99	....
Peak District & Potteries	£5.99	....
Welsh Borders (Shrops, Here, Worcs.)	£5.99	....
Heart of England (The Midlands)	£5.99	....
East Anglia (inc. Cambs & Essex)	£5.99	....
Cotswolds	£5.99	....
Wessex	£5.99	....
Devon & Cornwall	£5.99	....
Dorset, Hants, & I.O.W	£5.99	....
The South East	£5.99	....
Thames & Chilterns (Berks, Oxon, Bucks, Beds, Herts.)	£5.99	....

NB. FREE POSTAGE & PACKAGING

I enclose Cheque for £.................... made payable to:
M & M Publishing Ltd.

NAME..

ADDRESS...

....

POSTCODE...